Classroom Management
A Proactive Approach

Martin Henley
Westfield State College

PEARSON

Merrill
Prentice Hall

Upper Saddle River, New Jersey
Columbus, Ohio

KH

Library of Congress Cataloging-in-Publication Data

Henley, Martin
   Classroom management : a proactive approach / Martin Henley.
      p. cm.
   Includes bibliographical references and index.
   ISBN 0-13-093299-X
   1. Classroom management.   I. Title.
   LB3013.H464 2006
   371.102′4—dc22

2005009214

Vice President and Executive Publisher:
   Jeffery W. Johnston
Acquisitions Editor: Allyson P. Sharp
Editorial Assistant: Kathleen S. Burk
Production Editor: Sheryl Glicker Langner
Production Coordination: Karen Ettinger,
   TechBooks/GTS York, PA Campus
Design Coordinator: Diane C. Lorenzo

Photo Coordinator: Monica Merkel
Cover Designer: Ali Mohrman
Cover image: Index Stock
Production Manager: Laura Messerly
Director of Marketing: Ann Castel Davis
Marketing Manager: Autumn Purdy
Marketing Coordinator: Brian Mounts

This book was set in Palatino by TechBooks/GTS York, PA Campus. It was printed and bound by
R.R. Donnelley & Sons Company. The cover was printed by R.R. Donnelley & Sons Company.

Photo Credits: Scott Cunningham/Merrill, pp. 2, 214; Ken Karp/Prentice Hall School Division, p. 248;
Anthony Magnacca/Merrill, pp. 28, 120, 278; Anne Vega/Merrill, pp. 58, 180; Tom Watson/Merrill, p. 152;
David Young-Wolff/Getty Images Inc.—Stone Allstock, p. 86

Pearson Prentice Hall™ is a trademark of Pearson Education, Inc.
Pearson® is a registered trademark of Pearson plc
Prentice Hall® is a registered trademark of Pearson Education, Inc.
Merrill® is a registered trademark of Pearson Education, Inc.

Pearson Education Ltd.
Pearson Education Singapore Pte. Ltd.
Pearson Education Canada, Ltd.
Pearson Education—Japan

Pearson Education Australia Pty. Limited
Pearson Education North Asia Ltd.
Pearson Educación de Mexico, S.A. de C.V.
Pearson Education Malaysia Pte. Ltd.

10 9 8 7 6 5 4 3 2 1
ISBN 0-13-093299-X

2/8/07

For my wife, Teresa

Preface

When surveyed, beginning teachers consistently convey concerns about classroom "control." Likewise, national polls of parents, teachers, and administrators confirm that classroom discipline is a high priority. Without sound classroom management skills, even the most talented teacher will flounder. *Classroom management* is the study of how disciplinary practices and classroom structure influence students' behavior and productivity. *Classroom Management: A Proactive Approach* is based on three principles: First, classrooms should be learning communities; second, many behavioral problems can be prevented; and third, corrective interventions should promote positive behavioral change.

A teacher's philosophy of classroom management is based on his or her assumptions about learning and human behavior. Failing to reflect on one's assumptions about student behavior can lead to shortsighted practices such as the overuse of punishments and neglect of students' basic needs. Proactive teachers reflect on their assumptions. When students misbehave, proactive teachers look for causes and search for solutions.

Brian Sheehy, a third-grade teacher in an urban school, said, "I like the idea of choosing an approach that is compatible with your philosophy of education. Of course, this is valid only to the extent that your philosophy is based on an open-minded trial and error and honest rumination and reflection. If your philosophy is nothing more than a justification of your own personal biases and preconceived ideas, then this is an awful place to start."

My intention is to provide teacher educators with a practical and theoretically sound guide to proactive classroom management. This text provides an integrated approach based on strategies culled from theoretical principles encoded in psychodynamic, developmental, behaviorist, biophysical, and psychoeducational approaches. Within this text, theory is framed within the context of application. To this end, *Classroom Management: A Proactive Approach* combines the tenets of theories on human behavior with research-based recommendations for dealing with such contemporary concerns as cultural diversity, social skills instruction, and positive behavioral supports.

In such a comprehensive undertaking, bias is bound to emerge. Every written work requires thousands of conscious and unconscious decisions about how information is organized and presented. If the reader detects a slant in orientation, undoubtedly it will be in the direction of democratic classroom environments where students' feelings and perceptions are valued as much as their actions are.

Because classrooms are complex environments, teachers need to be flexible in their decision making. When a solution does not work, they need to step back and consider alternatives. This text highlights the key roles of reflection and problem solving in classroom management. I want to persuade the reader that planning is a better approach to classroom management than that of reacting to events as they unfold. Moreover, promoting responsible student behavior is a more worthwhile goal than controlling student behavior is. Throughout, the text emphasizes positive methods for binding individual students with their classmates into a community of learners.

Successful classroom management is based on a love for children and a will to succeed. Throughout my career, I have witnessed a simple but profound truth: Good teaching trumps problems in learning every time. When teachers believe in their students, remarkable things happen. My hope is to provide within these pages a useful guide that will enlighten and sustain the best efforts of the beginning educator.

ACKNOWLEDGMENTS

I want to acknowledge the many educators and students who have helped me learn that the human spirit expresses itself in many ways. Peter Knoblock, my mentor at Syracuse University, taught me that all feelings are legitimate and that young people have as much right to anger as they do to joy. Nicholas Long, William Morse, and Fritz Redl helped me understand that teachers need practical solutions for the complex behavioral issues they deal with daily. My sixth-grade students Debbie Tarson, Helen Wright, and Clarestine Hill taught me that discipline needs to be leavened with humor, that criticism is ineffective without caring, and that teaching without enthusiasm satisfies no one.

I am grateful to my undergraduate and graduate students at Westfield State College. Their questions, prodding, and challenges fired my ambition to author this text. I also want to thank the many reviewers of this text. They are W. George Scarlett, Tufts University; Roger Bass, Carthage College; Don Fennerty, Central Washington University; Eric D. Jones, Bowling Green State University; Brenda Scheuermann, Southwest Texas State University; Marshall Zumberg, Wayne State University; J. Cynthia McDermott, California State University–Dominguez Hills; Jack Prouty, Sam Houston State University; Judith A. McBride, California State University–Long Beach; Cynthia Northington, William Paterson University of New Jersey; Linda J. Button, University of North Colorado; Denise E. Salsbury, Ball State University; Carolyn M. Fink, University of Maryland; E. Paula Crowley, Illinois State University; Bruce Smith, Henderson State University; Jodi Katsafanas, LaRoche College; Ann Schulte, California State University–Chico; Amelia Blyden, The College of New Jersey; and John-Michael Bodi, Bridgewater State College. I learned from their comments, and the book is better because of them.

I want to thank Ann Davis, my original editor, for believing in this project. Allyson Sharp, my current editor, continued that support. Allyson encouraged me when I was discouraged, and she helped me to grasp the important relationship between teacher reflection and effective classroom management. Her guidance clearly helped me produce a more readable, useful text. Editorial assistant Kathleen Burk helped me keep my eye on the ball as she gently, but effectively, reminded me that deadlines need to be met. My graduate assistant, Shelby Marowitz, researched citations with steadfast determination. I owe a thousand thanks to my copy editor, Kathleen Riley-King. Her eye for detail and her passion for accuracy helped transform a decent manuscript into a polished professional publication. Karen Ettinger finished the project. The book you hold in your hands is testimony to the skills of the professionals at TechBooks/GTS.

My last, but most endearing, thanks is to you, the reader, for your attention and patience. Textbook writers and textbook readers are bound by a mutual desire to communicate. We may never meet, but our thoughts are nevertheless intertwined. I consider this a special and close relationship.

EDUCATOR LEARNING CENTER: AN INVALUABLE ONLINE RESOURCE

Merrill Education and the Association for Supervision and Curriculum Development (ASCD) invite you to take advantage of a new online resource, one that provides access to the top research and proven strategies associated with ASCD and Merrill—the Educator Learning Center. At **www.educatorlearningcenter.com**, you will find resources that will enhance your students' understanding of course topics and of current educational issues, in addition to being invaluable for further research.

How the Educator Learning Center Will Help Your Students Become Better Teachers

With the combined resources of Merrill Education and ASCD, you and your students will find a wealth of tools and materials to better prepare them for the classroom.

Research
- More than 600 articles from the ASCD journal *Educational Leadership* discuss everyday issues faced by practicing teachers.
- A direct link on the site to Research Navigator™ gives students access to many of the leading education journals, as well as extensive content detailing the research process.
- Excerpts from Merrill Education texts give your students insights on important topics of instructional methods, diverse populations, assessment, classroom management, technology, and refining classroom practice.

Classroom Practice
- Hundreds of lesson plans and teaching strategies are categorized by content area and age range.
- Case studies and classroom video footage provide virtual field experience for student reflection.
- Computer simulations and other electronic tools keep your students abreast of today's classrooms and current technologies.

Look into the Value of Educator Learning Center Yourself

A four-month subscription to Educator Learning Center is $25 but is **FREE** when packaged with any Merrill Education text. In order for your students to have access to this site, you must use this special value-pack ISBN number **WHEN** placing your textbook order with the bookstore: 0-13-155248-1. Your students will then receive a copy of the text packaged with a free ASCD pincode. To preview the value of this website to you and your students, please go to **www.educatorlearningcenter.com** and click on "Demo."

Discover the Merrill Education Resources for Special Education Website

Technology is a constantly growing and changing aspect of our field that is creating a need for new content and resources. To address this emerging need, Merrill Education has developed an online learning environment for students, teachers, and professors alike to complement our products—the *Merrill Education Resources for Special Education* Website. This content-rich website provides additional resources specific to this book's topic and will help you—professors, classroom teachers, and students—augment your teaching, learning, and professional development.

Our goal is to build on and enhance what our products already offer. For this reason, the content for our user-friendly website is organized by topic and provides teachers, professors, and students with a variety of meaningful resources all in one location. With this website, we bring together the best of what Merrill has to offer: text resources, video clips, web links, tutorials, and a wide variety of information on topics of interest to general and special educators alike. Rich content, applications, and competencies further enhance the learning process.

The *Merrill Education Resources for Special Education* Website includes:

Resources for the Professor—

- The **Syllabus Manager**™, an online syllabus creation and management tool, enables instructors to create and revise their syllabus with an easy, step-by-step process. Students can access your syllabus and any changes you make during the course of your class from any computer with Internet access. To access this tailored syllabus, students will just need the URL of the website and the password assigned to the syllabus. By clicking on the date, the student can see a list of activities, assignments, and readings due for that particular class.
- In addition to the **Syllabus Manager**™ and its benefits listed above, professors also have access to all of the wonderful resources that students have access to on the site.

Resources for the Student—

- Video clips specific to each topic, with questions to help you evaluate the content and make crucial theory-to-practice connections.
- Thought-provoking critical analysis questions that students can answer and turn in for evaluation or that can serve as basis for class discussions and lectures.

- Access to a wide variety of resources related to classroom strategies and methods, including lesson planning and classroom management.
- Information on all the most current relevant topics related to special and general education, including CEC and Praxis standards, IEPs, portfolios, and professional development.
- Extensive web resources and overviews on each topic addressed on the website.
- A message board with discussion starters where students can respond to class discussion topics, post questions and responses, or ask questions about assignments.
- A search feature to help access specific information quickly.

To take advantage of these and other resources, please visit the *Merrill Education Resources for Special Education* Website at

http://www.prenhall.com/henley

Brief Contents

Contents

CHAPTER 4

Developing Positive Student–Teacher Relationships 86

CHAPTER
7

Part III   *Positive Behavioral Supports   212*

CHAPTER 8   *Using Proactive Behavioral Intervention Strategies   214*

CHAPTER 9 *Managing Problem Behaviors   248*

CHAPTER 10   *Being a Reflective Teacher*   278

Note: Every effort has been made to provide accurate and current Internet information in this book. However, the Internet and information posted on it are constantly changing, so it is inevitable that some of the Internet addresses listed in this textbook will change.

Classroom Management
A Proactive Approach

Chapter 1

Introduction to Proactive Classroom Management

Chapter Outline

The Purpose of Education

Classroom Management and Achievement

Theories, Models, and Ecology

  Theories

  Models

  An Interactional Perspective

  Classroom Ecology

Structure, Instruction, and Discipline

  Structure

  Instruction

  Discipline

The Beginning Teacher

School Disciplinary Concerns

School Violence

Environmental Influences on Behavior

Proactive Classroom Management

  Can-Do Attitude

  Turnaround Teachers

  Accept-No-Excuses Motto

Textbook Organization

  Part I: Community

  Part II: Prevention

  Part III: Positive Behavioral Supports

Summary

What You Should Know

Applying the Concepts

 Key Terms

Behaviorist theory

Behavior modification

Biophysical theory

Can-do attitude

Classroom management

Community

Compliance

Developmental needs

Developmental theory

Discipline

Ecological approach

Gestalt

Instruction

Models

Positive behavioral supports

Prevention

Proactive

Psychodynamic theory

Responsible behavior

School achievement

School violence

Sociological theory

Structure

Theories

Turnaround teachers

Introduction

Classroom management is the essential teaching skill. Teachers cannot teach and students cannot learn in a classroom plagued with disruptions. How teachers maintain control of their classrooms is the central theme of this text. *Proactive* classroom management is based on the premise that discipline should be approached as an opportunity to teach students to be responsible for their behavior. Proactive teachers recognize that many disciplinary problems can be resolved by incorporating routines, lessons, and disciplinary practices that meet students' developmental needs. This approach can be achieved by adopting the three priorities of proactive classroom management: treatment of the classroom as a community, prevention of behavioral problems and provision of positive behavioral supports for students who exhibit disciplinary problems.

Proactive classroom management is the art and science of transforming a collection of young people into a cohesive group of learners. Just as an artist combines paint, brush, and blank canvas to create a memorable painting, a classroom teacher crafts a learning environment from the raw tools of books, paper, and curriculum. While artists are noted for their style of painting, teachers express themselves through their style of classroom management. The Association for Supervision and Curriculum Development (ASCD) defines *classroom management* as a gestalt combining several teacher traits, including reflection, skill in problem solving, skill in managing student behavior, and the ability to provide engaging instruction (Hansen & Childs, 1998).

A *gestalt* is a pattern or structure that is so integrated as a functional unit that it exceeds the sum of its parts. Coaches understand the meaning of *gestalt* when they attempt to mold individual players into a championship team. A gardener creates a gestalt by cultivating individual plants into a beautiful landscape. A poet selects individual words and composes verses; this, too, is a gestalt. Proactive teachers structure classroom interactions, routines, and activities so that all students, despite their strengths, weaknesses, and individual differences, become an integral part of a productive classroom *community*.

Although each teacher is alone in the classroom, his or her efforts are sustained by insights garnered by myriad researchers in the field of classroom management. This text provides beginning educators with the tools they will need to create a learning environment that is both productive and harmonious. The emphasis is on applied principles; however, application is worthwhile only when it is built on verified theory and principles of effective teaching. Therefore, throughout this text, the principles of classroom management that are presented are embedded in a sturdy theoretical and research foundation.

THE PURPOSE OF EDUCATION

How a teacher approaches classroom management—the priorities and techniques he or she uses—depends on his or her goals. If the purpose of classroom management is to elicit *compliance*, the methods chosen will reflect this choice. For example, the military requires behavior rooted in obedience. The methods used to foster compliant behavior include intimidation, drills, routine, and loyalty oaths. These methods are appropriate because the military needs to train soldiers and sailors who will follow commands unquestioningly.

The purpose of education is to teach students to be responsible citizens (Langdon, 1996). However, the word *responsible* is an abstract term that has different meanings for different people. To some people, responsible behavior in school means obedience to authority. To others, responsible behavior means exercising self-control without the need for constant supervision.

The definition of *responsibility* that guides the organization of this text is as follows: *Responsible behavior* is self-directed and is characterized by the ability to make socially appropriate choices, care for others, and be accountable for personal actions (Figure 1.1). Responsibility is girded by self-control, which guides individual behavior when the watchful eye of authority is turned the other way.

Marzano et al (2003) said the following about teaching responsibility:

> Ample evidence indicates that teaching responsibility is a high priority in U.S. education. Speaking of self-discipline, Bear (1998) explains that "the American public's belief that schools should play a role in teaching self-discipline has never been greater than it is today" (p. 15). He cites the 1996 Gallup study (Elam, Rose, & Gallup, 1996) indicating that 98 percent of the public believes that the primary purpose of public schools should be to prepare students to be responsible citizens. (p. 77)

FIGURE 1.1   Definition of *Responsibility*

The capacity to reflect on actions, to weigh choices, to make sensible judgments, and to act accordingly.

Compliance requires obedience.

Responsible behavior requires thinking.

If we as educators want students to be responsible rather than compliant, we must think carefully about how we can achieve this goal. The means used to manage students, the structures we develop, and the disciplinary techniques we use must be considered in relationship to what we want to accomplish (Charles, 2000). For instance, trying to teach students to make good choices while using overbearing tactics to force obedience would be foolish (Good & Brophy, 2000). Likewise, the teacher who extolls the virtues of student self-control as he or she doles out rewards and punishments to control students is preaching one set of values and exercising another. Kohn (2002) argued that teachers who "try to have it both ways" send mixed messages that undercut the value of each. Instead, to teach responsible behavior, teachers should structure classroom practices that invite participation and use disciplinary approaches that promote self-control.

CLASSROOM MANAGEMENT AND ACHIEVEMENT

The renewed vigor with which educators are attempting to improve *school achievement* underscores the importance of relating to students and managing classrooms (Moles, 1989; Snow, Burns, & Griffin, 2000). Teachers cannot teach and students cannot learn in a classroom marred by disciplinary problems. In many studies, researchers have identified a safe and orderly classroom as a prerequisite for academic achievement (Marzano, 2003).

Wang, Haertel, and Walberg (1993) asked 134 education experts to rank 228 variables of student achievement in order of importance. Skill in classroom management was ranked first. According to Marzano (2003), effective teachers perform three functions: They make wise choices about instructional strategies, they design the classroom curriculum to facilitate learning, and they use classroom management techniques effectively. These functions are interdependent. However, even skilled classroom managers are challenged by students with emotional or behavioral difficulties.

Meyers, Milne, Baker, and Ginsburg (1987) found that chronic misbehavior leads to low grades and low achievement test scores. Baker (1985) reported that a student with a D average is 9 times more likely to have trouble with the law, 24 times less likely to complete homework assignments, and about 3 times more likely to cut classes than is a student with an A average. This negative spiral is most acute in classrooms where the teacher's classroom management skills are weak.

All students, not just those who misbehave, are negatively affected when lessons are interrupted by disciplinary problems. Researchers at WestEd, a nonprofit educational research and development institute, described the devastating effect of weak classroom management skills on instruction (Aronson, Zimmerman, & Carlos, 1998):

> Several studies found that poor classroom management resulted in teachers and students losing considerable amounts of instructional time to student disruptions, waiting, long breaks between activities, student tardiness and various management

and discipline activities. One of the studies found that more than half of elementary school class time was occupied by non-learning activities, such as waiting, general management activities and other non-instructional activities. By one estimate, 70 percent of teachers need to improve their classroom management skills. (www.wested.org/wested/papers/timeandlearning/)

Proactive classroom management lays the foundation for successful learning (Edmonds, 1979; Meyers et al., 1987; H. Patrick, 1997). Virtually every action within the classroom—from distribution of materials to the tone students use when they are talking to one another—is influenced by the teacher's approach to classroom management. A survey of 118 school districts revealed that poor classroom management skills and disruptive students were the major reasons new teachers struggled in the classroom (D. T. Gordon, 1999). Problems with classroom management was the leading reason why new teachers left the profession.

Classroom management is an essential teaching skill, and effective classroom managers are proactive. Rather than simply reacting to classroom problems, they search out ways to improve their craft, they look for causes of disciplinary problems, and they realize that students will not succeed unless their *developmental needs* are tended with the same care as their academic needs.

THEORIES, MODELS, AND ECOLOGY

Healthy relationships and an understanding of human behavior form the bedrock on which proactive classroom management is built. Not only must teachers relate to their students, but teachers must also be able to analyze student behavior and make necessary classroom adjustments. Therefore, a discussion of theories and models of human behavior, as well as factors that influence behavior, is in order.

Theories

Several well-known *theories* of human behavior inform classroom management practices. What distinguishes each from the other is the relative emphasis placed on individual dynamics versus environmental influences. For example, in *biophysical theory*, human behavior is explained primarily in terms of individual metabolism, genetics, and neurology (e.g., a metabolic imbalance contributes to hyperactivity), whereas in *behaviorist theory*, human behavior is explained in terms of environmental factors that shape behavior (e.g., a student who is praised concentrates harder). Both interpretations are correct. Like the metaphorical blind men who felt the ear, leg, and trunk of an elephant and pronounced them, respectively, a fan, a tree trunk, and a snake, different interpretations of behavior hit part of the mark but miss the whole picture.

Three other theories of human behavior that inform understanding of student behavior are *psychodynamic theory*, which emphasizes personality formation (e.g., lack of reliable familial relationships leads to insecurity); *developmental theory*, which emphasizes basic needs that change as individuals mature (e.g., an adolescent dyes his or her hair neon red to establish identity); and *sociological theory*, which emphasizes culture and the effect of groups on individual behavior (e.g., Latino youths avert their eyes when they are reprimanded).

The relative merits of each theory have been debated for many years. However, one premise central to this text is that no single correct theory of human behavior exists. Each theory provides insights into how and why individuals behave as they do. Even though some professionals use theories compatible with their work—for instance, medical doctors use biophysical theory almost exclusively, and some psychologists and educators are strictly behavioral in their approach to students—most professionals integrate various theories. For example, a psychiatrist is a medical doctor who specializes in treating serious emotional problems. Confronted with a patient who is depressed, a psychiatrist might prescribe medication to alleviate anxiety (i.e., biophysical), provide therapy (i.e., psychodynamic), and recommend changes in the individual's routine (i.e., behavioristic). Chapter 8 includes more detail on how various theories shape how teachers interpret and respond to students' behavior.

Models

Whereas theories present abstract principles of human behavior, *models* describe practical guidelines. For example, *behavior modification*, which is frequently used in classrooms, is the application of behaviorism. Many well-known classroom management models are based on a single theme that gives each a distinctive identity, such as assertive discipline (Canter & Canter, 1992); discipline with dignity (Curwin & Mendler, 1988a); cooperative discipline (Albert, 1996); positive discipline (Nelson, Lott, & Glenn, 2000); and win–win discipline (Kyle, Scott, & Kagan, 2001).

Classroom management models such as these combine insights and principles from two or more theories. For instance, Curwin and Mendler's (1988a) discipline-with-dignity model emphasizes respecting students' basic needs (i.e., developmental), using effective teaching practices (i.e., psychoeducational), and implementing logical consequences (i.e., behavioristic).

Classrooms are complex social environments. To be effective, models of classroom management must provide practical guidelines on a number of overlapping classroom issues. The value of a model rests in its usefulness. Therefore, classroom management models need to respond to the teacher's primary concern: how to promote constructive and productive behavior in the classroom.

When misbehavior occurs, factors other than "What is 'wrong' with the student" must be considered. Dull lessons, disorganized classrooms, peer pressure, and overbearing disciplinary tactics contribute to disciplinary problems as much as an individual student's temperament does. Teachers who rely solely on a single model or a one-dimensional method of classroom management (i.e., "My way or the highway!") will, sooner or later, encounter a student who does not "fit" the system.

An Interactional Perspective

Many overlapping factors influence student behavior, including perception, temperament, developmental level, and physical well-being. The environment plays an equally essential role. Imagine an enthusiastic, healthy, and well-adjusted 6-year-old in a cheerless classroom where students are expected to sit quietly at their desks while the teacher doles out endless workbook assignments. Before long, the eager learner will either wilt into a compliant automaton, mindlessly finishing one task after another, or start to goof off in a vain search for stimulation.

In this case, if the student becomes a "disciplinary problem," the teacher is just as accountable as the student because a lack of imagination in lesson preparation set the stage for the student's misbehavior. This interactional point of view does not diminish the student's responsibility for his or her actions, but it does highlight the significant role that teacher organization and teacher attitude play in determining student behavior.

When teachers incorporate a variety of classroom models and theoretical viewpoints into their thinking about student behavior, they increase their options. Armed with knowledge about a range of approaches for understanding student behavior, a teacher becomes a proactive problem solver. When one system or idea does not work, instead of blaming the student, the proactive teacher moves on to another approach.

Classroom Ecology

The *ecological approach* blends several theories. In a classic treatise on application of different theories to the education of students Rhodes and Tracy (1975) wrote,

> Ecological theory is an encompassing framework, an umbrella, rather than a particular theory. It is a wholistic [sic] model, or model of models. It can be seen as a unifying framework, capable of embracing the biophysical, the behavioral, the psychodynamic and the sociological bodies of knowledge. (p. 26)

Throughout this text, an ecological point of view is incorporated.

In the ecological model, behavior is described as a function of the individual interacting within the environment $[B = f(I, E)]$ (Banning, 2001; Lewin, 1936). The ecological approach offers a variety of options for managing student behavior. Rather than focusing all their efforts on changing an individual student, teachers are encouraged to address environmental influences as well. The classroom is an ecosystem comprising physical and social environmental variables. Physical factors include schedules, space, chairs, color, sound, and lighting. Social characteristics include group dynamics, teacher disposition, rules for behavior, family involvement, and cultural differences.

Changes in physical or social characteristics will change individual behavior. Imagine trying to concentrate in a noisy or an overheated college classroom. Now consider how other elements of the college experience—such as quality of lectures, professors' enthusiasm, and anxiety about tests—can affect learning.

The ecosystem that supports learning also spreads beyond the classroom door. Events outside the classroom have a significant effect on behavior within the classroom. Although you as a teacher can control only the variables within your classroom, knowledge about your students' lives outside school will broaden your understanding and enhance your ability to communicate with your students.

FIGURE 1.2   Interaction of
Classroom Variables

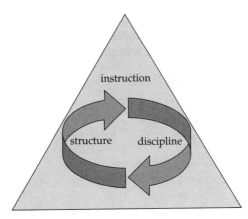

STRUCTURE, INSTRUCTION, AND DISCIPLINE

Proactive classroom management comprises three interactive features: structure, instruction, and discipline (Figure 1.2). How teachers structure their daily classroom program, the way they communicate with students, and the creativity they put into their lessons has as much to do with student behavior as the characteristics of individual students do.

Structure

Structure refers to organizational practices, routines, and procedures that form a platform for daily activities. Structure involves such concrete issues as how desks are arranged and influences such abstract concerns as group dynamics (Gunter & Denny, 1996; Hewett, 1968). Structure evolves with time. It is flexible and responsive to learners' needs. Flexibility allows for changes that will improve the learning climate. For example, a teacher notes that the formation of cliques in the classroom is leading to a spate of teasing and bullying. In response, the teacher reorganizes the structure of the classroom activities by emphasizing cooperative learning and de-emphasizing competitive group activities.

Instruction

Instruction is the centerpiece of successful classroom management. When students are engaged in their lessons, disruptions are minimal. Conversely, monotonous, dull lessons create boredom, which in turn leads students to seek out distractions. Effective classroom managers are enthusiastic, they know their curriculum, they take their students' needs and interests into account when planning, and they use a variety of teaching methods.

Instruction begins with a sound grounding in curriculum and human development. An elementary teacher who subjects students to a steady diet of drills and lectures is clearly unaware that the students' cognitive development requires regular doses of concrete learning experiences accented by learning centers and other activity-based methods. A secondary teacher who insists that students work in isolation overlooks the strong learning potential of instructional methods such as cooperative learning and brainstorming, which build on students' social developmental needs for affiliation and independence.

Discipline

Discipline refers to the approaches and strategies teachers use to guide and promote constructive student behavior. Discipline is as immediate as correcting misbehavior and as far reaching as developing a trusting relationship. Discipline is often misunderstood. Some people think of discipline as punishment. For example, Maria pushes a student in the hallway and she is "disciplined" with extra homework. Discipline involves more than simply reacting to misbehavior and punishing recalcitrant students, discipline is proactive, and it is educational.

The purpose of discipline is to teach students social skills they need for success both in and out of school. Social skills instruction involves more than students' sitting quietly in their seats and raising their hands. We as teachers want students to follow classroom rules, but we also want them to be cooperative and accountable for their behavior (Gaustad, 1992). Effective disciplinary practices teach students how to manage their feelings, behave appropriately, and respect others' rights. Table 1.1 lists the main points gleaned from 22 research reports on the classroom management skills of effective teachers.

TABLE 1.1   *Research on Effective Classroom Management*

Structure

Effective classroom managers do the following:
- Establish routines for all daily tasks and needs
- Orchestrate smooth transitions and continuity of momentum throughout the day
- Multitask

Instruction
- Strike a balance between variety and challenge in student activities
- Increase student engagement in learning and make good use of every instructional moment

Discipline
- Use consistent, proactive disciplinary practices
- Have a heightened awareness of all actions and activities in the classroom
- Include the use of space and proximity or movement around the classroom for nearness to trouble spots and to encourage attention
- Anticipate potential problems to limit disruptions
- Resolve minor inattention and disruptions before they become major problems

Note. Derived from *Qualities of Effective Teachers*, by J. H. Stronge, 2002, Alexandria, VA: Association for Supervision and Curriculum Development.

When combined, structure, instruction, and discipline have a dynamic effect on classroom management (Shores, Gunter, & Jack, 1993). Everything that transpires in a classroom—moment to moment, day to day, and week to week—is influenced by the teacher's approach to these three factors. In fact, the beginning teacher will quickly learn how structure, instruction, and discipline overlap.

THE BEGINNING TEACHER

The New York Times chronicled the first weeks of school for Donna Moffett, age 45, who left her comfortable job as a legal secretary to fulfill her dream of becoming a teacher (Goodnough, 2003). After completing a crash course in teacher preparation and passing an 8-hour certification examination, Ms. Moffett began teaching in a Brooklyn elementary school. Like many newcomers to teaching, Ms. Moffett quickly discovered how structure, instruction, and discipline affected her ability to manage her classroom. According to Goodnough,

> In these first few weeks of school Ms. Moffett is learning that teaching is only a small part of her job description—for now an achingly small part. She is already grappling with tardiness, and discipline problems, often spending far more time on "classroom management" as veteran teachers call it, than lessons. (p. A25)

In one month, Ms. Moffett did more learning than teaching. She discovered the interactive dynamics of structure, instruction, and discipline. She saw that reading cannot progress when students are not paying attention. She observed that "manipulatives" can be distractions as well as tools for teaching mathematics. She found that holding all the students back from lunch when one misbehaved was a mistake.

Like Ms. Moffett, many new teachers struggle to find their way. Success is built on the teacher's ability to manage a classroom productively. Creating such a climate requires mutual respect and engaging lessons. These commodities are generated in the thousands of person-to-person interactions that compose each school day. How daily interactions are carried out—the nature of how students relate to one another and their teacher—is a crucial element in determining whether school is a successful experience. Thus, cultivation of positive student–teacher interactions and student–student relationships is an essential aspect of classroom management.

SCHOOL DISCIPLINARY CONCERNS

The educational organization Phi Delta Kappa has conducted several polls of teachers' attitudes toward school (Langdon & Vesper, 2000). Since the polls were initiated in 1984, Phi Delta Kappa has compared teachers' and the general public's opinions about school discipline. Although both the public and teachers believe that maintaining student discipline is important, the findings indicate that, with regard to specifics, the general public and teachers have different views about school discipline priorities.

According to the Sixth Phi Delta Kappa Poll of Teachers' Attitudes Toward the Public Schools (Langdon & Vesper, 2000), nearly twice as many teachers (43%) as members of the public (24%) believe schools are safe and orderly. Whereas the public rated stricter discipline and control in schools as its first priority, this factor ranked fourth with teachers, who ranked parental involvement as their main concern. When teachers were asked how serious a problem discipline was in their school, only 13% reported a "very serious" problem.

The general public disagreed with teachers. Forty-three percent of the general public rated lack of student discipline a "very serious" problem. One possible explanation for the differences in perception between teachers and the public is that teachers have direct experience in school, whereas the public's perception may be shaped by media reports.

According to the National Center for Education Statistics (2002c), principals rated student tardiness, student absenteeism, and class cutting as their top disciplinary concerns. These factors were followed by physical conflicts between students, and tobacco use. Student possession of weapons, physical abuse of teachers, and sale of drugs on school grounds were the last three ranked items. Teachers' ranking of disciplinary problems centered on behaviors that interfered with instruction time. Incomplete schoolwork and homework, back talk, and noncompliance were the first three disciplinary priorities (Langdon, 1997). Teachers ranked drug use last under disciplinary concerns.

The National Center for Education Statistics (2002b) surveyed 10th graders about misbehavior. The students agreed that misbehavior that interferes with instruction is most problematic. Common misbehaviors cited by students included getting to class late, cutting class, and breaking school rules.

Gottfredson and Gottfredson (1985) analyzed data on disciplinary problems in more than 600 secondary schools. They reported the following schoolwide problems:

- Rules were unfair or perceived as enforced inconsistently.
- Students did not believe in the rules.
- Teachers and administrators disagreed on how to respond to student misbehavior.
- Teacher–administration cooperation was poor or lacking.
- Schools were too large or lacked adequate resources for teaching.

Two important ideas can be gleaned from these research studies: First, with regard to classroom management, one priority is getting students to participate more fully in their studies. School needs to be inviting so that students will strive to do well. Second, teachers must find ways to enhance cooperation among themselves, the administration, and students. If each group pulls in a different direction, problems that could be solved will seem intractable.

SCHOOL VIOLENCE

Although the juvenile homicide rate has declined since the mid-1990s, the media attention given to school shootings in particular has made the problem seem large. Of the approximately 2,300 annual homicides committed by youths younger than 18 years, only about 10 occur in or near schools (Rothstein, 2001). In 1995, 84% of all U.S. counties reportedly had no youth homicides. With regard to less violent crimes, Sauter (1995) reported that suburban and urban students are equally victimized. Skiba & Peterson (1999) underscored the misperception many individuals have about youth violence:

> When we watch the evening news or walk through the edgy and noisy corridors of urban middle schools, it is difficult to believe that school behavior is not worsening. But again the evidence seems to contradict our gut feelings. . . . Noted school violence researcher Irwin Hyman tracked a number of indicators of school violence over the past 20 years and concluded, "As was the case 20 years ago, despite public perceptions to the contrary, the current data do not support the claim that there has been a dramatic, overall increase in school-based violence in recent years." (p. 3)

Garbarino (2000) said that when *school violence* does occur, it is a symptom of larger underlying social issues. For example, each of the 2,300 annual youth homicides is matched by a youth suicide. A survey of youths by the Centers for Disease Control and Prevention (CDC, 2004) revealed that 15% of high school boys seriously considered suicide in 1997, and 5% attempted suicide. Girls plan and attempt suicide at a slightly higher rate than that for boys but are less successful because they often use pills, whereas boys use guns.

What causes youths to commit homicide or suicide? Among the factors psychiatrists identified is the sense that life is intolerable and no options for improvement exist. Such despair is hardened by a dysfunctional family life that reinforces feelings of shame, rejection, and depression. As at-risk factors accumulate, youths become more vulnerable to violent behavior. Table 1.2 summarizes at-risk factors for male youth violence.

Local schools and communities need to work in tandem to provide youths who are at risk with the social and emotional tools they need to cope with their difficulties and strive toward a brighter future. Four examples of successful community programs that support youths at risk are as follows:

1. **Boston Gun Project.**   In the Boston Gun Project, illegal gun suppliers are tracked down. In Boston, from 1995 to 1996, the homicide rate for males younger than 25 years old decreased by two thirds.
2. **Family Life Development Center.**   Located at Cornell University in Ithaca, NY, the Family Life Development Center helps vulnerable youths through research, outreach, and education programs that strengthen families and communities.
3. **Men and Women Against Domestic Violence (MADV).**   MADV is an Internet coalition that addresses the issue of domestic violence. This group

TABLE 1.2   *At-Risk Factors for Male Youth Violence*

Chances that a male youth will commit murder[a]	
Double[b]	**Triple**[c]
He comes from a family with a history of criminal violence.	He uses a weapon.
He has a history of being abused.	He has been arrested.
He belongs to a gang.	He has a neurological problem that impairs thinking and feeling.
He abuses alcohol.	He has difficulties at school and has a poor academic attendance record.

Note. Derived from *Lost Boys: Why Our Sons Turn Violent and How We Can Save Them* (p. 10), by J. Garbarino, 2000, New York: Anchor Books.
[a]The odds increase with the number of at-risk factors that apply.
[b]If one or more of the following are true.
[c]If, in addition to all the factors in the first column, one or more of the following are true.

provides educational information about prevention and treatment of physical, emotional, and sexual violence (www.silcom.com/~paladin/madv).

4. **Covenant House.**   In New York City, Covenant House provides shelter and emotional security for homeless boys and girls. More than 700 children a year stay at Covenant House.

Are current-day youths more aberrant than the youths of previous generations? Some indicators suggest that the current generation is more peaceful, less prone to promiscuity, and more ambitious than their predecessors (Schneider & Stevenson, 1999/2000). In 1997, the juvenile crime rate was the lowest since 1986. Since the mid-1990s, teenage pregnancy rates have decreased and high school graduation rates have increased. In addition, the percentage of students who pursued an advanced college degree doubled from 14% to 30% from 1972 to 1992.

ENVIRONMENTAL INFLUENCES ON BEHAVIOR

Factors outside school play a key role in shaping students' perception and behavior. Grinding poverty, overwhelming exposure to violence in the media (e.g., by the end of eighth grade, the typical U.S. child has witnessed more than 8,000 murders on television), accessibility to weapons, and a dysfunctional family life contribute to school misbehavior and violence. The American Psychological Association reported that the "strongest developmental predictor of a child's involvement in violence is a history of previous violence including having been a victim of abuse" (Sauter, 1995, p. K7).

Although teachers cannot assume the responsibility of primary caregivers for youths, teachers can provide students with a nurturing environment that emphasizes personal responsibility and caring for others. In many schools, conflict resolution and mediation programs help students learn to identify their anger triggers and to use peaceful coping strategies.

Of the environmental factors that have been correlated with misbehavior, the primary one is a school's location (Coleman, 1990; National Institute of Education, 1978). The strongest predictor of crime in school is the nature of the surrounding community (Gottfredson & Gottfredson, 1985). Schools situated in poor, high-crime neighborhoods will reflect these problems in the classroom. Frymier (1983), in his study of students at risk, concluded that neighborhoods with high crime rates are incubators for school disorder. He said, that the problems most children face lie outside the school rather than inside (cited in McClellan, 1994, p. 4).

Students do not leave their emotional baggage at home. Disruptive family relationships, drug problems, neglect, and myriad interpersonal problems haunt many schoolchildren's lives. Sometimes these personal problems are temporary; other times they are chronic. Invariably, personal problems at home or in the community affect student behavior in school. Noncompliance, low tolerance for frustration, and errors in judgment are a few ways students act out their emotional problems. Although poverty does not hold a patent on emotional problems, teachers within low-income schools deal with more intense problem behaviors than their peers in middle-class schools do.

W. Boyd and Shouse (1997) described two distinguishing characteristics of disciplinary problems in low-income schools. First, behavioral norms for students often run counter to teachers' academic goals for students. When students' personal experiences are bereft of concrete examples of a better life through education, the will to persevere academically faces a severe challenge from the stronger need for peer acceptance. One reason young people join gangs is to share a family atmosphere. An inner-city teacher told Boyd and Shouse, "To be intelligent around here is considered a crime. They don't bring in their books or supplies because of peer pressure. If you're making good grades and everyone else is not . . . you're just not going to be part of the group" (p. 3).

According to W. Boyd and Shouse (1997), problems typical of all schools are magnified in poor rural and urban environments:

- Students come to school on a few hours' sleep.
- Physical ailments such as colds and ear infections persist.
- Students who are displaced and homeless are common.
- Truancy and dropout rates are high.
- Grudges and gang rivalries form an undercurrent of tension.
- Low tax bases undercut school resources.
- Inadequate supplies, gloomy classrooms, and outmoded materials erode motivation.

Kozol (1991) chronicled the difficulties children who attend low-income, urban schools face. In *Savage Inequalities,* he described his thoughts about what the future held for a group of kindergarten children in Chicago:

I stand at the door and look at the children, most of whom are sitting at a table now to have their milk. Nine years from now, most of these children will go on to

Manley High School, an enormous, ugly building just a block away that has a graduation rate of only 38 percent. Twelve years from now, by junior year of high school, if the neighborhood statistics hold true for these children, 14 of these 23 boys and girls will have dropped out of school. Fourteen years from now, four of these kids, at most, will go to college. Eighteen years from now, one of those four may graduate from college, but three of the 12 boys in this kindergarten will already have spent time in prison. (p. 45)

Despite the problems, the situation is far from hopeless. Even under the most trying circumstances, inspirational teachers find ways to provide students with a safe and nurturing learning environment. Teachers, who relate in a positive manner to their students and their students' families, can achieve remarkable accomplishments. Kozol (1991) described a fifth-grade teacher, Corla Hawkins, who teaches in the same elementary school he described previously:

The room looks like a cheerful circus tent. In the center of it all, within the rocking chair, and cradling a newborn in her arms, is Mrs. Hawkins. The 30 children in the class are seated in groups of six in five of what she calls "departments." Each department is composed of six desks pushed together to create a table. One of the groups is doing math, another something that they call "math strategy." A third is doing reading. Of the other two groups, one is doing something they describe as "mathematical art"—painting composites of geometric shapes—and the other is studying "careers," which on this morning is a writing exercise about successful business leaders who began their lives in poverty. Near the science learning board a young-looking woman is preparing a new lesson that involves a lot of gadgets she has taken from a closet. "This woman," Mrs. Hawkins tells me, "is a parent. She wanted to help me. So I told her, 'If you don't have somebody to keep your baby, bring the baby here. I'll be the mother. I can do it." (p. 48)

At this point, you may be thinking, "How can Corla Hawkins be a model of an effective teacher when she is sitting in a rocking chair cradling a baby?" The answer is, simply, that she is managing her classroom. A manager directs the affairs of others. Sometimes this direction is obvious, and sometimes it is subtle. Think of a director of a play. Cast members need to know where to stand when they recite their lines, sets must be designed, actors need feedback and support, and the list of directional responsibilities goes on and on.

Now consider a classroom. Schedules must be made, furniture must be arranged, materials need to be distributed, a code of decorum must be established, and, central to everything else, the teacher must establish a classroom atmosphere that invites learning.

Corla Hawkins, like many other effective classroom managers, knows how to structure proactive classroom activities. She invites learning: Students are grouped so that they can share ideas and help one another, the curriculum is relevant and engaging, there are interesting activities, and the classroom activity is embedded in a communal atmosphere.

This brief vignette is only a snapshot of what occurs in Corla Hawkins' classroom each day. However, even in the most well-managed classroom, problems arise.

Unmotivated students need encouragement. Well-planned lessons flop, and frustrated students disrupt classroom activities. Nevertheless, the presence of difficulties need not confound the teacher; instead, the proactive teacher resolves to solve these difficulties.

Teaching is a challenging activity that requires quick thinking and good organizational skills. Lessons must be matched to curriculum frameworks. Instructional strategies for teaching lessons need to take into account the various abilities of students. Students require feedback that helps them understand their strengths and their deficiencies. Procedures for helping students get along need to be put in place. Personality differences need attention, and group dynamics require adjustments. The list might seem overwhelming, but proactive teachers like Corla Hawkins demonstrate that stimulating and supportive classrooms can be crafted even under the most difficult conditions.

PROACTIVE CLASSROOM MANAGEMENT

Proactive teachers do not avoid problems in learning or problems with behavior. These teachers accept responsibility for their students' successes and their students' failures (Brophy, 1983). Such teachers take pride in their ability to stand by all the students in their class, not just those who succeed. Proactive teachers understand that each student comes with strengths and weaknesses. Their challenge is to bring out the best in all students. When students present problems, proactive teachers accept responsibility for finding solutions. They recognize that schools are awash in explanations for students' difficulties, but they do not use these explanations as excuses. Table 1.3 summarizes variables that contribute to problem behaviors in classrooms.

TABLE 1.3   *Variables That Contribute to Behavioral Problems*

Individual Temperament and Background	Teacher Behavior
Dysfunctional family	Boring lessons
Neurological problems	Disorganized lessons
Emotional problems	Overreaction to misbehavior
Genetic predisposition	Stereotyping
Toxins or drug abuse	Burnout
Social skills deficits	Overreliance on punishment
Group Dynamics	**Classroom Organization**
Peer approval	Inconsistent routines
Dysfunctional group roles	Uncomfortable physical setting
Bullying and teasing	Irrelevant curriculum
Cliques	Inadequate materials
Student apathy or hostility	Obliviousness to cultural differences

Proactive teachers are distinguished by their positive approach to dealing with disciplinary problems. Rather than waiting for problems to develop and then re-acting, proactive teachers organize their classrooms to promote positive behavior. Such teachers think about problems with behavior in the same way they deal with problems in academics. They recognize that just as academic skills can be taught, so can appropriate social skills. These teachers incorporate social skills lessons into their daily activities and routines. They emphasize civility, and they model the qualities they want to develop in their students.

Rather than looking for a quick fix to behavioral problems, proactive teachers make a commitment to long-term behavioral change. Brophy (1983) listed three principles that guide the proactive teacher's approach to classroom management:

1. Rather than blaming students or families for behavioral problems, the teacher accepts responsibility for classroom control.
2. The teacher seeks long-term solutions to problem behaviors, rather than using short-term compliance strategies (i.e., overemphasis on rewards and punishment).
3. The teacher analyzes behavioral problems for possible causes, including developmental, emotional, and family factors.

Proactive teachers have three main characteristics. First, they have a "can-do" attitude. Second, they enable the growth of students at risk, and third, they adopt an accept-no-excuses motto.

Can-Do Attitude

Proactive teachers do not pass their classroom difficulties to someone else, nor do they give up on students labeled with such terms as *disadvantaged, learning disabled,* or *hyperactive.* Students note their teachers' *can-do attitude.* In an informal survey of education undergraduates, the following statements were representative of the re-ported characteristics of "best" teachers:

"He believed in me."
"She challenged me."
"He was always enthusiastic."
"She had a great sense of humor."
"He cared about me as a person."

Of a sample of 53 undergraduates, every respondent talked about personal quali-ties; no mention was made of specific instructional methods. The positive nature of the person mattered most (Henley, 2000).

Students are equally concerned about teachers who have difficulty maintain-ing order. One urban middle school student said,

The kids don't do the work. The teacher is hollering and screaming, "Do your work and sit down!" This makes the ones that want to learn go slower. It makes your grade sink down. It just messes it up for you. The teacher is trying to handle every-body and can't. (Corbett & Wilson, 2002, p. 19)

After comparing two junior high schools, Stanford (2000) found that successful and unsuccessful outcomes were directly related to teachers' and administrators' attitudes. Within Granite, the successful junior high school, were both a firm belief in students' abilities and a "no-excuses" attitude toward learning. The teachers at this school believed they were responsible for creating conditions within the school that fostered success. The notion of responsibility was reciprocal; that is, teachers also believed students should assume responsibility for their learning. High standards were anchored in supportive relationships between students and teachers.

Teachers at the less successful junior high had a poor attitude toward learners who had problems. Students' language and culture were widely viewed as insurmountable obstacles to learning, and "blaming the victim" was rampant. Teachers who subscribe to this deficit model see students through the myopic lens of stereotypes, which provide ready excuses for failure. Once the deficit model takes hold in a teacher's mind, it is not easily eradicated. The assumption is that because the student is "flawed," improvement will occur only if the student is "fixed" (Brendtro & Ness, 1995).

Problems in learning are interactional. Dull teaching, uninspired curricula, and a diffident administration contribute to behavioral and learning problems as surely as characteristics of individual students do (Blankstein & Guetzloe, 2000; Larrivee, 2005; Morse, 1987; Thorson, 2003). Proactive teaching is built on aspiration. If a student is struggling with mathematics, the first instructional step is to determine what calculation skills the student has. Dealing with problems with behavior is similar. All youths have strengths that can be used to move them toward constructive behavior. Consider the case study of Sylvia.

Turnaround Teachers

Benard (1997) studied characteristics of what she termed *turnaround teachers*. These teachers facilitate the self-righting mechanism of youths. According to Benard, teachers who enable the growth of students at risk establish a nurturing

 ## Case Study: Sylvia

Sylvia, a bright but temperamental 12-year-old, had developed a reputation as one of the most difficult students in her elementary school. Her temper tantrums were well known throughout the school. Despite constantly being rebuffed by Sylvia, the resource room teacher, Ms. Stanley, persevered. She talked with Sylvia at every opportunity—in the hallway, during lunch, at recess. Slowly, Sylvia's icy disposition began to thaw. She became more open about her feelings. She agreed to help tutor younger students in the resource room, and her temper tantrums decreased. Her sixth-grade teacher, who had experienced serious difficulties with Sylvia, began to remark about positive changes in her behavior. By the end of the year, Ms. Stanley concluded that Sylvia had turned a corner. For Sylvia, conversation as an alternative to acting out emotions had begun to take hold.

classroom environment. Specifically, turnaround teachers demonstrate the following attributes:

- Turnaround teachers provide emotional support, and when necessary, they provide basic necessities, such as snacks, hats, and personal hygiene items. In demeanor and action, they communicate the fundamental message "You matter."
- Turnaround teachers challenge students. They see possibilities by recognizing competencies that have gone undetected, often by the students themselves. These instructors teach students to understand themselves by understanding how their thoughts and feelings control their behavior.
- Turnaround teachers give students responsibilities. They cultivate and nourish outlets for students' contributions. They emphasize learning activities that encourage helpfulness and cooperation.

Underlying the qualities of turnaround teachers is the belief that all youths can grow and change. In his study on school effectiveness, Edmonds (1982) concluded that teachers can create a coherent environment, more potent than any combination of negative factors, and that for at least 6 hours a day, school can override negative outside-school factors.

Building on capacities to redirect youths has a rich, but overlooked, history among caregivers. Brendtro and Ness (1995) provided the following examples:

- Jane Adams saw delinquency as a spirit of adventure displayed by youth condemned to dreary existence on dead-end streets.
- Maria Montessori developed inner discipline in slum children at a time when others defined discipline as obedience training.
- Sylvia Ashton-Warner transformed unruly and unmotivated Maori students using competence and creativity as antidotes for aggression.
- Karl Wilker taught responsibility to youth in Berlin's youth prison and then gave them hacksaws to cut off the bars.
- In South Africa, Alan Paton transformed a wretched prison for black youth into a laboratory for positive moral development and gained worldwide recognition as a correctional performer. (p. 4)

Turnaround teachers possess a combination of behavioral and attitudinal qualities that enhance their ability to manage their classrooms and bring out the best in their students. In a turnaround teacher's classroom, the following are usually true:

- Most behavioral problems are handled within the classroom.
- Learning is viewed as a lifelong endeavor.
- Professional development and the acquisition of new skills are prized.
- Students are respected as individuals first. Success in school-based activities is secondary to the young person's overall welfare.

Accept-No-Excuses Motto

An apt motto to place over proactive educators' classroom doors would be "Accept No Excuses." Ginny Green, former principal at Stege Elementary School in Richmond, California, epitomizes a proactive administrator (May, 2000). When she took over leadership of Stege in 1997, it was one of the lowest scoring schools in one of the Bay Area's most impoverished neighborhoods. The school had no librarian, no computer room, and no field trips were taken. High teacher turnover rates plagued the school, no faculty meetings were held, and seagulls had invaded the playground with a voracity usually reserved for landfills. Even the flagpole had no flag.

Ginny Green directed her efforts toward restoring school pride and a sense of educational purpose. She set up teacher meetings so that teachers could share strategies, she put African cloth runners in the faculty room, and she cleaned the moldy bathrooms. She set her educational sights first on reading. She established a special reading room, which she helped staff with volunteers from the University of Berkeley. Teachers were instructed to tailor individual reading programs for students. Pride slowly replaced despair. Ginny Green's methods were unrelenting, and within 3 years, Stege showed triple-digit gains on the annual statewide Academic Performance Index. Students' scores in reading increased 37 points in the second grade, 18 points in the fourth grade, and 8 points in the fifth grade.

In many other schools and classrooms throughout the public school system, dedicated educators who do not shirk educational problems have replicated the Stege success.

TEXTBOOK ORGANIZATION

The information presented in this textbook is derived from theory and research that support a proactive approach to classroom management. Throughout, the emphasis is on positive practices that make school a more enjoyable and productive setting for both students and teachers.

Classroom Management: A Proactive Approach is divided into three parts: Community, Prevention, and Positive Behavioral Supports. Each of these elements of proactive classroom management complements the others. For example, a positive classroom climate (i.e., Part I, Community) provides a framework for preventing disciplinary problems (i.e., Part II, Prevention). Likewise, dealing with problem behaviors in a nonjudgmental and constructive fashion (i.e., Part III, Positive Behavioral Supports) helps prevent future behavioral problems from occurring (i.e., Part II, Prevention). Figure 1.3, the proactive classroom management pyramid, illustrates how the three priorities of proactive teaching—community, prevention, and *positive behavioral supports*—are linked by the three key features of classroom management—structure, instruction, and discipline.

Part I: Community

Proactive classroom management is built on a foundation of respect and rapport. Ask a third grader how he or she likes school, and you will probably hear "My teacher's nice" or "My teacher's mean." This response is more than an immature conclusion. It is a concise consumer statement about the classroom atmosphere.

FIGURE 1.3 Proactive
Classroom Management

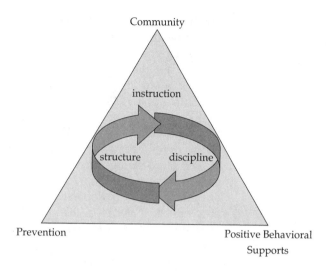

A classroom needs an inviting ambience. Student diversity requires teachers to find ways to expand interpersonal connections. Morale grows when teachers use principles of group process, listen to their students, empower students, and provide a nurturing environment. When respect and rapport are firmly in place, churlish behavior gives way to cohesiveness, dialogue supplants dissent, and enthusiasm overcomes apathy.

Part II: Prevention

Prevention is a proactive approach to discipline because the teacher establishes routines that support positive student behavior. Many disciplinary problems can be prevented by attention to the classroom structure, including group dynamics, motivation, physical layout, organization of activities, and quality of instruction. Students who are engaged in their schoolwork are less likely to be disruptive. Conversely, disorganized lessons and listless instruction incite classroom disturbances. Identifying classroom events and routines that contribute to disciplinary problems and making necessary modifications are key elements of preventive discipline. Teachers who practice preventive discipline look for causes of behavioral problems. They recognize that group dynamics influence individual behavior, and they establish a classroom structure and disciplinary practices that promote group cohesiveness.

Part III: Positive Behavioral Supports

Despite teachers' best efforts, some students will have difficulty adapting to classroom routines. The purpose of behavioral supports is to respond positively to student behavior, with confidence and flexibility. Teachers who use positive behavioral supports search for causes of behavioral problems and design proactive classroom interventions. Specific features of positive behavioral supports include identifying classroom events that trigger misbehavior; teaching constructive behavior to replace nonconstructive behavior; and defusing the impact of misbehavior through de-escalation strategies. Sugai et al. (1999) defined positive behavioral support as "the application of positive behavioral interventions and systems to achieve important behavior change" (p. 6).

How teachers think about students determines how they treat their students. In this part of the book, an attitudinal template for proactive behavioral intervention is provided, along with such best practices for supporting behavioral change as functional behavior assessment and behavior management plans.

Personal change is difficult. The slow and circuitous process of behavioral change requires student participation and empowerment to be successful. Readers are encouraged to depersonalize disciplinary problems, collect data, identify antecedents that trigger behavioral problems, and select the best approach for promoting behavioral change. An emphasis on problem solving and evaluation resonates throughout this part. Techniques such as applied behavior analysis, metacognitive strategies, and a variety of techniques for managing misbehavior positively are highlighted.

Summary

★ Classroom management is the essential teaching skill.
★ The purpose of proactive classroom management is to develop responsible student behavior.
★ A direct link exists between a teacher's classroom management skills and student achievement.
★ Three features of classroom organization that influence student behavior are structure, instruction, and discipline.
★ Proactive teachers believe in their students, they have high expectations, and they are responsive to students' developmental needs.
★ The three key elements of proactive classroom management are community, prevention of behavioral problems, and positive behavioral supports.

What You Should Know

Now that you have finished reading this chapter, you should know the following:

The meaning of *gestalt* and how it applies to classroom management
The difference between choosing compliance and choosing responsibility as a classroom management goal
The relationship between classroom management skills and student achievement
Some of the difficulties first-year teachers encounter
The three features of daily classroom activities that form the nexus for classroom management

How theories and models influence teaching practice
The role of the teacher's attitude in proactive classroom management
The meaning of *turnaround teachers*
How this textbook is organized

Applying the Concepts

1. Write a paragraph describing your favorite teacher in elementary or secondary school. List features of the teacher that were appealing and you would like to emulate. Using the list as a guide, have a classroom brainstorming session about the qualities of "best" teachers. How many of the listed qualities relate to disciplining students?

2. Interview a classroom teacher about classroom management. Ask the teacher to describe his or her philosophy of classroom management. Ask the teacher how he or she thinks the following influence classroom management practices: discipline, classroom routines, and instruction.

3. Using the Internet, search for the phrase "proactive classroom management." How many "hits" did you get? List the Web sites that discuss classroom management. Look for differences between and similarities in how the Web sites describe proactive classroom management.

4. In a cooperative learning group, list methods that teachers use to get their students to be compliant. List methods used to teach students to be responsible. Group members should reach a consensus on the following questions: How does a teacher's goals for behavior affect the way he or she sets up classroom routines? How does a teacher's goals for behavior affect his or her disciplinary practices? How does a teacher's goals for behavior affect lessons organization? Share your responses with the entire class.

5. Interview a classroom teacher about his or her first year of teaching. What were this teacher's primary concerns? What kinds of tips did veteran teachers provide him or her? What differences existed between what the teacher learned in college and the reality of the classroom? What types of disciplinary problems developed? What did the teacher learn about discipline the first year? How did the first year influence his or her current classroom management practices?

6. Observe a classroom and identify ways that the teacher interacts with students who are off task. Describe a few incidents, then analyze each in terms of how much the off-task behavior was related to student temperament and how much was related to the lesson quality.

7. What is the difference between a theory and a model? Give some examples of how educators translate theory into practice. Name and give examples of how a specific theory influences classroom management practices.

Part I

Community

All education proceeds by the participation of the individual in the social consciousness of the race.

John Dewey

Students who are given greater responsibility often develop a sense of responsibility. We tend to treat young people as citizens in preparation rather than asking to use their citizenship skills by becoming active members of the community.

S. Berman

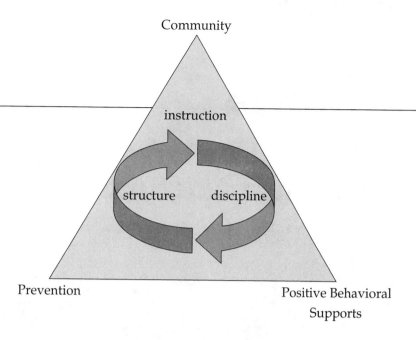

Proactive classroom management begins with community. Community fosters camaraderie and personal responsibility. Within a community classroom, students become decision makers about issues that relate to the organization and maintenance of the classroom. This daily involvement increases their personal investment and helps maintain a harmonious and productive atmosphere.

Chapter 2

Creating a Nurturing Classroom Climate

Chapter Outline

The Classroom Experience

Classroom Management Qualities
  Proactive Teachers Are Reflective
  Proactive Teachers Have High Expectations
  Proactive Teachers Are Problem Solvers

Four Myths About Classroom Management
  Myth One: A Well-Managed Classroom Is a Quiet Classroom
  Myth Two: Students Are the Most Common Cause of Classroom Disciplinary Problems
  Myth Three: Punishment Is an Effective Method for Changing Student Behavior
  Myth Four: Students with Emotional Problems Are in Special Education Programs

The Organizational Nature of School
  Classroom "Control"

Responsible Behavior

Democratic Values
  Choice, Not License

The Classroom Community
  Improved Productivity
  Improved Behavior
  Improved Citizenship

Classroom Space

Classroom Resources

Classroom Routines
  Movement and Transitions

Summary

What You Should Know

Applying the Concepts

Key Terms

80–15–5 rule
Ambience
Authoritarian
Authoritative
Autocratic teaching
Boss teacher
Choice, not license
Classroom community
Classroom control
Classroom organization
Cohesion
Compliance
Control theory

Democratic classrooms
Emotional intelligence
High expectations
Improved behavior
Improved citizenship
Improved productivity
Inclusion programs
Lead teacher
Learned helplessness
Myths about classroom management
Negative reinforcement
Obedience models
Proactive teacher qualities

Reflection   Self-fulfilling prophecy
Responsible behavior   Transitions
Self-efficacy

Introduction

Classroom "control" is a priority for new teachers. The control tactics teachers use are dictated by their beliefs. Proactive teachers reflect on their practices, they have high expectations for students, and they are problem solvers. Proactive teachers recognize that student behavior is influenced as much by the classroom climate as by individual student qualities. Proactive teachers also recognize the need to inject a sense of community into their classrooms. Community-based classrooms have a positive effect on students' behavior, citizenship, and productivity. Community is conveyed in many ways, including organization of space, development of daily routines, and implementation of procedures used to manage transitions.

Time spent in school is a significant part of an individual's childhood. On the basis of a 180-day school year and a 6-hour school day, a young person with perfect attendance spends 1,080 hours a year in school. Even when you consider periodic absences from kindergarten through 12th grade, the total time spent in classrooms exceeds 13,500 hours. Besides sleep, no other scheduled activity will absorb as much of a youngster's time than school. With that much childhood time invested in school, educators, parents, and students alike are naturally concerned about the quality of the classroom experience.

THE CLASSROOM EXPERIENCE

How students feel about school, the quality of their school experience, and their motivation to learn are linked. Teachers enhance the classroom climate by establishing procedures and routines that promote positive feelings about school. Sautner (2001) said the following about classroom climate: "Youth require a sense of belonging, opportunities for mastery, the ability to be responsible for one's self, and opportunities to provide a service to others" (p. 198). To provide such nurturing experiences, teachers must promote mutual respect and caring.

Like explorers, teachers begin each school year as an adventure. No two classes are alike: Each has distinct qualities. As teachers navigate both familiar and unfamiliar educational terrain, they need a compass to keep them moving toward their goal. Unfortunately, no mechanical device exists that can help teachers make the proper decisions about which course of action to follow. Instead, each teacher must depend on his or her internal compass, comprising a set of beliefs about what constitutes good teaching. The following section covers beliefs about classroom management that are guideposts for establishing a positive classroom climate.

Each belief is derived from a careful examination of effective teaching practices, empirical research, and educational theory. Taken together, these beliefs provide a road map for successful classroom management.

CLASSROOM MANAGEMENT QUALITIES

Outside their families, youths spend more time with teachers than with any other adult. How teachers approach their task—the attitudes and values they bring to the classroom—has a significant effect on students' attitudes and behavior. More than anything else, teachers need to demonstrate through their actions that they believe in their students. Three *proactive teacher qualities,* connect the pragmatic issues of managing student behavior with research on effective teaching practices. These three qualities provide a set of guidelines for implementing a proactive classroom management system. They are as follows: Proactive teachers are reflective, they have high expectations for students, and they are problem solvers.

Proactive Teachers Are Reflective

Dealing with classroom management issues requires thoughtful consideration (Gates, 2001). Classrooms are busy places, and teachers must make decisions on the spot. At any given time, a decision can either conclude or prolong a disciplinary problem. Thus, high on the list of teacher competencies is the ability to think through options before acting.

To manage classrooms effectively, reflective teachers must take two important factors into account: their emotions and their personal psychological needs. These factors are discussed next.

Restraint. When managing disruptive behavior, teachers must control their emotions. They must model the same restraint they seek to develop in their students. Thus, teaching requires emotional intelligence. *Emotional intelligence* is the ability to perceive a situation as stressful, reflect on the best course of action, and choose a reasonable action. Teachers who are quick to judge are unreflective. Instantaneous judgments have a serious drawback: They could be wrong (Goleman, 1995).

Thoughtless responses to student misbehavior can make a difficult situation worse. In the short term, a student may be embarrassed or humiliated. During the long term, student antipathy will grow with each unpleasant encounter (Braaten, Simpson, Rosell, & Reilly, 1988). Rezmierski (1987) stated,

> To me, the most critical aspect of disciplining youth is the maturity of the hand that provides the discipline. How far adults have advanced in their own schedule of development—how stable and mature they are—determines whether they provide discipline or punishment to the youth with whom they interact. (p. 5)

Personal Needs.   Reflective teachers understand that their personal psychological needs influence their behavior (Costa & Kallick, 2000). Teacher behavior is influenced by the need for control, the need for affiliation, the need for success, and the need to be appreciated. When these needs are frustrated by events either in school or out of school, the unreflective teacher risks projecting these needs onto students. Each frustrated need has a result: A frustrated need to be appreciated can lead to cynicism, a frustrated need for control can lead to an overbearing demand for obedience, and a frustrated need for success can lead to resignation and diminished creativity.

The teacher who engages in *reflection* takes a periodic personal inventory, and understands that students are not sitting in classrooms to meet his or her personal psychological needs. Costa and Kallick (2000) suggested that journal writing can help a teacher develop a reflective inner voice. Other recommendations for fostering a reflective attitude include partnering with a mentor teacher, attending professional conferences, and talking over issues with a trusted friend or colleague.

Proactive Teachers Have High Expectations

What teachers believe about their students goes a long way toward determining student success or failure (Brophy, 1983; Good & Brophy, 2000; Rosenthal & Jacobson, 1968). Teacher action is guided by beliefs about students, and these beliefs can turn into self-fulfilling prophecies. In 1968, Rosenthal and Jacobson documented the power of self-fulfilling prophecies. A *self-fulfilling prophecy* is a belief about an outcome that clearly influences the outcome. The more positive a person's attitude about achieving a goal, the more he or she will persevere to attain it.

In their study, Rosenthal and Jacobson shaped elementary teachers' expectations by telling the teachers that a small group of students in each class from first through sixth grade had been identified as intellectual "bloomers." In reality, the students were assigned to teachers randomly, and no intellectual difference existed among the students. At the conclusion of the academic year, the so-called bloomers showed more significant gains, particularly in the primary grades. The results of follow-up studies indicated that *high expectations* based on optimistic teacher beliefs about student potential produced clear-cut positive results often enough to demonstrate that teachers' expectations have a significant effect on student achievement (Good & Brophy, 2000, p. 27). Thus, teacher expectations shapes teacher behavior, which in turn influences student behavior.

Teachers with high expectations are faced with two challenges: encouraging students who are at risk and building students' self-efficacy. How teachers can meet these challenges is discussed next.

Youths Who Are at Risk.   The results of studies of youths at risk of school failure emphasize the positive impact of high expectations on student behavior. Students who are at risk are those whose life experiences have limited their ability to do well in school. See Figure 2.1 for factors that contribute to a student's being at risk.

Rutter (1981) reported that when teachers had high expectations, low-income schools in London had reduced delinquency rates, fewer behavioral disturbances,

- More than 900,000 children were confirmed victims of abuse and neglect in 1998.
- Black and Native American children are significantly overrepresented among victims of abuse and neglect—double their proportion in the national population.
- Three to 10 million children witness family violence each year.
- Young children are most at risk for being abused and neglected. Infants represent the largest proportion of victims; almost 40% of victims are younger than 6 years of age.
- A history of family violence or abuse is the single most significant contributor to delinquency.
- Children who witness domestic violence may display the following symptoms: sleep disorders, headaches, stomachaches, diarrhea, ulcers, asthma, enuresis, and depression. Such complaints are reactions to stress.
- Children of women who are battered have high rates of poor school performance, truancy, absenteeism, and difficulty concentrating.
- Children who witness domestic violence experience symptoms such as anxiety, aggression, temperament problems, depression, low levels of empathy, and low self-esteem. Lower verbal, cognitive, and motor abilities are also documented as symptoms in children who witness domestic violence.
- Juveniles make up 71% of all sex crime victims reported to the police.
- In 1998, firearms killed 10 children every day. Of these, 2,184 were murdered, 1,241 committed suicide, and 262 were victims of accidental shootings.
- Between 1979 and 1998, gunfire killed nearly 84,000 children and teens in America—36,000 more than the total number of American soldiers killed in Vietnam.
- Not all children exposed to violence suffer significant harmful effects. Resilient factors include a protecting family member, a caring teacher, and supportive peers. Resilient factors also include a child's internal capacity to cope with stress.

FIGURE 2.1 At-Risk Factors for U.S. Youths
From *Teaching Self-Control: A Curriculum for Responsible Behavior* (2nd ed., p. 3), by M. Henley, 2003, Bloomington, IN: National Educational Service. Copyright 2003 by National Educational Service. Reprinted with permission.
Original figure was compiled from *America's Children: Key National Indicators of Well-Being*, by the Federal Interagency Forum on Child and Family Statistics (1999) and *A Month of Mental Health Facts: Fact-of-the-Day*, by the New York University Child Study Center (2001).

and better attendance than those of comparison schools. Henderson (1997) found that teachers with high expectations used a meaningful curriculum, encouraged student participation, used heterogeneous groups for instruction (i.e., little or no tracking or labeling of students), and emphasized prosocial development of their students.

Many students who are at risk sit in classrooms without any sense of hope for the future. They look around their desolate urban or rural surroundings and find scant evidence that perseverance will be rewarded with a better life. These students present a profound challenge. They need to believe that they can succeed; they need hope. Making school a place where students want to spend time is the first stage of developing hope. Building alliances with communities and families, allowing students to make choices, bridging the gap between the curriculum and students' lives, and creating a classroom atmosphere that supports success are several ways proactive educators have improved both the attitudes and the achievement of their students.

Self-Efficacy.   Bandura (2000) defined *self-efficacy* as an individual's beliefs about personal capabilities, especially his or her ability to influence life events. According to Bandura, self-efficacy determines how students feel, think, behave, and motivate themselves, and it is closely aligned with hope (p. 18). Bandura proposed four self-efficacy builders that teachers can capitalize on to increase hope in the classroom: mastery experience, vicarious experience, social persuasion, and reduced stress response.

When students master skills in the classroom, their accomplishments promote confidence and perseverance. Conversely, failure breeds a sense of *learned helplessness*: the nagging belief that you cannot do well.

Vicarious experiences provide another avenue for strengthening students' perceptions of self-efficacy. Watching others succeed reinforces the notion that challenges can be overcome. This modeling effect, especially when the individuals who are observed succeeding have backgrounds similar to the students', is a persuasive method of increasing self-efficacy.

Although not as strong a reinforcer as modeling, social persuasion, particularly when accompanied by legitimate success, is an effective tool for instilling hope. The research on resiliency among youths at risk reaffirms the effectiveness of positive mentoring on young people's ability to rise above difficult challenges in life (Osher, Kendziora, VanDenBerg, & Karl, 1999).

Finally, according to Bandura (2000), self-efficacy is strengthened by reducing emotional distress. Physical symptoms of emotional distress include fatigue, aches, pains, and lack of stamina. Recognizing that persistent physical ailments are sometimes symptoms of chronic stress can provide clues about classroom conditions that might be contributing factors. Helping students recognize their stressors can alert them to negative mood triggers and sustain their efforts to develop coping mechanisms.

Proactive Teachers Are Problem Solvers

A reason for misbehavior always exists. Some students misbehave because they are upset about an event that happened outside school. Others misbehave because they have a temperamental, physical, or neurological problem. Still others misbehave because they have not yet learned how to adapt to the demands of school. Situations within school, such as frustration or competition, can also prompt misbehavior by stretching a student's inadequate impulse control (Henley, 1994a; Redl & Wineman, 1951).

The Phi Delta Kappa Commission on Discipline surveyed schools throughout the United States to identify hallmark qualities of schools that promote self-discipline in their students. In schools with effective disciplinary procedures, teachers looked for the causes of disciplinary problems rather than concentrating on the symptoms (Brophy, 1983; Wayson et al., 1982).

Thus, proactive classroom managers take time to look for the reasons for misbehavior. They problem solve: collect data, generate hunches, and provide positive behavioral supports (Scott, Liaupsin, Nelson, & Jolivette, 2003). This diagnostic approach to solving disciplinary problems in particular and aiding classroom management in general emphasizes solutions based on examination of student characteristics and an understanding of the impact of the educational setting on the individual student's behavior (Taylor-Greene et al., 1997).

Behavioral change is difficult to achieve. Think of unfulfilled New Year's resolutions, unsuccessful diets, and unmet fitness goals. Without commitment and perseverance, personal change is impossible. The poet W. H. Auden (1947) said the following about change:

> We would rather be ruined than changed
> We would rather die in our dread
> Than climb the cross of the moment
> And let our illusions die.
>   Epilogue, "The Age of Anxiety"

As difficult as changing ourselves is, changing another person is formidable. People naturally resist imposed change. However, by focusing on changing the classroom environment rather than on trying to directly change individual behavior, teachers can counter misbehavior without encountering individual resistance.

Teachers can alter their classroom environment in many ways to promote positive student change. Group dynamics, daily routines, lesson composition, delegation of responsibilities, rewards, and consequences are a sample of environmental structures that influence student behavior (Cooper, Heron, & Heward, 1990; Kazdin, 2001).

Group dynamics (i.e., environment) influence individual behavior when a student engages in a specific behavior to impress classmates. Routines established by the teacher influence student behavior by providing a framework for good work habits. Enthusiastic, interesting lessons promote student engagement. Teachers who have smooth *transitions* between lessons have fewer student behavioral problems than those encountered by teachers who begin and end lessons abruptly (Kounin, 1970).

Classroom ambience influences behavior. *Ambience* refers to physical factors such as classroom design and the arrangement of space, as well as elements that affect mood, such as movement and music. Research on brain function indicates that movement enhances memory and that music reduces classroom stress while improving learning (Jensen, 2000b). Changing the environment as an approach to solving problem behaviors is validated every day in classrooms (Chapter 9 covers problem solving in more detail). Consider the case study of Emily.

Reflection, high expectations, and problem solving are characteristics indicative of proactive classroom management. In combination, these teacher qualities help promote a classroom climate that fosters positive student behavior. In contrast, following are four common myths about classroom management that have

Case Study: Emily

Emily, a fifth-grade student, was having consistent behavioral problems in Mr. Allen's classroom. She was fidgety, and she often asked to get out of her seat to sharpen her pencil or get a drink of water. As Mr. Allen's patience wore thin, he became less inclined to grant her requests. Often, Mr. Allen and Emily ended up arguing.

Mr. Allen decided that maybe Emily would do better in Ms. Costa's fifth-grade classroom, which was more activity based than his. In Ms. Costa's classroom, students spent time at learning centers, engaged in cooperative learning activities, and were allowed to attend to minor tasks without asking for permission. Both the principal and Emily's family thought the switch was a good idea. Within a few weeks, Emily's behavior improved. No longer needing to sit for long periods, Emily was more relaxed and was better able to attend to her schoolwork.

evolved through the years, in some educators' minds, as "truths" about classroom structure and discipline.

FOUR MYTHS ABOUT CLASSROOM MANAGEMENT

Teaching is a complex endeavor. Sometimes, the task can seem overwhelming, particularly when you are confronted with students who seem more intent on avoidance than on learning. When classroom management problems arise, simple solutions seem appealing. The quest for finding an easy road to classroom management can sidetrack successful learning by creating detours that lead to dead-end solutions.

Common mistakes include using sarcasm to quiet noisy students, punishing an entire group for individual misbehavior, and neglecting to recognize the role dreary lessons play in fomenting student disruptions. These errors in judgment detract from the classroom climate. The following four *myths about classroom management* describe some basic flaws in thinking that can misdirect a novice teacher as he or she establishes classroom climate procedures.

Myth One: A Well-Managed Classroom Is a Quiet Classroom

Rows of students quietly sitting in their seats may seem like the ideal precursor to learning, but in fact long periods of passivity stifle rather than stimulate thought. Piaget, the father of developmental psychology, found that children learn by doing (Gardner, 1993).

Trial and error is the backbone of learning. As students mature, they proceed through stages of cognitive development that enhance their ability to handle abstract information. Students construct their understandings from their unguided interactions outside school and their guided interactions within school. To learn effectively, young people need opportunities to interact with materials and one another. These facts are well known to educators and for years have been the basis for organizing activity-centered classrooms.

Research on brain function and learning has bolstered developmental psychologists' findings (Sylwester, 2000; Wolfe, 2001). Positron-emission tomography and other technologies that allow direct observation of the human brain in action have added neuroscientific support for the activity-centered classroom. Movement is the only experience that unites all brain levels. Sitting for more than 10 minutes reduces a person's awareness of physical and emotional sensations (Jensen, 2000b). Restlessness, irritability, and attention problems are also exacerbated by long periods of sitting. Movement releases noradrenaline and dopamine, chemicals that enhance attention and behavior. The more opportunities students have to stand, move, walk, lie down, or change sitting positions, the better they will behave.

Individual lessons should include a variety of components to help students maintain attention. The brain discards information it does not perceive as relevant. Students' personal experiences provide a platform for introducing new ideas. Therefore, linking the curriculum to students' lives enhances motivation, attention, and retention. Students need opportunities to compare their perceptions with concepts. Measuring a desk, a book, and a classmate's height not only is more fun than doing calculations on a worksheet, but also sustains attention and minimizes misbehavior.

Well-managed classrooms are busy places where students are actively engaged in learning. Students move around the room. They talk together. They perform activities. The tools of passive learning, such as worksheets, texts, and workbooks, have their place, but they should not predominate. In activity-centered classrooms, teachers incorporate a variety of instructional procedures, including cooperative learning, peer tutoring, learning centers, role-playing, brainstorming, simulations, and class discussions. Each of these activity-based approaches stimulates motivation by meeting students' physiological and psychological needs.

Myth Two: Students Are the Most Common Cause of Classroom Disciplinary Problems

In their survey of school disciplinary problems, Hyman and D'Alessandro (1984) catalogued several causes of school misbehavior. Only two causes relate directly to students: inadequate parenting and inborn traits. Six relate directly to schools: ineffective teacher training, poor school organization, inadequate administrative leadership, inappropriate curricula, overuse of suspensions and punishment, and frustration with learning.

Kounin (1970) found that teachers cause disciplinary problems by neglecting to organize routines and lessons properly. When students are bored, lessons disorganized, and transitions abrupt, students act out more frequently. Kounin observed that teacher traits such as friendliness, humor, and compassion had less to do with preventing behavioral problems than did effective management of classroom routines.

Long (2000) reported that when teachers and students become embroiled in power struggles, 60% of the time teachers overreact and the problem escalates. He recommended that teachers learn not to take student provocations personally. Some specific teacher behaviors that contribute to student misbehavior are sarcasm, put-downs, attacks on students' character, yelling, and other reactions that cause students to "lose face."

Alderman and Nix (1997) said that admonitions should not include critical judgments but should concentrate on describing how behavior should change. Alderman suggested keeping track of negative and positive comments to ensure that criticisms do not outweigh praise. Finally, he allowed that change in students' attitudes and behavior is slow and circuitous.

Behavioral change also requires tolerance for setbacks on the part of both student and teacher (Long, 1986). The spiral model of behavioral change portrays alternative movement between behavioral improvement and regression. Long said,

> Behavioral and academic changes are not conceptualized as linear functions which improve over time but are viewed as a series of progressive loops in which the pupil moves ahead for a period of time, only to return to a lower level of functioning before developing new skills. (p. 6)

Setbacks are most likely to occur when students are distressed either physically or emotionally. The value of the spiral model is that it reminds individuals who work with difficult youths that a temporary regression is to be expected and is not necessarily a sign that classroom accommodations need to be realigned.

Myth Three: Punishment Is an Effective Method for Changing Student Behavior

No other disciplinary technique is more misunderstood than punishment. The use of punishment is based on principles of applied behavior analysis. Maag (2004) described punishment as a consequence that decreases the probability that a behavior will recur. In other words, if the misbehavior continues, punishment is not working and other, less aversive, approaches to changing behavior should be used. Often, punishment is used in schools to buttress authority without a clear sense of whether it is changing student behavior.

Why do teachers and administrators use punishment so liberally as a strategy for changing behavior? Ironically, the answer is found by examining another principle of applied behavior analysis called *negative reinforcement*. Consider the case study of Alan.

Punishment is particularly ineffective with students who display frequent behavioral problems. Redl said the following about punishment: "What counts most in punishment is not what we do to the kid but what the kid does with the experience to which we have exposed him" (cited in Brendtro & Long, 1997, p. 133). When teachers punish students, teachers assume that students understand the logical cause-and-effect relationship between their behavior and sanctions. However, chronic rule breakers do not perceive punishment in the same way that the adults

Case Study: Alan

Eleven-year-old Alan is sitting in the back of the room making sarcastic comments. Ms. Jones tells Alan, "Cut it out." Alan is embarrassed, and he complies. Ms. Jones's behavior is negatively reinforced because Alan's behavior has stopped, which has, in effect, rewarded her for her caustic remark. If Alan has learned his lesson Ms. Jones's response was fine. However, suppose Alan continues to make frequent, inappropriate comments: what should she do then? Teachers like Ms. Jones often find themselves punishing the same student repeatedly without gaining long-term behavioral change.

who are administering the punishment intend. Youths who are impulsive and aggressive, in particular, harbor cognitive distortions that serve as buffers between their behavior and their culpability. These cognitive distortions provide rationales for antisocial behavior. Examples of cognitive distortions include blaming their problems on someone else (i.e., projection); overlooking their own contributions to an unpleasant incident; and rationalizing (Goleman, 1995; Henley 1994a; Henley & Long, 1999; B. L. Lewis, 1992; Redl & Wineman, 1951).

For punishment to work, the student must accept both emotionally and cognitively that the punisher was justified. However, students with challenging behaviors often do not. Consider the case study of Wyatt.

Wyatt's reaction is a reminder that although punishment might temporarily stop a behavior, it does not teach new behaviors. In addition, it often breeds resentment and hostility (Skinner, 1978).

Myth Four: Students with Emotional Problems Are in Special Education Programs

A common misconception is that students with emotional problems are in special education programs. Although some are in these programs, students with emotional

Case Study: Wyatt

Wyatt is 16 years old. He attends an alternative school for students with behavioral problems. His teacher has warned him several times about playing "basketball" with wads of paper and the wastebasket. Finally, in desperation, the teacher sends Wyatt to the principal's office as punishment. The teacher believes this action will help Wyatt understand that his misbehavior has consequences, and the next time Wyatt is warned to stop goofing off, he will comply. However, Wyatt's thoughts on the matter are extremely different. First, he is glad to leave the "boring" class. Second, he is also resentful because other kids were goofing off during the morning and they did not get kicked out of class—more evidence, in Wyatt's mind, that the teacher does not like him. Finally, Wyatt decides that he is tired of being scapegoated, and he walks past the principal's office and out the front door. He hitchhikes home and spends the rest of the day drinking beer and smoking marijuana with his buddies.

problems are not found solely in special education classes. Many are educated in general education classes. Many students remain undiagnosed.

Included in General Education.   Under federal guidelines, students must be identified as "emotionally disturbed" to qualify for special education services. In 2000, approximately 8% of students aged 6 to 21 years received special education services because of an emotional disturbance (U.S. Department of Education, 2002).

Most students identified as emotionally disturbed have serious problems dealing with authority and school routines. A longitudinal study of students aged 9 to 21 years who were receiving special education services for serious emotional disturbance revealed that 70% of these students had a "conduct disorder" (Greenbaum et al., 1998). Students with such a disorder are aggressive and continuously violate rules for behavior. Anxiety disorder and depression disorder were the next most frequently reported psychiatric difficulties students receiving special education experienced. Many students have overlapping emotional problems. Among students with conduct disorder, 67% had a co-occurring disorder.

U.S. special education law—the Individuals with Disabilities Education Act (IDEA)—requires that students with disabilities, to the maximum feasible extent, be included in the general classroom. The "inclusion" movement has placed more responsibility on general education teachers for the overall instruction of students with emotional and behavioral problems. Thus, most students receiving special education services in 2000 spend the majority (80%) of their day in general education classrooms (U.S. Department of Education, 2002). In addition, most students with attention-deficit/hyperactivity disorder (ADHD) are taught primarily in general education classrooms (U.S. Department of Education, 2002).

Undiagnosed.   Mental health professionals have expressed widespread concern that special education services for students with emotional disturbance are provided principally for students who act out their problems, whereas students who keep their emotional problems to themselves are overlooked (U.S. Public Health Service, 2000). In the report of a study published by the Children's Defense Fund, entitled *Unclaimed Children,* Knitzer (1982) estimated that 3 million children have emotional problems and two thirds of them receive either no services or inappropriate services.

At the 2001 Surgeon General's Conference on Children's Mental Health, Forness (2001) stated that a study of 3,700 students conducted at the University of Alabama revealed that the majority of students with emotional problems go unrecognized. Because of inadequate mental health services, many youths go without needed professional help (Epstein, Kutash, & Duchnowski, 1998).

Consequently, sitting within every general education classroom may be two or three students who have an emotional or a behavioral problem serious enough to warrant professional help. Indicators of mental health problems that general education teachers should be alert to include chronic absenteeism, frequent physical complaints, and lethargy (U.S. Public Health Service, 2000).

THE ORGANIZATIONAL NATURE OF SCHOOL

Classroom management procedures are dictated by the organizational necessity of managing the interactions of hundreds of young people and dozens of adults within one building for 6 hours a day. Bells, schedules, lines, rules, and sanctions are bureaucratic staples of school life. Bureaucratic routines can dictate the school climate or be a backdrop to a more inclusive, community-based approach to education. An overly bureaucratic school provides scant opportunities for students to develop a sense of community. Finding ways to supplant bureaucratic procedures with community-based practices presents a challenge.

Meanwhile the major organizational consideration for teachers is maintaining classroom control.

Classroom "Control"

How students behave, how much effort they put into their schoolwork, and how much they enjoy school are directly related to the issue of *classroom control*. Learning cannot occur in a classroom where disruptions are commonplace and behavioral problems abound. In fact, for the novice educator, control of the class is paramount. The thought of managing the behavior of 25 young people for 6 hours with no backup or respite can be intimidating. Amanda, a graduate student who was making a career change into teaching, related the following conversation with her husband (Henley, Ramsey, & Algozzine, 2003):

> At the breakfast table last week I was talking incessantly about how well I was doing in my courses at the college and about how all the information I was getting about teaching was finally coming together. I was sure that I was soon going to be an English teacher extraordinaire, just like Robin Williams in the film *Dead Poets Society*. My husband was staring at me with his cold, calculating eyes and I knew what was coming; we had this conversation before. "What will you do when some kid acts up in your class?" he asked, a knowing smile on his lips. "Well that's easy," I said. "I will handle it in as mature and responsible a way as you would expect from someone of my obvious mental stature." And I smiled, but my husband did not. "You'll cry," he said, and then he smiled. (p. 292)

The traditional way for teachers to maintain classroom control is through autocratic classroom management. The goal of this type of classroom management is *compliance*.

Autocratic Classroom Management.   The pressure to maintain order in a classroom is omnipresent. The principal expects it, parents expect it, other teachers expect it, and students expect it. Many teachers report that losing control of their class is their greatest fear. For the new teacher, taking charge and showing students who is the boss might seem the reasonable course of action (Canter & Canter, 1992). In an autocratic classroom, the teacher dictates and students comply.

Nichols (1992) listed eight reasons why teachers gravitate toward autocratic classroom management styles:

1. Some children lack self-control skills, so the teacher must substitute external controls.
2. The teacher needs to maintain dignity and stop misbehavior in its tracks.
3. Teachers grow up with the notion, based on their personal experience, that teachers are the "boss" in the classroom.
4. Some teachers have a lurking belief that students are incapable of behaving in a self-directed, responsible manner.
5. A rudimentary knowledge of behavior modification leads some teachers to overemphasize external controls and overvalue punishment as a tool for behavioral change.
6. No teacher wants to be viewed as incapable of controlling a class. An authoritarian approach seems the best way to establish who is in charge.
7. Some teachers fear their students. They believe the adage "If you give them an inch, they'll take a mile."
8. For some teachers, silent, controlled classrooms are their model of the ideal learning environment.

Critics of *autocratic teaching* practices refer to such approaches as *obedience models* and *curricula of control* (Curwin & Mendler, 1997; Goodlad, 1984; Nichols, 1992). Curwin and Mendler (1997) argued that obedience models are popular because they are simple and they appear to produce immediate results.

If the teacher favors an autocratic approach, the pattern of classroom interactions is straightforward. The teacher is in charge and the students are expected to defer to teacher authority. Results will vary depending on how readily students bow to the teacher's will. If students comply, the climate will be one of studied passivity; if students do not comply, the climate will be adversarial. Peaceful coexistence usually depends on the teacher's ability to judiciously wield sanctions and rewards to elicit student conformity.

RESPONSIBLE BEHAVIOR

The purpose of education is to teach students to be responsible citizens. *Responsible behavior* is not acquired easily. To behave responsibly, an individual must reflect on actions, weigh choices, make sensible judgments, and act accordingly. You do not learn how to be responsible through dictum; it is acquired through practice (Goleman, 1995).

Horace Mann is widely credited with articulating the principles on which the U.S. public school system was founded. Mann believed that although reading, spelling, and writing were important, the primary mission of education was to build character. He often quoted the proverb "Train up a child in the way he should go; and when he is old he will not depart from it" (cited in Gibbon, 2002, p. 33).

When compliance is the main goal of classroom management, students do not have the opportunity to learn traits of responsible behavior such as cooperation, reflection, and respect for others. Sternberg (2002) said,

> When schools teach for wisdom, they teach students that what is important is not just what you know, but how you use what you know—whether you use it for good ends or bad. They are teaching for what some educators call the "fourth R" (i.e., "reading," "riting," "rithmetic")—"responsibility." (p. 42)

Sternberg (2002) listed egocentrism, pride, intolerance, and impulsiveness as four fallacies of thought that characterize clever but irresponsible people. Responsible students are emotionally intelligent (Goleman, 1995; Henley, 2003). They think about consequences before they act. They can see another person's point of view (i.e., are empathetic, not egocentric). They accept their frailties and resolve to do better (i.e., are humble, not proud). Emotionally intelligent individuals consider others' rights (i.e., are respectful, not intolerant) and the consequences of their actions (i.e., are reflective, not impulsive). The purpose of teaching academics is to help students learn to think. The purpose of teaching responsibility is to help students learn to be civil.

DEMOCRATIC VALUES

The classroom community models democratic values. Gathercoal (1993) maintained that a classroom management system should reflect individuals' basic rights as framed in the U.S. Constitution. When dealing with misbehavior, teachers should administer discipline "judiciously." Students have a right to due process, and this right should be reflected in school disciplinary procedures. As simple a gesture as allowing a student to tell his or her version of a misbehavior event exemplifies due process. Some schools have instituted peer review panels for mediation of cases of serious infractions. Allowing students to establish rules for behavior and sanctions is another example of due process in action. If we as educators want students to participate fully in a democratic society, we need to give them direct experience in how democracy works.

Coloroso (1994) and Kohn (1996) maintained that teachers should distribute power to students in doses that will facilitate their taking ownership for their personal behavior. Other people advocate *democratic classrooms* on the basis that it is sound educational practice. Students' motivation to learn is increased when they are allowed input into classroom activities. As student participation in learning increases, classroom management problems decrease (Glasser, 1990; Mendler, 1992).

Brendtro and Brokenleg (1993) argued that young people have deep-seated needs for autonomy, generosity, mastery, and independence. When these basic needs are met, students will participate more fully in classroom activities. Curricula of control strip young people of valuable learning experiences required to meet these needs. Unmet needs frustrate students and contribute to behavioral problems. All students have a basic psychological need for autonomy (Hall, Lindzey, & Campbell, 1998). Students who are given some control over their activities participate with enthusiasm, whereas students denied autonomy will still try to meet this need, but through nonconstructive behavior such as refusing to do work or talking back to a teacher.

Glasser (1986) espoused *control theory.* He stated that students need a certain amount of control over their environment or learning is desultory and fragmentary. He observed that while teachers are struggling to motivate students in their studies, the same students will enthusiastically participate in extracurricular activities. The difference in motivation, Glasser maintained, is that extracurricular activities afford students opportunities to exercise some control over their activities and to do things they care about.

Glasser's key words are *some control.* Adopting democratic values means allowing students *some* choice—but not complete license.

Choice, Not License

Allowing students some control over their school activities should not be confused with permissiveness or a lowering of standards. Landfried (1989) observed that sometimes teachers confuse *choice* with *license.* Responsible behavior means making choices and abiding by these decisions. Choice does not mean students are allowed to indulge in irresponsible behavior. They must be held accountable for their choices and their actions. Landfried cited some examples of how teachers inadvertently "enable" irresponsible behavior:

- Allowing students to sleep, read newspapers, or carry on irrelevant conversations with other students during classroom activities
- Making excuses for students so that they can avoid blame (e.g., "She didn't really mean it"; "He was tired from an after-school job")
- Accepting flimsy excuses from "good" students for inappropriate behaviors that would not be accepted from "troublemakers"
- Putting words into the mouths of students struggling to express thoughts or repeating questions for inattentive individuals
- Picking up trash left around the classroom by students or cleaning graffiti off desks or walls

Most students want to do well in school, and they look to their teachers for guidance. Corbett and Wilson (2002) interviewed inner-city adolescents about the type of teacher who helped them excel. Students consistently reported six qualities they admired in teachers. Good teachers, they said, did the following:

1. Pushed students
2. Maintained order
3. Explained until everyone understood
4. Varied classroom activities

5. Tried to understand students
6. Helped students

These traits suggest that students are most responsive to teachers who take an active interest in their welfare. Such teachers challenge their students. They have high expectations for student success and they push students to excel.

Responsible behavior cannot be taught without holding students accountable for their behavior. One of the most important lessons young people must learn is that consequences follow actions. Providing students with *choice, not license*—opportunities to make *some* decisions about how they spend their time in school—helps them learn valuable lessons in personal responsibility. Reflecting, weighing choices, working with others, and abiding by decisions are core skills of the responsible individual. Practice is required to cultivate these skills. A student does not learn to be responsible by hearing lectures about the topic. Providing students with experiences to learn responsible behavior is one of the primary goals of the proactive classroom manager. This goal is accomplished by establishing procedures and routines that actively encourage student participation in the classroom community. See Table 2.1 for a comparison of the democratic classroom with the autocratic classroom.

TABLE 2.1 *Comparative Features of Autocratic and Democratic Classrooms*

Autocratic Classroom	Democratic Classroom
Primary value: compliance	Primary value: cooperation
Teacher is "boss"	Teacher is leader
Rules made and enforced by teacher	Rules made by teacher and students; some consequences determined through consensus
Desks in rows to keep students isolated	Desks grouped to enhance student interaction
Instruction primarily lecture and independent seat work	Instruction multifaceted, utilizing a variety of methods, including cooperative learning, peer tutoring, lecturing, brainstorming, and learning strategies
One-size-fits-all approach to how students learn	Instruction modified according to student learning styles
Punishments used as sanctions	Logical consequences used as sanctions
Minimal student input into classroom affairs	Students encouraged to participate in classroom decisions
Low tolerance for students with behavioral difficulties	Positive behavioral supports used
Austere classroom ambience	Warm, user-friendly classroom climate
Students motivated to learn by use of rewards and punishments	Students motivated by the desire to succeed

THE CLASSROOM COMMUNITY

Schaps (2000) provided the following definition of the *classroom community*:

> A feeling among students of positive connection to peers and adults in the school, and a sense that they have a significant voice in at least some of the decision-making and problem solving that occur in the course of everyday classroom life. (p. 14)

Although no two classrooms are identical with regard to how a teacher can develop a community focus in them, several elements characterize classroom communities. Within classroom communities, positive student–teacher relationships and student–student relationships are cultivated. Students are allowed to make decisions about how they spend their time in school. Regular class meetings deal with issues relative to maintaining harmony and group cohesiveness. Learning is activity based, and teaching approaches that utilize students as resources, such as cooperative learning, are frequently used.

Classroom communities are student centered. Individual differences are prized, and students' interests, their culture, their developmental needs, and their individual concerns are emphasized. Because classroom communities prize diversity, this classroom management model is frequently incorporated within *inclusion programs*, programs in which students with special needs are maintained full time in the regular classroom.

Three benefits result from using a community approach as a foundation for classroom management. They are *improved productivity*, *improved behavior*, and *improved citizenship* (i.e., opportunities are provided for students to learn firsthand lessons for participating in a democratic society).

Improved Productivity

A community-based educational classroom increases productivity by building trust among adults and students. Bryk and Schneider (2003) analyzed trust in Chicago public schools. They found that trust rested on four supports: respect, competence, integrity, and personal regard for one another. In their analysis of 12 public schools, these researchers discovered that schools reporting strong trust links were 3 times more likely to report improvement on standardized tests in reading and mathematics than were schools where trust levels were low. In summarizing their findings, Bryk and Schneider said, "These data provide our first evidence directly linking the development of relational trust in a school community and long-term improvement in academic productivity" (cited in Gewertz, 2002).

Trust between individuals is the forerunner to group cohesion. *Cohesion* refers to the quality of a group that includes individual pride, commitment, and morale (Shepard, 1964). Cohesiveness is built through members' participation in decision making. Korinek, Walther-Thomas, McLaughlin, and Williams (1999) found that when students feel as if they are part of the classroom community, their cohesiveness has a positive effect on their attitudes, interests, and productivity. Cohesive classrooms provide opportunities for critical and creative thinking not found in traditional authoritarian classrooms.

Kensington Avenue Elementary School in Springfield, Massachusetts, used the *responsive classroom* (Eliot, 1993) as a model for establishing a community within the school. In 1999, despite a 92% poverty rate and the inclusion of 22% of students with mild disabilities in all general education classrooms, Kensington ranked first in Massachusetts for most improved fourth-grade standardized test scores ("Cheers for Kensington," 1999).

Other schools that emphasize school–community partnerships have reported similar results. For example, Charles Drew Elementary School in West Philadelphia, Pennsylvania, outdid every other school in the state in improving standardized test scores in math and reading. Likewise, Hampton Year Round Elementary in Greensboro, North Carolina, earned exemplary school status on the basis of state achievement test scores (www.communityschools.org/CCSDocuments/partner-ships.html). Architects of another community model—*consistency management and cooperative discipline*—documented statistically significant higher achievement test scores than those obtained by students who did not participate in community-centered classrooms. Three years after the initiation of the community model, students gained an average of three quarters of a year's achievement over that of comparison students (Freiberg, 1996).

At Hazelwood School in Louisville, Kentucky, second and third graders learned and worked together without the need for incentives or test scores. (C. C. Lewis, Schaps, & Watson, 1996). Their enthusiasm for study was reinforced by co-operative work. Before beginning a partners exercise, the teacher reviewed rules for helping. The students provided the guidelines:

"Disagree without being mean."
"If your partner says something that doesn't fit, then work it into another part."
"Let your partner say all they want to say." (p. 16)

The researchers in this study documented improvement in motivation and students' ability to collaborate.

To some extent, each community-based classroom model addresses the pivotal role of intrinsic motivation in learning. By capitalizing on students' interests, developmental abilities, and experiences, community-based models depend less on rewards or incentives to motivate students. Although the previously mentioned results are impressive, a caveat is warranted: Enhanced productivity does not necessarily translate into immediate improvement in achievement test scores. Several factors, including the quality of instruction, preschool readiness of the students, socioeconomic status of the students, and parental involvement, play a significant role in determining success on standardized achievement tests.

Improved Behavior

Schools emphasizing community in the classroom produce students who are more ethical and less prone to behavioral and drug problems (Bryk & Driscoll, 1998;

Hawkins, Catalano, Kosterman, Abbot, & Hill, 1999; Resnick et al., 1997). The W. T. Grant Consortium's study of prevention programs that seek to curb student drug abuse, smoking, teen pregnancies, and dropping out revealed that effective prevention programs teach a core of emotional and social competencies, including cooperation, conflict resolution, and management of impulsive behavior (Goleman, 1995). The classroom-as-a-community approach provides students with many opportunities to learn how to enhance their social competence. According to Panico (1997), empowerment promotes responsible behavior. Even for students with chronic behavioral problems,

> When our once disenfranchised students are empowered to help conduct community [i.e., classroom] affairs, make community decisions, manage community discipline, and mediate community conflicts, they have far better reasons to put limits on their own behavior than obedience-based programs could ever provide. (p. 37)

Glasser and Wubbolding (1997) differentiated between the *lead teacher* and the *boss teacher*. Whereas the boss teacher's management style is "My way or the highway," the lead teacher attempts to involve students in decision making and appeals to students' intrinsic motivation. Rather than following classroom rules because of teacher directives, students develop a sense of "ownership" for their behavior. The dual themes of personal responsibility and intrinsic motivation fostered by empowerment are found throughout the literature on community in classrooms (Coloroso, 1994; Freiberg, 1996; Glasser, 1986; Goleman, 1995; Kohn, 1996; Purkey & Novak, 1996). Schaps (2000) summarized research findings on the effectiveness of community models on student behavior. He reported that within a community climate, students were more ethical, more socially adept, and less prone to problem behaviors such as drug abuse and violence.

Advocates of character education and social skills programs alike strive to weave lessons in civil behavior throughout the academic curriculum:

> The common thread is the goal of raising the level of social and emotional competence in children as part of their regular education—not just something taught remedially to children who are faltering and identified as "troubled," but a set of skills and understandings essential for every child. (Goleman, 1995, p. 262)

Concurrently teaching academic skills and social skills establishes an experiential pattern for students. Contrast the effect of reading a chapter on "cooperation" as part of a social studies lesson with students' participating in cooperative learning groups to develop class presentations on global warming. Trying to teach social skills and civility through reading assignments or workbook exercises is a trivial exercise in miseducation. The classroom is a microcosm of society, and it provides a laboratory in which to study human relations. Students learn about cooperation by working together; they learn about taking responsibility by making decisions; they learn about diversity by helping one another. Students' feelings, their behavior, and their attitudes become topics in themselves. These topics are explored through both direct and incidental learning.

Improved Citizenship

Freiberg (1996) characterized high school students as "tourists" passing through the citizenship lessons embedded in the high school curriculum. He stated, "Although we teach about democracy, we rarely practice it in most schools and classrooms" (p. 23). Freiberg developed the Consistency Management and Cooperative Discipline (CMCD) project to serve as a model for implementing democratic principles in secondary classrooms. It merges five themes: prevention, caring, cooperation, organization, and community.

The CMCD model is based on Freiberg's (1996) conclusion that 80% of classroom management problems can be prevented by spending the first few weeks of school establishing democratic procedures for student participation in setting high standards for behavior. Each class lays a foundation by developing its own written "constitution" of individual rights. Caring is highlighted by periodic audiotaping of classroom discussions and replaying the tape to analyze how often negative comments seep into student and teacher conversation. Cooperation is built through teacher divestment of control and trust in students. Sergio, an eighth-grade student, wrote, "I feel lucky today because the day has just started and we have already been trusted in something we have never been trusted on, being alone. It is 8:15 and everything is cool. Nothing is even wrong" (p. 34).

Gathercoal (1993) said that the goal of discipline should be to help students make the transition from fear of authority to social responsibility. Like the constitution, rules should have a basis in fair and equitable treatment. Judicious rules are written in a positive form—for example, "Walk in the halls" rather than "No running." Judicious rules have a rationale and include due-process procedures so that violators can make appeals. When students see the reason for rules and participate in rule development, they are learning through direct experience about justice in a democratic society.

Fleming (1996), a seventh-grade teacher, believed that school should provide students with practice for participating in a democratic society. He asked his students to imagine a perfect society. They wrote autobiographies about their gifts, perspectives, and hopes for the future. Then Fleming organized them in groups of four and asked them to design a society that would accommodate each member's needs and wishes. They discussed the function of school and established a set of rules that would facilitate meeting their goals in school. After contrasting various ideas, the students voted on a constitution for the class. Sanctions were spelled out in four ascending, nonpunitive consequences. The collaboratively generated rules featured a provision that at any given time a student or teacher could ask for a class meeting to deal with an issue. Fleming maintained that the direct experience of designing a code for civility was a stronger lesson in civics than anything his students could have read in a textbook.

Before the rewards of creating a classroom community (i.e., improved productivity, behavior, and citizenship) can be obtained, the teacher must address three issues at the beginning of the school year. The teacher must, first, effectively arrange the classroom space; second, have the appropriate classroom resources; and, third, establish purposeful classroom routines.

CLASSROOM SPACE

The first priority at the beginning of the school year, even before the students arrive, is *classroom organization*—organizing classroom space and determining how students will use the space. How you go about this task is determined by your goals and your resources. The essence of community is the participants' active involvement; this means students must be able to move around the classroom with a minimum of fuss. Teachers who emphasize community configure their classrooms accordingly.

The single most visible indicator of the classroom climate is the physical ambience. Like a favorite restaurant, a classroom needs an inviting atmosphere. Several ways to achieve such an atmosphere are as follows:

- Survey students for their input on classroom decorations.
- Allow students to do the decorating.
- Have students meet in committees to decide on any classroom changes.

Student input enhances their sense of ownership of the classroom, which in turn increases their sense of personal responsibility. The more students care about their classroom, the more invested they will feel in their school activities.

Students who spend most of their day in a single classroom need storage areas for personal and school materials. Secondary classrooms have changing populations. Teachers in high school and middle school need to find creative ways to personalize these spaces so that students will feel comfortable.

The traditional, autocratic arrangement of desks is rows. The purpose of this linear structure is to prevent students from talking to one another. In a community classroom, desks are arranged to facilitate student interaction. Several ways of doing so are used. Desks can be arranged in small groups of four or six. This seating plan is preferred in many elementary classrooms. Other configurations include parallel seating, station seating, and alternative seating. Configurations used in secondary classrooms are tables, circles, or desks arranged in the shape of a horseshoe design (Figure 2.2).

Sometimes, teachers are concerned that students might have difficulty adjusting to more-interactive seating arrangements than those to which they are accustomed. In such a case, the teacher can initially begin with rows and gradually move into interactive seating patterns as the year progresses. This strategy is recommended for students who have been exposed to autocratic classrooms for a number of years. Also, students who have self-control problems need to be taught how to work cooperatively. (This topic is covered in more detail in the social skills section of Chapter 7.)

A temporary arrangement of desks facing the front of the room will cut down on peer distractions. However, as Knitzer, Steinberg, and Fleisch (1990) reported, although teachers often group students with behavioral problems in a way that

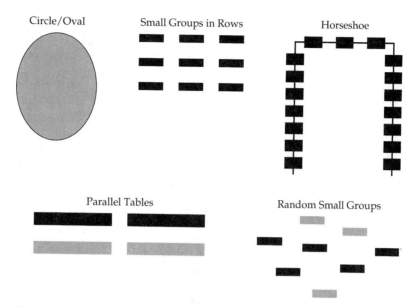

FIGURE 2.2 Desk Configurations

isolates them from one another, this arrangement should be only temporary, until students learn how to interact constructively.

Students should be assigned seats and told the first day that seating assignments will change during the year, as will desk arrangements. Although this directive might seem out of line with a community emphasis, the reasons for it are compelling. When students determine who sits with whom, cliques can quickly undermine the progress of turning a classroom into a community. In addition, a community classroom is organic. It changes form and structure according to the evolving needs of the community. Desks are portable. Because community classrooms emphasize activity-based learning, the physical configuration of the room will change throughout the year to reflect the evolving needs of both students and teacher.

CLASSROOM RESOURCES

The possibilities for arranging a classroom depend on the available resources. The size of the room, number of students, schedules, routines, equipment, and furniture all must be taken into account.

When resources (e.g., filing cabinets, tables and chairs, computers, rugs, comfortable furniture, room dividers) are meager, the teacher can solicit donations from local businesspeople. Furniture stores keep slightly soiled or scratched furniture in storage, and proprietors are often eager to donate marred items to a local school. Science equipment, computers, arts and crafts materials, and lumber are a few classroom materials that local businesspeople can provide. Parents are another source of materials and equipment. A letter to parents indicating specific items that are needed will always get a response from some. Yard sales and flea markets are another source of materials.

Principals like to know when their teachers are representing the school, so teachers should first clear any requests for donations with the building administrator. They should also talk with the building maintenance person about ideas for rearranging the classroom space, particularly if doing so would involve adding rugs or other materials that the maintenance person would be responsible for keeping clean.

Following are seven key concerns for teachers to keep in mind when they are arranging furniture (Evertson & Emmer, 1982b; Sylwester, 2000):

1. Keep high-traffic areas free of congestion.
2. Be sure you can easily see the students.
3. Keep frequently used teaching materials and student supplies readily at hand.
4. Be certain students can easily see whole-class presentations and displays.
5. Arrange furniture, room dividers, workstations, learning centers, and so forth in a manner that allows students to move easily throughout the room.
6. Create personal space for students.
7. Solicit student feedback on how they feel about the comfort level of the classroom.

Teachers can also draw a floor plan for the classroom. Get input from veteran teachers and keep in mind that even good plans need revising once the students arrive.

Following are some examples of how educators have embellished sterile space to enhance a sense of community:

- One special education teacher changed the conventional look of his classroom by adding a rug, tables, comfortable chairs, floor lamps, and a sitting area with large pillows for quiet reading.
- On bulletin boards throughout one elementary school, student art is displayed in professional-looking mats and frames.
- A middle school teacher set up rocking chairs near tables with lamps, similar to a living room.
- Each spring, elementary school students plant flowers around the school building.
- In lieu of using a rug to reduce the scraping noise of desk chairs, an elementary teacher inserted old tennis balls on chair legs.

CLASSROOM ROUTINES

Daily routines provide the infrastructure for all classroom activities. Well-organized routines decrease students' disruptive behavior, increase students' engagement, and increase students' achievement on standardized tests (Evertson & Harris, 1995).

Marzano and Marzano's (2003) analysis of effective classroom management organization indicated that a number of overlapping daily concerns need to be addressed. One priority is establishing participation guidelines.

How students should relate to one another and the teacher must be established the first day of class. Marzano and Marzano (2003) outlined priorities that elementary and secondary teachers typically address:

Elementary

- Politeness and helpfulness when dealing with others
- Respecting the property of others
- Not interrupting the teacher or others
- Not hitting or shoving others

Secondary

- Bringing materials to class
- Being in an assigned seat at the beginning of class
- Respecting and being polite to others
- Talking or not talking at specific times
- Leaving or not leaving the assigned seat
- Respecting other people's property

As mentioned, each of these priorities should be dealt with on the first day of class. Asking students to present their ideas on proper class decorum is a good beginning. Gaps in student input on the preceding priorities can be filled in by the teacher during the class discussion. Limits are particularly important for new teachers to establish because students need to know that their teacher is knowledgeable about behavioral expectations and that he or she is quick to assume a leadership role. Taking charge without sounding like a boss or a taskmaster is a characteristic of effective leadership. Leading a discussion about rules for behavior indicates to students that the teacher is *authoritative* (i.e., having or using authority) without being *authoritarian* (i.e., favoring complete obedience to authority).

Movement and Transitions

Teachers must establish two basic types of procedures for daily routines. First, procedures for movement around the classroom are needed. Second, procedures for transitions from one activity to another must be established.

Movement.   One routine to establish is how students move around the room. For instance, do students need to raise their hands to sharpen a pencil, throw away a piece of paper, or walk across the room to get some materials? Another issue that must be addressed are guidelines for changing activities, such as moving from a learning center to a quiet reading area or to a small group. Decisions about how to handle issues of movement and space are based on a number of factors, including the students' developmental level (i.e., younger students need closer supervision than older students do), the students' self-control abilities (i.e., whether students are impulsive, easily frustrated, or hyperactive), and conditioning (i.e., students who are accustomed to strict guidelines will need to be gradually introduced to more latitude).

In general, the less the teacher monitors student movement, the more time he or she has for teaching. Consider a sixth-grade teacher who requires students to raise their hands for permission to sharpen a pencil or get a dictionary. With a class of 25 students, this teacher will be sacrificing instructional time for traffic management duties. Yet, in even the best behaved classroom, some students will require more limits than others. Mendler (1992) argued that the *80–15–5 rule* applies in this case. According to Mendler, within a typical classroom, 80% of all students behave well, 15% require frequent reminders, and 5% display chronic disciplinary problems. He said that the goal is to provide structure for the 15% without overcontrolling the 80% or putting unreasonable limits on the 5%, whose insufficient self-control abilities must be addressed individually.

Transitions.   The school day is punctuated with transitions. Movement from one activity to another must be organized to eliminate disciplinary problems that may occur when students must make the change from unstructured to structured activity (Kounin, 1970). Key transitions include the following:

- The beginning of class
- A change in whole-class activities
- Return from special classes (e.g., art class, assembly, music class)
- Before and after lunch and recess
- Class interruptions (e.g., fire drill, teacher stepping outside the classroom)
- Sudden and unexpected changes in routine (e.g., an announcement that recess will not be outside or that a field trip must be postponed)

Depending on where they have been and what they have been doing, students will enter the classroom in various moods. Coming from the bus at the beginning of the day, students might be agitated or excited, or returning from recess or art class, students might be overstimulated. Establishing a routine helps students become focused on the next task at hand. For instance, in elementary classrooms, the schedule of daily activities should be clearly posted. In secondary classrooms, topics to be covered that period should be outlined before each class begins.

Teachers use a variety of ideas to focus student attention and help them adjust to transitions. Some of these ideas are as follows:

- Post an assignment, a question, or a brain teaser to help students settle in for the day or class period.
- Play quiet music.
- Delegate responsibilities for the week, such as taking attendance, watering plants, and tending to classroom pets.
- Provide students time to review and revise homework.

- Solicit students' input on transition difficulties and allow them to brainstorm solutions.
- Greet students at the classroom door.
- When students arrive at the beginning of the day in overlapping groups because of bus schedules, allow them to play games or work on puzzles.
- Have materials with directions organized ahead of time for changes in class activities.

When difficulties occur during transitions, examine classroom conditions that could be contributing to the difficulties.

Summary

★ Teachers' behavior is shaped by their beliefs about themselves and their students.

★ Proactive teachers are reflective.

★ Proactive teachers have high expectations for their students' success, and they are problem solvers.

★ Proactive teachers recognize that many disciplinary problems can be solved by changing elements of the classroom environment.

★ Even though institutional procedures exert pressure to control students, proactive teachers are not swayed by common school myths such as "Punishment helps change students' behavior" and "A well-managed classroom is a quiet classroom."

★ A strong body of research verifies the positive impact of a community environment on students' actions and productivity.

★ To build a sense of community, teachers must focus their efforts on changing how they and students typically interact. Doing so means thinking about how organization of the classroom space and procedures for handling daily maintenance will support the classroom as a community.

★ Democratic practices increase students' involvement in their learning and help students learn to take responsibility for their behavior.

★ Procedures for managing movement and classroom transitions influence students' behavior.

What You Should Know

Now that you have finished reading this chapter, you should know the following:

Three core beliefs that characterize the classroom management style of proactive teachers

Why "control" is such a major concern for new teachers

Four myths about classroom management

How a classroom community improves productivity and student behavior

Several comparison points between authoritarian and community classrooms
Ideas for arranging the physical layout of a classroom and developing classroom procedures that help maintain order

Applying the Concepts

1. Contrast authoritarian classrooms with community-based classrooms. How do they differ and how are they similar? What are the advantages and disadvantages of each? Which is easier for a teacher to establish and maintain?

2. View segments of the films *Lean on Me* and *Dangerous Minds*. What is the difference in how the main characters dealt with similar disciplinary problems? Critique Hollywood's approach to classroom management. Is it realistic? Compare segments of *Dead Poets Society* and *The Breakfast Club*. What was the impact of different teaching styles on how students felt about school?

3. At a field site, identify specific routines that build community and specific routines that foster authoritarian classrooms.

4. Interview several teachers about classroom control. What do they think is important and what advice would they give beginning teachers?

5. Review journal articles in *Educational Leadership* and *Phi Delta Kappan* on community in the classroom. Explain why authors support the idea of community. What are some ideas expressed in these articles for building community?

6. Interview parents of a school-aged child about how they feel about their child's school. Contrast this information with the annual *Phi Delta Kappan/ Gallup* poll on the public's attitude about schools.

7. Interview several public school students about how they feel about school. Use some of the topics in this chapter as probes. For instance, how do students "test" teachers? Why do students "test" teachers? What do students find appealing about their classrooms? What aspects of their classrooms do students find unappealing?

8. At your field site, observe how teachers interact with students with behavioral problems. Can you identify any aspects of classroom routines or structure that contribute to behavioral problems? Can you identify elements of teacher behavior that contribute to or minimize behavioral problems?

9. Draw a diagram for a classroom in which the teacher's goal is compliance. Draw a diagram of a classroom in which the teacher's goal is community. How does the physical layout differ for each? How do teachers who value

compliance differ in their approach to classroom procedures from teachers who value community?

10. Interview veteran teachers to solicit "tricks of the trade" that teachers use to manage group transitions in their classrooms.

11. Draw a floor plan for your ideal classroom. Explain how the floor plan will expedite transitions. What procedures will be put in place to deal with daily maintenance issues such as distributing materials, attending to students' requests for help, permitting students to leave their seats, and other typical procedural concerns?

Chapter 3

Building a Classroom Community

Chapter Outline

Elements of Community
    Empowerment
    Belonging
    Cooperation
Community in Action: Model School
Programs
    Places

Programs
Procedures
    People as Partners
Summary
What You Should Know
Applying the Concepts

 Key Terms

Acceptance
Attachment theory
Authoritarian group
Autonomy
Belonging
Brainstorming
Capability
Choice theory
Classroom meetings
Classroom space
Community
Community-based school
Connection
Contributions

Cooperation
CoZi initiative
Democratic groups
Empowerment
First weeks of school
Group structure
Interdisciplinary
Lead management
Mistaken goals
Procedures
Scapegoating
Service learning
Student choice

Introduction

A *community* is a group of individuals who share a vision. Within a classroom community many typical classroom management problems are reduced. In addition, in a classroom community, responsibilities for classroom maintenance are shared. Sharing responsibilities provides the teacher with more time to devote to instruction. Empowerment, belonging, and cooperation are three features of classroom communities. Advocates for classroom communities report benefits in student productivity, behavior, and citizenship. Parental involvement is also enhanced because parents are encouraged to become more actively involved in school affairs. No single best approach exists for establishing a community climate in a school or classroom. However, in model programs, efforts are focused on the four *P*s: places, programs, procedures, and people as partners. *Places* refers to arranging physical space to create a user-friendly ambience. *Programs* refers to planning curriculum that is interdisciplinary and collaborative. *Procedures* refers to daily classroom activities that foster a communal atmosphere, and *people as partners* means structuring experiences that give students the opportunity to serve others while learning.

A *community* is a group of individuals who share a sense of solidarity. Community is as much a feeling as it is a concrete entity. A small town divided by politics can advertise itself as a community, but without a communal feeling, it is simply an aggregate of houses, buildings, and roads bound by proximity. Members of a community share a vision, and they work together to achieve their goals. For a school to blossom into a community, the culture of the school must support every member as a valued participant. The value of community becomes a reality when daily procedures are established that ensure every member has a voice in decisions that affect him or her.

ELEMENTS OF COMMUNITY

Traits that typify community in schools and classrooms include the following:

- A strong student–teacher relationship
- Procedures that allow students to participate in classroom decisions
- A shared ethos of caring, concern, and support
- An emphasis on cooperation
- An appreciation of cultural diversity
- High expectations for student success, and commitment to challenging learning activities
- Connections to families and the local community

Community-based classrooms are founded on the premise that teachers and students are partners in the teaching–learning process (Albert, 1996; Sylwester, 2001). Educators have developed various approaches for fostering the democratic values of community within classrooms. In this chapter, descriptions of model programs illustrate the different social environments that educators have created to teach students to get along with others and to take responsibility for their behavior. However different they may be in design or emphasis, community classrooms share three values: empowerment, belonging, and cooperation.

Empowerment

Empowerment means providing students with opportunities to make decisions that affect their learning. Student empowerment enhances the perception that they have some control over their lives. Teachers will sometimes say the following about a student who is misbehaving: "He is out of control" or "She needs to learn to control herself." Students cannot practice self-control when they are under the teacher's thumb. The term *self-control* is oxymoronic if students are denied possibilities to assert themselves.

Much of students' disruptive behavior is an attempt to wrest some control of classroom activities from the teacher (Curwin & Mendler, 1988b; Mendler, 1992; Sylwester, 2000). Consider the student who refuses to complete an assignment because he or she dislikes reading, or the student who goofs off because he or she is bored. In each situation, the offending behavior is an attempt to gain a small amount of leverage over a situation in which the student is virtually powerless. Teachers empower students by organizing classroom activities and procedures that provide choices, elicit students' opinions, and foster interdependence. By channeling students' need for control, teachers provide students with constructive options for developing self-control. Consider the case study of Ginny Nelson.

The case study illustrates three of the four keys to empowering students: giving students autonomy, using the lead management teaching style, and providing students with choices. The benefits of allowing student choice extend not only to students in general education, but also to students receiving special education services. A fourth key to empowering students is helping students who are

 ## Case Study: Ginny Nelson

Ginny Nelson teaches fifth grade in an urban elementary school. Her 30 students' desks are arranged in groups of six. For most of the day, students work together in these small groups. Ms. Nelson moves around the room monitoring students' progress. She gives assignments, explains key concepts, and helps individual students. A relaxed sense of purposefulness accompanies each activity. Students require few directions to stay on task. Each day begins with a class meeting. Ms. Nelson reviews the agenda for the day and then asks students to offer suggestions for improving her plans. The class discusses upcoming projects, and Ms. Nelson encourages students to voice their feelings about how they are progressing in math, reading, and other key curriculum areas. This constant give-and-take helps Ms. Nelson monitor students' attitudes toward school, which, she believes, are a crucial determinant for success.

accustomed to a controlling classroom atmosphere in their transition to participatory learning.

Autonomy.   *Autonomy* is a powerful motivator (Reeve, Bolt, & Cai, 1999). Students will study harder when they have a voice in the curriculum; they will follow with more tenacity rules for behavior they have helped develop; they will care more about the physical condition of classrooms and a school they helped maintain. When researchers compared the performance of students in classrooms where teachers empower students with that of students in classrooms where teachers are controlling, autonomous students excelled in several key areas, including academic performance, motivation, emotional competence, and creativity (Boggiano, Flink, Shields, Seelbach, & Barrett, 1993; Koestner, Ryan, Bernieri, & Holt, 1984; B. C. Patrick, Skinner, & Connell, 1993).

Lead Management.   *Lead management* is the preferred teaching style Glasser and Wubbolding (1997) espoused to empower students. The concept of teacher as lead manager is derived from successful business management practices that have increased productivity by giving workers more control over their labor. When factory workers are allowed to critique manufacturing practices, recommend changes in assembly-line procedures, and share in profits, both productivity and morale increase (Peters, 1984). Glasser and Wubbolding (1997) contrasted the lead manager style with the boss manager style of teaching. The boss manager's motto is "My way or the highway" (p. 41). The boss manager is more concerned with controlling students' behavior than with fostering student empowerment. Whereas the boss manager is authoritarian, the lead teacher is authoritative. The boss manager attempts to control students' behavior; the lead manager promotes students' participation through democratic procedures. Reeve et al. (1999) found that lead managers give students fewer directions, empathize more with students, provide students with more choices, and respond more to student-generated questions than do boss managers.

Lead management is derived from Glasser's *choice theory*. It is a democratic teaching style based on the premise that misbehavior is the result of students' failing to satisfy the universal human needs for belonging, power, freedom, and fun. Specifically, the three main principles of lead management are as follows:

1. **Elicit student input.**   Hold regular class meetings. Arrange students' desks in a circle to promote interaction. Ask students about "quality" behavior and what their best effort is. Use a flip chart to keep track of students' suggestions. When a decision is reached on a discussion topic, have students sign a written agreement.
2. **Ask students what they want from themselves, their teacher, their school.** When discussing misbehavior, avoid asking "why"; doing so will generate only excuses. Ask students to evaluate their behavior, their effort, and their schoolwork. Then, make a plan of action with the students. Recognize that learning to plan takes time and that good planning will not occur during the first few meetings.

3. **Focus on meeting students' needs rather than on controlling behavior.**   Ask fundamental questions about how school can be made into a satisfying experience. Recognize that no easy answers exist but commitment to this process will make the school experience more meaningful to both students and teachers.

Student Choice.   *Student choice* means providing students with opportunities to make some decisions about how they spend their day in school. Researchers have documented, in both general and special education settings, the positive effect of providing students with choices as a path to empowerment (Goleman, 1995; Jolivette, Wehby, Canale, & Massey, 2001). Student choice enhances self-esteem, fosters resilience, and motivates students to excel (Benard, 1992; Lumsden, 1994). Involving students in their learning process has proved beneficial within all types of learning environments, including those designed for youths at risk and for culturally diverse students at both elementary and secondary levels.

As an illustration of how student choice influences motivation, contrast student behavior during the school day with student behavior during extracurricular activities. The same students who move without enthusiasm from class to class during the school day are energized during extracurricular activities. The school newspaper, the debate club, the drama club, and even to some extent sports provide the teacher and students with collaborative ways of interacting. During extracurricular activities, the students are the main participants, while the adults sit on the side to assist, direct, or coach. The students choose to be there, and they feel responsible for the outcome or product, whether it is a yearbook, a play, or a big game.

Each school day presents multiple opportunities for student choice. A few examples of how teachers can facilitate student choice and participation are as follows (Kordalewski, 1999):

- The teacher begins a new unit by determining what students already know about the topic, what they want to know, how they will locate this information, and how they will assess their new knowledge.
- The teacher negotiates aspects of the curriculum by soliciting students' input into the types of learning activities in which they would like to participate.
- The teacher bases writing assignments on students' experiences and interests.
- The teacher complements traditional lecture or direct instruction lessons with student-centered teaching strategies such as cooperative learning, peer tutoring, brainstorming, role-playing, and classroom discussions.
- Students set their own goals and evaluate their progress.

In a national survey of special education teachers, more than 90% reported that they believed student decision making and student goal setting were integral parts of classroom instruction (Wehmeyer & Schwartz, 1997). Furthermore, these teachers stated that promoting student autonomy was a "very helpful" way to prepare students for life after school. Seventy percent of the surveyed teachers reported that they incorporated some strategies for eliciting student self-direction or autonomy (Table 3.1).

TABLE 3.1   *Nine Core Empowerment Practices*

1. Classroom work is infused with student choice and design.
2. The teacher's role is collaborator and facilitator.
3. Schoolwork is characterized by active learning.
4. Learning activities are linked to student experience.
5. Emphasis is on small-group work and projects.
6. The overall school ambience is nurturing and supportive.
7. Space is used to promote civility and socialization.
8. Daily procedures are in place to promote feedback and communication.
9. The curriculum is integrated with a multidisciplinary perspective.

According to research, the incorporation of student choice into classroom instruction benefits students receiving special education services for emotional and behavioral disorders. In several studies, students exhibited less frequent misbehavior and more frequent appropriate behavior. Furthermore, students scored higher on achievement tests, when they were allowed to make choices (Cosden, Gannon, & Haring, 1995; Jolivette et al., 2001; Knoblock, 1973; Lovitt & Curtis, 1969).

According to Jolivette et al. (2001), choice improves student behavior for the following three reasons:

1. Choice allows students to select preferred tasks and assignments. Preference reinforces participation and decreases off-task behavior.
2. Students feel more secure because they are controlling predictable elements of their school day, such as what to do after a completed task and what task will come next.
3. Student–teacher relationships are improved. Students are not so inclined to compete for teacher attention because they are less dependent on teacher direction. Because they have more control of their environment, they are less likely to engage in noncompliant behavior.

Transition to Participatory Learning.   The longer students have been exposed to controlling autocratic teaching practices, the more difficult for them to make the transition to participatory learning. Moreover, some students lack the social skills and maturity necessary to accommodate democratic classroom practices.

One special education teacher, Panico (1997), outlined four guidelines for fostering student choice and empowerment among students who have difficulty taking responsibility for their learning:

1. **Expectations.**   At the beginning of the school year, teachers must explain to students their more active role in classroom affairs. For many students, this type of learning will be a new experience, and the students must understand

the connection between making decisions and accepting responsibility for these decisions. Taking a role in outlining class rules, planning projects, determining sites for field trips, and decorating the room are some preliminary choice opportunities that give students a feel for empowerment. Participation skills, such as listening and accepting different opinions, must also be taught.

2. **Commitment.**   Strong student–teacher relationships support empowerment by establishing a foundation of trust. Open communication provides a forum for setting group goals and writing group contracts. Community contracts can entail such mutual concerns as individuals' basic rights and responsibilities, rules for individual and group conduct, and sanctions for violations. Putting mutual issues on paper enhances accountability and helps teachers sidestep the power struggles that inevitably arise in the classroom.

3. **Knowledge.**   Teachers must instruct students in techniques for individual change. Basic information about psychological and physiological needs that affect behavior must be provided. Students will also need help assessing their individual needs and developing strategies to meet such needs as identity, competence, and affiliation. Accountability can be taught by highlighting the cause-and-effect relationship between choice and outcome.

4. **Skills.**   The class meeting can be used as a forum for teaching social skills such as verbalizing feelings, tolerating frustration, and recognizing the effect of behavior on others (Henley, 2003). The class meeting is a vehicle for students to practice communication skills, problem solve, and build group morale. Social skills instruction must also be incorporated into daily lessons and activities.

Belonging

People are, by nature, social beings. The word *society* is derived from the Latin *societas*, which means "companionship." Early childhood specialists use the term *parallel play* to describe the tendency of preschoolers to play alongside one another without interacting. At about age 4, parallel play gives way to *interactive play*. From this point on, children spontaneously seek out others with whom to share their time. By the time young people enter adolescence, peers, not the family, are the main source of social support.

Feeling disconnected from others contributes to many school disciplinary problems. Attention-seeking behaviors, withdrawal, and passive-aggressiveness are dysfunctional displays of the need to belong (Long & Long, 2001). Kohn (1996) said,

> Children may act in troubling ways because they are wanting for the sort of warm, caring relationships that enable and incline people to act more compassionately. They may have learned to rely on power rather than reason, to exhibit aggression rather than compassion, because this is what they have seen adults do—and perhaps what has been done to them. (p. 9)

TABLE 3.2   *Erikson's Eight Stages of Psychosocial Development*

Stage of Development	Psychosocial Crisis	Basic Strength	Core Deficiency
1. Infancy	Trust vs. mistrust	Hope	Withdrawal
2. Early childhood	Autonomy vs. shame and doubt	Will	Compulsion
3. Play age	Initiative vs. guilt	Purpose	Inhibition
4. School age	Industry vs. inferiority	Competence	Inertia
5. Adolescence	Identity vs. identity confusion	Fidelity	Prejudice
6. Young adulthood	Intimacy vs. isolation	Love	Loneliness
7. Adulthood	Generativity vs. stagnation	Care	Rejectivity
8. Old age	Integrity vs. despair	Wisdom	Disdain

The basic needs of *belonging* and *acceptance* are a common thread woven through the developmental theories of Adler (1939), Erikson (1950), Maslow (1971), and Glasser (1986). Each theorist highlighted the key role that affiliations play in human development in a slightly different manner. Adler (1939) emphasized the primacy of community and feeling connected to others. Erikson (1950) found that infants, children, and adults proceed through eight stages of socioemotional development (Table 3.2). Maslow (1971) believed that self-esteem was based in large part on gaining others' respect, and, finally, Glasser (1986) reasoned that the need to belong is genetic. He stated that whereas hungry students think of food, lonely students look for friends (M. Beck & Malley, 1998).

In the following subsections, five topics relating to belonging are covered. First, the role of parental attachment is discussed. Second, mistaken goals that relate to the need to belong are identified. Third, student–student and student–teacher relationships are examined. Fourth, family–school relationships are explored. Fifth and finally, community schools—including the CoZi initiative, an example of a community school—are defined and illustrated.

Attachment.   Infancy is a critical stage of human development. From birth to age 2 years, many children develop secure attachments with their parents or caregivers. As these children mature, the bonds connecting them to family carry over into their relationships with other adults and peers. Securely attached children are more trusting in later years, have good conflict-resolution skills, and can deal with stress and anxiety effectively. Conversely, insecurely attached infants, who have not developed a trusting bond with caregivers, can later develop emotional problems based on their difficulties with forming satisfactory adult and peer relationships (Ainsworth, 1989).

Attachment theory is an examination of mother–child bonds and the effect these bonds have on a child's emotional development. Ainsworth (1989) identified three types of attachment outcomes: securely attached, anxious or ambivalent, and avoidant. Securely attached children are the product of a loving relationship with the primary caregiver or caregivers. As adults, they are capable of stable, loving relationships, and they do not feel the need to constantly depend on others. Avoidants had minimal physical contact with their mothers as infants. As avoidants mature, they tend to be detached in their relationships and to shun overtures from nurturing adults. They react to stress with rage or flight. Anxious or ambivalent individuals had caregivers who were slow or inconsistent in responding to their infant needs. These individuals are overly needy and express their anger through passive-aggressiveness (Tully & Brendtro, 1998).

According to the results of studies of children growing into adulthood conducted by Bowlby (1973) and Ainsworth (1989), approximately one of every three students is either avoidant, or anxious/ambivalent. These students have difficulty sustaining relationships. Individual cases will vary, but misbehavior—particularly in terms of attention seeking—is characteristic of students who are anxious/ambivalent and students who are avoidant.

Tully and Brendtro (1998) speculated that without reciprocal attachment relationships, the part of the brain that regulates social behavior does not develop fully (p. 60). When young people are deprived of positive social relationships, their ability to form future relationships is impaired. Relationship-deprived youngsters have difficulty managing anger, sadness, and frustration. Their interpersonal relationships are marked by superficiality, distrust, and a need to control others.

Mistaken Goals.   Dreikurs and Cassel (1972) and Albert (1996) maintained that misbehavior is the result of students' unsuccessfully trying to fulfill their need for belonging. Dreikurs identified four *mistaken goals* that contribute to students' behavioral problems: attention seeking, power seeking, revenge seeking, and avoidance of failure. Teachers intuitively grasp Dreikurs' insight with comments such as "The problem with that student is that he's trying to get attention." Dreikurs' analysis helps teachers recognize that the need to belong, if not satisfied in a constructive fashion, will surface as misbehavior. Albert (1996) suggested "three Cs" for helping students to constructively meet their need to belong: capability, connection, and contributions:

1. *Capability* refers to the need for students to experience success. With so much attention given to the "right" answer, grades, and achievement test scores, increasing numbers of students with learning problems internalize failure and develop feelings of "learned helplessness." Efforts to provide successful school experiences for all students should begin with tolerance for mistakes, confidence-building experiences, and lessons that link the curriculum with real-life experiences.

2. *Connection* is the process of reaffirming students through attention, acceptance, and affection. Belonging is based on reciprocal respect and caring. Teachers need to communicate to students that they are valued as individuals first—above and beyond their academic achievements.

3. *Contributions* are intentional acts of generosity. Teachers should provide students with opportunities to help others and should search out possibilities

that reaffirm the students' sense that they are needed. Giving to others builds compassion and empathy: two emotions often cited as chronically underdeveloped in youths who are delinquent and violent.

Student–Student and Student–Teacher Relationships.   Supportive relationships play a central role in a youngster's ability to productively participate in classroom activities. Fahlberg (1991) made three recommendations for helping young people build relationships:

1. **Engage students in group activities that help them develop a sense of inclusive identity.**   Students could decide on a class color, select a class song, or design a class banner. Have students complete projects that require cooperation and team effort. Avoid competition. Be alert to cliques and other group-dynamic issues such as gender, race, or religion that separate students into "us" and "them."
2. **Support student activities outside school.**   Take an interest in the events that shape students' lives at home and in the community. Foster reciprocal relationships within the classroom. Provide opportunities for students to build camaraderie by having fun together.
3. **Support students during periods of high emotional arousal.**   During times of crisis, grief, illness, and frustration, students most need support. "As the adult walks through these storms of life with the child and alleviates psychological or physical discomfort, bonding and attachment are enhanced" (Brendtro & Brokenleg, 1993, p. 7).

M. Beck and Malley (1998) pointed out that institutional factors within schools can contribute to feelings of estrangement among youths. These researchers stated that the student–teacher relationship establishes the foundation on which a sense of belonging is built. Hewitt (1998) provided the following suggestions for fostering belonging in the classroom:

- Become familiar with students' faces and names before the first class. Look at yearbooks or class pictures.
- Ask each student what name or nickname he or she prefers.
- Smile, make eye contact, and exchange pleasantries.
- Notice what is important and of interest to students.
- Share information about your interests with students.
- Disapprove of misbehavior without degrading the student.
- Attend nonacademic functions such as sports events and concerts.
- Invite students to share their talents with the class.
- When confronted with misbehavior, teach prosocial skill alternatives.

The teacher sets the tone for interpersonal relationships in the classroom. The quality of student–teacher interactions, the methods used to handle misbehavior, and the ways students are organized for instruction all influence how connected students feel to classroom events. (Chapter 4 provides more details on how to develop effective student–teacher relationships.)

Family–School Relationships.   Students benefit from strong family–school ties. The National Committee for Citizens in Education (NCCE) reported that parent–teacher partnerships have a positive effect on grades, standardized test scores, attitude, and behavior (Henderson, 1997). In a review of 53 studies that measured the impact of parent–teacher partnerships, the NCCE did not find a single negative report. Students at risk of school failure gained most from parent–teacher collaboration.

For strong family–school ties to be established, barriers to such relationships must be overcome. Leitch and Tangri (1988) investigated barriers to family–school partnerships in two indigent Washington, DC, middle schools. Sixty families and 29 teachers participated in the study. The researchers reported that a parent from a single-parent household was less likely to be involved in school affairs than was a parent from a two-parent family. Parents of large families (six or more members) became involved with school affairs more than parents of small families did. Several conditions made attending school functions difficult for families. Chief among these reasons were lack of child care, no transportation, employment during the hours of school functions, and poor health.

Almost half the teachers surveyed blamed the parents for lack of participation. The most frequent criticism was "The parents don't care." In most cases, this generalization was based on an assumption rather than on the facts. In contrast, Leitch and Tangri (1988) reported that parents believed that teachers looked down on them. Parents said that the school did not work hard enough to involve them (Table 3.3).

Parent–teacher organization (PTO) meetings were the most frequent activity involving families. Unfortunately, these functions were controlled by a small

TABLE 3.3   *Eleven Worst Ways to Make a School Parent Friendly*

1. During back-to-school night or parent conferences, insist that parents squeeze into tiny tot furniture.
2. Hold all the meetings during the day.
3. Alternate from blitzing to boring communications.
4. Lock the doors, turn off the lights, and take the telephone off the hook at school by no later than 4 p.m.
5. When parents show up at meetings, sit behind a desk, do not smile, and use education jargon.
6. Design a report card that reads like a legal notice.
7. Make certain teachers do not introduce themselves to parents until late October.
8. Instruct secretaries never to welcome parents when they arrive at school.
9. Post "No Trespassing" signs outside external doors.
10. Open parent meetings with long speeches and wait until 5 minutes are left to ask if parents have any questions.
11. Make the first telephone call to parents a complaint about their youngster's behavior.

Note. Adapted from "The Ten Worst Ways to Make a School Parent Friendly," September 2000, *NEA Today.* Copyright 2000 by the National Education Association. Adapted with permission. Retrieved September 11, 2000, from http://www.nea.org/neatoday/0009/cover.html

group of parents, which left other parents feeling like outsiders. Often, parents said they did not receive notice of school functions.

Linking families and schools requires a total school commitment. The National Education Association (2000) outlined the following blueprint for action for enhancing parental participation.[1] Each item is followed by an example of teacher implementation:

- **Parenting.** Help families establish home support for academics.

  Example. "Our parent report card lists 19 items we suggest parents work on at home—limiting TV, encouraging cultural understanding, helping students with homework. Parents who check off seven or more items are commended in our newsletter."

  —Jean Campbell-Kuhn, Galax, Virginia

- **Communicating.** Reach out to families through home visits.

  Example. "Our home visit team includes teachers, a counselor, and a nurse who visit to discuss school programs. The focus is not on academic performance, so it's [the meeting is] more relaxed."

  —Patricia Lee, Tulsa, Oklahoma

- **Learning at home.** Provide parents with information for helping students with academics.

  Example. "Our family literacy program allows first graders to borrow books and cassettes to use at home."

  —Debra Carnes, Federal Way, Washington

- **Collaborating.** Identify resources and services from the community to strengthen families and student development.

  Example. "Our 'St. Pete Reads' program trains parents and other community residents to help increase literacy among disadvantaged students."

  —Elaine Davis, St. Petersburg, Florida

- **Volunteering.** Recruit and organize parental help and support.

  Example. "For parents who volunteer regularly, I hold workshops on how to read and write with young children, as well as how to handle problems or answer young kids' questions."

  —Becky Dixon, Bloomington, Indiana

- **Decision making.** Include parents in school decisions, developing parent leaders and representatives.

  Example. "As part of our Kids Vote program, political candidates speak on issues like the school budget. We ask families to write questions, and this gives kids a sense of real issues. One year, our work actually helped raise voter turnout 8 percent."

  —Maggie Mahland, Windsor, Connecticut

---

[1]Adapted from "A Blueprint for Action," September 2000, *NEA Today.* Copyright 2000 by the National Education Association. Adapted with permission. Retrieved September 11, 2000, from http://www.nea.org/neatoday/0009/cover.html

Community Schools.   A *community-based school* is a school whose administrators and teachers seek to extend services to the community at large. Some qualities of a community school are hosting community activities outside school hours; soliciting parental feedback and supporting parental participation in school decisions; encouraging students' participation in community affairs; providing families with child-rearing support and resources; and connecting families to needed mental health, immigration, and physical health services. Examples of after-hours community school programs are youth basketball, day care, mental health counseling, graduate equivalent degree (GED) classes, and English instruction for recent immigrants.

Community schools place a premium on parental involvement. Parents are encouraged to participate in such activities as volunteering in classrooms and serving on ad hoc committees that address school issues. In one New Haven, Connecticut, community school, parents volunteered in classrooms and tutored students in special activity groups, which integrated academics with the arts. Parents also planned activities such as a welcome-back-to-school dinner and a February "blues" party to attract other families. Parents reaching out to parents worked. Evaluation of the community school program revealed that students' achievement scores had increased, on average, 7 months beyond their grade level; attendance had improved to the number one ranking in the city; and many disciplinary problems had been eliminated (Comer, 1986).

According to a report issued by the Coalition for Community Schools (2004), growing evidence shows that community schools demonstrate positive effects on students, families, and their surrounding communities. An analysis of data retrieved from 49 community school programs indicated the following key results: Thirty-six programs showed gains in reading and math test scores; 19 schools reported improvements in attendance; several reported lower dropout rates; 11 schools had fewer suspensions; and 11 community schools reported a decrease in such high-risk behaviors as substance abuse, teen pregnancy, and disruptive classroom behavior (www.comunityschools.org/evaluation/evall.html).

The CoZi initiative.   *CoZi* is an acronym formed from the last names of two prominent educators: James Comer and Edward Zigler. Each developed a highly successful community school model. The *CoZi initiative* (Comer, Zigler, & Stern, 1997) is a collaborative effort that builds on the best each model had to offer. The guiding premise of CoZi is that schools can be transformed into full-service community hubs.

Bowling Park School in Norfolk, Virginia, was selected for the first implementation of the CoZi model. At Bowling Park, more than 75% of the students were eligible for free or reduced-price lunches. The school soon became a community center. Between 1992 and 1995, Bowling Park opened a child care program, four preschool classes, a summer vacation program, a home visitation program for parents of newborns, an adult GED class, a health clinic, and a family literacy program. Long-term effects at Bowling Park and other CoZi intitiative schools include improved teacher morale, enhanced academic performance, an increased high school graduation rate, reduced delinquency, and a decreased number of teenage pregnancies (Comer et al., 1997).

Cooperation

Cooperation is the bridge that connects the individual need for empowerment and the social need for belonging. Since primal times, cooperation has been the hallmark of productive and civilized cultures. Anthropological and archeological discoveries during the 20th century indicate that cooperation—as in the case of agriculture—not competition, propelled human civilization forward (Leakey & Lewin, 1977).

The biological inclination for social cohesion found in cooperation is firmly embedded in human nature. Anthropologists Richard Leakey and Roger Lewin (1977) said,

> Throughout the later stages of human evolution, from about three million years on-wards, there was . . . one pattern of social behavior that became extremely impor-tant, and we can therefore expect the forces of natural selection would have ensured its becoming deeply embedded in the human brain: this is cooperation. (p. 245)

Humans are a social species that prefers communal living to isolation. As our tech-nologically linked world grows closer, cooperation continues to be a unifying fac-tor in advancing human culture.

A group's cooperation is shaped by the group's structure (e.g., autocratic or democratic). In terms of classrooms, cooperative groups build students' social competence, which yields students many benefits. These two topics are covered next.

Group Structure.   A classroom is a microcosm of society. To be productive, stu-dents need to be able to work together, to share resources, and to follow rules for getting along. *Group structure* is the framework that establishes procedures for making decisions and shaping group interaction. For instance, a college basketball coach decides who will play and what plays to run. The group structure that fits the goals of an athletic team is the *authoritarian group.* Authoritarian, or autocratic, group structures are best suited for situations that require quick and decisive ac-tion. Another example is the military; soldiers have no time to vote on whether to charge a hill.

Some teachers believe that an autocratic group approach is needed to manage classrooms. While labeling such teachers domineering would be hyperbole, they clearly control almost all the class activities. William Shanker, past president of the American Federation of Teachers, once remarked that teachers are the most powerful professionals in the United States because no one else can tell a group of people when they may go to the bathroom.

Democratic classroom management is presented in this text as an alternative to the autocratic group structure. The advantages of *democratic groups* are many and were described in Chapter 2.

Social Competence.   Cooperation builds social competence. A socially competent individual is distinguished by the ability to develop interpersonal relationships and to work collaboratively with others (Goleman, 1995). Conversely, a lack of social competence leads to a variety of behavioral difficulties, such as chronic disciplinary problems, behavioral disorders, and delinquency (Rutherford, Mathur, & Quinn, 1998). Invoking cooperative activities in the classroom is both preventive and remedial. Social skills are developed and maintained through cooperative activities.

COMMUNITY IN ACTION: MODEL SCHOOL PROGRAMS

Educators have devised numerous ways to inject empowerment, belonging, and cooperation into schools and classrooms. The model programs discussed in this section present several such possibilities. These programs focus on the "four *P*s" of community in the classroom: places, programs, procedures, and people as partners (Purkey & Novak, 1996). These examples of model programs were drawn from successful classroom and school community programs.

Places

Winston Churchill once said, "We shape our buildings and they shape us" (Hebert, 1998, p. 69). Banning (1992) concurred that the physical environment leaves an indelible impression and has a clear impact on behavior. The look and feel of a building is an extension of the inhabitants' values. A warm, responsive learning environment is a proclamation for community. In such an environment, attention to the physical layout, arrangement of space, and use of common areas presents an invitation to participate that nourishes and sustains a model community. Not only must the building as a whole convey a sense of community, but the individual classroom must, too.

School Buildings.   More than any other feature, the physical environment establishes the identity of a school. The arrangement of furniture in classrooms, the type of displays on walls, and the look and feel of such common areas as hallways and cafeterias suggest either intimacy or isolation.

   The staff and students of Orem High School in Orem, Utah, created a school ambience that promotes school spirit and community. The hallways are accented with blue and gold, the school colors. Quotations from faculty and students adorn the walls. Open spaces in halls were converted into foyers where students can relax and socialize. The first thing people see when they enter the building, instead of dusty, old sports trophies, is an aquarium. The principal's office is decorated with antiques and sports memorabilia. When describing the principal's office, Hansen and Childs (1998) remarked, "A typical reaction of a student coming in for the first time is 'Gee, what a neat place!' Being sent to the principal's office is almost a treat!" (p. 16). Creating a warm, friendly physical environment at Orem gave the school a distinct personality, which was welcome relief from the sterile, neutral ambience that characterizes other schools.

Similarly, Freiberg's (1998) description of how he changed an unpleasant middle school cafeteria into a congenial, community dining area illustrates how even the most mundane aspect of school life can be improved with a little imagination and attention to detail. During Freiberg's first visit to the cafeteria, he found a space dominated by harsh sounds. Trays banging on tables, food being scraped into metal waste cans, and the cacophony of many voices speaking in unison created a distinctly unpleasant dining experience:

> The cafeteria was like many I have seen over the years. It had folding tables and chairs, and seated about 300 students. . . . What struck me immediately was the excruciatingly high noise levels. The machines in the cafeteria were running, an aide was using the public address system to tell Billy or Sarah to "find a seat and sit down," and the cafeteria workers seemed to be playing the *1812 Overture* with the stainless pots and pans. . . . Adults were shouting across the room, asking specific students to be quiet. When I said "good morning" to an older child, he looked at me as if I had called him a bad name. After thirty minutes in the cafeteria *I* was ready to fight. (p. 25)

Committed to improving the cafeteria climate, administrators, staff, and students worked together to make significant changes. Aides received training on relating positively to children. A teacher greeted students at the front of the serving line. Cafeteria workers stopped banging pots and pans. A sponge stick to clean plates was substituted for the old practice of banging plates against the metal trash can. Students were assigned regular tables and were allowed to talk with students across and next to them. The public address system was placed in mothballs (Figure 3.1).

Classrooms.   Classrooms with barren cement walls and desks arranged in rows facing the teacher present an institutional image that is bleak and uninspiring. Students have a biological need for spatial stimulation: A stimulating physical environment enhances the development of brain neurons (Diamond & Hopson, 1998). Within classrooms, spatial arrangements should be visually appealing, promote socialization, meet the need for privacy, and allow for movement (Sylwester, 2000). Breaking up the hard space formed by four block walls and tile floor advances the sense of friendliness that is vital to community. Soft music, plants, animals, comfortable seats, and nooks and crannies for private work all add to the comfort of a classroom.

Revitalizing *classroom space* provides an ideal opportunity to foster a sense of community by eliciting student input. Students can work in teams to design decorations for specific wall areas. They can bring in decorations and materials from home. They can share responsibility for taking care of the plants and animals and cleanup responsibilities can be rotated weekly or monthly. Giving students specific classroom responsibilities heightens their sense of ownership and reinforces the notion that to thrive, a community needs contributions from all its members.

If you hear...
- Announcements/public address system
- Adults talking to students across the room
- Banging of trays/clattering of silverware
- Machine noise
- Banging of pots and pans in the kitchen

Then...
- Do not use public address system.
- Provide lessons in table manners.
- Organize lunchtime (assign tables, limit time, appoint cafeteria managers).
- Create rules with the students.
- Play calm, relaxing music.
- Model the behavior you expect from students.
- Eat lunch with the students once or twice a week.
- Expand the overall lunchtimes for the school and shorten the actual lunchtime of the students. This will allow lines to move faster and students to find seating more easily.
- Make the teacher the cafeteria manager for his or her class for a week, or for however long it takes to establish a good climate. The teacher then trains six students as cafeteria managers.
- Appoint the principal or another authorized person to be always on duty in the cafeteria.
- Allow classes who behave well for a week to go on a picnic.

FIGURE 3.1 Cafeteria Ambient Noise Checklist
From "Measuring School Climate: Let Me Count the Ways," by H. J. Freiberg, 1998, *Educational Leadership, 56*(1), p. 26. Copyright 1998 by J. Freiberg. Reprinted with permission.

Programs

School programs that advance community do so by stressing common bonds and personal reflection throughout the curriculum. According to Simon (2002), "Every subject we teach would become more engaging if we considered how it links to the questions that human beings perennially ask and then structured learning around these questions" (p. 27) Examples of projects that hook students into "big questions" include cross-linked courses such as an investigation of diseases that begins in science class and continues with the study of the economic impact of diseases in social studies class. Or students can be asked to mull over such moral questions as "How should a society distribute its wealth?" and "What of anything constitutes a just war?" Existential questions such as "What does it mean to be a good human being?" encourage students to think about how their learning affects their beliefs and actions.

Other core questions intended to inspire reflection and class discussion among high school seniors in an English class were as follows: However you define the word *spirit*, tell us about a time when your spirit was nourished. What is it like to come into manhood or womanhood? How do we set goals and boundaries that will nourish us?

Interdisciplinary courses help students connect courses to the world outside school. An interdisciplinary program called *Unified Studies* included high school credits in science, language arts, social studies, and recreation (Hansen & Childs, 1998). A community service project, a skiing trip, and bird watching connected academics and direct experience.

At Graham and Parks School in Cambridge, Massachusetts, language arts was integrated with social studies (Carnegie Corporation of New York, 2001). Overarching questions were: What is courage? What does it mean to be a hero? and Why do individuals take action to change and improve the world around them? Standardized test scores at Graham and Parks were among the highest in the state, and the school had a long waiting list of families who wanted to enroll their children.

Programs supporting teachers are also important to promoting community. One irony of teaching is the term *public education* because for 5 hours a day most teachers work in virtual isolation from their peers. The rare instances when teachers observe each other are considered innovative. Lawyers, surgeons, judges, and businesspeople are always on display and subject to public scrutiny, but not teachers. The lack of sharing expertise and experience is a fact of life in public schools. When information is exchanged, the most likely forum is the teachers' lounge at lunchtime.

As a counterpoint, consider the Japanese approach to sharing expertise. In Japan, administrators organize study groups in which teachers can exchange ideas on teaching lessons. Stevenson and Stigler (1992) described the operation of a typical teacher study group in Japan:

> A glimpse of what takes place in these study groups is provided by a conversation we recently had with a Japanese teacher. She and her colleagues spend a good deal of their time together working on lesson plans. After they finish a plan, one teacher from the group teaches the lesson to her students while the other teachers look on. Afterward, the group meets again to evaluate the teacher's performance and to make suggestions for improvement. In her school, there is an annual "teaching fair." Teachers from other schools are invited to visit the school and observe the lessons being taught. The visitors rate the lessons, and the teacher with the best lesson is declared the winner. (p. 160)

When building administrators make a commitment to staff interdependence, the results can be satisfying. At the Lowell School in the District of Columbia, students are dismissed at 12:15 p.m. on Fridays so that teachers can use the afternoon to work together. Abigail Wiebenson, principal of Lowell, said (Strauss, 2001),

> Collaboration at so many levels occurs as we revise schedules, discuss behaviors, struggle to understand all the facets of learning, plan for events that will include cross-grade participation, revise curriculum, figure out how to turn toxic talk among parents into healthy information sharing and on and on. (p. A09)

Both teachers and students benefit when a school community is cohesive and working toward common goals. For students, demonstrating the connections among disciplines makes learning more relevant to the real world. For teachers, the opportunity to collaborate, which interdisciplinary courses offer, can re-energize them. The entire school is enriched when the community works together to establish common goals and meaningful change.

Procedures

Procedures are routines that facilitate communication and enhance a sense of togetherness among teachers and students. Procedures can be either classroom based or schoolwide. Three procedures within the classroom are discussed in this section: First, ideas for introducing the concept of community at the beginning of the school year are presented. Then, two methods for maintaining community during the school year—classroom meetings and brainstorming—are explained.

The First Weeks of School.   The first days and weeks of the school year set the stage for what is to come. During the *first weeks of school,* students are nervous, excited, and apprehensive. Teachers are filled with energy and ready to meet the challenge of a new year. This period is the time when the teacher should introduce the idea that the class will function as a community of learners. Many students will be puzzled. Others will be skeptical, and still others will test the limits. Virtually every school year begins with a discussion of classroom procedures and rules. Such a discussion presents an opportunity to describe what *community* means. Depending on the developmental level, age, and abilities of the students, their understanding will vary. The best approach is to keep the discussion simple and describe a community as a group of learners who care about one another and work together.

Establishing rules for conduct is a priority during the first class session. Students expect it and teachers need to set the tone for how business will be conducted throughout the year. Involving students in the development of classroom rules accomplishes two objectives: Students will more readily follow rules they help develop, and the process of agreeing on a common set of guidelines provides the students with their first positive community experience.

Other first-week exercises that promote community include the following:

- Allow students to decide how the classroom will be decorated. Assign students to decoration committees responsible for specific sections of the room.
- Select a class color, mascot, and motto. Humanize the room with plants, curtains, and small animals (e.g., gerbil, hamster, ant farm, etc.) for which students will have responsibility.
- Arrange furniture to enhance face-to-face interaction. Designate certain areas of the room for private work and group work. Move the teacher's desk from the front of the room to the side or back. Put cushions on the floor so that students have a comfortable area on which to work.

- Arrange fun group projects and mix up group compositions to deter the rise of cliques. One teacher challenged groups of four students to each design a structure built from plastic straws that could support a 1-pound bag of coffee.
- Give students specific responsibilities for classroom maintenance. Rotate responsibilities among all students, regardless of academic or behavioral considerations (often the student who misbehaves needs the teacher's trust).
- Set up a feedback system such as a suggestion box that will allow students to voice their ideas and feelings anonymously.
- Establish a peer review board so that students can appeal to it if they think they have been disciplined unfairly.

See also *101 Things You Can Do in the First Three Weeks of Class,* by Joyce Povlacs Lunde, at the following University of Nebraska, Lincoln, Web site: www.unl.edu/ gradstudies/gsapd/instructional/101things.shtml.

Classroom Meetings.   Regular meetings within the classroom enable social skills development and encourage communication. Following is a list of positive outcomes of *classroom meetings*:

- They help establish procedures for setting and achieving group goals.
- They provide a forum for making group decisions.
- They enhance group harmony by allowing expression of feelings.
- They present opportunities for eliciting student feedback.
- They enable group cohesiveness by strengthening group bonds and interpersonal relationships.

Students need to experience success in meetings so that they will continue to participate. Nelson, Lott, and Glenn (2000) proposed eight "building blocks" of class meetings. These building blocks provide a structure to help students and the teacher make the most of their meetings:

1. Form a circle.
2. Practice giving compliments and expressing appreciation.
3. Create an agenda.
4. Emphasize the use of *I* statements.
5. Learn about different perspectives.
6. Recognize different reasons for individual actions.
7. Practice role-playing and brainstorming.
8. Focus on nonpunitive solutions.

Zionts and Fox (1998) recommended two guidelines for classroom meetings. First, students must respect peer opinions. Everyone has an equal right to be heard. Students can be taught listening skills by requiring each speaker to paraphrase the preceding speaker's comments. Second, participation should be voluntary. Open discussion requires trust and emotional security. Listening is sometimes misconstrued as nonparticipation. Often, this belief is not true. Some students are more reticent than others. A quiet student is not necessarily an apathetic student.

When decisions are being made during classroom meetings, the teacher should strive for student consensus. Voting and majority-rules procedures separate a group of students into winners and losers.

A typical classroom meeting lasts 20 minutes, but the length may vary depending on the students' age, the students' developmental level, and the nature of the issue under discussion. Meetings can follow a regular daily or weekly schedule and a meeting can be called because of an important issue or problem that the teacher wants the class to consider. The teacher's role is to monitor student participation in much the way a chairperson guides a committee.

Problem behaviors will inevitably surface, especially when students lack experience with classroom meetings. Some typical problems are monopolizing, scapegoating, and being insensitive to others. Monopolizing can be dealt with by establishing individual "airtime" limits of 30 seconds to a 1 minute. *Scapegoating* is a form of ganging up on an individual by another individual or a small group. Teasing, criticizing, and bullying are typical scapegoating behaviors. One way to minimize such behaviors is to establish rules for civility beforehand and allow only the individuals who adhere to the rules to speak. Insensitivity, prejudice, and narrow-minded thinking are possible within any discussion group. Balancing expression of opinions with respect for differences promotes acceptance and mutual understanding.

When problems arise, the teacher as discussion leader must be cautious about jumping in to resolve the situation. Group members need the opportunity to work out some of their own difficulties. Clarifying, accepting feelings, questioning, and summarizing are helpful leadership behaviors that will move students toward a better understanding of themselves as individuals and community members.

Brainstorming. *Brainstorming* is a group method for generating new ideas and solutions. Teachers have successfully used brainstorming to teach lessons, lead classroom meetings, and launch new projects. Brainstorming requires a statement of purpose, a facilitator, and a secretary to record ideas. What makes brainstorming unique is the premise that no idea is a bad idea. Participants are encouraged to let their imaginations roam. While a brainstorming session is in progress, ideas are listed as quickly as they are pronounced. Free association and lateral thinking provide the underlying creative impetus. The only rule is that no idea can be evaluated until the brainstorming session is complete.

The stimulus for a brainstorming session can be a question (e.g., How can we fund a field trip to the state park?), a quotation (e.g., "Do not seek to follow in the footsteps of the men of old; seek what they sought"), a specific problem (e.g., How can we eliminate bullying on the playground?), or an academic stimulus (e.g., If you were President Truman, how would you have ended World War II?). After

Case Study: Ms. Wagner

After attending in-service training on cooperative learning, Ms. Wagner, a seventh-grade teacher, decided to introduce the technique to her seventh-grade social studies class. In her workshop, Ms. Wagner learned that the first step was to teach her students some basic ideas about group roles. She decided to use brainstorming as a teaching technique. Ms. Wagner began the class by asking students to list all the types of group activities in which they had participated. The students devised a list of activities including sports, extracurricular clubs, Scouts, and school committees. Then Ms. Wagner asked the students to describe some behaviors that helped each group and some behaviors that hindered each group. The students brainstormed for about 15 minutes and created a list of several behaviors for both categories. Ms. Wagner finished the assignment by asking the students to assign a name to each behavior to aid them in remembering helping and hindering group roles. For example, an individual who kept the group on track, a helping role, was called the *engineer*. A person who monopolized, a hindering role, was called a *chatterbox*. In the next class, Ms. Wagner followed up the brainstorming session by organizing students into cooperative groups and secretly assigning each student a different helping role. At the end of the class period, students tried to guess which role each had played.

various ideas are posted on a blackboard or a flip chart, the group can assess each and select the most favorable responses. Brainstorming appeals to students because it differs from the normal school protocol of giving the "right" answer. Consider the case study of Ms. Wagner.

Ms. Wagner could have taught the same lesson by listing helping and hindering roles on the board and describing each, but by directly involving the students through brainstorming, she was able to teach the same information through student participation. Teachers who use brainstorming report that students are more motivated to learn ideas that they have developed than ideas taught through lectures, reading, or worksheet assignments (Mendler, 1992; Marzano, Marzano, & Pickering, 2003). Brainstorming also helps the teacher maintain a group focus and in the process prevent behavioral problems.

People as Partners

Many successful school programs are partnered with the outside community. Advance placement courses, cooperative programs with colleges and businesses, and special electives take advantage of the myriad educational possibilities offered through community organizations outside school. Making connections between academic learning and real-life experience is a unifying principle behind community–academic programs.

Two nationally acclaimed programs infuse academics with community and family involvement. Expeditionary Learning Outward Bound (ELOB) and the

School Development Program (SDP) have been adopted by more than 200 schools nationwide.

ELOB is based on two key ideas: Students learn by doing rather than listening, and developing character and a sense of community is as important as developing academic skills. ELOB was established in 1992 and 65 schools in 13 states currently incorporate the approach. Teachers organize curriculum around central themes called *learning expeditions*. Rather than attending 50-minute-classroom, single-subject periods, students participate in 10- to 16-week projects. Staff are assigned to the same group of students for at least 2 years to build trust and a sense of community between teachers and students. Community members and parents are encouraged to contribute expertise and to attend student presentations at the end of each expedition. Internships with area organizations and businesses are commonplace. All members of the local community, especially parents, are encouraged to take an active interest in school affairs and decisions (www.elob.org).

Yale professor James Comer founded the SDP in 1968. The underlying assumption of the SDP is that children achieve when they have strong relationships with the adults in their lives (http://info.med.yale.edu/comer/). Social and moral development of children is enhanced when community members, particularly families, have direct access to school planning. The Parent Program provides structured opportunities for parents to participate in educational decisions within the school. Three principles guide the staff's behavior and actions:

1. **No-fault problem solving.**   When problems arise, the emphasis is on finding solutions rather than on assigning blame.
2. **Consensus decision making.**   Consensus requires discussion and negotiation. This process of coming together to reach decisions is preferable to voting and majority rule, which produces "winners" and "losers."
3. **Collaboration over fiat.**   Administrators, staff, and parents work together to enrich the curriculum and build school spirit.

In addition to ELOB and the SDP, service learning programs pair academics with community involvement. Service learning is described in detail next.

Service Learning.   The term *service learning* refers to school programs that expand learning into the community and in the process teach civic responsibility (Kielsmeier, 2000). Service learning is based on the philosophy that students learn best when they are actively involved and when their participation has a clear purpose. In 1999, 64% of all public schools and 83% of all public high schools provided students with some type of community service opportunities (Billig, 2000). The purpose of service learning is to foster active citizenship through volunteerism. Federal funding for service learning began in 1993 when the National and Community Service Act was amended to provide a stable financing base to each state. Funds are disseminated to Learn and Serve America programs housed in state education agencies (SEAs).

Service learning projects vary from community to community and from school to school. In Huntsville, Alabama, students found that a segregated cemetery in which only African Americans were interred had unmarked graves, missing headstones, and vandalized plots. Out of concern, students and teachers created the African American History Project, which included "a dazzling array of community contributions and learning experiences" (Kielsmieier, 2000, p. 654). In Columbia, South Carolina, 1,200 students distributed more than 20 tons of food, clothing, and medicine to indigent Hispanics who had recently moved into the area. Likewise, Crook County High School students in Prineville, Oregon, organized a community health fair that provided citizens with free blood pressure checks and updates on community health issues (Glenn, 2001).

The benefits of service learning are many fold. According to McLaughlin (2001), compared with their peers, students who participated in service learning were 26% more likely to have good grades, 20% more likely to go to college, twice as likely to view themselves as worthwhile persons, more than twice as likely to believe they have control over their lives, and more than twice as likely to express a sense of civic responsibility.

Service learning programs can be set up in various ways. Some pointers for beginning include the following:

- **Prefer direct service to fund-raisers.**   Holding a car wash to help fund a community kitchen is helpful, but it does not provide students with the experience of directly helping others.
- **Share school space and facilities.**   Grassroots organizations and neighborhood groups are always searching for places to hold meetings. Shared space creates connections where none existed.
- **Establish collaborative relationships with area agencies.**   Nursing homes, shelters, and food kitchens are examples of community programs that are always grateful for volunteers. Young people in particular are welcomed because of their enthusiasm. Contact local community organizations such as the Lions Club, the Rotary Club, or the Shriners. Query local clergy about families in need.
- **Invite guest speakers.**   Civic leaders can motivate students by sharing their personal experiences. Human service agency directors can provide information about volunteerism, and they can target special areas of community need.
- **Take a community tour.**   Inspect the local community for useful projects. Can a vacant lot be transformed into a vegetable garden or a playground? Perhaps river frontage begs to be cleaned up or graffitti-sprayed park benches need a fresh coat of paint. Scan the newspapers for articles about people in need.
- **Integrate local stories and history into the curriculum.**   Discuss the contributions of local citizens to the history of the community. Visit local cemeteries, museums, and monuments. Help students realize that behind each inscription carved into stone was a real person who faced many of the same problems

growing up as they do, yet that person managed to find a way to contribute to society.

As much as possible students should be allowed to choose their service learning projects. However, the teacher must temper their choices according to their developmental level. Older students need projects that are intellectually stimulating. Younger students require projects that are not too drawn out and that provide concrete gratification. Both younger and older students will need time to process their experiences through reflection and narration. Among other activities, journal writing, art projects, and song writing enable students to recognize more clearly the benefits both for themselves and for the people they assist.

Summary

- ★ A community is a group of individuals who share a sense of solidarity and work together to achieve common goals. Schools are by nature bureaucratic.
- ★ To change an institutional focus to a community focus, teachers and administrators must incorporate three principles of community into their dealings with students: empowerment, belonging, and cooperation.
- ★ When students have direct involvement in school decisions, they develop a sense of personal ownership for their learning and behavior.
- ★ Belonging fulfills a biological need to be a part of a larger social network.
- ★ Cooperation is a fundamental social skill that promotes community.
- ★ The glue that holds a community together is the active involvement of members in issues that directly relate to the community's goals.
- ★ The four *P*s of community—places, programs, procedures, and people as partners—illustrate the diverse ways educators have found to inject empowerment, belonging, and cooperation into schools and classrooms.

What You Should Know

Now that you have finished reading this chapter, you should know the following:

How fostering a classroom community yields improved productivity and behavior

Why empowering, belonging, and cooperation are key community values

Methods for enhancing family–school relationships

How a community classroom responds to the students' basic developmental needs

Specific procedures teachers use in the classroom to create a sense of community

How educators use places, programs, procedures, and people as partners to build community

Why some families fail to participate in school functions and some strategies educators use to forge closer links with families

Applying the Concepts

1. Form small groups of four, based on certificate level, then take 10 minutes to brainstorm specific strategies for meeting the following student needs in a community classroom:
   - Empowerment
   - Belonging
   - Cooperation

   Report your results to the entire class.

2. Interview a community leader. Ask how that leader got individuals involved in community affairs. What are a community leader's frustrations? What are the rewards? Ask a community leader to give a guest lecture on community organizing.

3. Using newspapers and magazines, cut out articles that describe how schools foster a sense of community among students and families. Have a classroom "media day" to share results.

4. Suppose students are accustomed to having teachers who control most classroom activities. What problems would this present for a teacher who wants to implement democratic practices? What strategies would help the teacher deal with the identified problems?

5. Research the "open education" and progressive education movements. Who were the leaders of these movements and what philosophies guided each? Analyze these reform movements in terms of the surrounding political climates. What events led to the decline of these movements?

6. Have a class discussion about the following questions: What social skills would students need for them to contribute to a community classroom? What social skills deficiencies would impede efforts to develop a community classroom? If many students lack such social skills development, what can a teacher do? How would a teacher respond to parents who want their children taught in a classroom that emphasizes the autocratic teaching style? Where could a teacher who is struggling with his or her efforts to build a community classroom go for assistance?

7. On the basis of field-site observations, contrast how community-centered teachers and autocratic teachers deal with the following: taking attendance,

transiting between activities, permitting students to get out of their seats, instructing students, and disciplining students.

8. Do a Web search on "community in the classroom." Follow the links. How much information is available? Identify useful Web sites and examples of how schools bolster a sense of community.

9. Visit a Head Start program. Gather information on how Head Start involves parents.

10. Research the theories of Abraham Maslow, Erik Erikson, Alfred Adler, Larry Brendtro, William Glasser, and Mary Ainsworth. Answer this question: How do their theories influence your understanding of creating a classroom that is responsive to basic student needs?

Chapter 4

Developing Positive Student–Teacher Relationships

Chapter Outline

 ## Key Terms

Advocacy
Authentic teaching
Body language
Cognitive development
Concrete operational stage
Cultural diversity
Culturally responsive classroom
Emotional arousal
Empathy
Gender bias
Gender equity
Girl culture
Grandiose ascension
Humor
Impulse control

Intrinsic motivation
Latchkey children
Mild disabilities
Mood regulation
Neural highjacking
Psychosocial crises
Respectful relationships
Social capital
Social competence
Socioemotional development
Stereotype
Stress
Students' feelings
Sympathy
Trust

Introduction

Students' behavior is directly related to how students feel about their teacher. Effective student–teacher relationships begin with trust. The better teachers understand their students, the more success they will have in developing a nurturing environment. U.S. society is *pluralistic,* which means teachers must be able to relate to a student population characterized by ethnic, religious, and cultural differences.

Understanding students' needs begins with learning more about their lives outside school. Additional insights into students' behavior are provided by developmental theories, particularly in relationship to cognitive and socioemotional needs. Stereotypes inhibit relationship building. Proactive teachers are sensitive to how educational labels, gender, and cultural differences create misperceptions that inhibit student–teacher relationships. Teacher behaviors that enhance student relationships are respecting students' feelings, having a sense of humor, conveying respect, and being authentic.

How students feel about themselves and school is directly connected to their feelings about their teacher and their classmates. If students feel threatened or if they are at odds with their teacher, schooling becomes a burdensome task (Rogers & Renard, 1999; Tomlinson, 2000). Teachers prevent disciplinary problems and foster learning by doing the following:

- Establishing trust
- Creating a nurturing environment
- Knowing their students
- Connecting with students' lives outside school
- Advocating for youths
- Understanding developmental needs
- Avoiding stereotypes
- Ensuring gender equity
- Dealing with cultural diversity
- Enhancing student–teacher relationships

ESTABLISHING TRUST

Bryk and Schneider (2003) reported that a trusting relationship among students and teachers enhanced students' standardized mathematics and reading scores. In summarizing their findings about improved schools in Chicago, Bryk and Schneider said,

> For successful learning to occur here, the trust built up in family life must be transferred to the classroom teacher. Assuming this happens, elementary grade teachers will hold diffuse affective power over their students. . . . The growth of trust depends primarily on teachers' initiatives. Such initiatives include both establishing a family-like climate in the classroom that builds on students's affective

experiences at home, and engaging parents in a supportive relationship around the child's learning. (pp. 31–32)

Walberg and Greenburg (1997) summarized the results of several research studies on the positive effects of the classroom social environment. They reported that trusting relationships among students and teachers positively influenced students' attitudes, interests, productivity, and achievement.

In addressing disciplinary concerns, Korinek, Walther-Thomas, McLaughlin, and Williams (1999) recommended that teachers build support networks that are responsive to students' emotional needs:

It is insufficient to address the problems displayed by individual students without examining conditions in the classroom that are not student centered and "child friendly." If students feel disconnected, disenfranchised, unwelcome, or unsafe in school, they will have great difficulty changing their behaviors or benefitting from instruction. (p. 4)

How students feel about school, their in-school relationships, and themselves influences both their classroom behavior and their academic standing. Specific benefits of positive relationships in the classroom include the following (Rogers & Renard, 1999):

- Students look forward to school because they feel physically and emotionally safe.
- Students are willing to take risks. They are not concerned about being criticized for mistakes.
- Students work harder because they feel secure and know their efforts are appreciated.
- Because emotions and cognition are intertwined, students can focus their attention better and think more clearly.
- Students are motivated because they feel valued as individuals.

CREATING A NURTURING ENVIRONMENT

In a nurturing classroom environment, the students' emotional needs are addressed. Emotionally, students need to feel safe, to trust their teacher, and to feel that they are capable. Socially, students need to feel appreciated and respected (Erikson, 1950; Maslow, 1970). Perhaps most significant, each student needs to know that he or she is accepted for both strengths and weaknesses.

Nurturing teachers find ways to foster personal pride. They support students' efforts and provide students with opportunities to succeed. Nurturing teachers give students a reason to hope that they can overcome any obstacle. Kohl emphasized the need for hope in current-day classrooms:

I want to convey that unless you project hope for your students, your efforts to teach them to read, write, and calculate won't make a profound difference. A teacher's task is not only to engage students' imagination but also to convince them that they are people of worth who can do something in a very difficult world. When children don't have access to resources, it's very easy for them to give up hope. And if you give up on hope, what's the point of learning to read? What's the point of passing a Regent's exam if you believe the college won't accept you? What's the point of doing well in school if you know at the end of schooling all you will get is a McDonald's job? (cited in Scherer, 2000a, p. 2)

How teachers consider their relationships with their students and how they act toward their students will, to a large extent, determine how students feel about themselves and how they perform. Ginott (1971) said,

> I've come to understand that I am the decisive element in the classroom. It is my personal approach that creates the climate. It is my mood that makes the weather. As a teacher, I possess a tremendous power to make a student's life miserable or joyous. I can be a tool of torture or an instrument of inspiration. I can humiliate or humor, hurt or heal. In all situations it is my response that decides whether a crisis will be escalated or de-escalated and a child humanized or dehumanized. (p. 38)

Every classroom teacher is in the unique position of helping to shape a young person's life. The student–teacher relationship gives direction and substance to daily interactions. It makes the difference between a student's wanting and not wanting to go to school each morning.

KNOWING YOUR STUDENTS

The media image of youths is often unfavorable. News reports about school killings have presented the violent side of some students, have revealed significant gaps in young people's moral character (Bushweller, 1999), have compared international academic achievement with that of U.S. students, and have underscored their academic failings. In short, the media have presented a steady picture of declining standards among current-day youth.

Public Agenda reported that 7 of 10 adults think teenagers are "rude," "irresponsible," or "wild" (Duffet, Johnson, & Farkas, 1999). Current-day students have been labeled the *E-Generation,* the *Ambitious Generation,* and the *Scapegoat Generation.* The media sensationalize their lives, entrepreneurs shape their image, and electronic entertainment (i.e., television and the Internet) insulates them from adult contact.

David Satcher (2000), former U.S. Surgeon General, said,

> We are doing a better national job at teaching children academic skills, reading and writing. Now we need to focus as well on social and emotional issues. Teachers need information on social and emotional issues and how to help children in trouble. (p. 2)

Understanding students—what motivates them, what is important to them, how they feel about themselves, and how they relate to the world around them— is a central issue in classroom management. As educators, we often know more about students in the abstract than we know about them individually. Students are routinely evaluated, analyzed, and categorized according to standardized test results. In fact, at no other time in an individual's life will he or she be scrutinized to the extent encountered during the school years. Student cumulative folders are filled with grades, test scores, and teacher comments on performance. So much emphasis on student performance can cloud our vision about the true nature of the young people who populate our classrooms.

To truly know students, we as teachers must also understand the changing demographics in the United States. Increasing *cultural diversity* and a mobile society are factors significantly affecting classroom composition throughout the nation.

Demographics

With regard to cultural diversity, by 2020, Latinos will comprise 24% of all children younger than age 18, and 15% of all children younger than 18 years old will be African American (www.childstats.gov/ac2004/index.asp). In addition, 40% of all Americans have had some racial mixing since the beginning of the 20th century (Hodgkinson, 2001). According to Hodgkinson, this blending of racial lines will continue at an unprecedented rate. Such blending is exemplified in Tiger Woods, whose "Cablinasian" heritage is a mixture of Caucasian, Black, Indian, and Asian.

In addition to cultural diversity, mobility is a significant factor in classroom composition. Approximately 40 million Americans relocate each year. Hodgkinson (2001) reported,

> Many teachers have 22 students in the fall and 22 in the following spring, but 20 out of the 22 are different students. Hospitals in these regions spend most of their time taking case histories from strangers. Each Sunday, ministers preach to a congregation, a third of whose members are new. (p. 8)

California, Texas, and Florida in particular are havens for more than 1 million immigrants a year.

Sharon Dreyfus, a second-grade teacher in Gaithersburg, Maryland, saw a new face in her classroom every few weeks. Typically, the youngster spoke little English and came from a family of recent immigrants. "The biggest challenge is to keep constantly changing the program around to meet the needs of the kids," said Dreyfus. "Not only are they learning a new language, but learning about life in the United States" (cited in Armas, 2001).

A pluralistic student base is one of the factors that makes teaching such a complex craft. To rise to the challenge of understanding and meeting the needs of our culturally and ethnically diverse students, we as teachers must focus more on what happens to students when they are not in school. Students' values and behavior are shaped in the home, the neighborhood, and the community. Understanding students—their needs, problems and aspirations—begins with learning about their lives outside school.

CONNECTING WITH STUDENTS' LIVES OUTSIDE SCHOOL

For every hour students spend in school, they spend 4 waking hours outside school. The nature of students' outside-of-school experience plays a crucial role in their behavior in school. What a student eats, how much sleep a student gets, the quality of a student's sibling and adult relationships, and the opportunities for wholesome leisure activities are factors outside school that influence student behavior in school.

One of the best indicators of student success is the level of parental involvement (Comer, 1986). Parent–teacher conferences and school open houses are the main sources of teacher-to-family contact. However, many families do not attend school functions. Lack of child care, failure to receive proper notice, work schedules, lack of transportation, cultural and language barriers, and negative feelings toward school authorities are some reasons families fail to meet with educators at school. Unfortunately, often the families who do not attend school functions are those with whom the teacher most needs to communicate.

Families want their children to be taught by a caring individual, and they have additional concerns: They want their children to be challenged, they want their children to behave, and they want their children to succeed. Teachers and families share these goals; thus, working together enhances the possibility that such goals will be met.

Newsletters, telephone calls, and home visits help teachers initiate and maintain contact with families. Newsletters provide families with ongoing reports about their children's classroom experience. Too often, telephone calls are made only when a problem occurs. Instead, telephone calls can be used to introduce a child's new teacher, to keep families abreast of important news, and to share an interesting anecdote about a child. Many schools use Web sites, e-mail, and distribution lists to enhance family–school relationships and to provide families with key information. Likewise, a home visit can provide insights

 ## Case Study: Mr. Torres

Mr. Torres, a sixth-grade teacher, was having difficulty getting Juan to stop making sarcastic classroom remarks. When Mr. Torres visited Juan's apartment, he discovered that Juan's mother was raising five children on her waitress's salary and public assistance. She relied on Juan to help supervise and care for his siblings when she was at work. Juan's mother was pleased that Mr. Torres took the time to visit her. She told him that none of Juan's previous teachers had shown that much interest in Juan.

Juan, too, seemed pleased with the attention, particularly when he realized that the purpose of Mr. Torres's visit was to meet his mother and not to complain about Juan's caustic comments. During the weeks following Mr. Torres's visit, Juan settled into the regular classroom routine. Juan's need for attention seemed less frantic, especially after Mr. Torres took a hint from his home visit and gave Juan some specific classroom duties.

and ameliorate niggling school behavioral problems. Consider the case study of Mr. Torres.

Distance, unsavory neighborhoods, and lack of time have limited the once-common home visit. Driving through a student's neighborhood, shopping at a student's local market, identifying youth recreational spaces, or visiting a student's place of worship is an indirect, but effective, method for learning more about the social influences on a student's life.

Spending time outside school with students also reveals much about their temperament, values, and needs. Field trips, mentoring programs, and community service projects provide novel ways for teachers and students to interact and build their relationships. Ultimately, each relationship is built on the quality of shared experience. As Garbarino (2000) stated, "We need to return to this understanding of the aliveness and interconnectedness of all things" (p. 30). When the classroom climate is based on a spirit of community, each youngster is valued as an integral part of the whole.

ADVOCATING FOR YOUTHS

Coleman (1990) used the term *social capital* to describe the network of human relationships and institutional supports that guide and nurture youths. Social capital is developed and sustained by interpersonal relationships. Many childhood experiences that characterized social capital for earlier generations are gone. This depletion can be observed across socioeconomic boundaries.

In many locales, the walk to the neighborhood school has been replaced with a lengthy school bus trip. The front porch, which was once a contact point for neighbors, has been exchanged for the isolated backyard deck. Lengthy telephone conversations with friends have lost their allure to Internet chat rooms, where the identity of a conversational partner is sometimes in doubt. Likewise, running freely around the neighborhood is often a high-risk activity for children.

For youths who are disadvantaged and living in densely populated urban areas, staying away from neighborhood activities is a survival strategy. Parents are afraid to allow their youngsters to go outside for fear of putting them in harm's way. Some youths find family connections by joining gangs. Those that join gangs for protection, have real concerns. According to the Children's Defense Fund (2004, 2005),

- One in every 2 children lives in a single-parent family at some point during his or her childhood.
- One in 5 children is born poor.
- One in 8 children has no health insurance.
- One in 7 children never graduates from high school.
- One in 9 children is born to a teenage mother.
- One in 12 children has a disability.
- One in 13 children will be arrested at least once before age 17.

- One child or teen is killed by gunfire nearly every 3 hours.
- One in 83 young people will be in a state or federal prison before age 20.

Garbarino's (2000), pleas to strengthen supports for young people to help them resist the dangers of toxic social environments has registered with many educators. Educators reconnect with youths by establishing classroom environments that meet students' basic socioemotional needs. One of the best ways to understand students—how they feel and why they behave the way they do—is to move past the stereotypes and go directly to the source.

In *A Tribe Apart*, Hersch (1998) chronicled the lives of teenagers in Reston, Virginia. She found that even in what appeared to be a nurturing community, youths struggled to find a sound mooring within the constantly changing currents of adolescence. She encountered many *latchkey children*. These young people returned home from school to empty houses, where they spent from 3:00 to 6:00 p.m. alone or with their peers and siblings. Hersch reported that the most stunning change for current-day adolescents is their aloneness. Adolescents are now more isolated and more unsupervised than the youths of any other generation. According to Hersch,

> It used to be that kids sneaked time away from adults. The proverbial kisses stolen in the backseat of a car, or the forbidden cigarette smoked behind the garage, bestowed a grown-up thrill of getting away with the forbidden. The real excitement was in not getting caught by a watchful (or nosy) neighbor who'd call Mom. Today Mom is at work. Neighbors are often strangers. Relatives live in distant places. This changes everything. It changes access to a bed, a liquor cabinet, a car. The kids have all the responsibility for making decisions, often in a void, or they create an ersatz family with their buddies and let them decide. These youngsters can easily do more good or bad without other people knowing about it. (pp. 19–20)

The resultant problems have yielded much criticism of youths. Criticism is acceptable if it leads to solutions, but what is lacking is concern about issues that influence students' development. Youths need advocates. Students do not have the maturity or the resources to effectively advocate for themselves. Teachers who get involved in their communities invariably become advocates for young people. Advocates listen to youths and take their concerns seriously. When youths get into trouble, advocates try to understand why, and advocates look for solutions where others see only problems. Four examples of community youth *advocacy* follow:

Problem.   Teenagers are congregating and skateboarding in a business district.
Solution.   The community builds an in-line skate park and follows that with construction of an ice-skating rink.

Problem.   Teens are hanging out on street corners and selling and buying drugs.
Solution.   A police-sponsored evening basketball league is formed.

Problem. Few community activities exist for preschoolers and primary-grade children.

Solution. A community-sponsored and -supported interactive children's science center is opened.

Problem. Attendance at school open houses and parent–teacher conferences has decreased.

Solution. Day and evening hours are staggered for conferences, with transportation and child care provided.

By advocating for students, educators help provide young people with the community supports they need to avoid troubles and put their best effort forward in school.

UNDERSTANDING DEVELOPMENTAL NEEDS

Much of what is known about students' needs is encoded in the rich and varied body of developmental psychology. Areas of human development include four major domains: language, socioemotional, cognitive, and motor. A developmental perspective helps educators understand what students' learning needs are as they grow and mature. Developmental theories are framed by the following assumptions:

- Normal development is the product of both biophysical and environmental factors.
- Development progresses through stages from simple to more complex.
- Developmental stages are culture free and universal.
- Each stage of development is characterized by observable behaviors (i.e., developmental milestones).
- Although often marked by chronological age; developmental change varies with individuals.
- The stages and developmental milestones can be arranged into a predictable sequence.
- Each stage of development contains elements of the preceding stages.
- An individual can be delayed or fixated at one stage when development does not follow the normal course.
- Every individual who is developmentally delayed or disabled has acquired elements of normal behavior.
- Planned educational interventions can overcome developmental problems.

Whereas texts on developmental psychology present developmental theory in the abstract, the classroom presents the beginning teacher with a laboratory for real-life application. In terms of issues related to classroom management, key areas are socioemotional and cognitive development.

Socioemotional Development

The proactive teacher is responsive to students' social and emotional developmental needs. Chief among these are the basic needs of safety, trust, control, belonging, and mastery. In fact, as several prominent contributors to classroom management research have pointed out, disciplinary problems are often a consequence of students' trying in vain to have their basic developmental needs met (Curwin & Mendler, 1988a; Nelson, Lott, & Glenn, 2000).

When students cannot meet their socioemotional developmental needs through constructive behavior, they will continue to strive even though their behavior is unconstructive and self-defeating. For example, Dreikurs and Cassel (1995) maintained that students have a basic need to be accepted by their peers. When this need for belonging is frustrated, students will attempt to achieve recognition through whatever means necessary, including disrupting lessons, arguing with teachers, and refusing to follow directions (Charles, 1999; Table 4.1).

Psychosocial Crises.   Erikson (1950) applied psychoanalytic theory to human development in his quest to describe the stages of socioemotional growth. (See the

TABLE 4.1   *Examples of Frustrated Basic Needs*

Frustrated Basic Need	Unconstructive Behavior
Need for autonomy or control	Not complying, being tardy, stalling, not hearing directions, arguing, engaging in other passive-aggressive behaviors
Need for mastery	Being apathetic, lacking motivation, hesitating to take a risk, avoiding, being resigned to failure, displaying learned helplessness
Need for belonging or affiliation	Engaging in attention-seeking behaviors, being the class clown, teasing, bullying, withdrawing socially, joining a gang or a cult
Need for physical well-being	Showing signs or fatigue, being absent frequently, having unexplained bruises, having frequent stomachaches, having infections, squinting, having earaches, being irritable

Factors Outside School That Contribute to Unmet Developmental Needs
Poverty
Placement in foster care
Family history of mental health problems
Maternal depression
History of neglect or abuse
Family trauma
Sleep disturbance

introduction to Erikson in Chapter 3.) According to Erikson, individuals confront a series of *psychosocial crises* as they mature and develop. Successful movement through a stage is marked by the emergence of a developmental strength. Conversely, difficulties in resolving a stage can lead to a socioemotional deficiency. (See Table 3.2.)

Both strengths and deficiencies carry over to successive stages. Therefore, an infant in the first stage of *socioemotional development* who develops trust acquires a sense of hope about the future. In contrast, difficulties at the trust stage, explained Erikson, can lead to a sense of withdrawal and resignation that undermines hope at later stages.

Note that when students are beginning school, they are confronted with the psychosocial crisis of industry versus inferiority. The result can be either a sense of competence or inertia. Students who experience early school failure face a difficult road, which is complicated by their sense that they cannot succeed. In general, early childhood educators are best at including developmental exigencies in their daily routines and interactions with youths. Unfortunately, students' social and emotional needs are less a priority as they make their way through elementary, middle, and high school.

Adolescents.   The adolescent struggle for identity often puts teens at odds with parents and teachers. In the National Longitudinal Study of Adolescent Health (1994), researchers collected data on 12,000 middle school students. Whereas 60% of seventh graders believed their teachers cared about them, only 45% of ninth graders thought the same. Furthermore, school problems such as having difficulty paying attention and feeling isolated from others increased from seventh to ninth grade. Suspensions and expulsions also peaked during the middle school years. Laurence Steinberg, a psychology professor from Temple University, summarized the findings with a caustic comment, "Schools seem to dislike young adolescents nearly as much as young adolescents seem to dislike school" (cited in Olson, 2002, p. 9).

As they enter young adulthood, adolescents are preoccupied with the benefits of freedom and are less attracted by the encumbered responsibilities. They yearn to escape the fetters of adult supervision. The poet Robert Bly (1990) referred to this adolescent trait as *grandiose ascension*. Thus, the middle school teacher who is dismayed by a teenager's noncompliance may need to remind him- or herself that such adolescent behavior is normal before launching into a lecture directed at the young rebel. At this stage, the youngster might be much more concerned about what peers think than about the teacher's opinion. Savvy middle school teachers recognize that "saving face" is a central developmental issue for adolescents and talk with recalcitrant students in private.

Cognitive Development

Developmental needs in the realm of cognition also have an effect on students' behavior. All students, regardless of culture or ethnicity, go through the same sequence of sensorimotor, preoperational, concrete operational, and formal operational stages of *cognitive development* (Piaget, 1954). Embedded in each of these stages are characteristic ways that students perceive the world around them. Teachers who use instructional approaches that are out of sync with cognitive development risk missing the mark with their lessons and inadvertently increase the possibility of classroom management difficulties.

Consider a fourth-grade teacher who ignores that most of his or her students are at the *concrete operational stage* of intellectual development. At this stage, students are beginning to think logically. They can follow a sequence of ideas to a conclusion, and they can flesh out abstract ideas through imagination. At the concrete operational stage of thinking, students are also here-and-now oriented, they focus intently on subjects that spark their interest, they enjoy organized social activities, and they learn best through direct experience. Like props on a stage, students' interests, day-to-day activities, and personal priorities provide the backdrop for key learning "scenes" in their lives. If these fourth-grade students are taught principally through texts, workbooks, and individual seat work, their teacher will have failed to capitalize on how his or her students think best. Rather than letting students help one another, such a teacher insists on solitary effort. Classroom information is derived straight from textbooks and no attempt is made to bridge the mental distance from the abstract to students' direct experience. If the teacher's approach is curriculum driven (i.e., emphasizes information) rather than developmentally oriented (i.e., emphasizes student perception), the teacher runs the risk of teaching "facts" at the expense of not communicating effectively with his or her students. Student interest in black holes in space, horses, time travel, and cartoons is ignored because these subjects are not in the school curriculum for fourth graders.

If the mismatch between developmental stage and instructional methods continues, students find maintaining attention more difficult. Classroom management problems soon follow. Bored students goof off. Distracted students are reprimanded, and the frustrated teacher leans more and more on incentives and threats to compel students to finish classroom tasks.

Elementary Students' Thinking.   An elementary student listened to a health teacher's lecture on the circulatory system. The teacher explained that the arteries carry oxygen-rich blood and the veins carry oxygen-depleted blood. The student raised her hand and asked if something was wrong with the "blue blood" in her arm. The health teacher reassured her that the darker oxygen-depleted blood in veins was normal. After the presentation, the student approached a teacher, rolled up her sleeve, and pointed to her blue veins. "See," the student said, "I have all these blue veins. And I have sickle-cell, and I want to know if that's the bad blood." The fourth grader's perception of the lesson was based less on facts than on her personal experience.

Katherine G. Simon, Director of Research at the Coalition of Essential Schools, in Oakland, California, related the preceding anecdote. In Simon's (2002) view, "All too often, curriculum planning focuses on inventories of facts. But when designing curriculum, it's [sic] helpful to step back and ask *how* human beings have acquired the knowledge that we now want to transmit" (p. 24).

Student-Centered Perspective

Proactive classroom management is student centered. It embraces developmental principles that highlight the value of the students' perspective. Ultimately, every student constructs his and her own sense of the how the world operates. The purpose of proactive classroom management is to help students develop meaningful cognitive and social skills through classroom experiences that take into account the student's view of reality.

AVOIDING STEREOTYPES

At school, important decisions about a student are made on the basis of traits and categories. For instance, Ellen is a student who is "at risk" because her family is poor and she is failing eighth-grade math and literature. Mark is an "honors" student because he achieved an A average during his first 3 years of high school. Third-grader Juan has "ADHD" (attention-deficit/hyperactivity disorder) because he has difficulty sitting still and concentrating for more than 10 minutes. Travis has accumulated a steady string of Fs in math, but when classified by his IQ score, he is "above average," so he sprouts a new identity: "learning disabled with dyscalculia."

This ongoing process of sorting students and typecasting them by educational categories holds on inherent danger: It creates a false impression that, once labeled, students' educational needs are clear-cut. Imagine a sixth-grade classroom filled with 25 students, all of whom scored 140 on an IQ test. As a category, these students are classified "geniuses," but individually they are as different as any other group of sixth-grade students. Some are boys, others girls; some are African American, others Latino, and still others White. One half of the students live in single-parent families. Three students receive free school lunches. One student is a Boy Scout, and 4 students play Little League baseball. Two of the students have a learning disability. Five students are frequently absent. Two make no secret about the fact that they "hate" school. Four students like math; 10 students like reading; 7 students say their favorite subject is art. Each has a different family history and varied interests outside school.

Thus, the prudent, and proactive, educator is not quick to *stereotype* students. Instead, he or she takes into account all the variables in a student's life to determine the student's developmental and educational needs. In particular, the proactive teacher realizes that labels are a double-edged sword, particularly with regard to students who receive special education services.

Special Education

Approximately 6 million students aged 3 to 21 receive special education services (U.S. Department of Education, 2002). Approximately 80% of these students were not identified as having special needs until they began school. Some of these students with *mild disabilities* were placed in special education because of speech or language impairments. Others receive special education services because of difficulties in behavior or with academics. To receive special education, a student must be evaluated as having a disability. The federal special education law—the Individuals with Disabilities Education Act (IDEA)—lists 13 disability categories (Table 4.2). More than half the students in special education programs are identified as having a learning disability. Other common disability categories to which students are assigned are "emotionally disturbed" and "mildly mentally retarded."

As mentioned previously, some educators are concerned that terms or labels used to identify a special need can work against a youngster (Lipsky & Gartner, 1991). Critics contend that the educational practice of labeling students who have problems with learning and behavior undercuts teacher expectations. Furthermore, the argument goes, labels inhibit teacher creativity and perseverance. Terms such as *mildly retarded, emotionally disturbed, hyperactive,* and *learning disabled* imply that the student is the sole source of the problem, in much the same way the medical diagnosis "diabetic" conjures the image of an ill individual who will improve only when treated by a specialist.

TABLE 4.2   *Number of Students Ages 6 Through 21 Served Under IDEA During 1991–1992 and 2000–2001*

Disability	1991–1992[a]	2000–2001	Percent Change in Number
Specific learning disabilities	2,247,004	2,887,217	28.5
Speech or language impairments	998,904	1,093,808	9.5
Mental retardation	553,262	612,978	10.8
Emotional disturbance	400,211	473,663	18.4
Multiple disabilities	98,408	122,559	24.5
Hearing impairments	60,727	70,767	16.5
Orthopedic impairments	51,389	73,057	42.2
Other health impairments	58,749	291,850	396.8
Visual impairments	24,083	25,975	7.9
Autism[b]	5,415	78,749	1,354.3
Deaf-blindness	1,427	1,320	−7.5
Traumatic brain injury[b]	245	14,844	5,958.8
Developmental delay	—	28,935	—
All disabilities	4,499,824	5,775,722	28.4

Note. IDEA = Individuals with Disabilities Education Act. From *Twenty-fourth Annual Report to Congress on the Implementation of the Individuals with Disabilities Education Act* (p. II–20), by U.S. Department of Education, 2002, Washington, DC: Author.
[a]Data from 1991–1992 include children with disabilities served under the Chapter 1 Handicapped program.
[b]Reporting in the autism and traumatic brain injury categories was optional in 1991–1992 and required beginning in 1992–1993.

The three designations of a mild disability—learning disabled, emotionally disturbed, and mildly retarded—are not clear-cut medical conditions but categories assigned as a result of school-administered evaluations. For the most part, these evaluations consist of a composite of standardized test scores, teacher reports, and grades. A determination of whether a mild disability exists is made when school officials compare a student's evaluation results with disability criteria established by each state department of education. In summary, most students who receive special education (i.e., learning disabled, emotionally disturbed, and mildly mentally retarded) are determined to need services on the basis of an administrative review of their lack of progress in general education, not because they have a medically based disability (Henley, Ramsey, & Algozzine, 2003).

Although some students profit from being identified as a student with special needs, others do not. The same label that opens the door to special education service can also brand a student as a chronic failure. The problem of negative stereotypes associated with students in special education was addressed by the reauthorization of two federal laws: IDEA in 2004 and the No Child Left Behind Act in 2002. Each law raises the standard for academic progress of students with disabilities. IDEA requires the general education classroom to be the first option considered during determination of special education placement. The No Child Left Behind Act mandates that the educational progress of students with special needs be evaluated with the same standardized tests as those taken by students without disabilities. By 2007, the educational progress of all students in Grades 3 through 8 must be measured by standardized achievement tests. In many states, passing standardized achievement tests is a graduation requirement. Advocates of these inclusive education measures hope that raising the bar of educational expectations will offset the negative stereotyping of students with special needs.

ENSURING GENDER EQUITY

Understanding students requires uncovering the unique individual behind the facade of labels and categories. Because female students present fewer disciplinary problems in schools, the special problems they face are often overlooked (Jones & Jones, 2004). For instance, compared with female students, 4 times as many male students are referred and placed in special education programs because of emotional problems (Henley et al., 2003). So, do female students have fewer emotional problems than boys do? The answer is unequivocal: No. However, female emotional problems are often internalized, less obvious than those of male students, and thus addressed less often. For example, concerns about female body image can lead to low self-esteem, depression, anorexia, and bulimia (Graber, 1996).

Harter (2000) reported that at the third-grade level, girls and boys feel equally good about their appearance, but by the end of high school, girls' self-perceptions of their physical appearance are significantly lower than those of boys (pp. 134–135). Likewise, an estimated 60% of U.S. women and girls older than 10 years will, at any given time, report that they are dieting (Whitehead & Hoover, 2000).

Conversely, male emotional problems are likely to be externalized through aggressive behavior. An experienced social worker said, "Disturbing males go to jail; disturbed females get pregnant."

Some believe females internalize their feelings because they have not been encouraged to be outspoken. One 10th-grade student, Bettina, unconsciously echoed this sentiment, "What gets me in trouble is—my big fat mouth." J. M. Taylor, Gilligan, and Sullivan (1996) argued that female students need opportunities to express their thoughts and feelings. These researchers found that adolescent girls at risk of failing school felt disconnected from others. Taylor et al. described two types of adolescent female reactions to alienation: First, "loud" girls spoke or acted out their resentments against others who they thought were limiting their relationships, and second, other girls adopted a "deliberate silence" (p. 69). These researchers summarized their findings as follows:

> Inclusion of the voices of girls is essential in the development of any program that is intended for their benefit. Without girls' voices informing the direction of policy and programs, girls' needs are likely to be misconstrued and their strengths and resilience ignored or lost behind the focus on need. (p. 73)

Stein (2000) wanted to learn more about what she called *girl culture*. She said, "Girls are too varied and vibrant for labeling, and as soon as you think that you have one pegged, she changes" (p. 19). Stein dispelled some common stereotypes about girls. She reported that school-aged girls were independent, technologically astute, socially assertive, and expansive in their views on traditional gender roles. For instance, some girls countered standard cultural messages about feminine appearance in fashion magazines by creating *zines*, self-designed magazines that girls write, design, and circulate among themselves. Stein said, "Zines are a backlash against mainstream fashion magazines. Often in zines, girls complain about too-skinny fashion models, articles and advertisements that encourage girls to try to live up to someone else's ideals, and stupid and/or sexist boys"(p. 19).

Jobe (2003) said, "The goal of *gender equity* [italics added] is to build learning environments where neither boys nor girls feel confined by stereotypes and expectations about who they are" (p. 65). Jobe recommended the following guidelines for helping females succeed in school:

- Recognize and address issues such as sexual harassment, substance abuse, and pregnancy.
- Design collaborative science, math, and technology lessons that appeal to both male and female students.
- Infuse math, science, and technology into other subject areas such as music, art, and history.
- Highlight contributions of females to math, and science, as well as history and literature.
- Reflect on hidden biases such as calling on males more often or organizing classroom responsibilities into stereotypical roles (e.g., the boys do the heavy lifting jobs and the girls decorate).
- Provide collaborative activities that require males and females to work together.

- Infuse such interpersonal skills as cooperation, conflict resolution, and negotiation into male and female classroom activities.
- Avoid any activity or discussion that pits females against males.

Gender Bias

Gender equity begins with teacher perception. Teachers vary in their tolerance of student behaviors. P. B. Taylor, Gunter, and Slate (2001) found that teachers rated the behavior of African American females "inappropriate" more frequently than the behavior of White female students. Likewise, white male students were rated as exhibiting more inappropriate behavior than that of White females. Researchers have pointed out that elementary teachers tend to be female, whereas males often favor secondary teaching positions (Heard, Divall, & Johnson, 2000; McIntyre & Tong, 1998). This separation of genders within the teaching profession may explain why boys are more frequently identified as having behavioral problems in elementary school and girls lag behind in science and math achievement in secondary school.

Copeland and Hess (1995) studied adolescents' coping strategies. They reported that girls tend to use more diverse coping strategies than those that boys use. Girls will talk with friends, seek spiritual help, look for social distractions, and use positive images. Boys will avoid problems, use humor, and rely on passive distractions such as video games. Male and female students are more alike than different, yet the differences must be respected. A sulking female student may have been sexually abused. An unruly male student may also have been sexually abused. An underlying reason always exists for inappropriate behavior. The literature on gender differences cautions teachers against making quick judgments solely on the basis of surface behavior. An understanding of the varying needs of male and female students requires teacher reflection. Teachers must confront their own gender-based stereotypes and recognize the role gender plays in learning and behavior.

The following guidelines can help teachers limit *gender bias* in the classroom:

- Be alert to curriculum bias. An example of curriculum bias is the idea that females are not well suited for math and science and boys do not excel in the arts.
- Look for gender bias in textbooks. Point out instances of gender bias and discuss these instances with students.
- Discuss bias in the cultural media with students. An example of media bias is that the idea women must be beautiful to be a main character in a movie and men must be handsome.
- Use non-gender-specific language. Say "police *officer*" rather than "police*man*" and "fire*fighter*" rather than "fire*man*."
- Encourage both male and female students to discuss their feelings.
- Challenge female students and male students alike to excel.

Gender bias is extensive, and it is reinforced by unchallenged assumptions. Gender bias limits opportunities for male and female students alike. Teachers need to create learning environments in which no member dominates and no student is silenced. This goal can be accomplished by minimizing gender-segregated activities, encouraging independent thinking, and highlighting a curriculum that is gender equitable, presenting women in nontraditional roles.

Zittleman and Sadker (2002) recommended the following strategies for teaching students about gender bias:

- Ask students to review school texts and identify forms of bias. Ask them to suggest ways of improving gender representation in texts.
- Ask students to identify gender bias in magazines, television programming, and advertising.
- Find examples of bias that negatively affect males, people of color, or the poor. Ask for suggestions to overcome these examples of bias.
- Ask students to identify how gender bias is evident in their schooling: for example, teachers' asking only males to help with physical tasks and studying women's contributions only during "Women's History Month."

CULTURAL DIVERSITY

As mentioned at the beginning of this chapter, Latinos and Asians will continue to outdistance Whites and African Americans in number as the century progresses (www.childstats.gov/ac2004). With an increase in diversity will come new challenges for teachers. Different languages and different cultures can either subtract from or contribute to the American mosaic. Teachers can celebrate differences and forge bonds among young people by tightening the interpersonal links that connect students to one another.

Sheets and Gay (1996) reported that students of color are disciplined more frequently than White students are. Disciplinary actions are directed most frequently at African American students, followed by Latino students, and then Filipino students. According to Kea (1998), tension and negative consequences seem to intensify when teachers or students feel threatened. O. L. Taylor (1990) identified the eight most common cross-cultural disciplinary problems:

1. Challenging teacher authority
2. Interrupting
3. Talking out of turn
4. Responding loudly
5. Arguing
6. Not walking away from an altercation
7. Losing emotional control during a confrontation
8. Socializing in class

Teachers can overcome such problems and deal with other challenges that cultural diversity presents by doing the following. First, teachers must recognize cultural differences; second, they must create a culturally responsive classroom; and third, they must understand and be sensitive to students' beliefs and value systems.

Recognition of Cultural Differences

With cultural differences come different behaviors. For example, Latino children may avert their eyes when a teacher is talking with them about their behavior. Young African American males sometimes engage in spirited insults that include family members. This practice of *woofing* is common in urban areas. Southeast Asian students who are reprimanded might smile out of guilt rather than a lack of respect for authority (Sileo & Prater, 1998).

According to the National Center for Education Statistics (2002a), 90% of public school educators have European ancestry. Meanwhile, the cultural roots of public school students continue to change. While the African American population is expected to slowly expand beyond 13% of all students, the Latino (currently 13%) and Asian American (currently 4%) populations are projected to double by 2020. Changes in urban areas will be even more pronounced, especially in large cities such as New York, Miami, and Los Angeles (Hochschild & Scovronick, 2003).

Unless taken into account, the attendant cultural and linguistic differences between teacher and students can lead to misunderstandings about both intentions and behavior. Consider the case study of "Michael."

 # Case Study: "Michael"

Donna Marriott taught in a multiaged (5–9 years) inclusion classroom. One day in the middle of a busy morning, a new student arrived. The school secretary introduced "Michael, who doesn't speak English." He was welcomed and provided with a series of bus, rug, water, and lunch "buddies." He was well mannered, neat, respectful, and withdrawn. A week later, the bilingual teacher said to Ms. Marriott, "You might have better results, dear, if you call him Miguel." Ms. Marriott was embarrassed and dismayed. Why hadn't Miguel's parents corrected her? Why hadn't Miguel said something? How could the school secretary make such a mistake?

As often happens in urban schools, within a few weeks Miguel moved away. Three weeks later, his records arrived and Ms. Marriott read something that made her catch her breath. "His name wasn't Michael. It wasn't Miguel. His name was David," she said. In trying to understand what had gone wrong, Ms. Marriott arrived at some insightful conclusions. She guessed that David was told to respect "la maestra," and if the teacher decided to change his name, so be it. She expected that David would stand up for himself, but in retrospect, Ms. Marriott saw that the power differential dictated opposite behavior. She was White; he was Brown. She was the teacher; he was a student. She spoke English; he spoke Spanish. She believed in the "system"; David accepted the inadequacies of the system. In summary, Ms. Marriott (2002) said,

> I have learned many difficult lessons in the years since David sat submissively on the edge of my classroom. I have learned lessons about passive racism—the kind that we cannot see in ourselves, don't want to see in ourselves, and vehemently deny. I have learned lessons about implicit power and explicit powerlessness—about those voices we choose to hear and those voices we unknowingly silence. I have learned that being a good teacher is as much about rapport and relationships as it is about progressive curriculum, pedagogy, and assessment. (p. 35)

Also consider that African American boys are overrepresented in special education programs for students with behavioral disorders. Weinstein, Tomlinson-Clarke, and Curran (2004) reported that some African American students participate by making enthusiastic comments or having enthusiastic reactions. Teachers may find such behavior disturbing.

Creation of a Culturally Responsive Classroom

The *culturally responsive classroom* is a classroom in which each student feels that his or her culture is valued (Table 4.3). Following are four recommended guidelines for establishing a culturally responsive learning environment (Weinstein et al., 2004):

1. **Recognize your ethnocentric biases.** The predominantly White teacher population considers its cultural norms as neutral and universal. This bias sets the stage for interpreting different behaviors as abnormal. Cultural biases and assumptions must be articulated and examined.

TABLE 4.3   *Questions to Guide Culturally Competent Teaching*

Questions About Cultural Context

1. How much information is available about this student's linguistic, ethnic, and cultural background?
2. How would this student's family explain the student's behavior?
3. Do other students with similar cultural backgrounds exhibit similar behaviors?
4. Does anything indicate that the student's behavior has a cultural explanation?

Questions About Classroom Rules and Explanations

1. In what ways are students expected to respond to questions and directions?
2. In what ways are students expected to signal attention?
3. In what ways are students expected to behave toward authority?

Questions About Classroom Practices

1. In what ways is the teacher using flexible grouping?
2. In what ways is the teacher promoting interdependence?
3. In what ways is the teacher differentiating instruction?
4. In what ways is the teacher celebrating diversity?

Questions to Promote Classroom Accommodations

1. Do any rules, expectations, and response behaviors need to be explicitly taught to this student?
2. Do any classroom practices need to be added, refined, or eliminated to more effectively support this student?
3. Does the teacher need more information about this student's background and sociocultural context before further adaptations are made?

Note. Derived from "Promoting Cultural Competence Through Teacher Assistance Teams," by S. Craig, K. Hull, A. G. Haggart, and M. Perez-Selles, 2000, *Teaching Exceptional Children, 32*(3), p. 10.

2. **Learn how students' cultural backgrounds influence how they learn.**
   Values, standards for achievement, rules of decorum, communication styles, learning styles, and motivational systems vary by ethnic group (Sheets & Gay, 1996). Attempting to delineate specific differences among the many cultural groups represented in public schools would be an overwhelming task. However, an understanding of some basic areas includes emphasis on the collective versus the individual, active versus passive learning styles, and cultural expectations about how children should interact with adults. Learning key phrases in a student's native language also helps a teacher develop a relationship with the student.

   Visiting students' families and consulting with community leaders provide important information and build trust. Searching out resources that provide background information on specific cultural and ethnic groups is a worthwhile strategy. In her book *Subtractive Schooling: U.S. Mexican Youth and the Politics of Caring,* Valenzuela (1999) explained that Mexican youths need to feel "cared for" before they will care about school.

3. **Identify cultural heritage details from students' lives.**   What foods do they eat? What religious beliefs do they hold that might restrict classroom activities? What cultural celebrations do they follow? What norms do they follow in terms of psychological or emotional support? Many of these questions can be included in student surveys; others can be answered by family members and professionals who share the students' cultural background.

4. **Determine what disciplinary and classroom management practices are equitable for all students.**   Disciplinary procedures should be evaluated to determine whether cultural inequities exist. For example, African American students are suspended more often than are European Americans, who are more often given in-house suspensions. Caution must also be used to ensure that stereotypes based on dress, haircuts, tattoos, and piercings do not influence how often students are disciplined. Hyland (2000) reported that when teachers march young students down the hall for disciplinary reasons, some teachers hold African American students by the wrist and White students by the hand. One high school teacher even warned her students that if they did not shape up, they would end up as prostitutes (Katz, 1999).

   Other common errors that reflect a lack of cultural knowledge are not recognizing that in the Latino culture the group contribution is emphasized and singling out an individual's achievement may be embarrassing; reprimanding Filipino American students, who are brought up dependent on adult authority, for a lack of independence; and encouraging Chinese American students, who have been raised to listen respectfully to adults, to express their opinions.

   Determining how to treat students in a culturally equitable fashion requires self-reflection coupled with an interest in how people in different cultures raise their children. Most of all, teachers need to be open to parental feedback. Many cultural differences become apparent only after an event triggers a parent's attention, such as when a Mexican father disapproved of his kindergartner son's playing in the classroom housekeeping area or a Muslim father did not want his fifth-grade daughter sitting next to a boy (Weinstein et al., 2004).

Sensitivity to Students' Beliefs and Values

Generalizing about how values and beliefs shape the behavior of individual students within specific cultural groups is always risky. No two students or families are alike. Broad statements entail the danger of being viewed as stereotypes or even prejudicial. The following information is presented with this disclaimer firmly in mind.

Many times students, regardless of ethnicity, believe they are not given a fair chance to tell their side of a story in a dispute with a teacher. However, students *might* feel differently about discipline as a result of their ethnicity. For instance, African American students tend to place more emphasis on feelings and their relationship with their teacher. Whereas White students are less likely to be upset by impersonal teachers, students of color are sensitive to being "dissed" by teachers, and they might perceive that teachers favor White students. When African American students feel unjustly accused, they are less likely than other ethnic groups to concede to authority. The actions of African Americans are more likely to be driven by personality, loyalty to friends, and their own sense of what is right.

Chicano and Filipino students are more sensitive to embarrassment. They would rather avoid conflict than bring shame on their families. They are particularly sensitive to teachers who yell at them. They will walk out of a classroom rather than endure acrimonious comments (Kea, 1998; Sheets & Gay, 1996).

Some Latino students are polychronic (i.e., address many things at one time), whereas some non-Latino students are monochronic (i.e., address one thing at a time). In conversation, Latino students may seem to all be talking at the same time and may be perceived as wanting immediate attention even though the teacher is involved with someone else. Latinos often interact at a closer distance than non-Latinos do and are more accepting of close physical contact. Smiling among Latino youths is a way of saying "hello," "please," and "thank you." Also, Latinos are taught to lower their eyes when reprimanded. This lack of eye contact is not a sign of defiance (Irujo, 1989).

Teachers should always be alert to the possibility that, instead of being difficult, students are simply exhibiting behavior that reflects differing values and beliefs. Keeping this idea firmly in mind may prevent misunderstandings and students' loss of *trust* in their teacher.

ENHANCING STUDENT–TEACHER RELATIONSHIPS

Knowing students—what they care about, how development influences their behavior, and their cultural backgrounds—provides a sound underpinning for cultivating good student–teacher relationships. The student–teacher relationship provides an anchor for students who are buffeted by the demands of a fast-paced, world. When students trust their teacher, they are more secure and productive (Bryk & Schneider, 2003). Time spent developing a good relationship with students is a sound investment.

A positive student–teacher relationship inspires through example. Positive relationships between teachers and students establish common ground for directing the efforts of each day. Conversely, a negative student–teacher relationship numbs students' desire to learn and is the source of many disciplinary problems. The following subsections cover four factors that influence student–teacher relationships: students' feelings, teacher authenticity, sense of humor, and respect for students. The guidelines that are offered are based in both theory and research on effective teaching practices.

Students' Feelings

Emotions play an important role in behavior. The seat of emotions is the limbic system, which is buried deep in the center of the brain. Millions of neural fibers link the limbic system to the neocortex—the thinking part of the brain. When a student feels *stress*, the brain "downshifts" from the reasoning neocortex gear to the emotional limbic system. When this happens, emotion overrides thought. Anyone who has had the experience of "going blank" when confronted with a test question is familiar with the downshifting phenomenon. Thus, a negative student–teacher relationship can numb a student's desire to learn and be the source of disciplinary problems. Goleman (1995) called this takeover by emotions a *neural hijacking*, which is a protective function. Students cannot flee from a stressful classroom situation. To compensate, they will either act out or withdraw. Fatigue, noncompliance, distractibility, and defiance are some of the classroom behaviors of "downshifted" students (R. N. Caine, 2000).

Robert Sylwester, author of *A Biological Brain in a Cultural Classroom* (2000), is a leading authority on using brain research in the classroom. In his book, Sylwester frequently refers to the role feelings play in behavior. He said, "Young people need to create a functional balance between unconscious *emotional arousal* [italics added] and conscious rational response" (p. 28). In reviewing the important role that emotion plays in brain function, Sylwester highlighted several abilities teachers can foster in students to help them be emotionally secure:

- **Intrinsic motivation.** *Intrinsic motivation* is the ability to persist in frustrating situations. Activities that help students develop this ability provide a forum in which to discuss feelings. The teacher should also encourage cooperative approaches to problem solving and student self-assessment.

- **Impulse control.**   *Impulse control* is the ability to reflect on choices and delay gratification. Activities that help students develop this ability focus on long-term projects with some immediate goals. The idea is for students to appreciate experiences that develop slowly.
- **Mood regulation.**   *Mood regulation* is the ability to moderate moods, especially those having to do with anger. Activities that help students develop this ability teach students to express both positive and negative feelings. Allowing for retreat from social interactions when emotions become overwhelming helps students learn to calm down and reflect before reacting.
- **Empathy.**   *Empathy* is the ability to connect with another person's feelings. *Sympathy* is a kindhearted response to another person's situation. Empathy implies more of a sharing of feeling. Activities that help students develop this ability encourage open discussion to help students tune in to one another's feelings. Engaging in activities that promote conversational skills such as listening and responding is a suitable way to foster empathy.
- **Social competence.**   *Social competence* is the ability to assess and respond appropriately to a social situation. Activities that help students develop this ability provide constant informal interactions and teach group social skills. Cooperative learning, games, field trips, peer tutoring, and brainstorming promote social competence.

Teachers who are responsive to *students' feelings* solicit feedback, listen to students, and revise classroom procedures to accommodate students' concerns.

Teacher Authenticity

An authentic teacher is trustworthy and sincere. One common mistake novice teachers make is to confuse the *role* of teacher with *authentic teaching*. Rather than naturally allowing their personalities to emerge, they project an image of how they think a teacher should behave. Their conception of the role of teacher is influenced by a variety of factors, including advice from veteran teachers (e.g., "Don't smile until Christmas," "Show them who is the boss"), concerns about "controlling" their class, and memories of how past teachers treated their students. The primary reason individuals enter the teaching profession is because they like children. An authentic teacher allows this caring attitude to show.

Many teachers have encountered a wide-eyed student at a supermarket or shopping mall. "Gee, Mr. Riley, you buy groceries" and "Wow, Ms. Abraham, I didn't know that you went to the mall" are common student reactions after seeing their teacher outside school. Students are pleased to see that their teacher is a "regular" person. Allowing your personality to shine through in the classroom helps students feel more comfortable. If you listen to students talking about a new teacher during the first day of school recess, you will likely hear a critique based on one of two criteria: "She is mean" or "She is nice." Teachers do not have to be "mean" to gain students' respect, and being personable does not imply weakness. Students are keen observers of their teachers and believe in teachers who believe

Authentic teachers do the following:
- Admit mistakes and correct them immediately
- Listen to students and respect their opinions
- Share information about their personal lives
- Display a sense of humor
- Enjoy being around young people and communicate this joy every day
- Become involved in students' extracurricular activities
- Respond to students with respect, even in difficult situations
- Do not jump to conclusions about causes of student misbehavior
- Recognize that students have lives outside school
- Challenge students to achieve their best
- Enjoy teaching and expect students to enjoy learning
- Have one-to-one conversations with students
- Address students by name
- Do not talk to another adult about students in the students' presence

FIGURE 4.1   Characteristics of Authentic Teachers
Adapted from *Qualities of Effective Teachers*, by J. H. Stronge, 2002, Alexandria, VA:
Association for Supervision and Curriculum Development.

in themselves. Teachers who are self-assured have a natural authority that does not require threats or gimmicks to control students' behavior. Figure 4.1 lists personal characteristics of authentic teachers.

A natural reaction to entering a new profession and taking on the responsibilities of a professional role is to want to appear confident and in charge. Likewise, students will naturally test a new teacher. Authentic teachers trust their abilities. They are upfront and direct. When students test their teacher, it is a probing strategy. They want to see what kind of reaction they can get. Students need to know what to expect. They are searching for boundaries. Testing the limits tells them a great deal about the person whom they are dealing. An authentic teacher short-circuits the testing process by clearly stating expectations. Authentic teachers are assertive. They tell students what they like and what they do not like (Canter & Canter, 1992). They follow through on consequences, without rancor. When dealing with misbehavior, the authentic teacher conveys the key message "I care about you, but your current behavior is unacceptable."

Teachers also express authenticity through body language (F. Jones, 1987). *Body language* includes tone of voice, carriage, eye movements, position of the arms, hand gestures, posture, and facial expressions. Body language speaks volumes about what a person is thinking and feeling (Figure 4.2).

Imagine being a student entering a classroom. The teacher is standing at the door with his hands on his hips and a scowl on his face. Now contrast this with a teacher greeting students at the door with high fives and a smile. Body language communicates more effectively than words. Positive body language includes confident movement, an erect posture, good eye contact, and a steady tone of voice that does not rise and fall with anger or resentment (F. Jones, 1987).

> *The Eyes.*   The eyes communicate more than any other part of the body. Relaxed and comfortable eye contact communicates self-confidence. A shifting gaze suggests discomfort. Staring or a steady gaze can be interpreted as hostility. Steady and friendly eye contact suggests sincerity.
>
> *Touching.*   Touching should be restrained to such accepted practices as handshakes and high fives. Comforting a young child who has scraped a knee is acceptable as well. Some students are "tactilely defensive." They shirk from physical contact. Always check with the school administration about specific school policies on touching.
>
> *Gestures.*   Posture, gestures, and facial expressions indicate an individual's comfort level. An erect posture indicates confidence and self-assurance. Crossed arms suggest defensiveness. Hand signals communicate as effectively as speech.
>
> *Smile.*   Nothing invites participation more readily than a genuine smile. More than 50 types of human smiles can be expressed. Authentic smiles begin with a small facial movement and expand to a broad expression.

FIGURE 4.2   Body Language

Sense of Humor

The authentic teacher has a genuine commitment to the interpersonal process. Authentic teachers allow their humanity to show (Clark, 2000; Moustakas, 1971). They appreciate the value of *humor* as a way of connecting with youths and elevating the joy of coming to school. The entertainer Victor Borge often said, "Laughter is the shortest distance between two people" (Saltman, 1995). Humor overcomes barriers, invites participation, encourages risk taking, and bonds people.

Nevertheless, teachers must discriminate between negative and positive humor. For instance, sarcasm might seem funny, but it hurts the target person and undercuts trust. Humor begins with lightness, a sense that each day will unfold in a positive way. Smiling at students, laughing at their jokes, poking fun at your foibles, and observing the incongruities in everyday situations are some ways of injecting a sense of humor into the classroom climate. According to Carlson and Peterson (1995), "Teachers, like cooks, need spice to keep their hungry customers coming. Humor can be that necessary spice" (p. 8).

Some educators believe humor captures students' attention and enhances memory (Larrivee, 2005; Teachers.net, 2005). Hauck and Thomas (1972) found that elementary schoolchildren remembered humorous associations better than those that were nonhumorous during spontaneous classroom discussions. Humor can also turn dead spots in the day into lighthearted moments. One high school science teacher was getting nowhere with his lecture–question format approach to astronomy, so he told his students that for the next 10 minutes all he wanted to hear was wrong answers—the more imaginative the better. Students who had been sullen a moment before started talking. The ensuing discussion concluded with students' writing short essays on topics such as What If Gravity Were Switched Off for the Day? and Searching for Extraterrestrial Life in a Molecule. The creative ideas that this lighthearted approach to astronomy generated provided grist for several classes on quantum physics and relativity.

Everyone enjoys humor, but not everyone can be spontaneously funny. The following guidelines can help a teacher inject a humorous mood into classroom activities:

- **Look for incongruous ideas or situations.** Woody Allen is a master of humorous juxtaposition. A few samples of Allen humor on the usually unhumorous topic of death are as follows: "It's not that I'm afraid to die. I just don't want to be there when it happens." "Why are our days numbered and not, say, lettered?" (www.quotationspage.com/quotes/Woody_Allen)
- **Acknowledge and elicit student humor.** A first-grade teacher gave each student in her class the start of a well-known proverb and asked the students to finish the proverbs. Following are some of the results:

  > "As you shall make your bed so shall you . . . mess it up."
  > "Better be safe than . . . punch a 5th grader."
  > "Strike while the . . . bug is close."
  > "You can lead a horse to water but . . . how?"
  > "The pen is mightier than the . . . pigs."
  > "A penny saved is . . . not much."
  >   (http://www.thehumorarchives.com/humor/0000558.html)

- **Incorporate humor into the daily routine.** One idea is to have a joke or cartoon corner of the classroom. First, the class must discuss what is in good taste: What constitutes a good joke or a bad joke? Then, each day, a different student is responsible for bringing in a funny joke or cartoon. To get their jokes, students can join joke-a-day e-mail lists (e.g., www.joke-of-the-day.com or www.laffaday.com).
- **Incorporate humor into the curriculum.** Stimulus questions for research include Why do we laugh? What do humorists contribute to society? What is the value of humor? and Does humor vary by culture? Students can analyze political cartoons and report on how political cartoons influence public perception. Other topics include the cultural role of comics, humor as propaganda, violence in comics, and gender stereotypes and humor.

Respect for Students

From 1990 to 2003, Sister Mary Rose McGeady was the director of Covenant House, a crisis and rehabilitation facility for New York City street youths. Many of the youngsters she encountered distrusted adults. According to Sister McGeady (1997), these youngsters need "respectful acceptance":

> When a hurt kid is greeted gently, called by name, encouraged to speak, and really listened to, they [sic] hardly know how to respond. It is a new experience to many. Such an approach indeed needs to be our stock in trade. (p. 9)

Respect can be conveyed in many subtle ways. Speaking courteously, using the student's name, and remembering something personal about the student convey respect. One of the most disturbing scenes in school is a teacher yelling at a student. Teachers who model the behaviors they want to elicit from their students are respectful, and they earn their students' respect. Special education teacher Linda Goulet (1997) listed the following seven guidelines for building *respectful relationships* with students:

1. **Begin each day with an upbeat greeting and a smile.**   Give handshakes and slap high fives to set a friendly mood.
2. **Discover "generational" student interests.**   Youths' interests change with each generation. Identify the music, television shows, and athletes that students appreciate. Talk about their interests in class. Let students bring in posters and music they enjoy. Show respect for their generational culture.
3. **Share your personal interests.**   Tell students about your life outside school. Students are immensely interested in their teacher as a human being. Two or three times a week, begin class with a personal anecdote.
4. **Look for decency.**   Even the most outwardly offensive student has some decency. Cultivate seeds of decency by bringing them into the daylight and providing nourishment.
5. **Be honest and nonjudgmental.**   Avoid cryptic and evasive comments. Be direct. Students know when they are being patronized. Do not overreact to comments or behaviors that strike you as rude or inappropriate.
6. **Practice forgiveness.**   Hold students accountable for their actions, but allow for mistakes and provide fresh starts.
7. **Enjoy your students.**   Look for moments in which to share laughter. Genuinely appreciate students' qualities as youths. Do not allow external pressure to shape your behavior in the classroom. Standardized tests may need to be passed, but not at the sake of sacrificing the joy of teaching and learning.

Too often, respect is doled out to students on the basis of merit. Each student needs to be valued as an individual. Not all students can garner top grades, or be elected to the student council, or win the big game, or take the top prize in the science fair. However, all students deserve to be respected.

Favoritism.   Overindulgence in rewards, incentives, and praise for students who achieve in school is discouraging to students who are not singled out for their accomplishments (Kohn, 1993). Favoritism toward specific students can have a negative effect on the entire class. Some ways of avoiding favoritism are as follows (Cotton, 2001):

- Avoid unreliable sources of information about students, including stereotypes and other teachers' biases.
- Emphasize that different students are good at different things. Create situations in which students can display their unique talents.

- Show warmth, friendliness, and encouragement to all students.
- Give all students generous amounts of time in which to formulate answers.
- In your feedback, stress continuous progress relative to mastery. Avoid comparisons with other students.
- Give useful feedback of effort, not just an evaluation of success or failure.

Students' Uniqueness and Perceptions.   All students have some quality of value. Taking time to identify the personal attributes of students is one way to build respect. Listening to them is another. Too much one-way teacher talk inhibits communication. Even when students are angry or plain wrong, a subtext in their conversation needs attention. Anger may need to be ventilated. Confused feelings may need to be accepted. How a student perceives a situation is important information for problem solving. Each student's perception, right or wrong, guides his or her behavior. Information about a student's perspective enhances understanding about the student's behavior.

Summary

- ★ A strong research base supports the idea that the quality of the student–teacher relationship sets the stage for learning.
- ★ Students learn best in nurturing environments where they feel accepted and trust their teachers.
- ★ Teachers foster positive relationships by advocating for youths, understanding how development influences behavior, and establishing a classroom climate that prizes cultural diversity.
- ★ Proactive teachers take the initiative to enhance their relationships with students.
- ★ Proactive teachers are authentic. They have a sense of humor and respect young people for who they are, not just for what they accomplish.
- ★ By valuing students, their backgrounds, and their feelings, teachers establish a climate in which students feel physically and emotionally safe.
- ★ Students who trust their teachers are willing to take risks. This willingness translates into a higher level of commitment to school and school-related goals.

What You Should Know

Now that you have finished reading this chapter, you should know the following:

Why trust between teacher and student is an important quality to nurture .
Several ways of enhancing the student–teacher relationship.
How child and adolescent development influences students' behavior.

Why proactive teachers value a developmental perspective.

The changing demographics of U.S. schoolchildren.

Behavioral differences you might observe because of students' differing cultural backgrounds.

How to recognize gender and special education stereotypes.

Ways of incorporating humor, authenticity, and respect into student–teacher relationships.

Applying the Concepts

1. In a cooperative group, exchange stories of times in elementary or high school when you felt distress because of something that happened in school. What could your teacher or teachers have done to alleviate your distress? Brainstorm a list of recommendations for decreasing classroom stress. Share your ideas with other groups.

2. Interview parents about their visits to their child's school. Ask open-ended questions such as Did you feel welcome? Did you feel comfortable? and What were your feelings after the visit? If the parents rarely attend school functions, ask why and what the school could do to involve them more regularly.

3. At a field site, select a level of cognitive development that matches the students' age. Observe how the teacher presents lessons in a way that stimulates students. Observe how teachers present lessons in ways that fail to take into account students' level of cognitive development. In both instances, describe how the manner in which a lesson is presented influences students' behavior.

4. Review several textbooks used in either elementary or secondary schools. Identify how the textbooks deal with gender equity and cultural diversity.

5. Select a public school in an affluent area. Walk or drive through the area, visiting local stores, businesses, and youth recreation areas. Select a public school in an economically deprived area and take the same tour. Contrast your experiences. Discuss your observations in class. How did the tours help you better understand the students who attend each school?

6. Do a Web search on using humor in the classroom. Make a list of Web sites that offer humorous ideas that a teacher could use. Do not limit yourself to education Web sites. Brainstorm a list of regular routines or procedures that a teacher could use to maintain a cheery classroom atmosphere.

7. Visit an inclusion program and visit a self-contained special education program. What differences do you note in terms of student motivation, student behavior, and teacher expectations? What are the advantages and disadvantages of inclusive education programs compared with those of self-contained special education programs?

8. What are some daily routines that teachers follow to demonstrate their respect for all their students? Recall your days as a student in elementary or secondary school. Did teachers have favorites? How do teachers single out students as favorites? What is the effect on other students? What are some ways of avoiding the pitfall of playing favorites?

Part II

Prevention

Any idiot can face a crisis; it is this day-to-day living that wears you out.

Anton Chekhov

If school is not inviting, if the tasks are not clear, interesting, and at an appropriate level, how can we expect students to be on task? Adverse student reactions should be expected when classes are dull, teaching is uninspired, and failure built in.

William Morse

I heard teachers talking about people, saying, "Those kids can't do nothing." Kids want teachers who believe in them.

Inner-city middle school student

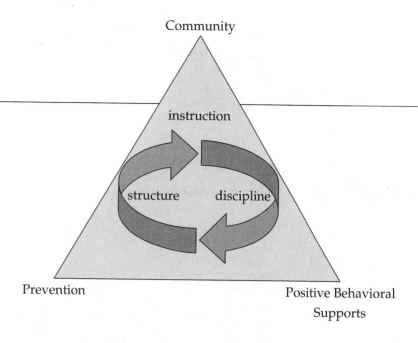

The art of classroom management is preventing students from engaging in behavior that disrupts their work and the work of those around them. One of the more interesting revelations about classroom management is that in some cases the teacher is the source of student misbehavior. As disconcerting as this statement may appear, it substantiates the fact that teachers are influential determiners of student behavior. If, as researchers indicate, disorganized routines, strained peer relationships, and uninspired lessons contribute to disciplinary problems, then well-organized lessons, trusting relationships, and interesting lessons can improve student behavior.

Each aspect of classroom structure has a significant effect on student behavior. Students who are bored, students who feel isolated, and students who do not know what is expected of them are at risk for developing disciplinary problems. When students are motivated, they turn their attention and energy to learning, which eliminates the teacher's need to deal with behavioral problems that interfere with instructional time.

Chapter 5

Managing Groups

Chapter Outline

 Key Terms

Introduction

Teachers spend most of their day in group situations. A class of students is more than simply an aggregate of individuals. Groups develop their own personality. Teachers often comment on how one "class" is different from another. When the focus is on prevention of problem behaviors, the starting point is adopting effective practices for managing students within groups. Most behavioral problems within a group setting are minor distractions, such as students' not paying attention or "goofing off." These mild disciplinary issues are best dealt with nonverbally. When a teacher directs a verbal comment to a student, the flow of a lesson is disrupted and others are distracted. The goal of preventive discipline–oriented teachers is to develop group cohesiveness. To attain this worthwhile end, teachers need to understand the following: group dynamics and group process, including how to foster peer relationships, the stages of group development, how to handle cliques, and classroom interventions to suppress bullying.

With properly guided groups, the group potential can surpass the talents of individual members. For example, the Miami Dolphins is the only National Football League team to complete a season undefeated. They were anchored by the "No Name Defense." That is, individually the players were anonymous; together they were champions.

Teachers spend most of their time working with groups of students. This fact is self-evident. Less clear is how essential being skilled in group management techniques is for teachers. The ebb and flow of classroom activity is constant. Teachers must attend to individual students while simultaneously monitoring the behavior of the entire class. Some group activities pertain directly to instruction, others deal with such "housekeeping" issues as attendance and distribution of materials, and still others involve transitions from one activity to another. Distractions are constant. Students clowning around, pleas for extra help, and transitions between activities permeate the school day. Each of these situations requires an efficient teacher response. Managing the flow of group activities and minimizing interruptions is central to good group management.

Prevention and Group Management

Kounin (1970) was one of the first researchers to observe the impact of group management skills on both group and individual behavior. Kounin was an educational psychology professor at Wayne State University in Detroit, Michigan. One day he saw a student reading a newspaper during one of his lectures. When Kounin reprimanded the student, he noticed that the other students became more attentive. This accidental observation, which he called the *ripple effect*, piqued Kounin's interest in learning more about the dynamics of group process in the classroom. He observed and videotaped students and teachers interacting in hundreds of classrooms. Kounin wanted to determine how teachers minimized behavioral problems while keeping students focused on their work.

Kounin's (1970) emphasis on prevention was based on his findings that effective teachers were no different from ineffective teachers in dealing with student behavior *after* misbehavior occurred. The difference, he noted, was that effective teachers *prevented* misbehavior. His conclusions based on preventive group techniques were far reaching. Kounin said,

> An analysis of real classrooms reveals that there *are* concrete techniques of managing classrooms that relate to the amount of work involvement and misbehavior in learning situations. These skills go beyond those required to manage individual children. They are group management skills that apply to boys as well as to girls, to emotionally disturbed children in regular classrooms as well as to nondisturbed children, and to both recitation and seatwork settings. (p. iv)

The techniques Kounin (1970) reported involved teachers' keeping their classroom groups functioning smoothly while preventing minor individual behavioral problems from escalating into large group distractions. The following subsections summarize some of Kounin's principal findings about group management and preventive discipline.

Withitness and Overlapping

Withitness is a teacher's ability to communicate to students that he or she knows what is going on throughout the classroom. Kounin (1970) noted that teachers had proverbial "eyes in the back of their head," and the teachers who communicated their alertness through verbal remarks prevented misbehavior. Some ways teachers demonstrate withitness include the following:

- Correcting the appropriate student for misbehavior, rather than the wrong child or an onlooker
- When two problem behaviors occur simultaneously, attending to the more serious infraction
- Intervening quickly when a misbehavior has the potential to spread beyond one or two students

Overlapping refers to what teachers do when they have two situations that need to be dealt with simultaneously. Consider Marilyn, a first-year fifth-grade teacher. It is reading time, and her students are divided into several groups. Alan needs help and raises his hand, but Marilyn is so immersed with helping Angela that she does not look up and see Alan, who is steadily growing impatient. Tired of waiting, Alan puts his head down on his desk. Marilyn looks up, spies Alan, and admonishes him for not getting his work done.

Teachers who become immersed in one issue and miss other events in the classroom are prone to the following group management mistakes: acting on a misbehavior after it has escalated, identifying the wrong student as misbehaving, and overlooking students who need help. Teachers do not have the luxury of focusing entirely on an individual student for more than a minute. Teachers need to be masters of *multitasking*.

Maintenance of Group Focus

Teachers hold students' attention by creating a sense of suspense about who will be called on. Repetitive response routines undermine the *group focus*. For example, Mr. Estrada, a seventh-grade social studies teacher, often has students take turns reading paragraphs from their text. His students sit in rows and read aloud, one after the other. Students count ahead to see when they will read. Once students have read a paragraph, they can spend the rest of their time daydreaming or goofing off.

In contrast, Ms. Klapletzky keeps her students guessing. Her tenth-grade English literature students never know when she might call on them. Whether a student raises or does not raise his or her hand makes no difference. Ms. K asks a question and then slowly scans the room. If she favors any student, it is the one with averted eyes. Because students never know when they will be called on, Ms. K's students are attentive.

Alerting.   *Alerting* is the ability to keep nonreciting students involved while others are speaking. Even experienced teachers have gazed out over a bored group of students as one selected to speak drones on. Teachers use alerting techniques when they do the following:

- Create suspense; pause and look around; ask students to follow up on what a previous student said
- Search for contrary opinions; seek creative answers by asking for possible alternative solutions
- Tell specific students that they will be called on shortly
- Do not allow frequent contibutors to monopolize discussions
- Consciously make errors (humor works best) and challenge students to catch mistakes

Accountability

Kounin (1970) found that students worked harder when their teacher frequently provided feedback on their performance. Accountable teachers hold students responsible for their work. A teacher who gives an assignment to groups of students and at the end of the class tells them to put it away without checking it is demonstrating a lack of accountability. So-called "busywork" tells students that their time and effort are unimportant. The students know they will not be held accountable, so they put minimal energy into their work. Kounin observed that accountable teachers use the following techniques:

- They ask students to hold up their work for a visual scan.
- They have students recite in unison.
- They have one student follow up on another student's comments.
- They ask prepared students to raise their hands and check on those who do not.
- They circulate among students, checking progress while other students are reciting.

Checking student progress and providing students with timely feedback is the key to accountable teaching. Even with large groups, the teacher can develop methods for keeping track of students' work. Some methods of assessing student progress include the following:

- Students exchange and correct each other's work.
- Students keep portfolios of their progress.
- Students update charts that track their progress.
- Students provide the teacher with anecdotal feedback on the effectiveness of his or her teaching.
- Students periodically rate their progress in terms of level of improvement: improved, much improved, no improvement.
- The teacher sends samples of students' work home to parents.
- Students do presentations.
- Students write tests and supply correct answers.

Students need teachers to notice their effort. Frequent feedback encourages students to persevere, whereas absent feedback causes students to surmise that their work is not valued. Lack of feedback leads to apathy and a host of related classroom problems, including being absent frequently, being tardy, goofing off, and failing to complete assignments.

Management of Movement

Kounin (1970) said that, on average, elementary classroom activities change 33 times a day. His count included only academics. Recess, lunch, and housekeeping routines add even more transitions to a typical class day. All these changes must be managed smoothly, and special attention must be paid to maintaining momentum.

In trying to determine how teacher management influenced movement in the classroom, Kounin (1970) asked, "Do activities continue to move at an appropriate pace, or are activities slowed down, held back, and made to appear draggy? What is it that teachers do to keep activities moving forward or to hold them back?" (p. 95). After analyzing the hundreds of actions of teachers, Kounin identified three specific teacher behaviors that inhibit the smooth flow of classroom activity: stimulus-boundness, flip-flops, and dangles:

1. *Stimulus-boundness* is the habit of diverting a lesson to tend to a minor detail. Ms. Raymond's fourth-grade math students have their books out and are ready to hear their assignment. Annie has a question about their assignment. Just as Ms. Raymond is about to answer, she notices a paper bag on the floor. "What is that lunch bag doing there?" she asks. Suddenly, everyone is looking around the room and pointing to different suspects. Ms. Raymond starts walking around the room looking for more lunch bags instead of answering Annie's question and moving the lesson forward.

2. A *flip-flop* occurs when the teacher impulsively switches from one activity to another and then back to the first activity. Mr. Williams is leading a discussion

on black holes in space with his tenth-grade science class. The students are interested and have many ideas about where black holes come from and where they go. Then Pablo raises his hand and asks, "Mr. Williams, is all this stuff going to be on the test?" "Of course," Mr. Williams replies. A chorus of groans annoys Mr. Williams. He drops the topic of black holes and spends the next 10 minutes talking with his students about the value of standardized tests. Then, he says, "Now, back to black holes."

3. A *dangle* refers to starting an activity and then suspending it. Ms. Lopez tells her first-grade class to line up quietly for lunch. Following her practice, she names students to get into line when they appear quiet and ready for the transition. She calls several names, then she spies another teacher in the hallway. She tells her students she will be right back and leaves the room. When she returns 5 minutes later, students in line are pushing, while others are running around the room. A *truncation* is similar to a dangle, except the teacher does not resume the suspended activity.

How teachers initiate and maintain activity flow in the classroom is central to keeping students' attention. Kounin (1970) reported significant differences in how teachers approach this mundane, but nevertheless important, managerial task. Teachers who maintain a smooth flow when teaching lessons and directing transitions experience significantly fewer problem behaviors. Kounin found that teachers who were susceptible to one behavior that interfered with the smoothness of activity (e.g., dangles) were also likely to exhibit other disrupting behaviors.

MINOR DISRUPTIONS

Keeping minor disruptions from growing into major disruptions is a key element of preventive discipline (Viadero, 2003). Fooling around, being silly, whispering, and engaging in other nonattentive behaviors are commonplace in classrooms. Such transgressions erode teachers' efforts to maintain a group focus. Both students and teachers work best when these distractions are minimized. The best approach for teachers to take is to intervene before misbehavior escalates into a more serious disciplinary problem. The term *intervention* refers to a teacher's response to a disruptive behavior. The more interventions a teacher is skilled in, the more options he or she has available for efficiently managing a classroom. F. Jones (1979) reported that more than 90% of student misbehavior consists of minor issues such as talking without permission, goofing off, and not paying attention. Although relatively insignificant taken alone, these incidents can accumulate at the rate of almost 600 events a day in unruly classrooms (Charles, 1996). With this many daily disruptions going unchecked, imagine how much instructional time could be wasted during the year. Often, simple nonverbal interventions can solve such problems.

Nonverbal Interventions

Actions communicate more clearly and directly than words do. Most minor classroom disturbances can be extinguished by using *nonverbal interventions*. Nonverbal interventions are preferred to verbal interventions for three reasons:

1. **Nonverbal interventions do not draw attention to the student.** Some students misbehave to gain peer attention, teacher attention, or both. A good example is the "class clown." Focusing attention on his or her wisecracks provides positive reinforcement, which encourages the student to continue. Nonverbal interventions are unobtrusive and thus short-circuit the behavior–reinforcement cycle.
2. **Nonverbal interventions do not detract from the flow of activity in the classroom.** Each time a teacher verbally corrects a student, the lesson is interrupted. Students who were concentrating on their work are distracted, and their attention turns to the teacher–student interaction.
3. **Nonverbal interventions are nonconfrontational.** Words invite a response, which sometimes leads to what teachers commonly refer to as *power struggles*. For example, a teacher tells a student, "Get to work." The student says, "I don't know how to do it." The teacher says, "You've done these problems before; you are just stalling." The student says, "I'm not doing it," and the verbal exchange escalates in terms of both emotions and consequences as teacher and student struggle with each other, the teacher to take control and the student to save face.

Consider the case study of Mr. Morris, a teacher who tries to maintain a group focus by using verbal reprimands. Several nonverbal interventions are offered next as alternatives to his approach.

Proximity.   By remaining stationary in the front of the room, Mr. Morris limited his ability to stop problem behavior. If Mr. Morris had moved around the room as

 ## Case Study: Mr. Morris

Mr. Morris, a tenth-grade geometry teacher, was reviewing theorems. He stood at the front of the room next to an overhead projector. Diagrams and key points were displayed on the transparencies. He was about 5 minutes into his talk when he noticed some shuffling and muttering. "José," he said, "stop playing with that compass; you need this review." He waited for José to look up, then he proceeded. No more than a minute later, he corrected Andrew for slouching in his seat. Less than 30 seconds later, he told Fran to stop whispering to Maria. And so it went: a few comments about theorems punctuated by reprimands.

As the lesson proceeded, Mr. Morris became more frustrated. "Don't you realize how important this information is?" he said, "These theorems are going to be on your standardized achievement tests." In desperation, Mr. Morris started threatening individuals with extra work. For the next 20 minutes, his lesson deteriorating, Mr. Morris struggled to maintain his students' attention.

he lectured, his physical presence next to a student would have eliminated many minor student disturbances. He would not have indicated a student problem, thus no attention would have been drawn to the student. As the need arose to change transparencies, he could have asked various students to do so—another subtle move that keeps students' attention focused on the front of the room. Rarely does a teacher need to say anything to a student when he or she uses *proximity* as a preventive intervention.

Planned Ignoring.   Under the best circumstances, sitting still and listening to a lengthy group lesson is difficult. Invariably, some students will look around the room, others will doodle, and items will be dropped on the floor. According to Jensen (1998), the average sustained attention span is approximately equivalent in minutes to a student's age in years. Thus, the optimum sustained attention span for a first grader is 6 consecutive minutes. Likewise, research on neural functioning indicates that after 15 consecutive minutes, a high school sophomore's attention will waver. Most minor distractions are self-terminating. Paying attention to such misbehavior can be reinforcing, even when the attention is a reprimand. Thus, *planned ignoring*—consciously choosing to ignore restlessness and brief episodes of inattention—is nonreinforcing and prevents other students from being distracted. Some of the behaviors Mr. Morris was concerned with would have subsided if he had ignored them.

Signal Interference.   Gestures communicate as clearly as words. A finger to the lips means "Silence." A hand extended palm down means "Settle down." A steady gaze means "I'm aware of what you are doing." A smile says, "Ok; now let's move on." Writing an assignment on the board is a signal that it is time to start working. Following are some practical examples of how signals can focus students' attention:

- **The music box.**   Buy an inexpensive music box and wind it up at the beginning of the day. Tell the class that if any music is left at the end of the day, they will get a group reward. Just reaching for the music box will often be sufficient to quiet a noisy group.
- **The quiet game.**   Give students 3 seconds to make as much noise as they want, then, at your signal, they must become silent for as long as possible. Calling it a game seems to be the prime motivator. Use a timer to keep track of their efforts.
- **Eye the clock.**   Let students know that whatever time they waste will be subtracted from free time. Each time they get loud, eye the clock or a watch. Keep track of how much time is lost, perhaps by writing it on the board. After a while, a mere glance at a timepiece will be all that is necessary to quiet students.
- **Hands up.**   When the class gets noisy, raise your hand. This action signals that all students should raise their hands. As hands go up, noise goes down. This suggestion has been used in many elementary schools and seems to be extremely effective.
- **Flick the light switch.**

Mr. Morris could have used a spontaneous or prearranged signal or simply stopped talking until he got the attention he wanted.

Restructuring.   Mr. Morris's presentation was tedious, but on any given day even the best constructed lesson can fizzle. The source of student inattention could be the weather, the time of day, or some other innocuous event independent from teacher preparation. At times like this, simply changing the routine is a reasonable alternative. The idea is to shift students' attention without blame. The teacher simply decides to halt the activity that is not working and move on to something else.

Teachers need to think on their feet. Mr. Morris could have assessed the situation and decided that a transparency-based lecture was not practical that day. Experienced teachers know that having backup activities available and ready to go is always a good idea. However, for Mr. Morris to say, "This lesson isn't working, so we'll get back to our cooperative group project" would be a mistake. If he told his students why he was changing gears, they might get the idea that all they have to do to avoid a boring lesson is to start fooling around. Thus, *restructuring* should be done without indicating to students that their behavior prompted the change.

Removal of Tempting Objects.   Paper-maiche is for molding, pencils are for writing, and rulers are for measuring. These self-evident functions of classroom paraphernalia are sometimes lost on students who would prefer to throw, poke, and sword fight than use materials appropriately. Knowing how to present manipulatives in a way that will advance learning and not interfere with an activity requires experience and a knowledge of the students.

Impulsive students are especially prone to misusing objects. Redl and Wineman (1951) called this impulsive tendency *gadgetorial seduction*. Organizing activities so that only one object is presented at a time helps eliminate the distraction of several objects presented simultaneously. Giving directions on how to use an object in an activity before passing out materials helps students resist the temptation to misuse materials. If a student does misuse an object, the teacher can simply remove it, explain why, and describe the conditions that need to be met for the object to be returned.

Younger students often bring favorite objects to school. Setting these aside until a prescribed time of day alleviates the distraction for them and others.

Mr. Morris could have started his talk by asking students to put all their materials away except paper and pencils for notes. Alternatively, he could have walked over to José, put his hand out (a signal to hand over the compass), and continued walking around the room as he pointed out features on the transparencies.

A Caveat

None of the nonverbal interventions will work all the time or in the same situation. Selecting the proper intervention requires knowledge of students' tendencies and a little common sense. A week after the author of this book explained nonverbal interventions in one of his education courses, a disillusioned undergraduate student approached him. "Professor Henley, I tried planned ignoring yesterday when I was helping to supervise recess at my field site, but it didn't work," he said. "They kept right on fighting!"

Sometimes nonverbal interventions are the best choice; other times more extensive interventions are warranted (see Chapter 8). In general, nonverbal interventions are best suited for minimizing the effects of minor classroom disruptions.

PEER RELATIONSHIPS

Peers have a strong influence on individual behavior, and this influence grows through the years. Half of an 11-year-old child's social activity is with peers. By adolescence, time spent with peers exceeds time spent with family (Hartup, 1992). Relationships with peers provide the main entry into adulthood, and *peer influence* can be both positive and negative.

Positive peer relationships foster tolerance of others, build effective interpersonal skills, and promote self-confidence. Negative peer relationships undermine social competency and can expose young people to a number of risk factors such as alcohol abuse, smoking, and criminal behavior.

Positive relationships among students help eliminate tension. When students feel comfortable and safe in the classroom, distress and problem behaviors are minimized. Positive relationships also bind students together. As social ties develop, common values emerge. Students care about one another and express this concern through respect, kindness, and a concern for the common good.

Cultivated properly, peer relationships help young people acquire social status, realize their identity, and exchange emotional support. Taking time to build student relationships not only helps individual students learn important social skills such as how to work effectively in a group, but also keeps classroom activities moving along smoothly.

Classroom Supports

Korinek, Walther-Thomas, McLaughlin, and Williams (1999) suggested that teachers practice preventive discipline by fostering student support networks:

> It is insufficient to address problems displayed by individual students without examining conditions in the classroom and school that are not student centered and "child friendly." If students feel disconnected, disenfranchised, unwelcome, or unsafe in school, they will have great difficulty changing their behaviors or benefitting from instruction. (p. 4)

Supportive relationships play a central role in a youngster's ability to productively participate in classroom activities. Fahlberg (1991) recommended three practices for helping young people develop supportive relationships:

1. **Engage students in group activities that help develop a sense of inclusive identity.**   Students could decide on a class color, select a class song, or

design a class banner. Have students complete projects that require cooperation and team effort. Avoid competition. Be alert to cliques and other group-
dynamic issues, such as gender, race, or religion, that separate students into
"us" and "them."

2. **Support student activities outside school.**   Take an interest in the events
that shape students' lives at home and in the community. Foster reciprocal
relationships within the classroom. Provide opportunities for students to
build camaraderie by having fun together.

3. **Support students in periods of high emotional arousal.**   Crisis situations,
grief, illness, and frustration are examples of times when students most need
support. "As the adult walks through these storms of life with the child and
alleviates psychological or physical discomfort, bonding and attachment are
enhanced" (Brendtro & Brokenleg, 1993, p. 7).

ACHIEVEMENT AND SOCIAL COMPETENCE

According to H. Patrick (1997), "A substantial body of evidence suggests that a
positive association exists between students' social competence and their academic
performance, including achievement, school adjustment, and motivation for
schoolwork" (p. 209). *Social competence* is the ability to maintain peer relationships
and exhibit prosocial behavior in school. Students who are rejected or isolated are
at risk of low social competence, as are students who exhibit regular behavioral
problems (Bukowski, Newcomb, & Hartup, 1996). In contrast, when students feel
positive about their relationships, their confidence is enhanced. (H. Patrick &
Townsend, 1995; Wentzel, 1991).

Bryk and Schneider (2003) identified *relational trust* as a critical factor in students' academic success in several low-income Chicago schools. The researchers
coined the term *relational trust* to describe a school climate based on mutual respect,
competence, integrity, and personal regard for others. Bryk and Schneider reported
that the Chicago schools in which students scored in the top 25% on standardized
tests recorded higher levels of relational trust than those of the schools in which
students scored in the bottom 25%.

Ladd (1984) found that students who made new friends scored higher on
achievement tests than did students who were unable to develop friendships.
Alexander and Entwisle (1988) observed that as early as first and second grade,
peer popularity was correlated to high test scores in reading and math.

Conversely, as might be expected, students who experience problems relating
to peers often have difficulties with academics. According to H. Patrick (1997),
"About 25 percent of those children who were poorly accepted in elementary
school were found later to have dropped out of school, whereas only about 8 percent of the other children dropped out" (p. 211).

Peer Acceptance

Statistics are revealing, but they do not convey the emotional challenges students cope with in their search for peer acceptance. Hersch (1998) chronicled teenagers struggling to define themselves. Central to their quest is dealing with peer intimidation. Consider the emotional impact of the following scene:

> The front doors of South Lakes High School burst open and the "ghetto boys" swagger in. Like Old West outlaws charging through the saloon doors, these dudes of all races command attention as crowds of students milling in the vestibule part to let them through. Sometimes defiant, challenging with a look or a gesture, they just as often keep their faces set in expressionless poses, their hands shoved in their pockets as they make their way through the halls. "Yo, wassup man," they call out to friends. The response is a cool, smooth high five. Modern day Pied Pipers of Bad, these young men set the style of the nineties high school. (p. 81)

Some students might admire these youths, others might feel intimidated, and still others might resent them. However a student feels about the "ghetto boys," one thing is clear: No student would want to be on the nasty end of their attention.

From the primary grades through high school, students continually strive to find their place among their peers. Bad results such as isolation, rejection, or enmity can make school an awful place to be.

During adolescence, young people search for their identity (Erikson, 1950). Paradoxically, this striving for individuality comes primarily through bonding with a peer group. "Fitting in," being accepted, having friends, and being popular are crucial personal issues. However, peer relationships are unpredictable. A student might experience ridicule on Tuesday from the same group that expressed affiliation on Monday. How a youth weathers and overcomes the vicissitudes of peer relationships has a profound effect on his or her sense of self-worth and ability to develop new relationships.

Hoffman (2002) wanted to learn what high school meant to students. She pored over yearbooks, interviewed students, and immersed herself in ethnographic accounts of adolescence.[1] She found that in school, adolescents were more concerned with peer acceptance than with academics. Students saw high school as a rite of passage, with many interpersonal shoals and narrow social channels to navigate. Academics were lowest among the students' priorities.

Hoffman found that adolescents cared most about issues that related to "growing up." Gaining independence and getting along with peers were their primary concerns. Hoffman concluded her analysis of adolescent priorities by asking

> If these essential "adolescent ethos" elements were recognized as the center-piece of the high school program, rather than elements to ignore, suppress, or work around, how might high school be? (p. 38)

---

[1]See, for example, *Adolescent Life and Ethos: An Ethnography of a U.S. High School,* by Heewon Chang, 1992; *A Tribe Apart: A Journey into the Heart of American Adolescence,* by Patricia Hersch, 1998; and *Makes Me Wanna Holler: A Young Black Man in America,* by Nathan McCall, 1994.

The results of numerous research studies have substantiated the observation that "adolescent ethos" is a primary influence on students' behavior. For instance, Walberg and Greenburg (1997) summarized several research studies on the classroom social environment. They found that the relationships among students had a significant effect on virtually every facet of their school experiences. Relationships with others shaped attitudes, piqued interest, enhanced or diminished productivity, and ultimately influenced academic achievement.

Students Who Have Low Status

Students who feel detached and isolated from others can present a number of problems in the classroom. They have difficulties maintaining friendships and are easily discouraged by failure and criticism. Students with low status talk less, and when they do speak up, they are virtually ignored. They may even be physically excluded from activities. Students with high status are good talkers, and the group usually acts on their suggestions.

Status problems are influenced by group dynamics and individual temperament. J. Kagan (1998) estimated that about 10 to 15% of all individuals are inhibited or fearful, and about 20 to 40% are uninhibited. These traits are inborn but are amenable to environmental intervention. M. Beck and Malley (1998) maintained that many children fail in school because they feel detached or alienated from the general student body. Violent episodes reported by the media have highlighted the need to attend to such students. Five types of students need special attention to feel as though they belong (Wallace, 2000):

1. **Nonathletes.**   Bright, high-achieving male atheletes rank highest in status among peers. Lowest ranked are high-achieving nonatheletes. The dominance of the "jock" mentality makes life difficult for students who are labeled "nerds" by schoolmates. Often, these students are victims of teasing or bullying.

2. **Students who are low achieving but gifted.**   Unchallenging school programs can turn students away from exploring their talents. Equally problematic is the lack of opportunities for students with abilities outside the typical curriculum (e.g., students with social leadership skills or special talents in chess, model building, dance, or music).

3. **Introverts.**   Whereas extroverts gain support and comfort from one another, introverts spend most of their time alone. They write poetry, interact through the anonymity of computers, and read instead of initiating contact with others. Lacking the temperament to reach out to others, these students will remain outsiders without adult or peer intervention.

4. **Counterculture youths.**   Students who identify with mainline peer groups are easily accepted, whereas students who identify with fringe groups run the risk of being ostracized. Intolerance toward differences adopted by youths pushes them farther away and increases their sense of alienation. As Wallace (2000) commented, "In the aftermath of the Columbine massacre,

some school districts banned black trench coats. We must take care to differentiate between dark clothing and dark intentions" (p. 46).

5. **Students with special needs.**   Special education is federally mandated by the Individuals with Disabilities Education Act (IDEA). More than 6 million students receive special education services. The inclusion movement in special education has led to an increase in the amount of time students with disabilities spend in the regular classroom. Most of these pupils include students with special needs, those with speech and language disorders, students with learning disabilities, and students with physical disabilities. The benefits of special education are sometimes offset by the stigma of being labeled a "special education student." Students who receive special education services need to be included in normal classroom routines as much as possible.

Norton (1995) identified the "six Rs" of withdrawal that typify estranged students:

1. They become *resentful* and withdrawn.
2. They become *resistive* of additional efforts to gain their trust.
3. They become *rebellious* and refuse to cooperate.
4. They *retreat* by becoming truant, by dropping out, or by turning to drugs.
5. They become *reluctant* to do anything.
6. They become *revengeful* and engage in overt activities designed to get even. (cited in M. Beck & Malley, 1998)

The following sections address how the potential of democratic groups can be used to help promote a general sense of acceptance and caring within the classroom.

GROUP DYNAMICS

Group dynamics is the study of how groups and individuals influence each other's behavior. One of the first researchers to highlight the powerful role of the group in shaping individual behavior was Fritz Redl (Charles, 2002). The typical youngster, said Redl, "carries the image of his or her reference group as a 'shadow' even in the midst of a vigorous discussion about discipline" (cited in Morse, 2001, p. 78).

Students are keenly aware that two audiences are observing them: the teacher and the other students. Student actions can be directed toward grabbing the attention of either or both audiences, and the reaction the student gets will, in a reciprocal fashion, influence future actions. Figure 5.1 illustrates the reciprocity of interactions between individual students, the teacher, and the group.

Redl recommended that professionals analyze the groups they work with to better understand individual student behavior. For instance, Redl and Wineman (1951) observed a group-dynamic phenomenon they called *group contagion*. Group contagion is an unplanned, impulsive reaction to a situation that sets one or two group members off and quickly spreads among the rest. Even normally well-behaved students can get caught up in the excitement of the moment.

FIGURE 5.1 Interactions Affecting Classroom Behavior

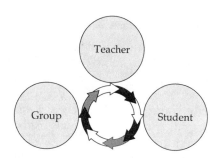

In the same way that a crowd can reach a state of frenzy at a sporting event or a rock concert, students can become "infected" by the behavior of excited or agitated peers. From an outside observer's viewpoint, group contagion implies that a teacher has lost control of the class. Some teachers are so concerned about group contagion that they resort to overbearing tactics to ensure they never lose the reins of control (Canter & Canter, 1992; Nichols, 1992). Substitute teachers are especially vulnerable to group contagion, which is triggered by the absence of the teacher, a familiar authority figure.

Group contagion is only one example of how the group and individuals influence each other's behavior. Just as teachers need to know individual students' traits, teachers also need to understand how their students relate to one another within the large group called a *class*. Temperament, intelligence, motivation, and development are some of the qualities that influence individual behavior. Likewise, roles, cliques, and leadership styles influence group behavior.

GROUP PROCESS

Group process refers to the stages of group development. Not all groups develop in a positive fashion. Some groups move forward, others stagnate, and still others achieve a level of functioning that gets things done, but without enthusiasm or joy.

Autocratic groups are most susceptible to stagnation. When the group leader controls all group decisions, individual members' talents are underused. In addition, positioning for influence in autocratic groups frequently promotes such negative features of group life as cliques, favoritism, and apathy.

Democratic groups respond to the needs of all members. Within democratic groups, the ability to influence events is predicated on equal participation. Consequently, democratic groups are flexible and can adapt to changing circumstances. Previous sections of this text covered how democratic groups foster a sense of community. This section covers the stages of progression that characterize democratic groups. Each stage is unique and requires different skills on the part of the group leader (i.e., teacher). Properly managed, democratic groups progress through five stages of development: forming, storming, norming, performing, and adjourning.

The Group Leader

Prior to learning about group stages, you must understand what teaching within a democratic classroom community does and does not mean. The teacher is the executive in charge. The teacher does not acquiesce authority, but delegates authority at opportune times to enable participation. Student-centered activities support a democratic structure. The teacher is responsible for changing these or any other routines that fail to meet group goals. Although students are given opportunities to make choices, provide input, and give feedback, the students are not ultimately responsible for group success or failure. Final responsibility for all decisions rests with the teacher.

Stages of Democratic Group Development

As groups progress through the *stages of group development*, the teacher's role must be adjusted. Sometimes students need direction, other times they need gentle guidance, and still other times they need to be left alone. Making the proper judgment about when to intervene and how to intervene in group situations requires knowledge of how democratic groups evolve. The following description of group stages outlines how a democratic group process can meld an aggregate of individual students into a harmonious and productive class (Tuckman, 1965).

Forming.   During the first stage, the *forming* stage, the teacher explains his or her goals for the class. The concept of community is described, and students are given an opportunity to provide input and ask questions about a community learning environment. The older the group, the more likely students are accustomed to a more teacher-directed system. Doubts about how a community in the classroom will work are bound to surface. The teacher's role is to provide continuity through predictable routines.

Activities that require student participation are a priority, including agreements about a classroom code of behavior. At this time, the teacher should survey students about their interests and concerns. Figure 5.2 presents a sample survey used to identify students' concerns about making the transition from sixth grade to middle school.

Games and classroom activities that are noncompetitive facilitate group bonding. Students can decorate the room, discuss class projects, and select symbols such as a mascot or class colors to provide the class with its own identity. At this point, each class member must be clear about the purpose and advantages of a classroom community. Routines that structure democratic participation, such as brainstorming, class meetings, and cooperative learning, are initiated during this phase.

Storming.   A democratic structure is more complex than an autocratic structure. In an autocratic group, the leader is both decision maker and enforcer. This arrangement is simple and straightforward. In a democratic group, however, each member is expected to participate and contribute to the group goals. This arrangement is more complicated, and personality clashes are inevitable as members try to find their place.

Not Worried	Hardly Worried	Worried	Very Worried
(about this)	(about this)	(about this)	(about this)
1	2	3	4

___ Being different from others
___ Drugs
___ Failure
___ Giving a presentation in front of others
___ Being picked on
___ Being made fun of
___ Being sent to the principal
___ Getting lost
___ Hard classwork
___ Getting along with other students
___ Homework assignments
___ Unkind people
___ Lockers
___ Getting on the wrong bus
___ Lunchroom

___ Getting to class on time
___ Keeping up with assignments
___ Making friends
___ Not having an adult who listens
___ Moving from classroom to classroom
___ Length of class periods
___ Not knowing what is expected
___ New rules and routines
___ Textbooks
___ New teachers
___ Size of the building
___ Taking tests
___ Club activities
___ Opportunities for after-school activity
___ Physical education program

Other concerns not listed:

_____

_____

_____

_____

FIGURE 5.2   Student Survey: What Students Worry About When Transitioning to Middle School
Adapted from "Measuring School Climate: Let Me Count the Ways," by H. J. Freiberg, 1998, *Educational Leadership, 56*(1), pp. 22–26. Copyright 1998 by H. J. Freiberg. Adapted with permission.

How the group manages during the second phase depends on teacher leadership and the resources of individual members. This *storming* stage is characterized by doubts and competition. Each person is coming to grips with the realities of the democratic process, and limits are tested. Some common results are that students who usually take charge feel a loss of power, those who are accustomed to "sitting on the sidelines" feel threatened, and students who are accustomed to being told what to do have difficulty making decisions. This stage is a period of adjustment.

Such turmoil is a natural and predictable stage of democratic group development as individuals vie for status. Resentments are expressed and some students may want to revert to a teacher-controlled classroom. Rules, sanctions, and responsibilities must be reviewed daily. Some students may need to be taken aside and privately reassured.

Time may appear to be lost on too many personality issues, but it will be more than made up in later stages. The teacher's role is to provide predictable routines, to allow students to express their opinions, and to abide by previous agreements.

Norming.   In the *norming* stage, although growing pains continue, interpersonal strife decreases as the class moves toward cohesiveness. Cohesion is the sum of attractions group members have for one another, the morale of the group, and the level of group motivation. The term *norming* refers to standards for interacting that begin to typify the conduct of group members. The ability to plan and carry out group projects is growing in this stage. Students begin talking about "our" classroom, cliques begin to loosen, and new leaders emerge. Problems and issues are dealt with routinely through meetings and individual conferences. A sense of belonging among students signals that the group has come together, and creativity is high.

Cliques are the most serious threat to cohesion. The teacher should observe students in informal settings such as the cafeteria and during recess to identify cliques and isolated students. The teacher's primary role is managerial. He or she may need to make adjustments in group activities to highlight the contributions and talents of all students. Routines that emphasize student participation should be maintained. The teacher should also look for ways to incorporate students' interests and cultural diversity into the curriculum.

Performing.   *Performing* is the group's productive stage. Individuals are secure, and many group problems have been resolved. Students work well in pairs, in subgroups, or as a unit. Group unity exists. Commitment to tasks is high, and the need for teacher prodding is minimal. The class develops its own identity. However, not all is smooth sailing. As Seldes (1985) pointed out, "Liberty is always unfinished business" (p. 10). Individual and group problems surface, but the general mood is upbeat. The teacher's main responsibility is to clarify learning objectives and provide enough stimulation to help productivity keep pace with student involvement.

Adjourning.   When any successful group activity nears termination, members go through a mourning phase. During *adjourning*, past problems may resurface as a result of the difficulties some students have with detachment. Reassurances and acceptance of feelings can help students with this transition. The teacher should focus on the high points of the activity and give students time to discuss their experiences.

GROUP COHESION

Teachers who seek to develop inclusive peer relationships work to build group cohesiveness. *Cohesive groups* are characterized by respect for individuals, commitment to group goals, high group morale, and resourcefulness in dealing with group problems (Shepard, 1964). The more cohesive the group, the more productive. The relationships among group members—how they feel about one another, how well they communicate, and how well they treat one another—are a key determinant of whether cohesion has been achieved.

Strategies for Building Group Cohesiveness

Merging a disparate group of individual students requires a keen eye for elements of group dynamics that join and separate students. Group cohesion is the glue that binds supportive relationships. The *level* of group cohesion refers to the tendency of a group to bond in pursuit of similar goals and objectives.

Not all cohesive groups are productive. For example, members of gangs, cults, and hate groups feel a strong sense of belonging, and they identify with group goals. However, their beliefs and actions are antisocial. In contrast, groups that stress tolerance and value individual differences promote positive interactions among all members. Positive student relationships are reinforced by the feeling of belonging as group cohesiveness grows.

Affective features of cohesiveness include high morale and identification with group values. Properly guided, cohesive groups not only enjoy their classes more, but are more productive as well. Engagement in classroom activities accelerates and behavioral problems decrease as tensions caused by cliques and social rejection are alleviated.

Strategies for promoting group cohesiveness vary according to grade level and educational setting. Primary and elementary teachers, as well as teachers in self-contained special education programs, have an advantage because they spend most of their day with the same group of students. Teachers at the secondary level work with many groups, which gives them less time to concentrate on cohesiveness. Whatever a teacher's situation, the dynamics of the group that tend to separate students can always be improved. The following recommendations are divided into elementary and secondary subsections. These activities are examples that should be adapted as necessary:

Primary and Elementary

The First Weeks
- Continually emphasize the value of a "community of learners."
- Along with the students, design a class bill of rights.
- Experiment with desk arrangements. Explain that you will change furniture around during the year.
- Develop a class identity. Have a class mascot, class colors, a class coat of arms, and so forth.
- Have each student sit with a peer with whom he or she is unfamiliar and interview each other. Then, have each introduce the other to the class.

During Instruction
- Use instructional techniques that foster social skills development and student interaction (e.g., cooperative learning, peer tutoring, projects, brainstorming).

- Read stories that describe authentic problems of young people and discuss such problems in class.
- Emphasize class participation over getting the "right" answer.
- Allow students to help one another rather than waiting for the teacher.

Classroom Maintenance
- Assign students to decoration committees and give each committee a section of the room to decorate and redecorate as the year progresses.
- Keep a revolving schedule of students' responsibilities. Do not link jobs to "good" behavior.
- Institute a buddy system to introduce new class members to the school.
- Develop a revolving student system for getting information (e.g., homework assignments) to sick and absent students.
- Make the physical space attractive and functional. Divide the classroom into areas. Use carpets, dividers, and beanbag chairs to invite participation in activities.
- Establish a suggestion box or some other method for acquiring anonymous feedback.

Secondary

The First Weeks
- Through teacher behavior, highlight the values of empathy, perseverance, and tolerance. Model such interpersonal skills as listening, smiling, using praise, and using humor.
- Ask students for suggestions about making the class interesting and relevant.
- Arrange desks in a way that promotes interaction (e.g., a horseshoe shape).
- Have students fill out an interest survey describing how they feel about the subject and their hopes for their class.
- Decorate the classroom. Make it an appealing space in which to spend time.

During Instruction
- Highlight cooperation and friendship values in lessons (e.g., the role of cooperation in science and friendships in literature).
- Use instructional techniques that foster social skills development and student interaction (e.g., cooperative learning, peer tutoring, projects, brainstorming, teaming).
- Include in the curriculum current events and local issues that affect young people.
- Give a grade for class participation, and reward students for "wrong" answers that are partially correct.
- Vary the classroom routine. Intersperse lectures with group work, projects, and discussions.
- Explain directions until you are certain all students understand assignments.
- Turn some learning activities into games based on team competition rather than on individual competition.

Classroom Maintenance
- Understand that peer acceptance takes priority over learning for many young people.
- Recognize that conflict with authority is a normal adolescent rite of passage.
- Avoid favoring individual students.
- Value young people as individuals first and students second.
- Liven up the classroom with posters, pictures, and plants. Ask students for suggestions.
- Identify emerging cliques and intervene (see the following sections on cliques and bullying).
- Take time to discuss schoolwide issues that are important to students (e.g., the junior prom is canceled because of drinking).
- Look for opportunities to deflate stereotypes (e.g., "jocks" are dumb; girls are the weaker sex).
- Identify students who are lonely, rejected, or isolated. Find ways to highlight their abilities.
- Regularly elicit feedback on how students feel about class.
- Become involved with extracurricular affairs (e.g., chaperone dances, attend sporting events and school plays, advise an extracurricular club).

A key indicator of group cohesion is student conversations about class. Students' comments about "our" classroom rather than "Ms. Allen's classroom" is an indicator of cohesiveness. Another observable indicator is students' behavior when the teacher leaves the room. Students who continue to work and behave have internalized the value of group responsibility. Students who misbehave still depend on teacher control.

CLIQUES

A *clique* is an exclusive group of individuals who are bound by mutual interests or goals. Cliques are a ubiquitous form of human bonding. When individuals seek out like-minded persons, cliques develop. They provide members with a sense of identity and belonging. Cliques are both inclusive and exclusive. In schools and classrooms, cliques can undermine efforts to foster a sense of community and well-being among all students. Factors that contribute to the formation of cliques include socioeconomic status, gender, aggressiveness, common interests, and low status (Bagwell et al., 2000). Although people often label cliques in terms of popular and nonpopular students, the reality is much more complex.

Cliques are as diverse as the mixture of students who attend a school. In 1999, the *Washington Post* identified the following cliques in a suburban high school in Littleton, Colorado: jocks, preppies, headbangers, skaters, trenchies, techies, and nerds (Wilson & Mishra, 1999). Any high school or middle school student could easily add names to this list. Within the classroom, cliques can cause friction between students. Unattended, these frictions can develop into teasing, harassment, and bullying. For this reason, any formation of cliques should be observed carefully to determine the effect on the class as a whole.

Strategies for Managing Cliques

Attempts to directly disband cliques will harden rather than soften them. The best approach is to build ties that traverse boundaries that separate students. S. Boyd (1997) suggested using the following nine icebreaker activities to help students get to know one another at the beginning of the school year:[2]

ACTIVITY 1
What's Different, Partner? (partners; 5 min.)

Ask everyone to team up with a partner (someone whom the student has not met or who has the same eye color). Ask the partners to turn back to back and change five things about their appearance, one that is silly. When they are ready, the partners should turn around and try to guess the five things that were changed.

ACTIVITY 2
Four Facts (teams of 4–6 people; 10–15 min.)

Each person writes down four facts about him- or herself, one of which is a lie. Each person takes a turn reading his or her list aloud, and the rest of the team members write down the one item they think is a lie. When all the students are done reading their lists aloud, the first person reads his or her list again and identifies the lie. The team sees how well they did. Then each remaining team member identifies the lie on his or her list.

ACTIVITY 3
Four Cs (teams of 4–6 people; 10–15 min.)

Each person writes, on an index card, his or her favorite color, cuisine, country to visit, and closet dream. The cards are shuffled and redistributed. Each student reads aloud from the card he or she picked, and each person guesses, in writing, who wrote that card. At the end, the team determines who guessed the most correct responses.

ACTIVITY 4
Let's Make a Deal (teams of 4–8 people; 10 min.)

Make up a worksheet with six to eight items listed that the team members would likely have with them or on them. List one or two items that are uncommon. Choose someone to be the recorder according to a certain criterion (e.g., person

[2]Adapted from *Ten Ways to Break the Ice!* by Susan Boyd, 1997, Philadelphia: Susan Boyd Associates, Inc. Copyright 1997 by Susan Boyd, Susan Boyd Associates. Adapted with permission. Retrieved from http://www.susan-boyd.com/tenways.htm

whose birthday is next, person with the longest last name). The team gets points for *each* person who has these items. Only one of each item per person can be counted, and the team with the most points wins. The list could include a pencil, an unusual keychain, something red, a calculator, blue buttons, and so forth.

ACTIVITY 5
Birth Order (all participants; 10–15 min.)

Make up four signs, one each saying the following: Only Child, Oldest Child, Youngest Child, Middle Child. Put one sign in each corner of the room. Have each student go to the corner of the room that is labeled with his or her birth-order position. When all the students are assembled, ask the groups to discuss the special characteristics of their particular birth order and to record them. Choose a recorder according to a certain criterion (e.g., student who was born the farthest away, tallest student). Have the groups report to the class.

ACTIVITY 6
The Mingle Game (works well with larger groups–15–20 people; 15–20 min.)

Create a worksheet listing 12 to 15 criteria. The criteria can be, for example, as follows: is wearing contact lenses, has brown socks, saw the movie _____, has gone to Europe, plays a musical instrument, has an unusual hobby, and so forth. Below each criterion, leave a blank space. Give each student a worksheet. Ask the students to walk around the room, collecting signatures from other students who meet the criteria. A person can sign the sheet only once. If students finish early, have them help the others finish their sheets. Collect the completed sheets and select three as winners.

ACTIVITY 7
Team Brainstorming (groups of 4–6 people; 10–15 min.)

Ask teams to list things that are round, things associated with a holiday, things that are red, things you can make out of tires or coat hangers, or something else. Allow no discussion among team members. Choose a recorder according to a certain criterion (see the criteria for activity 4 and activity 5). The team with the most items on its list wins.

ACTIVITY 8
Beach Ball Brainstorming (entire group; 5–10 min.)

Announce a topic (e.g., things associated with a season, a holiday). Then, have everyone stand and pass around an inflatable beach ball. When someone catches the ball, he or she must shout out something related to the topic and then toss the ball to someone else. If the group is small, the members can pass the ball in a circular chain.

ACTIVITY 9
Mind-Reading Attention Getter (entire group; helps build listening and following-directions skills; 5 min.)

Tell the students you have extrasensory perception (ESP) and can read their minds. To prove it, ask each student to do the following: Step 1: Think of a number from

1 to 9. Step 2: Multiply that number by 9. Step 3: Add the digits of the result (e.g., 72 = 7 + 2; 9 = 0 + 9). Step 4: Take that number and subtract 5. Step 5: Equate the result with a letter of the alphabet (i.e., 4 = D). Step 6: Think of a country name that begins with that letter. Step 7: Think of an animal name that begins with the *second* letter of the country name. Then ask the students, "How many of you are thinking of elephants in Denmark?" This exercise works because any number they think of for step 1 will result in an answer of 9 for step 3. From that point on, the country name will begin with D (Denmark is one of a few), and *elephants* is typically used for *E*.

Negative Consequences of Cliques

On April 20, 1999, tragedy struck Columbine High School in Littleton, Colorado. Two students in black trench coats killed 12 students and a teacher. After terrorizing the school, they climbed onto the roof and shot themselves to death. They were called the "Trenchcoat Mafia," a clique formed out of a sense of rejection and isolation from other students.

Cliques breed an *us-versus-them* mentality. A common result is *scapegoating*: enmity directed at one group or individual by others. The target of scapegoating experiences exclusion, ostracism, and isolation. Given such negative social effects, it is not surprising that students who are scapegoated will seek comfort in their own clique. Although blaming cliques for the Columbine tragedy would be oversimplistic, the shootings certainly demonstrate the value of managing group dynamics in a classroom to avoid negative fallout from clique formation.

BULLIES

Seventy-five percent of high school graduates report being bullied at some point in their schooling (Hoover & Oliver, 1996). *Bullying* begins with teasing and harassment around third grade and continues through high school (see Figure 5.3). Approximately 15% of fourth through eighth graders suffer severe emotional distress due to bullying. A survey by the Centers for Disease Control and Prevention (1997) showed that 10,000 students stayed home from school at least once a month because they feared bullies.

Bullies are not just instigators; they are victims of their own abuse. Bullies identified by age 8 are 6 times more likely to be convicted of a crime by age 24 and 6 times more likely than nonbullies to end up with serious criminal records by age 30 (Hoover & Oliver, 1996, p. 3). A National Institute of Child Health and Human Development study revealed that both bullies and victims are at risk of loneliness, difficulty making friends, school failure, and addictions (Ericson, 2001).

Bullying involves more than physical intimidation. Teasing, taunting, hazing, threatening, hitting, sexually harassing, socially isolating, and excluding others are all bullying behaviors. Whereas boys are more likely to engage in physical intimidation, girls are more likely to spread rumors and isolate victims. The key component in bullying is a pattern of physical or psychological intimidation.

Physical Aggression

Mild		Moderate		Severe
Pushing Shoving Spitting		Defacing property Stealing	Physical acts that are demeaning and humiliating but not bodily harmful (e.g., de-panting) Locking in a closet or confined space	Physical violence against family or friends	Threatening with a weapon Inflicting bodily harm
Gossiping Embarrassing someone	Setting up to look foolish Spreading rumors	Ethnic slurs Setting up to take the blame	Publicly humiliating (i.e., revealing personal information) Excluding from group Social rejection	Maliciously excluding Manipulating social order to achieve rejection Malicious rumor-mongering	Threatening with total isolation by peer group
Mocking Name-calling Dirty looks Taunting	Teasing about clothing or possessions	Teasing about appearance	Intimidating phone calls	Verbal threats of aggression against property or possessions	Verbal threats of violence or of inflicting bodily harm
Threatening to reveal personal information Graffiti Public challenge to do something	Defacing property or clothing Playing a dirty trick	Taking possessions (lunch, clothing, toys)	Extortion	Threats of using coercion against family or friends	Coercion Threatening with a weapon

FIGURE 5.3 Bullying Behaviors

From "Bully-Proofing Your School: A Comprehensive Approach," by C. Garrity, K. Jens, W. Porter, N. Sager, and C. Short-Camilli, 1996, *Reclaiming Children and Youth, 5*(1), p. 36. Copyright 1996 by Compassion Publishing Ltd. Reprinted with permission.

The emotional effects of bullying can last a lifetime. In 2000, Ann Landers, the syndicated advice columnist, published an open letter from a woman who refused to attend her 20th high school class reunion. In the letter, the woman told her classmates that they had made her 4-year high school experience a living hell; they never got to know her and laughed at everything from her hair to her parents' strict rules. She told them she was miserable then but tried not to show it and stuck it out till graduation. Through subsequent counseling, she overcame the emotional abuse they inflicted on her, but she would not voluntarily re-enter an abusive situation by attending the reunion. She told them that although she did not want to see them again, she did not bear them ill will. However, she hoped that they raised their children to be less cruel. Her letter clearly showed that bullying is more than a childhood rite of passage. It is a vindictive assault on an individual's physical and emotional well-being.

Victims

The relationship between victims and bullies is complex. Apparently bullying behavior is spurred by a need for power and control (Hoover & Oliver, 1996). Bullies buttress their lack of compassion for their victims with the rationalization that they were provoked in some way. This lack of empathy is supported to some extent by the generally permissive attitudes of other youths and adults toward bullying. Notions such as "Bullying is always going to happen," "It helps toughen a young person," and "It is a rite of passage to adulthood" help sustain the bully's conviction that his or her actions are acceptable.

Victims of bullying often experience emotional problems, including anxiety, depression, and suicidal tendencies. Fourteen percent of students bullied in Grades 8 to 12 reported negative effects on their ability to learn. Females, more than males, experience chronic distress.

Students who do not fit in are easy prey for bullies. Victims are selected for a number of reasons: The most common is appearance. Physical features such as weight, size, facial appearance, and clothing place a young person at risk. Distinguishing social factors such as high or low grades, a reputation of sexual promiscuity, and lack of friends also place students at risk of becoming victims of bullying. Unpopular students are easy prey. (See Table 5.1.)

To some degree, familial patterns play a role. Whereas families of bullies have been characterized as emotionally cold with tendencies toward physical and verbal abuse, families of victims are characterized as overprotective (Hodges & Perry, 1996).

While not minimizing the impact of family on bullying, Hoover and Oliver (1996) reported that accepting attitudes embolden bullies to continue their behavior.

> In our research we were struck by the degree to which young people saw bullying as part of the natural order of things. A lack of concern about bullying has also been noted among teachers in secondary schools. American high school students felt that teachers knew of their plight but were unwilling to intervene, perhaps another sign of the seemingly normative nature of bullying. (p. 4)

TABLE 5.1 *Why Students Are Bullied*

Rank	Males	Females
Grades 8–12		
1.	Did not fit in	Did not fit in
2.	Was physically weak	Had a facial characteristic that was the subject of scorn
3.	Was short tempered	Cried or was emotional
4.	Associated with the "wrong" friends	Was overweight
5.	Did not wear the "right" clothes	Had good grades
Grades 4–8		
1.	Did not fit in	Did not fit in
2.	Associated with the "wrong" friends	Associated with the "wrong" friends
3.	Was physically weak	Did not wear the "right" clothes
4.	Was short tempered	Had a facial characteristic that was the subject of scorn
5.	Did not wear the "right" clothes	Was overweight

Gilbert (1999) cited two studies that underscored the complex relationship between bullies and victims. A study of 16,410 Finnish students aged 14 to 16 years reported that nearly one third of admitted bullies also identified themselves as victims. In a second study in Australia, researchers surveyed 3,918 children aged 11 to 15 years and reported the same results. Apparently, bullying is a learned behavior prompted by loneliness and frustration. Dr. Susan Limber, assistant director at the Institute of Families in Society at the University of South Carolina, stated that many victims may have attention-deficit hyperactivity disorder (Gilbert, 1999). Their irritability and low impulse control prompt others to bully them, and they in turn switch from victims to bullies. Most experts agree that bullying is a learned behavior that can be ameliorated through school intervention programs.

Strategies for Preventing Bullying

The political philosopher Edmund Burke wrote, "All that is necessary for evil to succeed is for good men to do nothing." For too long, bullying has been accepted as a natural part of growing up. William Modzeleski, head of the federal Safe and Drug-Free Schools Program, said, "Bullying was accepted as part of the tradition of the school. That has to change. We're starting to recognize that this is a serious issue and beginning to address it" (Donald, 2002; www.detnews.com/2002/schools/0212/10/schools-32460.htm).

An increased awareness of the negative consequences of bullying has prompted many educators to initiate antibullying intervention programs. One difficulty that must be overcome is that most bullying occurs out of adults' sight. Although other students are often present, those who would like to do something may not know how to help. Given the circumstances, the best intervention is a schoolwide program. Smith and Sharp (1994) emphasized a comprehensive program of prevention and counseling for bullies and victims alike. Successful school programs have the following elements, summarized by Banks (1997):

- Students are surveyed with questionnaires. This survey provides data on the extent of the problem, helps justify intervention efforts, and serves as a benchmark to measure the effectiveness of school improvements in climate and other interventions.
- A parental awareness campaign is conducted during parent–teacher conferences, through newsletters, and during parent–teacher association (PTA) meetings. The intent is to invite parental cooperation and support for school-wide programs.
- Schoolwide information is disseminated at assemblies. An antibullying advertising campaign is launched by using buttons and posters. Students are given recognition for civil behavior.
- Within the classroom, teachers and students develop antibullying rules. Role-playing is used to teach students how to manage a bullying situation. Cooperative learning and peer tutoring help break down cliquish behavior that contributes to bullying. Children's and young adult literature stimulates discussions about coping strategies such as how students can come to each other's aid. This use of literature to explore emotional issues is called *bibliotherapy*.
- Counseling is provided for identified bullies and victims. Adult supervision is increased in informal areas where students congregate during breaks in the academic program.

Bully prevention programs can make a difference. Figure 5.4 lists curriculum materials that provide guidelines and activities for reducing bullying behavior (Banks, 1997; Hoover & Oliver, 1996).

In schools where educators and parents have joined forces to combat bullying, the incidence has decreased by as much as 50% in 2 years (Ericson, 2001). Furthermore, antibullying campaigns have helped reduce the overall rate of antisocial behavior, including theft, vandalism, and truancy.

Summary

- ★ Within the classroom, groups orchestrated in a democratic fashion can be an enriching and productive experience for students and teacher alike.
- ★ In autocratic groups, power is distributed linearly: The teacher controls almost all activity, and individual members vie for status among themselves. When

Publications

Besag, V. E. (1989). *Bullies and victims in schools: A guide to understanding and management.* London: Taylor & Francis.

Derman-Sparks, L. (1989). *Anti-bias curriculum: Tools for empowering young children.* Washington, DC: National Association for the Education of Young Children.

Drew, N. (1987). *Learning the skills of peacemaking: An activity guide for elementary-age children on communicating, cooperating, resolving conflict.* Rolling Hills, CA: Jalmar Press.

Foster, E. S. (1989). *Energizers and icebreakers.* Minneapolis, MN: Educational Media Corporation.

Garrity, C., Jens, K., Porter, W., Sager, N, & Short-Camilli, C. (1995). *Bully proofing your school: A comprehensive approach for elementary schools.* Longmont, CO: Sopris West.

Gibbs, J. (1987). *Tribes: A process for social development and cooperative learning.* Santa Rosa, CA: CenterSource Publications.

Hoover, J. H., & Oliver, R. (1996). *The bullying prevention handbook: A guide for principals, teachers, and counselors.* Bloomington, IN: National Educational Service.

Judson, S. (1984). *A manual on nonviolence and children.* Philadelphia: New Society.

Olweus, D. (1993). *Bullying at school: What we know and what we can do.* Cambridge, MA: Blackwell.

Pikas, A. (1989). The common concern method for the treatment of mobbing. In E. Roland & E. Munthe (Eds.), *Bullying: An international perspective* (pp. 132–144). London: Fulton.

Webster-Doyle, T. (1991). *Why is everybody always picking on me: Guide to handling bullies.* Middlebury, VT: Atrium Society.

Videotape

National School Safety Center. (n.d.). *Set straight on bullies.* Malibu, CA: Author and National Educational Service.

Internet

Anti-Bullying Network (www.antibullying.net)
Bullying Online (www.bullying.co.uk)
Bullying.org (www.bullying.org)
Bullying at School (www.scre.ac.uk/bully)
Dealing with Bullies (www.safechild.org/bullies.htm)
Take Action Against Bullying (www.bullybeware.com)

FIGURE 5.4   Bully Prevention Curriculum Materials

teachers lead their groups autocratically, they are usually unconcerned about group dynamics and overlook the harmful effects of cliques and bullying.

★ Teachers who recognize the potential of group process pay attention to group dynamics. They strive to develop a sense of cohesiveness among their students, and they implement interventions to offset negative group issues.

★ Teachers keep group activities moving smoothly by avoiding distracting behaviors such as dangles and flip-flops. When minor classroom misbehaviors surface, they intervene nonverbally so as not to draw student attention away from the classroom activity.

★ Teachers can incorporate specific classroom strategies to prevent the negative effects of cliques and bullying.

What You Should Know

Now that you have finished reading this chapter, you should know the following:

Why group management is such a vital teaching skill
The advantages of nonverbal behavioral interventions
Several specific nonverbal behavioral interventions
How teachers manage movement in the classroom to prevent behavioral problems
Methods for fostering student relationships and group cohesiveness
How to identify behaviors that undercut cohesiveness, such as cliquishness, bullying, and social isolation, and interventions to prevent such behaviors
Characteristics and stages of democratic group development

Applying the Concepts

1. In a cooperative learning group, share personal group experiences outside the classroom, perhaps as a counselor at a summer camp, on a sports team, or in a club. Did the group leader (i.e., coach, adviser, or you) help the group become more cohesive? What did the leader do to enable cohesiveness? What group-dynamic factors impeded cohesiveness? Try to identify in your own words the changes the group went through with time. How could you apply this analysis of your personal group experience to teaching a class of students?

2. Interview three students (pick an age that corresponds to your course) on their experiences with bullies. Ask whether bullies are a problem at their school. Ask if they have ever bullied another student. If so, why? Ask if they have ever been a bully victim. What do they believe causes a student to be a bully? What causes a student to be a victim? Ask what they think teachers

and parents can do about bullies. Contrast your interview answers with those of other members in your course. What can you conclude about bullying?

3. At a field site, note each time a teacher uses a nonverbal intervention. What type of intervention is used? Does the teacher use nonverbal interventions not described in this chapter? What effect did the nonverbal intervention have? Select two nonverbal interventions you can try at a field site. Make a commitment to use such interventions at a field site or during practice teaching. Keep a record of your results.

4. Interview an individual who has substitute taught or share your own views on substitute teaching. What are some group-dynamic issues that a substitute teacher must contend with? Are these group issues different than what a regular classroom teacher would deal with? Discuss similarities and differences. Name group-dynamic issues common to both substitute teaching and regular teaching. Name group-dynamic issues that are distinctive. Select three key group issues for substitutes and regular educators and develop a plan for how a teacher would deal with each.

5. In a cooperative learning group, select one of the phases of group development: forming, storming, norming, performing, or adjourning. As a group, brainstorm ideas for supporting students during each stage. Share these ideas with the entire class.

6. Using professional books, journals, and Web sites, research group cohesion. Rather than locating information in education sources, search the sources for other disciplines, such as social psychology, sociology, and social work. Create an annotated bibiliography of 10 articles, book chapters, and Web sites. Write a two-page summary of your conclusions.

7. Select two of the following concepts detailed by Kounin—withitness, overlapping, dangles, flip-flops, stimulus-boundness, and alerting. At a field site, observe and provide examples of each in a classroom setting.

8. The study of groups and group dynamics has a rich tradition in sociology and social psychology. Search for articles written 50 or more years ago on group dynamics. Select two or three articles that could be considered classics. Explain why you selected each and discuss how the information in the articles informs practice in current-day classrooms.

Chapter 6

Enhancing Student Motivation

Chapter Outline

Key Terms

153

Introduction

Motivated students present few disciplinary problems. Finding ways to keep students interested in their schoolwork is a basic preventive discipline strategy. Boredom and apathy are not compatible with a preventive discipline approach. Providing students with incentives and rewards for work accomplished has a strong tradition in public schools. However, frequent use of extrinsic rewards raises fundamental questions, including what happens when students do not care about the rewards and what happens to motivation when rewards are terminated. As dropout rates continue to climb, many educators and researchers agree that motivational strategies should bolster students' belief in their capacity to learn. This goal can be accomplished by encouraging effort and creating a climate in which students are not afraid of making a mistake.

"What can I do to motivate my students?" is the question every worthwhile teacher seeks to answer as he or she sits down to plan the lesson for the next day. This question has launched hundreds of "can't miss" instructional strategies and libraries brimming with educational research. If teachers were dealing with only a single student, the question would be difficult enough to answer, but teachers deal with many students. Lessons that hit the mark with some students miss with others. In a classroom, a teacher is dealing with multiple temperaments, interests, ability levels, and work habits.

Student motivation is directly related to preventive discipline. Motivated students are less likely to disrupt classroom activities than are students who lack interest in their studies. Phi Delta Kappa, a national educational association, regularly polls teachers about their attitudes toward schooling. In 1996, 1997, and 2000, elementary and secondary teachers identified students' failing to complete their assignments as a serious concern (Langdon, 1996; Langdon, 1997; Langdon & Vesper, 2000).

STUDENT MOTIVATION

How students feel about school significantly influences their motivation to learn. Students who believe in themselves are willing to take risks; those who lack confidence put their energy into avoiding failure rather than into trying to succeed (Viadero, 2003). According to Marzano and Marzano (2003), student surveys indicate a declining interest in school. In 2000, 28% of 12th graders said that school was meaningful. This percentage reflects a significant decrease from the 40% who reported their classes meaningful in 1983. Reversing this trend of student dissatisfaction requires an understanding of the complex variables that shape students' attitudes toward school.

TABLE 6.1   *Largest High School Completion Gaps*

		Gap (%)	
Rank	**State**	**White/Hispanic**	**White/Black**
1	New York	43.4	40.2
2	Wisconsin	28.0	41.3
3	Pennsylvania	40.4	35.4
4	Michigan	40.3	n/a[a]
5	Iowa	38.8	31.3
6	Massachusetts	37.6	24.3
7	Nebraska	34.8	36.5
8	Ohio	32.7	36.3
9	Illinois	25.1	35.1
10	Connecticut	31.8	21.2

Note. From "Report Urges Focus on Graduation-Rate Gaps," by K. S. Reid, 2004, *Education Week*, *23*(25), p. 5. Copyright 2004 by Editorial Projects in Education. Reprinted with permission.

According to a National Research Council and Institute of Medicine report, by the time most students reach high school, they have lost a sense of purpose in their education (Gehring, 2003). Whereas students from advantaged backgrounds still manage to get by, many students from disadvantaged backgrounds fail to graduate. In 2004, researchers at the Civil Rights Project and the Urban Institute released a study indicating major gaps in graduation rates between White and minority students (Swanson, 2004). Table 6.1 shows the discrepancies in graduation rates in selected states. Reid (2004) reported that only about one-half of African American, Latino, and Native American youths are graduated from high school in four years.

Some recommendations for closing the graduation gap between Whites and ethnic groups are as follows (Gehring, 2003):

- Tailor instruction to draw on students' cultures and real-world experiences.
- Make greater efforts to coordinate with community social and health services.
- Break down comprehensive high schools into smaller learning communities.
- Eliminate formal and informal tracking of students.
- Pair students and families with an adult advocate who can help them navigate academic and personal challenges.

Finding ways to entice disenchanted and reluctant learners to believe they can succeed in school is at the core of classroom management. Traditionally, the carrot-and-stick approach to motivation has been used in classrooms. However, the efficacy of this technique has been disputed, and students' lack of motivation often leads to disciplinary problems that affect all the students in a class. Both the carrot-and-stick approach, and the ramifications of motivational problems for a class are discussed next.

The Carrot-and-Stick Approach

The *carrot and stick* is a metaphor used to describe a system of rewards and punishments. According to *Merriam-Webster's Collegiate Dictionary* (2003), this term originated from the "traditional alternatives of driving a donkey on by either holding out a carrot or whipping it with a stick" (p. 189). The carrot-and-stick approach to motivating students has a long tradition in schools: pass–fail, good grade–bad grade, and praise for correct answers–criticism for incorrect answers. The administration of achievement tests is an attempt to make students care more about their learning. If students are tested regularly, the thinking goes, they will study harder and get better grades—the carrot. In some states, education administrators have upped the ante by requiring students to pass standardized tests to graduate—the stick.

Many educators think the carrot and stick helps students to take school more seriously. Other educators believe carrot-and-stick tactics backfire because they do not take the students' concerns into account, and, as a result, these procedures undermine motivation. One of the primary rationales for so called "high-stakes" tests (i.e., tests required to pass in order to graduate) is the belief that achievement tests improve both teaching and learning.

Amrein and Berliner (2003) disagree. They reported that dropout rates were 4 to 6% higher in schools where exams determined eligibility for graduation. These researchers said,

> When rewards and sanctions are attached to performance on tests students become *less* intrinsically motivated to learn and less likely to engage in critical thinking. In addition, they [researchers] have found that high-stakes tests cause teachers to take greater control of the learning experiences of their students, denying their students opportunities to direct their own learning. (p. 32)

Amrein and Berliner believe that test-driven classrooms exacerbate boredom and anxiety, which leads to an increase in attentional and behavioral problems.

Motivation and Discipline

Motivational problems with individual students can lead to disciplinary problems that impact all students. In the Louisiana School Effectiveness Study, schools in which students had serious academic problems were characterized by frequent classroom interruptions (Stringfield & Teddlie, 1988; Teddlie & Stringfield, 1993). Conversely, students in schools with few classroom disruptions uniformly outperformed students in schools where classroom disruptions were common (Stallings, 1980).

Throughout this chapter is a discussion of how educators grapple with the fundamental question of how to motivate students. The question is far reaching because it touches on virtually every facet of classroom management. No clear-cut solution exists for problems with motivation. Each approach—whether the traditional carrot and stick or a more recent method based on student self-efficacy—must be examined in terms of individual goals and group goals. Ultimately, each teacher must make an informed decision about which motivational technique will inspire his or her students.

THE STUDENTS' VIEWPOINT

According to Hoffman (2002), three factors motivate high school students: relationships, involvement, and independence. *Relationships* refers to spending time with peers in various activities, including sports, clubs, lunch, and hallway chats. "Students care deeply about their friends and the acquaintances that make up the age group with whom they attend school. They revel in the relationships with close friends," Hoffman said (p. 34).

Hoffman (2002) also said that students equate *independence* with "being grown up." Students crave the freedom extended by a driver's license and earning their own money. They also value their relationships with adults. According to Hoffman, students feel more mature when they earn an adult's trust. Hoffman encouraged educators to respect the "adolescent ethos" and to strive to find ways to incorporate students' interests and concerns into academic programming.

Holloway (2002) reported that students gravitate to extracurricular activities because these events provide them with substantial and positive experiences that tap into the adolescent ethos. Extracurricular activities require cooperation, build student–adult relationships, connect students to school, and entice students to try new activities. Holloway exhorted educators to replicate some of the positive features of extracurricular activities in the general and academic curriculum.

Middle and High School Students

A survey of 40,000 middle school and high school students revealed that African American and Latino students, despite having lower achievement scores, care just as much about succeeding in school as their White and Asian peers do (Gewertz, 2002a). The results of this study challenge the stereotype that fundamental differences exist in the motivational makeup of students from different ethnic backgrounds (p. 5). Reflecting on the study results, Ronald Ferguson, a lecturer on public policy at Harvard University's John F. Kennedy School of Government, said that students lacking academic skills sometimes act tough and adopt a cavalier attitude toward school. He said that such students are attempting to mask deficiencies and that they are actually deeply concerned about their academic status (p. 5).

As mentioned in Chapter 2, Corbett and Wilson (2002) interviewed nearly 400 inner-city middle school and high school students. These students identified six qualities of good teachers. Each of the six points is followed by a student comment: [1]

1. **Good teachers push students.**

   "If they don't keep after you, you'll slide and never do the work. You just won't learn nothing if they don't stay on you." (p. 19)

2. **Good teachers maintain order.**

   "The kids don't do the work. The teacher is hollering and screaming, 'Do your work and sit down!' This makes the ones that want to learn go slower. It makes your grade sink down. It just messes it up for you." (p. 19)

3. **Good teachers explain until everyone understands.**

   "The teachers are real at ease. They take the time, you know, go step-by-step. We learn it more. It seems like they got the time to explain it all. We don't have to leave anyone behind." (p. 20)

4. **Good teachers vary classroom activities.**

   "I prefer working in groups. You have more fun and you learn at the same time. You learn quickly. So, you have fun and you do the work." (p. 21)

5. **Good teachers try to understand students.**

   "I heard teachers talking about people, saying, 'Those kids can't do nothing.' Kids want teachers who believe in them." (p. 21)

6. **Good teachers are willing to help.**

   "A good teacher takes time out to see if all the kids have what they're talking about and cares about how they're doing and will see if they need help." (p. 20)

Primary and Elementary School Students

One of the ironies of schooling is that before students begin their formal education, they want to learn everything they can about the world around them. Once school begins, however, children's natural proclivities are restrained by such organizational necessities as sitting still, waiting, and following teachers' directions.

In school desks, workbooks, primers, paper, pencil, and schedules compose the template for learning. Information is divided into "right" and "wrong" answers, and making a mistake is a behavior to be avoided. Some students make the adjustment and move on; others do not. Those who encounter difficulties become discouraged and hold back.

School for the learner who is at risk becomes an exercise in avoidance: Avoid making a mistake, avoid being wrong, and avoid a demonstration of ignorance.

---

[1]From "What Urban Students Say About Good Teaching," by D. Corbett and D. Wilson, 2002, *Educational Leadership, 60*(1), pp. 18–22. Copyright 2002 by the Association for Supervision and Curriculum Development. Reprinted with permission.

Avoidance gradually evolves into distrust of one's own abilities and presents the teacher with a motivation problem. An unmotivated student will not try, and a student who will not try is a student who will continue to fail (Viadero, 2003).

When students do not fully participate, they continue to lose ground academically, but their problems do not end there. Inevitably, difficulties in learning turn into behavioral difficulties. Apathy becomes noncompliance; learning deficits lead to frustration and acting-out behavior. When school no longer meets such basic needs as mastery, belonging, and control, students will still strive to meet these needs through such nonconstructive behavior as acting out for attention or by such passive-aggressive behavior as not completing assignments (Erwin, 2003).

SCHOOL DROPOUTS

At a minimum, a high school diploma and the skills it represents provide entry to jobs. Without employable skills and adult guidance, young people are vulnerable to toxic social situations that lead to crime, drug abuse, gang involvement, and teenage pregnancy. Students at risk of dropping out are usually those who can least afford to pass up an opportunity to improve their lives. Pikes and Daniels (2000) profiled the academic and social characteristics of typical *dropouts*:[2]

> We found that dropouts and students at risk of dropping out displayed identical behavior, except that dropouts, having already left school, were further along the continuum. While in school, both sets of students exhibited poor academic performance, high absentee and truancy rates, low self esteem, histories of repeated failure, recurring discipline problems, and socialized-aggressive behaviors. Some had experienced suspension and/or expulsion because of their rebellious attitudes and inability to relate to school authorities.

When asked about why they dropped out, young people who felt disenfranchised directed the brunt of their criticism at teachers and the quality of instruction (Pikes & Daniels, 2000). Low teacher expectations, placement in classes for low achievers, and lack of teacher interest in their lives typified most of the students' complaints. Following is a sample of their replies:[3]

> "They [the teachers] don't give you any high school work. What's the sense of going?"
>
> "Teacher attitudes. Some kids . . . make you want to fuss at them, but don't bring your attitude from that person to the next one. That's what [teachers] are doing."

[2]From "Listen to Us! Voice of Despair," by T. Pikes and V. I. Daniels, 2000, *Reaching Today's Youth, 4*(4), p. 6. Copyright 2000 by the National Educational Service. Reprinted with permission.

[3]From "Listen to Us! Voice of Despair," by T. Pikes and V. I. Daniels, 2000, *Reaching Today's Youth, 4*(4), p. 7. Copyright 2000 by the National Educational Service. Reprinted with permission.

"Teachers' attitudes. Same stuff [classwork, worksheets] over and over, year after year."

"Too old, had to start over at 9th grade. Picture you 20 years old in the 10th grade."

"Because I was embarrassed, ya'll dig! I can't hack the special ed class. They's always ask you like, 'What do you want to achieve?' and they'd try to put you down and say, 'Think of something else, because you'll never become that.'"

The economic repercussion of dropouts touches nearly everyone. According to a congressional estimate, school dropouts cost individual taxpayers $800 a year (Joint Economic Committee, 1991). In 2000, 35 of the largest cities in the United States graduated less than 50% of their high school freshman classes (Harvard Graduate School of Education, 2001).

Finding ways to encourage at-risk youths to persevere and finish high school presents a massive motivational challenge. Many educators believe that the solution is to instill within students who are at risk the hope that they can succeed in school and that a high school diploma is a harbinger of a brighter future. Instilling optimism and providing students with the ability to gain control of their lives are two ways for educators to help students develop such hope.

Optimism

Optimism is the bedrock of perseverance. Students at risk of dropping out of school need to believe that school can make a difference in their lives. Blankstein and Guetzloe (2000) encouraged educators to help students develop "a sense of the possible." They emphasized the complementary roles of hope and optimism:

> For the purpose of this discussion, we will define hope as a sustaining life-force that provides meaning, reason, and direction for one's existence. Having hope is an essential part of one's social, emotional, and spiritual sustenance. It gives us strength to live and continually move forward, even when conditions seem hopeless. A key factor in working successfully with young people is the development of a sense of the possible, as well as the faith, courage, and means to pursue it. (p. 2)

According to Seligman et al., students can learn to monitor, identify, and change thoughts that undermine their self-confidence and performance. Seligman et al. call this approach the *ABC model*.

ABC Model

Seligman, Gillham, and Reivich (2000) said that optimism is more than slogans, happy thoughts, and the elimination of negative emotions. Rather, optimism begins with self-knowledge—a belief that you are fully capable of directing your life in a positive manner. These researchers also argued that optimism can be taught. They identified four basic skills for achieving optimism: catching automatic thoughts, evaluating automatic thoughts, challenging automatic thoughts, and decatastrophizing. *Automatic thoughts* are unbidden thoughts that cross our minds during times of worry or stress. An automatic thought is the voice in the mind that says that something cannot be done. Automatic thoughts are self-destructive because they undermine optimism and set the stage for self-fulfilling prophecies. For instance, a female basketball player who stands on a foul line during a game and says to herself "I can't make this shot" has clearly put herself at a disadvantage. *Decatastrophizing* refers to eliminating thoughts of the most dire consequences when you are reflecting on a problem or concern. The notion of creating positive visual images is well known in sports psychology.

The ABC approach is based on the premise that thoughts and feelings are just as real as behavior and, like behavior, can be analyzed and changed. Following is a summary of the four steps that can help students learn to reflect and change pessimistic internal dialogue:

1. **Introduce internal dialogue.**   Discuss the natural tendency to "talk to yourself." Encourage students to think about a recent time when something went wrong and to remember what they were thinking. The goal is to help students recognize and pay attention to unbidden internal dialogue.
2. **Match thoughts to feelings.**   Provide activities for students to match their thoughts with their feelings. For example, which feeling best matches the thought "Now I don't have any friends"—mad, okay, or sad? Through such exercises, students slowly realize that they can change their feelings by revising how they think about situations, particularly those that undermine optimism.
3. **Provide sample activities for analysis.**   Provide examples of adverse situations. Ask students to analyze each case study in terms of what happened, how key individuals interpreted the situation through internal dialogue, and what the consequences of the interpretations were. This process is the basis of the ABC model—A, adversity; B, beliefs; C, consequences. The ABC model says that when adversity (A) strikes, our beliefs (B) about what caused the adversity determine the consequences (C), both emotional and behavioral.
4. **Apply ABC to real-life problems.**   Once the students have a handle on the ABC method, begin to use the model in conversations about students' problems. Continue to encourage students to reflect on their internal dialogue and its effect on their feelings and behavior (Seligman et al., 2000).

THEORIES OF MOTIVATION

Historically, the study of what motivates individuals was divided into two camps: those who argued that motivation was extrinsic and those who argued that motivation was intrinsic. A student who is extrinsically motivated undertakes an activity to obtain a reward or avoid a punishment (Lepper, 1988). A student who is intrinsically motivated undertakes an activity because of enjoyment or a feeling of accomplishment. Beliefs about using *intrinsic incentives* for motivation are buttressed by developmental theories that explain how *basic needs* influence behavior. Developmental theorists believe that individuals are motivated by specific intrinsic needs such as the need to belong and the need to experience a sense of mastery (Erwin, 2003; Glasser & Wubbolding, 1997).

A third viewpoint is social learning theory. This school of thought highlights the role of individual perception in motivation.

Extrinsic Motivation

Proponents of using *extrinsic incentives* believe individual motivation is propelled by environmental stimuli that reinforce behavior (Canter & Canter, 1992; Skinner, 1978). Stickers, grades, praise, and rewards are a few of the ways teachers motivate students extrinsically.

Skinner elucidated the psychological principles that provide the framework for using incentives as motivation. He explained that specific behaviors can be shaped by following them with a positive reinforcer. *Positive reinforcement* is an event whose presentation increases the possibility of a behavior, or response, that it follows (Kazdin, 2001). For example, when third-grader Alicea satisfactorily completes a worksheet (i.e., "response"), she is rewarded with a sticker (i.e., "event"). If Alicea continues to complete worksheets for stickers, her motivation is extrinsically reinforced.

Teachers use two forms of extrinsic reinforcement—*tangible incentives*, such as stickers, and *social incentives*, such as praise. Both are discussed next.

Tangible Incentives.   Giving students a reward for good work seems a reasonable way to motivate them. In school, the reward might be a sticker for a correct answer; at home, it might be a piece of cake for eating vegetables. The use of incentives as positive reinforcement appears to be efficient and simple, but problems can arise. Unintended effects can undermine teachers' objectives.

Natalie, a first-year teacher, attempted to motivate her students with candy rewards. At first, Natalie saw improvement in student participation, but soon Natalie's plan backfired when the only questions students cared about answering correctly were those for which a candy reward was offered. Tangible rewards used as incentives, whether candy, stickers, or prizes, can distract students from the behavior a teacher is trying to shape. Therefore, the decision to use tangible rewards should not be made lightly.

Kohn (1993) noted that when students work for a reward, they do what is necessary to get it and no more (p. 63). Deci, Koestner, and Ryan (1999) reviewed 128 studies in which researchers examined the effects of incentives on intrinsic motivation. They found that tangible rewards worked until the novelty wore off or the incentives were terminated.

Researchers also discovered that rewards used as incentives undermined students' desire to complete tasks that they originally found interesting. For example, 51 preschool children were given the opportunity to draw with felt-tip pens—something young children enjoy doing (Lepper & Greene, 1975). Some of the children were told that if they drew pictures, they would get certificates decorated with red ribbons. Other children were simply allowed to draw with the felt-tip pens. After two weeks, the students who received the certificates lost interest in drawing while the students who received no incentive continued to enjoy the activity.

Not all educators agree that extrinsic rewards undermine intrinsic motivation. However, the evidence dictates that teachers should carefully consider the unintended negative consequences of using incentives to motivate students.

Social Incentives.   In addition to using tangible reinforcers to motivate students, teachers use social incentives, such as positive feedback. Maag (2001b) pointed out that, on average, teachers give twice as much attention to negative behavior than to positive behavior. He recommended that teachers increase their positive comments to students. Positive remarks are more likely to support appropriate behavior than are reprimands. However, the cautions enumerated about tangible incentives also apply to praise. Too much praise can distract students from the task at hand if they switch their attention to pleasing the teacher.

Ginott (1971) distinguished between appreciative praise and effusive praise. *Appreciative praise* draws attention to effort; *effusive praise* is evaluative and creates dependency. Ginott advised teachers to avoid directing praise at a student's character, such as "You are really smart," and use descriptive comments instead, such as "Thank you for working quietly." His criticism of evaluative praise echoes the findings of Dweck (1999) and Kohn (1993): A "peril of praise" is that students will work for praise rather than for accomplishment.

Cangelosi (2003) said that teachers' word choices can mean the difference between motivating and demotivating students. According to Cangelosi, students feel less threatened and more willing to engage in learning activities when working with teachers who use descriptive language than with teachers who use judgmental language.

Descriptive language verbally portrays a situation, a behavior, an achievement, or a feeling. *Judgmental language* verbally summarizes an evaluation of a behavior, an achievement, or a person. Judgmental language that focuses on personalities is particularly detrimental to a climate of cooperation (Ginott, 1971). Descriptive language concentrates on circumstances, learning tasks, and situations.

When Ms. Alvarez asks Caitlyn to stop drumming her pencil because it is distracting, the youngster is more likely to comply without feeling embarrassed than if Ms. Alvarez had said, "Caitlyn, cut it out." Descriptive statements tell a student explicitly what the teacher wants. Ginott (1971) called descriptive statements *sane messages* because they do not attack a child's character. Judgmental statements complicate student–teacher communication because the student feels put down. When talking to students and to other professionals about students, teachers should avoid terms that indicate negative qualities, such as *lazy, immature, hyperactive, slow, retarded, uncoordinated, silly, careless,* and *sloppy.*

Best Practices for Using Extrinsic Incentives.   Following are recommendations for using tangible and social incentives to motivate students:

- Link positive feedback to specific criteria, such as willingness to take a risk, putting effort into a project, or helping another student.
- Give the class preferred activity time (PAT) as an incentive. When a student misbehaves, reduce the time by the amount of time squandered.
- Praise effort rather than intelligence. Use comments such as "You put a lot of work into this paper." Do not use comments such as "Again you demonstrated that you are a smart student."
- Inform parents of noteworthy accomplishments.
- Instill a sense of personal satisfaction, such as "You achieved your goal."
- Pair tangible rewards such as stickers and points with positive verbal comments.
- Use tangible rewards sparingly. Avoid having tangible rewards take the place of personal satisfaction.
- Incentives work best when dull tasks need to be completed. Avoid pairing incentives with tasks that hold the promise of natural satisfaction (see the following section on intrinsic motivation).
- Direct positive feedback at competent behavior rather than negative feedback at problem behaviors.
- Give incentives in a low-key, noncontrolling manner.

Intrinsic Motivation

Developmentalists maintain that intrinsic needs are central to motivation. Maslow (1971) believed that people instinctually strive to grow and blossom. This development proceeds through a hierarchy of needs from the basic physiological needs such as safety and shelter to actualizing full potential (see Figure 6.1). Hall, Lindzey, and Campbell (1998) explained Maslow's hierarchy of needs:

> The lower a need is in the hierarchy, the more prepotent or dominant that need is. In other words, when several needs are active, the lowest need will be the most compelling. As needs are satisfied, new and higher needs emerge. In addition, needs at the lower levels of the hierarchy entail *deficiency motivation*, because they are triggered by some deficit or lack within the person, while needs at the highest level entail *growth motivation*, because they entail the person's striving after goals and personal growth. (p. 449)

Within each broad area of needs are several embedded needs. For example, arranging experiences that help students meet their esteem needs, including competence, mastery, independence, and achievement.

Other intrinsic needs described by educators who view motivation from a developmental viewpoint include the need for control (Glasser, 1986), the need for generosity (Brokenleg, 1999), and the need for fun (Mendler, 1992). Teachers try to meet intrinsic needs in a variety of ways, including providing successful experiences to meet students' need for mastery and allowing student choice to meet

FIGURE 6.1   Maslow's
Hierarchy of Needs

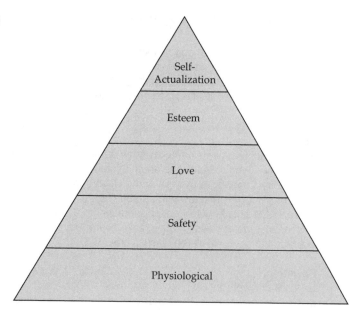

students' need for power and control. Figure 6.2 lists recommendations for meeting intrinsic needs in the classroom.

Wehlage, Rutter, Smith, Lesko, and Fernandez (1989) said that students with chronic behavioral problems improve when their intrinsic needs are taken into account. These researchers described how an alternative school for students with chronic disciplinary problems succeeded in motivating alienated students by establishing a school climate that emphasized membership (i.e., belonging), engagement (i.e., usefulness), and commitment (i.e., potency and optimism).

The intrinsic view of motivation takes personal initiative into account. Although teachers cannot control students' needs, they can attempt to meet students' intrinsic needs through lessons, routines, and disciplinary practices. Whereas the extrinsic view of motivation emphasizes the need for the student to adapt to school, the intrinsic view emphasizes the need for the school to adapt to the student. Teachers can help students meet their intrinsic needs by taking advantage of natural incentives.

Natural Incentives.   The strongest incentives occur naturally. The joy in reading an entertaining story or the feeling of competence after solving a mathematical problem reinforces the desire to read or calculate. Maag (2001b) said that the most effective classroom managers analyze and modify environmental, curricular, and instructional variables to take advantage of naturally occurring incentives. Not only do interest, success, and enjoyment motivate students to strive, but because the reinforcement is intrinsic, the results are more durable. Which has a more lasting impact on a student's reading: getting a prize for finishing five books or enjoying the five books read?

Survival

- Provide students with opportunities to get food, fresh water, and fresh air by allowing snacks, regular water fountain breaks, movement, and open windows.
- Maintain behavioral guidelines that support safety and respect.
- Develop consistent classroom procedures and routines that add to a sense of security and order.

Belonging

- Learn each student's name as soon as possible and engage students in activities that allow them to learn one another's names.
- Greet all students as they enter the classroom.
- Let students get to know you personally.
- Teach students how to work cooperatively.
- Conduct regular class meetings to encourage problem solving, group cohesion, and academic-content-related discussions.

Power

- Solicit students' input.
- Discover students' instructional level and meet them where they are.
- Teach to a variety of learning styles.
- Hold regular classroom meetings to discuss the value of the curriculum in students' lives.
- Use research-based instructional practices such as cooperative learning, authentic assessment, and mastery teaching methods.
- Instead of giving low or failing grades, give students second and third chances to improve.

Freedom

- Provide students with choices.
- Ask students to help decide the sequence of academic material to be covered.
- Listen to students.
- Allow students to decorate the classroom.
- Go on field trips.
- Set classroom goals together. Collaborate on group rewards.

Fun

- Begin class with team-building activities.
- Incorporate music and art into lessons.
- Adapt television game show formats for reviews.
- Use adventure-based learning games such as those described in *Adventure in the Classoom* (Henton, 1996).
- Play drama games that relate to course content, such as role-playing and charades.
- Use brain teasers—for example, *What's This Got to Do with Anything?* (Craigen & Ward, 1996) and *Great Lateral Thinking Puzzles* (Sloane & MacHale, 1994).

FIGURE 6.2   Meeting Students' Basic Needs

Natural incentives include activities in which students are allowed to socialize, such as brainstorming, peer tutoring, and cooperative learning. Likewise, lessons that relate to students' interests or connect to their lives outside school inject relevancy into the curriculum.

Best Practices for Using Intrinsic Incentives.   Following are recommendations for using natural incentives to motivate students:

- Meet students' trust and competence needs by giving students responsibilities.
- Help students set daily, weekly, and monthly goals.
- Attribute students' success to things students can control, such as planning and effort.
- Look for ways to increase student decision making in the classroom. For instance, let students help make rules, decide how to arrange furniture, choose decorations, and decide on class projects, class colors, and a class motto.
- Recognize that misbehavior can be caused by unmet needs for attention, mastery, and belonging.
- Try to inject fun into activities. For example, turn a drill into a fast-paced game. Use materials that are concrete, meaningful, and relevant to students.
- Inject enthusiasm into teaching. Demonstrate a high energy level.
- Develop procedures that help students track incremental advances in their skills.
- Focus on mastery.
- Provide learning activities that encourage socialization and affiliation.
- Remember that deadlines, evaluations, and imposed goals undermine intrinsic motivation.

Social Learning Theory

A third motivation approach melds ideas from the extrinsic and intrinsic theories. *Social learning theory* introduces the element of individual perception into the explication of motivation (Bandura, 1977; Kelly, 1955).

Bandura (1986) postulated that humans are capable of thought and self-regulation. These attributes allow us to both control and be shaped by our environment. The reciprocal exchange between environment and individual is the hallmark of social learning theory. Social learning theorists argue that human behavior can be understood in terms of the reciprocal interaction between external stimuli and internal cognition (Hall et al., 1998).

Reciprocal Determinism.   Individuals make predictions about what is rewarding. Then, they strive to maximize rewards and minimize punishments. For example, the boy who is "punished" with suspension may view the suspension as a "reward" because he is getting exactly what he desires—time away from school. Bandura (1986) called this interaction between extrinsic stimuli and intrinsic perception *reciprocal determinism*.

Central to reciprocal determinism is the concept of self-efficacy. Positive learning experiences build self-confidence; negative learning experiences undermine efficacy and retard the will to persevere. Students will strive with tasks and activities that they believe they can perform competently and will avoid tasks that make them feel incompetent (Pajares, 2000). Thus, students and their environment are reciprocal determinants of each other (Bandura, 1986). In other words, students both control and are shaped by their environment.

To understand reciprocal determinism in school, you must understand how students think about an event. Consider this example: A teacher decides to give her students tokens to motivate them to raise their hands and answer questions correctly. These tokens are chips that students can trade for trinkets at the classroom "store." Almost immediately, she gets the response she is looking for: An eager bevy of hands greets each question. The teacher is pleased because class participation has increased.

However, Bandura (1986) suggested that all is not what it appears to be. Why are the students raising their hands? Are they interested in the topic, or are they more interested in acquiring tokens? What about students who do not care about tokens, or students who are afraid of making a mistake? How will students feel about the token program as more and more tokens are collected by a few who know the answers while students who do not know the answers are left out? The questions could go on and on. Bandura said, "What people think, believe, and feel affects how they behave" (p. 25).

How students perceive attempts to motivate them is just as important as the strategies teachers adopt to influence their behavior. The teacher who bases lessons on students' interests, surveys students about their goals, and links lessons to students' lives outside school recognizes the important role students' perceptions play in their motivation to learn.

Best Practices for Using Social Learning Theory.   Following are recommendations for using social learning theory to motivate students:

- Praise students for effort rather than intelligence.
- Praise the process (i.e., effort, strategies, ideas that go into work), not the person.
- State your confidence in students' ability to complete a task.
- Structure tasks so that students can complete them with reasonable effort and a high success rate.
- Refrain from characterizing tasks as "easy."
- When students are having difficulties or fail, redirect their thinking from personal evaluation—such as "It's too hard" or "I'm dumb"—to reminders of past successes.
- When students fail, remind them about past strategies that worked and strategies that did not work.
- Emphasize the value of learning over grades.
- Portray effort as investment rather than risk.
- Build on students' mistakes or partially correct answers.

- Give reasons to strive.
- Demonstrate how achievement benefits students' lives.
- Acknowledge your own mistakes.

In summary, behaviorists emphasize the role of extrinsic variables, developmentalists emphasize meeting intrinsic needs, and social learning theorists emphasize the power of individual beliefs about your ability. Each of these contrasting ways of thinking about motivation has merit. Taken together, they provide teachers with an assortment of strategies for motivating students, particularly those who experience failure more often than success.

STUDENTS WITH FAILURE SYNDROME

Failure syndrome, learned helplessness, and *low self-esteem* are a few of the terms teachers use to describe students who have lost confidence in themselves and their ability to learn. Such students are in every classroom. They give up easily; they avoid work; they dislike school. A frequent lament is "I can't do it." Students with failure syndrome routinely engage in behavior that is self-defeating. They fear appearing "dumb" to their peers and thus engage in self-handicapping strategies to draw attention away from their lack of success. Likewise, even some successful students shy away from challenges because they fear making mistakes.

Students' Self-Handicapping Strategies

Turner and her colleagues (2002) surveyed 1,092 sixth graders in three midwestern states. They found that in classrooms where teachers emphasized correct answers and publically displayed grades, students who were unsuccessful developed "self-handicapping strategies." The students went to great lengths to avoid looking "stupid." Purposely goofing off, forgetting assignments, procrastinating, and giving up easily were common self-handicapping strategies these students used. Apparently, from some students' viewpoint, seeming lazy, giving excuses, or seeming too busy is better than appearing "dumb" in front of classmates and teachers. Students exhibited fewer self-handicapping strategies in classrooms where the teachers emphasized understanding and effort rather than achievement. In these classrooms, students asked questions, helped one another, and tried harder. According to Viadero (2003), fifth grade through middle school is the period when self-defeating behaviors seem to take hold.

Daphne Gregory teaches students who are at risk in a New Jersey high school. She includes abusing drugs and alcohol, sleeping during class, acting out in class, and even dressing outrageously as self-defeating strategies students use to avoid schoolwork. Gregory said, "Kids who dress that way think people will look at them and say, 'Well, he's a weirdo, anyway' and not expect them to do well." She said, "It's our job as teachers to help them understand that they aren't stupid, that taking risks is a wonderful thing, and it's good to make a mistake" (cited in Viadero, 2003, p. 8).

Beginning in the primary grades, students cultivate strategies to fake learning. In his timeless book *How Children Fail*, John Holt (1964) catalogued several covert strategies students use to hide their inadequacies:

- **Guess and look.**   The teacher stands at the blackboard. She has two columns listed. One is labeled "Nouns." The other is labeled "Verbs." She says a word and asks in which column the word belongs. She calls on a student. The Student starts to say an answer, all the while watching the teacher. Unconsciously, the teacher stands next to the appropriate column, waiting to write the correct response. Her body position gives her away, and the student uses this information to answer correctly.
- **Follow the eyes.**   A student must select the correct answer from a workbook while the teacher is standing at his desk. The student positions his pencil over the options while following the teacher's eyes for a clue about the correct answer.
- **Wait for the cave-in.**   A teacher is listening to a student read. The student starts to sound out a word, then pauses, waiting for the teacher to provide the next clue. After a few seconds, the teacher runs out of patience and caves in.
- **Keep a poker face.**   A teacher is reviewing multiplication facts with a group of five students. She holds up a flash card, and in unison the group responds with 100% accuracy for each card. The teacher is pleased and commends the students. At recess, a student tells her that she was sitting next to a sunny window and the students could read the correct answers printed on the back of the cards.
- **Memorize and recite.**   The special education teacher follows the same routine daily. He places placards with numbers from 1 to 10 on the chalk sill under the blackboard. Then he names a number and asks a student to walk up and point to it. The students point to *1, 2, 3*, and so forth without difficulty. One day, he decides to mix up the numbers. To his dismay, the students get every number wrong.
- **Disappear.**   Perhaps the most successful strategy is to seek invisibility. Sitting in the last seat in a row, rarely volunteering to answer a question, finding an excuse to leave the classroom, doing the minimal amount of work, and avoiding eye contact with the teacher are common avoidance techniques. Collectively, these strategies help students get through the school day with a minimum amount of attention drawn to their incompetence.

Other means of avoiding work are more overt. José, a student in special education, would irritate his teacher until he was sent to the principal's office. When queried about his motive, he simply stated, "I hate math."

Truancy, feigned illness, and the final act of resignation—dropping out of school—are lamentable consequences of students' giving up on their ability to learn. Failure syndrome begins in the early years of school, and if unchecked, it continues. Instead of developing a work ethic, the student with failure syndrome builds an avoidant ethic.

Most children enter school enthusiastic about learning, but as they encounter frustration, anxiety about failure supercedes curiosity. As failures accumulate, students abandon serious attempts at learning and instead focus their efforts on protecting whatever fragments of self-esteem remain (Brophy, 1998). Sooner or later, the *avoidant behavior* causes problems. Early indicators include poor grades, incomplete work, and noncompliance. Unchecked, these problems escalate into more serious behavioral difficulties. Therefore, teacher interventions to support flagging student motivation are critical, especially during the early years of schooling.

Good Students Afraid of Failing

Ironically, a track record of school achievement is no guarantee that a student will persevere in the face of new challenges. According to Dweck (1999), no relationship exists between a history of success and seeking out challenges. She found that good students are often afraid of taking risks. They back away from challenges because they worry about making mistakes and appearing "dumb."

Mueller and Dweck (1998) reported that praising students for their intelligence after an outstanding performance temporarily produced positive effects, but with time the effect was nagative. Whereas students who were praised for their intelligence backed off from challenges, students who were praised for their efforts perceived setbacks as a signal that they needed to persevere. According to the researchers, praise should be directed at the processes students use to succeed, such as setting goals, planning strategies, and learning from mistakes.

SELF-EFFICACY

Mendler (2000), said that students who demonstrate negative behaviors or give up are covering up their concerns about being perceived as stupid. "They are protecting themselves from the embarrassment of looking dumb in the eyes of their classmates, parents, and selves," Mendler said (p. 3). *Self-efficacy* is confidence in your ability to succeed. According to Bandura (1977), people confidently take on tasks they believe they can master but fear and avoid situations they perceive as beyond their abilities. This assertion helps explain at least some of the avoidant behavior students demonstrate in the classroom. Failure to complete assignments accompanied by a negative attitude toward schoolwork is characteristic of school apathy.

Bandura (2000) outlined four sources of self-efficacy—mastery experiences, vicarious experiences, social persuasion, and a reduced stress response:

1. **Mastery experiences.** Successes build self-confidence; failure undermines effort. Even students who are marginal—students who do not understand the system, students who have not done well in school in the past, and students

who do not feel as if they have any hope for a brighter future—have strengths that can be capitalized on to bolster a sense of mastery. Identifying students' strengths and interests and finding ways to accentuate their abilities is key to mastery building.

2. **Vicarious experiences.**   Other people's example can inspire effort. The strength of the modeling effect depends on the similarity of the model to the observer. The observer must be able to identify with the model. If the observer sees the model as too different, the effect on self-efficacy is negligible.

3. **Social persuasion.**   Using verbal encouragement coupled with successful experiences, teachers can persuade students to achieve. Key to a teacher's persuasiveness is the quality of the student–teacher relationship. Students are most likely to believe teachers whom they trust. Efficacy builders avoid placing students in situations in which they are likely to fail and encourage students to measure success in terms of self-improvement rather than comparisons with others.

4. **Physical and emotional states.**   Bandura (2000) said, "Another way to positively influence perceptions of self-efficacy is reduce people's stress reactions and help them alter their negative emotional proclivities and misinterpretations of their physical states" (p. 19). When faced with a stressful situation, confident students turn their stress into an *adrenaline rush*—think of the burst of energy that makes meeting a term paper deadline possible. Students who lack self-efficacy interpret nervousness and anxiety as a physical sign of incompetence. In both cases, the stress is the same—the difference is in the perception and behavior. Students need help understanding that fear and anxiety are normal stress reactions, not a sign of vulnerability.

The critical element in self-efficacy is the mind-set students bring to each new situation. The belief students have about their ability to master a task will determine how hard they work to achieve their goal. Confidence fuels commitment. This all-important mind-set is the result of both personal experience and observations of others.

A student who is observing another student's being put down for an incorrect answer is less likely to risk the same result. Conversely, a student who observes a teacher using a wrong answer as a springboard to deeper understanding would be more willing to risk making a mistake. Key, then, to improving students' efforts is to accept mistakes as part of the learning process and to value the child over the answer. Nel Noddings (1984) said,

> When a teacher asks a question in class and a student responds, she receives not just the "response" but the student. What he says matters, whether it is right or wrong, and she probes gently for clarification, interpretation, and contribution. She is not seeking the answer but the involvement of the cared for. . . . The student is infinitely more important than the subject matter. (p. 39)

Valuing students more than their correct answers motivates students to try harder. Students who believe they are capable are more likely to put forth the effort needed to overcome obstacles than are students who view themselves as incompetent.

HOW TO ENCOURAGE EFFORT

Teachers need to find ways to revitalize students' desire to learn. Effort is the key. Students cannot succeed unless they try. Often when students fail, they blame lack of ability rather than lack of effort. Exposure to media stars in the movies, in the music industry, and in sports creates a perception of effortless success. Finding a shortcut to being rich and famous is a national passion. Lotteries, instant-celebrity television shows, and million-dollar athletes suggest that the road to fortune in life is divided into two lanes: luck and ability. Idealistic images of instant success contrast sharply with the day-to-day grind-it-out experience. A shift in emphasis from achievement to effort is more than a method for motivating students; it is a valuable life lesson.

Great accomplishments follow effort. Samuel Beckett said, "Ever tried? Ever failed? No matter. Try again. Fail again. Fail better." Few things in life come easily. Sigmund Freud was booed from the podium when he first presented his ideas to the scientific community (Pajares, n.d.). Abraham Lincoln failed as a businessman and was defeated in his first attempt to be nominated for Congress. Vincent Van Gogh sold only one painting in his lifetime. What teachers need to nourish in their students is the desire to strive despite failure.

Praise directed at effort does more to motivate students than does praise garnered from achievement. More than any other single trait, effort girds against collapse in the face of adversity. Consider the bumpy road the following successful individuals traveled (Pajares, n.d.):[4]

- In 1954, Jimmy Denny, manager of the Grand Ole Opry, fired Elvis Presley after one performance. He told Presley, "You ain't going nowhere, son. You ought to go back to drivin' a truck."
- Winston Churchill failed sixth grade. He was defeated in every election for public office until he became prime minister at the age of 62.
- Michael Jordan and Bob Cousy were each cut from their high school basketball teams. Jordan once observed, "I've failed over and over again in my life. That is why I succeed."

[4]From "But They Did Not Give Up," by F. Pajares, n.d., Lecture delivered at Emory University, Atlanta, GA. Copyright F. Pajares. Reprinted with permission. Retrieved from http://www.emory.edu/EDUCATION/mfp/pajaresgtl.html

- Walt Disney was fired by a newspaper editor because "he lacked imagination and had no good ideas." He went bankrupt several times before he built Disneyland. In fact, the city of Anaheim rejected the proposed park on the grounds that it would attract only riffraff.
- Every cartoon Charles Schulz, creator of the cartoon strip *Peanuts*, submitted was rejected by his high school yearbook staff, and Walt Disney would not hire him.

Mendler (2000) and Marzano (2003) offered the following recommendations for encouraging effort in the classroom:

- **Dignify "wrong" answers.**   A college professor stands in front of a group of 30 students and asks a question. Two students raise their hands. They think they know the "right" answer, and the rest of the students abstain because they do not want to risk being "wrong." This conditioned response to avoid failure begins early in school. Encourage all answers. Remind students that any answer requires thought. Build on partial answers and praise students for trying. Remember, effort, not success, is the basis for learning.
- **Allow the "three *R*s": redo, retake, and revise.**   A common anecdote about Thomas Edison is that a reporter asked him how it felt to have failed 1,000 times during his attempts to invent the lightbulb. Edison supposedly replied, "I didn't fail 1,000 times. The lightbulb was an invention with 1,001 steps." Every worthwhile effort requires diligence and revision. Allow students to re- take tests and revise projects. Give deadlines for partial completion of projects and grade those as well. Adding redo, retake, and revise options encourages students to keep trying and lets them know that effort can lead to success.
- **Provide students with frequent feedback about their progress.**   Students need to see that effort is worth the time spent. Frequent feedback encourages students to improve on one thing each day. If a student gets a math problem wrong, indicate parts of the problem that were correct. Allow students to chart their personal progress rather than comparing their progress with that of other students. Assess a student's achievement level at the beginning of a unit of instruction and compare it with an end-of-unit assessment. Show students how to chart their progress with frequency counts and graphs. Lindsley (1990) observed that learning can be enhanced by frequent self- recorded responses on standardized charts. He called this approach *precision teaching*. Daily recordings of progress by students allows them to see the out- comes of their efforts in a measurable way.
- **Reframe unmotivated behavior.**   Identify positive aspects of what students do and highlight these over the negative. Mendler (2000) pointed out, for ex- ample, that a student who arrives 5 minutes late for a 50-minute class is pres- ent 90% of the time, which would be an A or A− on a graded measure. Affirm what students present rather than criticizing what they lack. All students have strengths and positive aspects not ordinarily displayed in school. Learn about students' interests and hobbies. Find ways to incorporate their strengths into classroom activities.

- **Give students a reason to strive.**   Constantly search out examples of the connection between effort and accomplishment. Biographies, and lessons in history, science, and mathematics, offer myriad examples of individual perseverance. Invite adults into class to tell their stories. Redirect students from the antics of celebrities to the strivings of "ordinary" people.

ATTRIBUTION TRAINING

Attribution training is a method for teaching students to attribute success to factors they can control, such as time spent studying, effort, and planning. Attribution training in schools has proved effective in a variety of situations, including getting fifth-grade students to clean up after themselves, raising second graders' math scores, and enhancing the performance of eighth-grade females in physics (Pierce, 1999; Ziegler & Heller, 2000). Attribution training teaches the following (Brophy, 1986):

To concentrate on a task rather than thinking about past failures
To deal with frustration by determining mistakes or alternative procedures
To attribute failure to lack of effort rather than lack of ability or external
sources such as a boring textbook or bad teaching

The purpose of attribution training is to help students learn to be accountable for their behavior by providing them with positive feedback about their effort and accomplishments. When students do not do well, the teacher does not accept excuses but helps the student pinpoint mistakes made along the way. Rewards, threats, or lectures about how a person *should* behave are omitted. Teacher feedback describes student behavior, particularly with respect to the student's effort. Figure 6.3 contrasts attribution statements with persuasive and reinforcement statements.

Persuasive Statements
"You should be good at math."
"You should behave yourself."
"You should listen to my directions."

Reinforcement Statements
"I'm proud of your work in math."
"I'm pleased with your behavior."
"Good listening."

Attribution Statements
"You really are working hard on your math."
"It's clear you are trying to behave yourself."
"Your effort in following directions is obvious."

FIGURE 6.3   Comparison of Teacher Statements

FLOW

Csikszentmihalyi (1990) coined the term *flow* (Scherer, 2002) to describe the time when an individual is completely involved in a task. Flow is characterized by deep concentration, high motivation, and clarity. For example, a musician experiences flow when he or she moves effortlessly from one note to the next. As young children learn to walk and talk, they experience flow.

About 15% of all adults experience flow regularly through favorite activities such as cooking, gardening, athletics, and writing. A hallmark of the flow experience is focused attention and concentration. Students report experiencing flow when engaged in group work, computer-assisted instruction, and vocational subjects. Meanwhile, teacher lectures, audiovisual presentations, and independent tasks reduce flow.

Flow is realized when students are immersed in their learning. Observing students engaged fully in their lessons is one of the most rewarding aspects of teaching. A few examples follow:

> Mrs. Allen, a third-grade teacher, steps into the hall to discuss an issue with a colleague. The class is so fully engaged in their cooperative learning activity that they do not even realize she is out of the room.
>
> Mr. Melindez, a middle school teacher, is brainstorming with his class about the hypothetical social and economic effects if the South had won the Civil War. The bell rings to change classes and the students moan, "Do we have to stop now?"
>
> Mr. Torres, a special education teacher, is talking with Gregory about his reading progress: "Greg, you have done great; you finished the book. You can give it back to me now." Greg reluctantly hands the book back. Mr. Torres says, "Greg, would you like to keep this book?" Greg's face lights up, "Thanks, Mr. Torres."

Each of the preceding examples illustrates Ginott's statement that teaching is a series of small victories (cited in Charles, 1999). Getting students to fully participate in their schoolwork and thereby achieve during lessons is every classroom teacher's goal.

When students are motivated, they care about their studies, school is important, and they give their best effort. Motivation is more than achievement; it is the ability to persevere despite obstacles. In Chapter 8, teaching approaches that help engage students more fully in their learning are described.

MOTIVATIONAL GUIDELINES

By now, you should clearly see that the question about how to motivate students is not only important, but also widely discussed anywhere educators congregate either figuratively in journals or literally in school hallways, classrooms, and teacher lounges. The following four practical recommendations are derived from both the research on motivation and observations of effective classroom practices:

1. **Use novelty to hold attention and create interest.** Vary teaching methods. If a lesson requires a lot of teacher talk and student listening, follow it up with a lesson that elicits student participation and input. Student interest in such teacher-directed lessons as lectures and demonstrations can be sustained by teacher enthusiasm.

2. **Every day, allow students to make some choices about how or what they learn.** Control empowers students and gives them a personal stake in their learning. The results of studies on responsibility in a variety of organizations clearly indicate that personal input and decision making enhances accountability and motivation (Miller, Brickman, & Bolen, 1975; Wehmeyer & Schwartz, 1997).

3. **Encourage students to set their own goals and evaluate their learning in terms of incremental progress.** Goal setting gives direction to learning and jump-starts effort. Students are more likely to overcome obstacles if they are working toward their own goals rather than someone else's.

4. **Use tangible incentives such as prizes only as a last resort.** Incentives seem so natural and useful that their use can lull a teacher into believing that they are the foundation of good motivational technique. Paradoxically, tangible incentives undermine intrinsic motivation. By nurturing intrinsic incentives such as personal satisfaction and accomplishment, a teacher helps create a self-sustaining motivational attitude. Students who dislike reading are more likely to change their attitude if they are provided with high-interest reading materials than if they are given a sticker for every reading assignment completed.

For some, motivation becomes more of a problem each year. By the time they reach high school, many students lack any sense of purpose or connection to their schoolwork. The problem of student alienation is most acute in disadvantaged urban and rural schools.

According to the National Research Council and Institute of Medicine report *Engaging Schools: Fostering High School Students' Motivation to Learn* (2004), high schools should attempt to tailor instruction in an effort to match curriculum to students' cultural backgrounds. Additional recommendations included coordinating with community social and health agencies, creating smaller learning environments with more personable student–teacher relationships, and eliminating both informal and formal ability tracks.

Summary

★ Various approaches, including using incentives, meeting students' instrinsic needs, and encouraging effort, have proved successful in motivating students.
★ Motivation plays a key role in classroom management.

★ Unmotivated students often exhibit behavioral problems.
★ Students who have a history of school failure are most susceptible to motivational problems.
★ Rewarding effort encourages students to take risks.
★ Attribution training helps students gain confidence in their ability to complete tasks successfully.
★ Incentives and rewards can distract students from the purpose of a learning task.
★ Students experience "flow" when they are absorbed in a task.

What You Should Know

Now that you have finished reading this chapter, you should know the following:

Some of the reasons for student apathy and high dropout rates
The difference between extrinsic motivation and intrinsic motivation
The advantages and disadvantages of tangible, social, and natural reinforcers
The connection between social learning theory and motivation
Best practices for enhancing motivation by using incentives
Best practices for enhancing motivation by meeting students' intrinsic needs
Best practices for enhancing motivation by boosting students' self-efficacy
How to spot self-defeating student behaviors that undermine perseverance
The principles of attribution training
How a lack of motivation is a source of disciplinary problems

Applying the Concepts

1. Review the criticisms of extrinsic rewards that are described in *Punished by Rewards: The Trouble with Gold Stars, Incentive Plans, A's, Praise, and Other Bribes*, by Alfie Kohn (1993), published by Houghton Mifflin. Compare Kohn's arguments with the positive presentation of incentives found in many behavior modification textbooks. Conduct a classroom debate on this topic: Resolved that grades and other incentives should be eliminated as motivational techniques (or a similar debate topic).

2. At a field site, make a list of tangible reinforcers used. Present your findings to your class. Do you believe teachers use too many or not enough tangible reinforcers? Also, at the field site, pick an hour at random and count how many persuasive statements the teacher makes and how many attribution statements he or she makes. Compare the data.

3. In a cooperative learning group, each member should select a specific job or profession (e.g., a physician and an auto mechanic) and list and compare specific extrinsic and instrinsic motivators that influence job performance.

What can you conclude about the relative value of external and intrinsic motivation in an individual's career?

4. Have you ever experienced flow? If so, under what conditions? Is creating the same conditions in a classroom possible? Brainstorm ways that flow is achieved outside school and how flow can be achieved within a classroom.

5. Recall your school days. Did you have particular subjects or particular grades in which your sense of self-efficacy was undermined? If so, how did it affect your feelings about school? How did you behave? What are the long-range effects of this experience on you today?

6. Interview a primary, an elementary, or a secondary student. Ask how the student likes school. Ask if the student works hard in school. Follow these probes with other questions such as why the student feels the way he or she does about school. What goes on in school that shapes the student's perceptions? Ask the student if he or she has any "tricks" to get out of work or to avoid looking "dumb." If so, what are they? Finally, ask what the student's teacher could do to make learning more interesting. Report your findings to the class.

7. Interview a teacher about using rewards in the classroom to motivate students. Why does the teacher use rewards? What are some difficulties that arise from the use of rewards? What does the teacher value more—achievement or effort? How does the teacher's value influence his or her behavior?

8. Analyze the No Child Left Behind Act from the viewpoint of the principles explained in this chapter. In what ways is the Act congruent with chapter information on motivation? In what ways does the information in this chapter deviate from the principles outlined in the Act? If a teacher were to emphasize self-efficacy over rewards, how would that teacher justify such actions in light of No Child Left Behind?

Chapter 7

Instructing Classes

Chapter Outline

No Child Left Behind Act
Engaged Learning
Boredom Busters
  The Drive for Mastery
  The Drive to Understand
  The Drive for Self-Expression
  The Drive to Relate
Differentiated Instruction
  Community-Based Learning
  Cooperative Learning
  Peer Tutoring
  Theme-Based Learning
  Entrepreneurial Projects
"Brain-Compatible" Instruction
Direct Instruction
The Right Balance
Teacher Qualities

Organization of Instruction
Help for Students with Learning Problems
  Easily Distracted
  Difficulty Completing Tasks
  Incomplete Homework
  Difficulty Following Directions
  Disorganized
  Failure to Try
Social Skills Instruction
  A Different Way of Thinking About
  Discipline
  Social Skills Programs
  How to Teach Social Skills
Character Education
Summary
What You Should Know
Applying the Concepts

 Key Terms

Boredom
"Brain-compatible" instruction
Character education
Classwide peer tutoring (CWPT)
Community-based learning
Cooperative learning
Cross-age peer tutoring
Differentiated instruction
Direct instruction
Engaged learning

Entrepreneurial projects
Learned helplessness
Mnemonic
No Child Left Behind (NCLB) Act
Peer tutoring
Social competence
Social skills instruction
Social skills programs
Standards-based education
Theme-based learning

Introduction

Academic success and classroom management go hand in hand. The more adept teachers are at minimizing classroom disturbances, the more effectively they can meet their students' learning needs. While test scores measure achievement, student participation in their lessons is a measure of their interest. Interested students are engaged in their learning. They see meaning in their lessons, and they understand the relevance of what they are expected to learn.

Various instructional approaches promote student engagement by aligning lesson presentation with basic student needs. Cooperative learning and peer tutoring allow students to interact as they mutually solve learning problems. Theme-based learning helps students link concepts by providing a scaffolding of interdisciplinary experiences. Preparing students for standardized tests without resorting to "drill-and-kill" tactics is a conundrum for teachers. Using direct instruction methods with clearly defined learning objectives and providing students with reliable feedback is one approach that has a proven track record.

Striking a balance between teacher-directed lessons and student-centered learning is key to covering requisite material without losing students' interest. Students with special needs and other learners who are at risk often require instructional accommodations. In addition, many students go to school lacking the social skills they need to successfully participate in their lessons. When social skills instruction is merged with the curriculum, students learn valuable lessons in getting along with others as they master key academic skills.

Each year, students and teachers embark on a journey together. From September through June, galaxies are explored, eons of history are surveyed, and the composition of molecules is dissected. Minds are challenged, friendships are forged, and lives are changed. Remarkably, all this activity transpires within a succession of solitary rooms linked in eggbox-type buildings called *schools*. Each room is populated with approximately 25 young people and one or two adults. While they meld the exuberance of youth with the experience of maturity, students and teachers navigate their way through thick textbooks, unbending schedules, and challenging examinations.

At school, the stakes are high, and the pressures are real. Current-day teachers face intense public scrutiny coupled with high expectations for student success. The crucial role instruction plays in preventing disciplinary problems cannot be overstated. Teachers cannot teach and students cannot learn in classrooms disrupted by student misbehavior. Boring, uninspired lessons invite such mischief, whereas interesting lessons focus attention. Enthusiastic teaching encourages participation, and challenging activities inspire effort. This chapter covers how teachers keep their students involved in their learning through well-organized, meaningful instruction.

No Child Left Behind Act

On January 8, 2002, President George W. Bush signed into law the *No Child Left Behind (NCLB) Act.* This reauthorization of the Elementary and Secondary Act of 1965 set challenging new academic standards for the education of U.S. youths. The Act is based on four educational reform principles:

1. Stronger school accountability is needed for improved student learning.
2. Local schools need increased flexibility to be able to respond to specific student needs.
3. Expanded educational options should be made available to parents.
4. Teaching methods should have a strong positive research basis.
   (www.nclb.gov/next/overview/index.html)

Throughout the 670-page document, one central theme clearly emerges: Schools and teachers are accountable for the academic achievement of *all* students—including those in traditional "at-risk" categories, such as students with special needs; students who are economically disadvantaged, homeless, disabled, or migrants; and students with limited English proficiency. The urgency of meeting these federally mandated standards may cause teachers to lose sight of the key role classroom management plays in academic performance.

To attain the lofty achievement goals set by education reformers, teachers must find ways to increase the amount of time they spend teaching and decrease the amount of time they spend attending to misbehavior (Wang, Haertel, & Walberg, 1993). Persistent and severe misbehavior problems have a devastating effect on learning. Students with chronic behavioral problems have a dropout rate of more than 50% (U.S. Department of Education, 2000). The renewed vigor with which educators are attempting to improve student achievement underscores the importance of skillfully managing classrooms (Moles, 1989; Snow, Burns, & Griffin, 1995).

Aronson, Zimmerman, and Carlos (1998), researchers at WestEd, a nonprofit educational research and development institute, found that 70% of all teachers need to improve their classroom management skills (www.wested.org/wested/papers/timeandlearning/). Likewise, a major study conducted by the National Center for Education Statistics (2002b) revealed that classroom disorder eroded the academic environment for both students who were achieving and those who were underachieving.

Engaged Learning

Motivational problems are diminished and achievement is enhanced when students are actively engaged in their studies. According to the results of several research studies, the amount of time in which students are engaged in their learning varies from 28 to 56% of the school day (Goodlad, 2000; B. Jones, Valdez, Nowakowski, & Rasmussen, 1994; Stallings, 1980). Observable indicators of *engaged learning* include participating in classroom discussions, answering questions, asking questions, having peer discussions, and engaging in creative writing.

Student participation is the critical factor in engaged learning (Stronge, 2002). Goodlad (1984) reported that students spend too much of their school day listening to lectures and filling in blank spaces in workbooks. Similarly, Katims and Harmon (2000) reported that middle school students typically spend 75% of their classroom time and 90% of their homework time using textbooks and worksheets.

Like radar, the human mind is constantly scanning for new stimuli. If lessons are irrelevant, pedestrian, or disorganized, students will seek alternative ways to occupy their minds. The more fully students are engaged by their lessons, the less likely they are to misbehave. *Lessons that focus student attention and encourage student participation increase motivation and prevent disciplinary problems.* Attention and participation are promoted by lessons that allow students to interact, exchange ideas, and capitalize on their individual strengths.

One way to promote engaged learning is to stymie boredom. The next section covers methods for doing so.

BOREDOM BUSTERS

Think back to your elementary and secondary school days. Can you recall when you daydreamed, stared at the clock, or looked for patterns in the walls? If you have such not-so-fond school memories, you are not alone. *Boredom* is as common a school experience as are soggy pizza, warm milk, and hall passes. It is the bane of every teacher and the torment of every student. Boring lessons squelch interest in learning, waste instructional time, and invite misbehavior.

The German philosopher Arthur Schopenhauer said, "The two foes of human happiness are pain and boredom" (cited in Seldes, 1985, p. 375). Phillips (1993) described boredom as a form of depression coupled with a deeply felt need for stimulation. Strong, Silver, Perini, and Tuculescu (2003) said the following about boredom:

> This double aspect of boredom—its negative brooding and its positive yearning—makes it difficult to deal with in the life of classrooms. Its dark, depressive side tends to provoke our anger and defensiveness (I am *not* boring!), even as its searching quality stirs up fears of our own insufficiency. (p. 24)

Teachers can counter boredom by examining how well a lesson or a unit incorporates the following four natural human interests (Strong et al., 2003; Figure 7.1):

1. The drive for mastery
2. The drive to understand
3. The drive for self-expression
4. The drive to relate

Think of a unit you teach. Place a number between 1 and 4 in each box to indicate your unit's strengths or weaknesses in each area (4 for *strong*, 1 for *weak*). What do you notice?

MASTERY

- Is the goal of the unit defined in terms of a product or performance?
- Have students been involved in analyzing the competencies and qualities of the product or performance?
- Have the constituent skills been clearly modeled?
- How well has on-the-spot feedback and refinement been built into the work?
- Total:

INTERPERSONAL

- How closely connected to the real world are the content and products of the unit?
- How well designed is the use of audiences, clients, and customers as ways to stimulate reflection and improvement?
- How carefully modeled are strategies for collecting real-world information and communicating with authentic audiences?
- How vital a role do real-world samples of products and performances play in the unit?
- Total:

UNDERSTANDING

- Is the unit organized around provocative questions?
- Are the sources used in the unit sufficiently challenging and based on powerful ideas?
- Does the unit teach students strategies for evaluating ideas and evidence?
- Are students able to critique and correct their own and others' products and ideas?
- Total:

SELF-EXPRESSION

- How strong a role does choice play in the unit?
- How regularly are strategies for creative thinking modeled?
- How rich a set of sample is available for student study?
- How well are discussions of student work used to drive student progress?
- Total:

FIGURE 7.1   Student Interest Rubric for Curriculum Design
From "Boredom and Its Opposite," by R. Strong, H. Silver, M. Perini, and G. Tuculescu, 2003, *Educational Leadership, 61*(1), p. 26. Copyright 2003 by the Association for Supervision and Curriculum Development. Reprinted with permission.

The Drive for Mastery

Some students are apprehensive before a lesson begins. They are unsure of what is expected of them, and they question their competence. Student angst leads to avoidance and boredom. This negative student reaction can be overcome by describing the goal or outcome of the lesson. What is the student expected to produce or how is the student expected to perform? Teachers should provide students with examples of competent performance or the expected product, model skills that students will need to incorporate, and provide students with on-the-spot feedback. Rubrics, samples, minilessons, and models are examples of common tools used to lighten students' anxiety about expectations.

The Drive to Understand

Even the best organized lesson needs to spark curiosity. The drive to understand is a natural human capacity that students express by asking questions, pointing out errors, and voicing their opinions. Without these student behaviors, a lesson is one-sided, dry, and tedious. Therefore, teachers should organize units around questions that will elicit student concern. One way to hook student interest is with controversy. For example, how do the current-day terrorist tactics compare with the tactics used by fighters in the American Revolution or Civil War? In addition, texts and written information should represent more than a single viewpoint. Teachers should show students how to identify, collect, and analyze data and provide forums for student debate and discussion.

The Drive for Self-Expression

Imagine a sixth-grade lesson on ancient Egypt. In Ms. Alford's classroom, students take turns reading a paragraph in the text and then answer the questions at the back of the chapter. In Mr. Reiser's classroom, he shows a 5-minute clip from the movie *The Mummy*. Then he shows pictures of the Sphinx, a pyramid, and a sarcophagus and asks his students why they think the movie put so much emphasis on life after death. He asks his students to form pairs and discuss what is fact, what is fiction, and what they would like to know about Egyptian history. After a brainstorming session, he records their ideas and questions and uses the students' input to plan the rest of the unit.

Tedium is the handmaiden of boredom. Whereas Ms. Alford stifles self-expression, Mr. Reiser promotes and builds on student participation. Teachers allow for student self-expression by providing opportunities for student choice. They provide illustrations and artifacts that represent real-life scenarios and events. Most of all, teachers who nurture self-expression use projects to add vitality and realism to their lessons.

The Drive to Relate

Teachers spend a lot of time and energy trying to stifle student-to-student conversation. Passing notes and whispering provide stimulation for bored students. The need to socialize is hardwired into the human brain; thus, students have difficulty shutting down this basic biological need (Sylwester, 2000). Consequently, rather than expending energy trying to stop students from socializing, teachers should develop classroom methods that capitalize on socialization as an instructional tool. Students can be provided with activities that allow them to work together—such as class meetings, brainstorming, cooperative learning, peer tutoring, and community-based learning.

DIFFERENTIATED INSTRUCTION

Whenever teachers offer a varied approach to learning, they are differentiating instruction. The purpose of *differentiated instruction* is to enhance student engagement by adapting instruction to the students' needs. Differentiated instruction is characterized by the following set of beliefs (Tomlinson, 2000):

- Students differ in their readiness to learn, learning styles, and interests. Successful learning experiences encompass such differences.
- Student differences significantly affect the pace of their learning and their need for teacher support.
- Students learn best when they can make a connection between the curriculum and their life experiences.
- When schools and classrooms create a sense of community, students are more effective learners.
- The goal of education is to maximize each student's capacity.

Examples of differentiated instruction include community-based learning, cooperative learning, peer tutoring, theme-based learning, and entrepreneurial projects. Each of these instructional methods has successfully enhanced both student engagement and student achievement.

Community-Based Learning

Within every town, city, or community, certain issues and concerns can be used as a jumping-off point for interesting lessons. Community-based projects are multidisciplinary; they require mutual problem solving and are relevant to students' lives outside school. Some examples of community-based projects are as follows:

- After a young boy sustained a head injury while riding his bike, elementary school students organized a successful citywide campaign to pass an ordinance requiring bicycle riders to wear helmets.
- Middle school students organized and participated in a series of cleanup campaigns along the banks of a river that flowed through the center of town.
- High school students organized a walk-a-thon to raise money for a student who was seriously ill.
- Elementary students made and sold artificial floral arrangements to help finance a skateboard park for teenagers in their community.

Community-based learning requires students to demonstrate a variety of skills, including budgeting, writing, organizing, committing to a project, planning, and collaborating with community leaders. Strong et al. (2003) provided four suggestions for helping students organize community-based projects:

1. Teach students strategies for collecting and organizing data, such as using surveys, doing Web searches, performing library searches, and conducting interviews.
2. Provide samples of products that students can use as a model for their endeavors.
3. Outline rubrics to help students evaluate and improve their performance.
4. Identify target audiences, clients, or customers.

Cooperative Learning

Cooperative learning is a teaching strategy that infuses social skills development into group work. Students are separated into groups of five or six. Teachers attend to three aspects of group dynamics. First, certain behaviors help or hinder communication within small groups (Table 7.1). Students need help identifying specific behaviors that move the group toward success (e.g., listening, questioning, providing feedback, staying on topic, and summarizing). Second, thought must be given to the group's composition so that the group is balanced in terms of students' abilities. Third, a system must be put in place for ensuring each group member's accountability. For example, many teachers use the "jigsaw" approach. Each student is assigned a specific task within the group. An alternative method is to have students decide, among themselves, each person's assignment.

The benefits of cooperative learning are twofold: students are more productive than when they engage in traditional group work, and they practice interpersonal skills such as listening, mutual problem solving, and working as a team

TABLE 7.1 *Cooperative Group Behaviors*

Helpful Behaviors	Hindering Behaviors
Ask questions	Monopolize conversation
Keep the group on track	Go off on tangents
Provide information	Do not contribute
Summarize	Become bogged in detail
Problem solve	Generate problems
Give supportive feedback	Criticize
Share ideas	Remain silent
Be enthusiastic	Be apathetic

(Johnson and Johnson, 1986). Berman (1997) reviewed many research studies on cooperative learning. He reported the following positive effects (cited in M. Beck & Malley, 1998):

- Students care about one another and are committed to one another's welfare.
- Prosocial behavior and social competence increase.
- Students develop skills in conflict resolution.
- Commitment to democratic values increases.

The four leading cooperative learning models are as follows (Walters, 2000):

1. **Student team learning (STL).**   Robert Slavin, at Johns Hopkins University, developed the STL model. He designed this approach to cooperative learning for learners who are at risk. In this approach, teams earn certificates or awards for achieving above a performance standard set by the teacher. Individual performance and team performance are rewarded. Three STL strategies are appropriate for students in Grades 3 through 12: Student Teams Achievement Division (STAD), Team–Games–Tournaments (TGT), and Jigsaw II. Each has a different focus. With STAD, students study together, and individual quiz scores are averaged into team scores. With TGT, students play academic games rather than take quizzes, and with Jigsaw II, students become "experts" on assigned topics. (For more information, contact the Director of Training Projects, Center for Social Organization of Schools, 3505 North Charles Street, Baltimore, MD 21218; www.ed.gov/pubs/EPTW/ eptw10/eptw10u.html).

2. **Learning together.**   David and Roger Johnson, at the University of Minnesota, developed the learning together cooperative learning approach. In learning together, students work in heterogeneous groups of four to five members. A single product is the assigned group goal. The group is rewarded for successfully reaching the goal. Team-building activities and discussions about how well the group is working together are regular features of this model.

3. **Jigsaw.**   In the jigsaw method, students are placed in six-member groups. Each student has an individualized assigned reading. "Expert groups" are set up to allow the assigned readers from each group discuss what they learned. Students then return to their own groups and take turns teaching their group members what they learned from their readings and the expert-group discussions. Elliot Aronson and his colleagues at the University of California at Santa Cruz are credited with the development of the jigsaw model. This method is useful when the main source of student information is an assigned text.

4. **Group investigation.**   In group investigation, students form their own two- to six-member teams. Each team chooses a subtopic of a curriculum unit and develops a team report. When the report is completed, the students give classroom presentations. Shlomo Sharan and Yael Sharan, from Tel Aviv University, developed the group investigation method.

On the basis of a national survey, Walters (2000) reported that 79% of elementary teachers and 62% of secondary teachers used cooperative learning in their lessons. Cooperative learning is an ideal venue for meshing the varied skills and aptitudes of students in elementary and secondary classrooms. Augustine, Gruber, and Hanson (1990) reported positive academic results with students who were low achieving, gifted, and disabled. S. Kagan (1994) reported that cooperative learning was also an effective way to improve race relations among students.

Cooperative learning provides a structure for daily review of social skills. The following four suggestions are a guide to beginning cooperative learning activities:

1. On the first day of class, communicate to students clear expectations about cooperative learning. Students need information on how they will be graded, what happens if they come to class unprepared, and how individual and group grades will be determined.
2. With the entire class, brainstorm specific roles that move group projects along and roles that hinder group efforts. Make a list of helpful and hindering behaviors. Have students role-play different behaviors in a group.
3. Provide a nonthreatening, hands-on introduction to cooperative learning that students can easily accomplish. One fifth-grade teacher divided students into teams and gave each team member a different magazine or newspaper section. She told them to search for words that rhymed with the assigned spelling words for the week. For a final product, the teams had to write a group poem using as many of the spelling and rhyming words as they could. The class then voted on the silliest poem, the cleverest poem, and the best-rhyming poem.
4. After students have had several cooperative learning experiences, ask them to develop group-process ground rules. Write the rules on poster board and review them periodically, adding and subtracting from the list as needed.

Goodwin (1999) noted that cooperative learning is more complicated than it might first appear. She recommended that teachers keep tasks short and simple until students become proficient at some of the social skills they need to work together. Teachers should start with students in pairs or groups of three, then select one model—such as the jigsaw or group investigation model—and make incremental adjustments as needed. Finally, she suggested that cooperation does not take root spontaneously. It requires careful planning and a willingness to persevere through inevitable bumps in the road.

Peer Tutoring

Peer tutoring is the arrangement of students in pairs for instruction. One student—the tutor—is the instructor. The other student—the tutee—is the learner. Peer tutoring is an effective instructional method for all grade levels and subject areas. It benefits both the tutor and the tutee. It improves time on task, lessens duress over errors, enhances motivation, and improves social relationships (Haskell, 2000; Lloyd, Crowley, Kohler, & Strain, 1988; Prater, 1999).

Some variations of the peer-tutoring format are classwide peer tutoring and cross-age peer tutoring. *Classwide peer tutoring (CWPT)* involves an entire class in reciprocal teaching. Each class member takes a turn as tutor and tutee. CWPT is recommended as a review strategy, after new material has been introduced and discussed (Haskell, 2000).

Cross-age peer tutoring is the systematic tutoring of younger students by older students. This approach is particularly useful with students who are having academic difficulties. Students who are low achieving get a boost in confidence by helping younger students learn. In addition, tutoring a younger student helps the tutor review previous concepts that might be a contributing factor in his or her learning difficulties.

Henley, Ramsey, and Algozzine (2003) outlined the following four steps for implementing peer tutoring:

1. **Start small.**   Slow development allows for modifications as the tutoring program evolves.
2. **Prepare students for tutoring.**   Both tutors and tutees need to know what is expected of them. If students go to different classrooms, schedules must be balanced and agreements reached among teachers about specific tutoring objectives. Tutors need clear guidelines about their responsibilities.
3. **Arrange a tutoring schedule.**   Half-hour sessions produce the best results. Time constraints and spatial requirements need to be surveyed. Build in consistency by establishing a set time each day. Recognize that initial adjustments in schedules will probably be necessary. Make provisions for student absences. Develop a list of alternative tutors.
4. **Inform parents.**   Parents are curious about novel teaching methods. Assure parents that peer tutoring is not depriving students of the teacher's instructional time. Explain the benefits of peer tutoring. Locate professional journal articles that support your program and send copies to parents. Identify Web sites that provide further information about peer tutoring.

At Danville High School in Kentucky, peer tutoring began as a program for providing students with disabilities with individualized help from non-disabled peers. As the program grew, the tutors started to develop deeper insights into human relationships and social policies that affected the lives of individuals with disabilities. Teachers recognized that tutorial experience could help students meet state academic standards dealing with social justice and critical-thinking skills. Peer tutors delved into such topics as the meaning of friendship and the pros and cons of the Americans with Disabilities Act.

Longwill and Kleinert (1998) summarized the reciprocal benefits of peer tutoring:

> Peer tutoring has thus evolved more into a context of learning *together,* helping one another and supporting each other's efforts. Such a context provides a more fertile ground for the development of genuine friendships, and lessens the potentially negative impact of peer tutors seeing themselves as extensions of the teacher, as opposed to participating as true learning partners. (p. 64)

Theme-Based Learning

Traditionally, school curricula have been arranged in a ladder-type sequence. New ideas and concepts are built on previously learned material. Sets of ideas are categorized within subjects. This view likens thinking to an escalator—climbing one idea at a time. This static, one-dimensional view of learning does not do justice to the remarkable activity we call *thinking.* The human mind works more like a popcorn machine than an escalator. Thoughts and ideas spring up spontaneously; the work is in making the connections (K. W. Fischer & Rose, 2001).

In contrast, theme-based programs help students link concepts by providing a scaffolding of interdisciplinary experiences. *Theme-based learning* allows students to follow their natural inclination as they construct personal thought patterns. Emotion, intuition, artistic expression, and spontaneity all have a role in theme-based learning. Students are encouraged to trust their natural learning styles. When students use information in different contexts, they achieve a deeper understanding than that produced through compartmentalized learning (Scherer, 2001).

At the Westmark School in Encino, California, the home economics program combined the joy of ethnic cooking with literature, mathematics, and social studies. Students in science class used humidifiers, music, sound effects, and wall decorations to replicate a rain forest in their classroom (Wagmeister & Shifrin, 2000). In theme-based learning, students' questions are prized as much as their answers are.

One eighth-grade class learned about the U.S. Civil War through a process of guided experience. Teachers began by identifying a core set of facts they wanted their students to learn. They engaged their students' interest by reading a story about Sarah Rosetta Wakeman, a female soldier in the Union Army. They followed the story with a short excerpt from the video *Gettysburg.* The teachers added emotional intensity by substituting an audiotape of Charlotte Church singing "Pie Jesu" for the soundtrack. Last, the teachers presented data revealing that 51,000 people died at Gettysburg, Pennsylvania.

Students asked insightful questions: "Why did they fight?" "Why did soldiers walk into gunfire?" "Were women really fighting?" The students' questions were used to group the students into research teams. By the time the unit had ended, the teachers believed that not only had the students covered all the core facts, but their level of understanding exceeded teacher expectations (G. Caine, Caine, & McClintic, 2002, p. 71).

G. Caine et al. (2002) found that the academic benefits of theme-based learning are complemented by an increase in appropriate in-school student behavior. They said,

> Discipline problems diminish when students' concerns and questions lead the learning and their intrinsic interests drive participation. And although the approach is nonlinear, our own experience over many years shows that students who have experienced the exhilaration of this kind of learning also do better on standardized tests. (p. 73)

The preceding remark is good news for teachers who fear that "high-stakes" achievement tests leave them few options except to teach to the test. Bergstrom and O'Brien (2001) reported that theme-based programming is most successful when students' interests are considered. These researchers recommended using the following questions to identify students' interests:

- What do you know a lot about?
- What kinds of people, animals, or places would you like to know more about?
- In what places in the community do you like to do things? Why?
- What kinds of materials, equipment, experiences, or tools interest you?
- What is your favorite topic or theme to pursue outside school?
- What kinds of hobbies and interests could you share with others?
- What strategies would help you implement activities based on a specific theme?
- What strengths do you bring to a theme-based program?

Entrepeneurial Projects

The Council for Children with Behavioral Disorders, a division of The Council for Exceptional Children (CEC), awarded Sylvia Rockwell the Outstanding Professional Performance Award. She taught students with emotional disorders in Pinellas County, Florida. Although she strove to develop her students' interpersonal skills, Rockwell (1997) thought something was lacking in her ability to get students to manage peer pressure that was inhibiting their learning:

> Time and time again, I have come up against student belief systems that at are odds with the goal of establishing responsible behavior patterns. Peer pressure kept one group from completing and returning homework until we as a class devised a temporary system for students to bring work to me without others knowing it had been done. The fear of looking like a "geek" or a "nerd" was just too great. In another group, being the first one to voluntarily answer an academic question during lessons was a badge of dishonor. (p. 44)

Rockwell (1997) recognized that she needed more than the traditional curriculum to motivate her students to work together. Her novel solution was to involve her students in establishing their own minibusinesses, or *entrepreneurial projects.* One class decorated T-shirts with appliqués and paint in preparation for a winter holiday sale. Other projects included class anthologies, newspapers, cards for the elderly, simple cooking activities, and crafts.

The minibusiness enterprises provided students with authentic experiences for sharpening their interpersonal skills and experiencing success in group projects. Rockwell's minibusiness approach underscored the importance of engaging students in their classroom activities in a manner that connects them to learning in a meaningful way. Rockwell (1997) suggested some other successful minibusiness ideas:

- Make books for preschool or kindergarten children.
- Make specialty food items; for example, put frozen fruit juice drinks in small paper cups and sell them to teachers and students.
- Locate a local business or organization that needs a service performed. For example, a bank needed plastic bags stuffed with pens, keys, and bank service information for customers.
- Make and sell seasonal gifts. A primary-level class decoratively arranged different-colored beans in Mason jars. They attached a poem about diversity and included a recipe.
- Search out a need for a special service and find a way to satisfy it. One class offered a word-processing service for a small fee. Another class made picnic tables for the school yard.

"Brain-Compatible" Instruction

The infusion of research on how the brain functions has created a stir among educators. Braced with the imprimatur of neurological science, many forms of *"brain-compatible" instruction* have found their way into classrooms. The early 1990s witnessed the advent of left- and right-hemisphere teaching. Students were sorted on the basis of teachers' judgments about a student's preferred mode of instruction. After a few years, this "innovation" was realized to be an oversimplification, and it faded. More recently, educators have been writing about the connections between emotions and learning and how hormones affect learning.

Sylwester (2000), one of the leading advocates of applying the principles of neural function to learning, argued that brain research supports democratic, cooperative classrooms. He contended that the historic teacher-oriented focus of limiting student input, using rewards and punishments to encourage compliant behavior, and emphasizing teacher-directed, "efficient" instructional methods is incompatible with the natural functioning of the human brain.

Many brain-compatible methods match long-standing beliefs about teaching and learning. However, the speed with which brain-compatible ideas are proselytized warrants caution. Sometimes, the desire to be on the cutting edge can outpace good sense. Ronald Brandt, past editor of the journal *Educational Leadership*, once said that the American highway of education reform is littered with the wrecks of famous bandwagons. Calling an educational method "brain-compatible instruction" sounds good, but initially all bandwagons sound good.

Jensen (2000a) has written extensively about brain research applied to educational settings. He said, "Neuroscience has much to offer our understanding of

Myth. Early childhood experiences stimulate neuron growth.
Reality. During the first 5 years of a child's development, neurons are pruned, not added.

Myth. Learning should involve low stress.
Reality. A moderate level of stress enhances learning.

Myth. Rote memorization is antagonistic to how the brain works.
Reality. Repetition is bad only when it is boring.

Myth. Most individuals use only 5 to 10% of their brain.
Reality. No scientific validation exists for this comment.

Myth. Emotions and intelligence are separate.
Reality. Emotions and intelligence originate in separate places, but their paths cross in the orbitofrontal cortex.

Myth. Learning styles and multiple intelligence are brain-based educational models.
Reality. These methods are based on psychology and social science.

Myth. An enriched environment contains posters, mobiles, music, and manipulatives.
Reality. Enrichment comes more from the process of challenge, feedback, and novelty than from equipment.

Myth. From age 4 to age 10, children learn more quickly than older children do.
Reality. All we know for sure is that between age 4 and age 10 a child's brain uses more glucose.

Myth. Brain-based reasons exist for adopting specific instructional approaches.
Reality. Neuroscience has produced no evidence for brain-based instruction.

FIGURE 7.2 Myths About Brain Function and Learning
Adapted from "Brain-Based Learning: A Reality Check," by E. Jensen, 2000, *Educational Leadership, 57*(7), pp. 76–78; and "In Search of . . . Brain-Based Education," by J. T. Bruer, 1999, *Phi Delta Kappan, 80*(9), pp. 648–657.

teaching and learning. But we must be cautious about taking research out of the laboratory and into the classroom" (p. 77). In Figure 7.2, several educational myths about the relationship between brain function and learning are enumerated.

DIRECT INSTRUCTION

In contrast to differentiated instruction, with an emphasis on adapting to the student, *direct instruction* has an emphasis on teacher control. Whereas differentiated instruction is student centered (e.g., cooperative learning), direct instruction is teacher centered (e.g., lectures). *Direct instruction* is a generic term educators use to describe teaching methods that emphasize carefully sequenced, teacher-directed lessons. Examples of standards-based direct instruction include phonological instruction, effective instruction, precision teaching, programmed learning, mastery learning, and behavior modification.

Direct instruction is usually conducted with groups of students in the following manner:

1. Prior to the lesson, the teacher clearly states the goal and objectives of the instruction.

   Example.   Each student will demonstrate, with 90% accuracy, the addition of whole numbers by adding columns of figures with pencil and paper.

2. During the lesson, the teacher demonstrates the skills to be mastered. Some teachers use predesigned or scripted lessons.

3. After the presentation of new material, the teacher guides students through practice sessions and frequently checks on the students' understanding of the material.

4. The teacher systematically evaluates student learning.

In their analysis of 228 classroom variables, Marzano and Marzano (2003) found that classroom management had the largest effect on student achievement (p. 6). Throughout their report, these researchers emphasized that students need to clearly understand what is expected of them in terms of academic performance, and teachers need to give students reliable feedback about their progress. Direct instruction is the teaching strategy that most closely approximates the key elements of teaching that Marzano and Marzano identified.

Gunter and Denny (1998) encouraged teachers of students with behavioral and emotional problems to include "effective instruction" (i.e., direct instruction) in their plans. These researchers pointed out that the academic progress of such students would improve if teachers modeled behaviors (academic and social), provided guided practice, used positive reinforcement, and modified instructional procedures to meet students' needs.

Scheuermann (1998) contended that academic programs for students with behavioral and emotional problems would be vastly improved if teachers adopted principles of direct instruction. She said, "Unfortunately, classes for students with EBD (i.e., emotional/behavioral disorders) are not widely characterized by high quality academic instruction. In fact, it appears that systematic, teacher-directed presentation of carefully planned curricular sequences is the exception, not the rule" (p. 3).

Darch (1998) applied principles of direct instruction to teaching social skills to students with behavioral difficulties. In describing their program—Instructional Classroom Management (ICM)—these researchers stated that social skills should be taught as systematically as academic skills. They said, "The basic assumption of the Instructional Classroom Management (ICM) approach that we are proposing is that teachers must first *teach* students how to behave in every circumstance for which the teacher expects appropriate behavior" (p. 16).

Some of the advantages of direct instruction are the following:

- Students understand what skills they are expected to demonstrate.
- New material is introduced to many students simultaneously.

- Teachers frequently check on students' understanding of material.
- Teachers are assured that all students have been exposed to the same information.

THE RIGHT BALANCE

Debates about the best way to teach are as common in education journals as blackboards are in classrooms. Basically, the lines of demarcation are drawn between teacher-directed instruction and student centered learning. As the years pass, each position is remade with a new name.

Currently, many advocates of teacher-directed instruction use the term *standards-based education*, and student-oriented methods morphed into *differentiated instruction*. Standards-based education highlights teacher-led instruction of skills that will be measured by achievement tests. Differentiated instruction underscores teaching techniques that enhance student engagement.

Critics of direct instruction methods claim such methods are rigid and boring. Advocates of direct instruction claim it is scientific and the best way to prepare students for standardized tests. From a motivational viewpoint, standards-based teaching emphasizes incentives—pass the test and be recognized as proficient, or in some states pass the test and be allowed to graduate.

On the other hand, differentiated instruction is aligned with developmental and social learning theories of motivation. Tests are deemed necessary, but passing tests is not the standard for excellence. Rather, teaching effectiveness is judged by students' enthusiasm and interest in their learning. Critics of differentiated instruction claim it is unfocused and lacks standards. Advocates claim it matches students' developmental needs and encourages critical thinking.

So, who is right? As most experienced teachers know, the answer is "Both" (Council for Exceptional Children, 1986). The unifying principle that brings out the best in each approach is presentation of a lesson in a way that captures students' interest and matches curriculum goals. If students lack motivation to participate, no instructional approach, no matter how elegant, will succeed. Conversely, without clearly stated outcomes, neither teacher nor students can assess the value of a lesson.

A balance of direct instruction and differentiated instruction injects novelty into classroom activities. It keeps both teachers and students on their toes. A combination of instructional approaches helps teachers determine which approach is most effective with specific students. For teachers who want to determine ways of balancing direct instruction with differentiated, Tomlinson had this advice (cited in Scherer, 2000b):

- Take notes on your students each day. Be conscious of what works and what does not.
- Assess students before you begin to teach a skill or topic.

- Look at the work your students do as an indicator of student need.
- Create at least one differentiated lesson per unit.
- Give students structured choices about how to work or which homework assignments to do.

TEACHER QUALITIES

Shellard and Protheroe (2000) identified specific teacher behaviors that are key to engaging instruction:

- Planning for instruction
- Combining instructional strategies
- Using differentiated instruction
- Having an interactive teaching style

Although matching the best teaching method to instructional goals is important, even more important is how the teacher approaches his or her task. Teachers who are organized, who give clear directions, who monitor students' progress, who provide immediate feedback, and who use effective questioning techniques enable learning (Cotton, 2000). Teachers who are vague, who do not anticipate problems, and who have difficulty individualizing instruction are less effective (Emmer, Evertson, & Anderson, 1980).

ORGANIZATION OF INSTRUCTION

Teaching is a public performance before a select audience. As in the theater, success depends on audience attention. If students are distracted, confused, or bored, the lesson will degenerate into a series of teacher prompts for attention as students look for something else to occupy their minds. An unprepared teacher will almost assuredly encounter a number of disciplinary problems. Stronge (2002) suggested using the following research-based ways of developing well-organized lessons:

- Clearly identify specific outcomes—for example, "After a 15-minute brainstorming session, students will list five causes of the Civil War."
- Plan a variety of activities to fill an instructional time slot. A 45-minute high school math class might be divided into a 15-minute teacher presentation, a 20-minute cooperative learning activity, and a 15-minute period in which each group briefly presents its findings.
- Recognize the importance of linking instruction to real life.
- Use advance organizers, graphic organizers, and outlines to alert students to key points.

- Consider students' attention spans and learning styles when planning lessons.
- Develop objectives, questions, and activities that reflect higher order cognitive skills.

HELP FOR STUDENTS WITH LEARNING PROBLEMS

Some students—especially those with special needs and those who are at risk—require assistance in learning how to learn. The scenario of a student hurrying into class late, without homework and minus pen and notebook, is all too familiar to many teachers. Laments such as "Rosie can't follow directions!" "Lucia is always forgetting assignments!" and "Jose is so disorganized!" underscore how the absence of self-management abilities can impede school performance. Following are two *mnemonic* organizational strategies for helping students overcome common learning problems (Mastropieri & Scruggs, 1998).

HOW.   HOW reminds students what a written essay should look like. Each letter cues a student to an important step.

H.   *Headings, which include name, date, subject, and page number.*
O.   *Organization reminders; for instance, starting on the front side of the paper, including a left and right margin, and leaving at least one blank line at the top and bottom of the page.*
W.   *Writing; is the paper written neatly?*

TOWER.   TOWER is an acronym for think, order, write, (look for) errors, and revise. TOWER provides a note-taking procedure and a system for drafting essay exams.

T.   *Think about the content.*
O.   *Order the topics.*
W.   *Write a rough draft.*
E.   *Look for mechanical errors.*
R.   *Revise and rewrite.*

Hammeken (2000) provided the following suggestions for teachers to use to help students organize materials and activities (cited in Henley, 2004):

- Write the daily schedule on the board.
- Color code folders for each subject.
- Provide a specific location in the classroom for daily assignments, for late assignments, and to pick up take-home materials.
- Stick to the daily classroom routine.
- Allow time for students to share their individual organizational strategies.
- Keep all student supplies in a central area.
- Break long assignments into shorter units.
- Help students create daily to-do lists.

- Enlist parent cooperation in setting a specific time for homework.
- Use plastic ziplock bags to store writing materials in students' desks.
- Alert students to a change in activities through visual and auditory cues.
- Use graphic organizers to provide a visual overview of specific topics.

Following are sample suggestions for accommodating specific student learning and behavioral problems.

Easily Distracted

Learning begins with attention. Look for aspects of the physical environment that can be distracting, such as fluorescent lights (i.e., the flickering), a seat near the door or window, other students, noise from water pipes, or even the ticking of a clock. Parcel assignments into units. Using peer tutoring, computer-assisted instruction, and hands-on activities, as well as relating tasks to students' interests, is a useful modification.

Difficulty Completing Tasks

Allow students extra time to complete assignments. Shorten assignments and praise work completed. Allow for different outcomes depending on ability level. Emphasize correct responses rather than errors. Give alternative assignments. Praise effort.

Use visual aids, give concrete examples, and provide hands-on activities. Simplify directions and make sure the student is clear about what is expected. Provide an overview of assignments and due dates. Allow students to use aids, such as calculators and computers.

Sometimes tangible rewards help, but they should be used only as a last resort. The most reinforcing reward for completed work is success. Most important, consider the nature of the task. What about the task invites or discourages participation? Good students seem to find a way to adjust to boring tasks, but problem learners do not. Nothing kills motivation more quickly than a dreary assignment. Also, check students' medications to determine whether side effects are hampering student performance.

Incomplete Homework

Communicate with the student's family and request that a specific homework time be established. Have a family member sign each homework assignment. Provide extra credit for homework completed. Use negative reinforcement; for example, homework completed Monday through Thursday is rewarded by no weekend homework. Use homework as a review, not as a method for learning new material, and coordinate with other teachers. The more time homework takes, the less likely it will be completed. Do not use homework for punishment. Provide a homework "hotline" so that students can call each other for help. If feasible, set up a homework support Web site or Listserv. Provide class time in which students may start homework.

Difficulty Following Directions

Use visual aids. Do not begin directions until all students are ready. Clarify directions by speaking slowly, simplifying vocabulary, checking for understanding, and writing directions on the board. Ask students to repeat the directions. Allow students to work together. Appoint student "teacher aides."

Disorganized

Provide students with an assignment notebook. Conduct periodic notebook checks. Provide assignment sheets. Write assignments at the same place on the blackboard. Explain why assignments are necessary. Include a rubric with specific grading criteria. Provide bonus points for good organization. Be organized yourself. Have students keep work in folders. Provide instruction in organizational skills. Encourage students to share organization tips.

Failure to Try

Learned helplessness is a term applied to students who no longer believe in their capacity to learn. Avoid too much one-on-one attention, which breeds dependency. Recognize that some students are clever about getting others to do work for them. Confidence builds through incremental success. Allow students some choice in their assignments; for example, incorporate learning centers, contracts, and personal goal setting. Use media- and computer-assisted instruction.

Adapt the number of items that a student is required to learn. For example, reduce the number of science terms a student is expected to know. Gradually increase the difficulty level of the classroom work. Emphasize effort and give more positive feedback than negative. When grading papers, use green or blue ink rather than red. Use a slash rather than an *X* for wrong answers. Mark the number of correct answers out of the total rather than subtracting the number of incorrect answers. Maintain expectations for high success (Henley, 2004).

The preceding suggestions relate directly to classroom instruction. However, teaching involves more than meeting students' academic needs. Many students come to school bereft of the social skills required for academic success.

SOCIAL SKILLS INSTRUCTION

In a U.S. census survey of 3,000 small businesses, employers were asked, "When you consider hiring a new non-supervisory or production worker, how important are the following [traits] in your decision to hire?" ("Qualities That Count," 1995,

TABLE 7.2   *Qualities That Count with Employers*

Question: "When you consider hiring a new non-supervisory or production worker, how important are the following in your decision to hire?"

Factor	Rank[a]
Attitude	4.6
Communication skills	4.2
Work experience	4.0
Recommendations from current employer	3.4
Recommendations from previous employer	3.4
Certifications in your field	3.2
Years of schooling	2.9
Scores on interview tests	2.5
Grades	2.5
Reputation of school	2.4
Teacher recommendations	2.1

Note. Data from U.S. Census Bureau.
[a]On a scale from 1 (*not important*) to 5 (*very important*).

p. A13). The results (Table 7.2) might seem surprising, particularly in view of widespread media comments about U.S. students' leaving school academically unprepared to compete in a world economy. However, consider the kind of employment positions for which a young person without a college education would be applying. Restaurant employee, salesperson, and retail worker are three possibilities. Each requires a dependable person who can work with others. As the United States moves farther from an industrial economy and closer to a service-oriented economy, social competence plays a more significant role in employment opportunities.

Social skills instruction is a proactive approach to helping students who have deficits in social competence. *Social competence* refers to an individual's ability to monitor his or her emotions and to weigh alternatives before acting. Social competence is the hallmark of civility. Patience, tolerance, and consideration typify the individual who is socially competent (Henley & Long, 1999).

In social skills instruction, lessons in self-awareness, cooperation, self-control, stress management, and conflict resolution are typically incorporated. While traditional disciplinary efforts focus on stopping school misbehavior, social skills instruction teaches skills such as cooperation and conflict resolution.

Students with deficits in social competence include but are not limited to those with chronic disciplinary problems, those who are aggressive or act out, those who are hyperactive, and those with special needs (e.g., emotional disabilities, nonverbal learning disabilities). Cox and Gunn (1980) listed three reasons students come to school lacking social competence:

1. The student does not know appropriate behaviors.
2. The student may know appropriate behaviors but may lack practice.
3. Student emotional reactions to situations may inhibit performance of desired behaviors.

To these three, one more can be added:

4. The student may have a neurological or metabolic problem (e.g., attention-deficit hyperactive disorder) that interferes with the execution of an appropriate behavior.

Social skills instruction is a different way of thinking about discipline.

A Different Way of Thinking About Discipline

Teaching social skills may seem like an additional burden, but in actuality social skills instruction is embedded in student–teacher interactions throughout the school day. Every conversation about behavior is a social skills mini-lesson. Classroom rules that encourage students to respect others and cooperate are codified social skills. Likewise, teachers who treat students with respect and dignity model social skills.

Social skills instruction is proactive and preventive. It is proactive because teachers are not simply reacting to students' behavioral problems; instead, teachers are promoting positive behaviors. Social skills instruction prevents disciplinary problems through instruction in such social skills as managing frustration, anticipating consequences, and selecting stress-reducing activities (Henley, 2003).

Social Skills Programs

Even the most talented teacher would have difficulty teaching science, math, or reading without a curriculum. Curricula provide goals and objectives, assessment tools, and teaching methods. Many published social skills curricula are available to teachers. A sound *social skills program* should be field tested, and identified social skills should match problem areas.

Schumaker, Pederson, Hazel, and Meyen (1983) posed five key questions to guide teachers in selecting a social skills curriculum:

1. Does the curriculum promote social competence?
2. Does the curriculum accommodate the students' learning characteristics?
3. Does the curriculum target social skills deficits?
4. Does the curriculum provide training for supportive routines (i.e., structure) as well as intervention skills (i.e., discipline)?
5. Does the curriculum include instructional methodologies found to be effective with the population of students for whom it is intended?

Case Study: Mrs. Anderson

Consider the case study of Mrs. Anderson. Mrs. Anderson, a third-grade teacher, was concerned about the frequent teasing she observed among her students. She believed that teasing was a precursor to more serious problems such as bullying and harassment. Mrs. Anderson realized that punishing offenders might temporarily stop the problem, but it would not teach her students alternative, positive ways of relating to one another. She needed a proactive social skills program that taught students empathy, compassion, and caring for others. After a review of publishers' catalogs and an Internet search, Mrs. Anderson selected the *Responsive Classroom* program (www.responsiveclassroom.org).

Mrs. Anderson liked this program because it addressed both structure and discipline. Structural recommendations included having morning meetings and arranging furniture to support positive student interactions. The program also provided ideas for involving parents. A recommended format for using rules and logical consequences provided Mrs. Anderson with a consistent approach to discipline that fostered responsibility and self-control. In addition, *the Responsive Classroom* program provided a range of support materials, including staff training, videos, and books on specific components of the program.

A sound social skills curriculum includes the following elements:

- A description of the research base for the program
- An assessment instrument to determine social skills strengths and weaknesses (see the self-control inventory in Appendix A)
- A practical method for teaching social skills
- A component for including family and student input
- Behavior management strategies
- A detailed description of social skills
- Sample units and lessons

Figure 7.3 provides a list of well-known social skills programs.

How to Teach Social Skills

Teaching social skills is as valuable a use of instructional time as teaching academic subjects is. Some social skills programs are structured as separate subjects. Others merge with the academic curriculum. Some accomplish both. Immersion of students in social skills throughout the day is preferable to setting aside one period a day for social skills development. Weaving lessons in social skills into academic lessons promotes generalization. Figure 7.4 provides an example of how social skills can be merged with the academic curriculum.

Adolescent Curriculum for Communication and Effective Social Skills (ACCESS)
Walker, H. M., Todis, B., Holmes, D., & Horton, G. (1988). *The Walker social skills curriculum: The ACCESS program.* Austin, TX: PRO-ED.

Aggressive Behavior Management
Rockwell, S. (1995). *Back off, cool down, try again: Teaching students how to control aggressive behavior.* Arlington, VA: Council for Exceptional Children.

Anger Management
Eggert, L. L. (1994). *Anger management for youth: Stemming aggression and violence.* Champaign, IL: Research Press.

Developmental Therapy–Developmental Teaching
Wood, M. M. (1996). *Developmental therapy–developmental teaching: Fostering social-emotional competence in troubled children and youth* (3rd ed.). Austin, TX: PRO-ED.

EQUIP Program
Gibbs, J., Potter, G., & Goldstein, A. P. (1995). *The EQUIP Program: Teaching youth to think and act responsibly through a peer-helping approach.* Champaign, IL: Research Press.

Improving Social Competence
Campbell, P., & Siperstein, G. (1994). *Improving social competence: A resource for elementary school teachers.* Boston: Allyn & Bacon.

Prosocial Skills Development
McGinnis, E., & Goldstein, A. P. (1997). *Skillstreaming the elementary school child: New strategies and perspectives for teaching prosocial skills* (Rev. ed.). Champaign, IL: Research Press.

Reconnecting Youth (RY) Prevention Research Program
Eggert, L., & Nicholas, L. (n.d.). *Reconnecting Youth: A peer group approach to building life skills* (2nd ed.). Bloomington, IN: National Educational Service.

Resolving Conflict Creatively Program (RCCP)
Lantieri, L., & Patti, J. (1996). *Waging peace in our schools.* Boston: Beacon Press.

Second Step: A Violence Prevention Curriculum
Committee for Children. (1992). *Second Step: A violence prevention curriculum.* Seattle, WA: Author.

Self-Control
Henley, M. (2003). *Teaching self-control: A curriculum for responsible behavior* (2nd ed.). Bloomington, IN: National Educational Service.

Social Skills Intervention for Young African-American Males
Taylor, G. R. (1997). *Curriculum strategies: Social skills intervention for young African-American males.* Westport, CT: Praeger.

Teaching Children to Care
Charney, R. S. (2002). *Teaching children to care: Management in the responsive classroom* (Rev. ed.). Greenfield, MA: Northeast Foundation for Children.

Tribes
Gibbs, J. (1995). *Tribes: A new way of learning and being together.* Sausalito, CA: CenterSource.

FIGURE 7.3   Social Skills Programs

Social Skill: To help others.

Mathematics: Begin a math peer or cross-age tutoring program. Start with once-a-week tutoring sessions. Provide tips on how to tutor. After each tutoring session, solicit feedback from students. Use feedback to make program adjustments. On a more informal level, allow students who are finished with math assignments to wander around the classroom to help others.

Social Studies: Do a community survey of social programs. Take a class trip to a homeless shelter, soup kitchen, or nursing home. Invite a representative of a community social program to speak to the class. Select a social program for the class to support. Do bulletin boards, a fund drive, a car wash, and other activities to highlight and promote community service.

Language Arts: Read "Helping" from *Where the Sidewalk Ends,* by Shel Silverstein (1974). Ask students to brainstorm behaviors that help one another and behaviors that do not help. Have each student commit to one helping behavior (pp. 112–113) for a week and keep a daily journal of the experience.

Social Skill: To describe consequences.

Language Arts: For primary students, read *Enid Blyton's The Night the Toys Had a Party,* by Enid Blyton (1989). Discuss the consequences of Ben's behavior. Elementary students should read *Just a Dream,* by Chris Van Allsburg (1990). Discuss the consequences of pollution. For secondary students, read an article from a local newspaper and discuss how behavior and consequences contributed to the incident.

Social Studies: Organize students into cooperative learning groups. Have each group brainstorm consequences for the following scenarios:

- The British win the Revolutionary War.
- The South wins the Civil War.
- The United States does not drop the atomic bomb on Hiroshima and Nagasaki.
- The ozone layer continues to deplete.
- Schools decide to stop using grades to evaluate students' work.
- A live Tyrannosaurus Rex is discovered in Zaire.
- Radio astronomers pick up signals indicating intelligent life in a distant galaxy.
- A state law is passed that prohibits parents from punishing their children.

Science: Conduct various demonstrations and ask students to predict the effect—for example, simultaneously drop different-sized objects, place a glass over a burning candle, put objects made of different materials in a tub of water, or mix food colors.

FIGURE 7.4 Sample Lessons: Social Skills Lessons Across the Curriculum
Adapted from *Teaching Self-Control: A Curriculum for Responsible Behavior* (2nd ed., pp. 150–151), by M. Henley, 2003, Bloomington, IN: National Educational Service. Copyright 2003 by National Educational Service. Adapted with permission.

Teachers use a variety of instructional approaches to teach social skills. Chief among these are the following:

- **Discussion.**   The teacher poses a problematic situation to the class, and members brainstorm solutions or alternative behaviors.
- **Modeling.**   The teacher role-plays a problematic situation. The group observes. Individuals then practice various positive ways of interacting.
- **Rehearsal.**   A step-by-step plan provides students with a "script" for positive behavior. Students are provided with a mnemonic or an acronym as a behavioral guide, such as STAR (stop, think, act, review consequences).
- **Feedback.**   Role-plays or videos provide prompts and students recommend appropriate responses.
- **Cooperative learning.**   Productive group work requires students to demonstrate a variety of prosocial skills. Teachers rehearse specific skills with students first, then students provide one another with feedback about performance following a cooperative group activity.
- **Peer and cross-age tutoring.**   Helping other students helps a tutor learn and practice social skills. Tutoring sessions must be monitored so that tutors can discuss interpersonal issues and receive feedback on their performance.
- **Bibliotherapy.**   Children's and young adult literature is used as a springboard for discussing how events, emotions, and relationships affect outcomes.
- **Service learning.**   Students help needy residents or agencies that provide services within the community.
- **Class meetings.**   Daily, students share their perceptions about social issues that affect them. Students are encouraged to verbalize feelings, listen, and offer solutions.
- **Academics.**   Teachers use the academic curriculum as a backdrop for discussing social issues and social outcomes. Literature, history, social studies, and the arts in particular offer diverse opportunities for social skills instruction.
- **Applied reinforcement.**   Students are provided with incentives when they exhibit specific social skills. These reinforcers are usually positive (i.e., a pleasant consequence following a behavior) or negative (i.e., following a behavior, an aversive is eliminated).
- **Natural reinforcement.**   Teachers arrange naturally occurring positive reinforcement. For example, students take part in extracurricular activities, such as drama and sports, that build social skills.
- **Behavior contracts.**   Students agree in writing to practice specific social skills.
- **Self-monitoring.**   Students systematically observe and record aspects of their behavior.
- **Journal writing.**   Students describe events and their feelings.
- **Cognitive behavior modification.**   Students are taught to examine their thinking processes in relationship to their behavior. Self-defeating thoughts are examined in terms of real outcomes, and students are taught to reflect on their feelings before taking action.

As this list indicates, each school day presents many opportunities to foster positive social skills development.

Teachers are most effective at teaching social skills when they demonstrate through their interactions the same respect, compassion, and emotional intelligence they seek to develop in their students. Social skills instruction transforms the notion of discipline from a reactive, "What must I do to control my students?" attitude into a proactive, "What skills do my students need in order to exercise self-control?" perspective.

CHARACTER EDUCATION

Concerns about the moral state of youths have found voice in renewed efforts to incorporate values into the curriculum. The *character education* movement is based on the premise that the ethical development of youths has deteriorated. Brogan and Brogan (1999) defined character education as the teaching of virtue. They maintained that helping students learn to be courageous and willing to take risks for their beliefs is as integral a part of the mission of schools as the teaching of mathematics and science is. "One can be taught to be a good mathematician," Brogan and Brogan said, "but to be a good person is not just to act properly or to know what to do. It has to do with the interior life of the person and cannot be just a matter of training" (p. 349). Within this view of character

 ## Case Study: Cheating

A 1998 survey of 356 high school teachers revealed that 9 of 10 teachers believe cheating is a serious problem (Bushweller, 1999). Half the surveyed teachers reported that students routinely cheat in their classes. Broader concerns about ethics among youths were addressed more recently in the *2004 Report Card on the Ethics of American Youth* (Josephson Institute of Ethics, 2004). Among the highlights of this nationwide survey of 25,000 high school students were findings that, during the past 12 months, 82% of the youths lied to their parents, 27% stole something from a store, and 62% cheated on an exam.

The negative picture of the ethical status of today's youths needs some perspective, however. For instance, cheating has more to do with the situation than the student's moral fiber (Woolfolk, 1990). Students who would not consider lying or stealing might cheat if either the pressure to succeed was great or the chances of being caught were minimal. Schab (1980) asked 1,100 high school students why cheating was common. Three primary reasons were that they were too lazy to study, afraid of failure, and under parental pressure. Within the past several years, standardized testing of high school students has increased the pressure on students to perform well on achievement tests. When high-stakes results such as college admission, the reputation of an individual school, and high school graduation rest on a test score, the instinct to survive can supercede ethical concerns.

education, the teacher is the moral model (Hayden, 1997; Leming, 1993). Character is drawn out by ennobling the goals of education to supercede mundane goals such as test scores and to elevate education to a higher plane where learning is a virtue in itself. The learning environment enhances character by presenting students with opportunities to celebrate diversity, community, and civility.

Lickona (1991), a leading proponent of character education, argued that youths lack strong personal character. His view of character education is embodied in three principles: moral knowing (i.e., awareness, reasoning, decision making), moral action (i.e., competence, will, habit), and moral feeling (i.e., conscience, empathy, self-control). Within the ethical person, each moral principle informs and interacts with the others. Advocates of character education believe that academics should be supplemented with regular teaching of such values as respect, honesty, and empathy in the classroom (Hayden, 1997; Leming, 1993). Consider the case study Cheating.

Youths have instant access to both the best and the worst aspects of what society has to offer. The Internet catapults children into the world of adulthood with a flip of the switch on the family computer. Cable television offerings range from smut to sublime. Movies, video games, and music extol the virtue of violence. With so many accessible distractions and temptations, young people can easily lose track of more significant human values. Classroom management strategies based on moral virtues such as honesty, mutual respect, and empathy help provide students with concrete illustrations of ethics in action.

Summary

★ Engaging lessons, which enhance student participation, are the most effective means of preventing misbehavior.

★ Active participation enhances motivation.

★ A variety of differentiated instruction strategies effectively engage learners. These strategies include, but are not limited to, community-based learning, cooperative learning, peer tutoring, theme-based learning, and entrepreneurial projects.

★ Even within the best organized classroom, teachers encounter problem learners. Sometimes students have attentional difficulties; other times students have problems staying organized and completing assignments.

★ Specific classroom accommodations can help problem learners stay focused and complete assignments.

★ Social skills programs boost social competence and prepare students for employment in service-oriented workplaces.

★ Concern about the ethical standards of youths has generated a variety of character education programs.

★ Social skills programs focus on skills to improve interpersonal relationships; character education fosters specific values such as honesty and trustworthiness.

What You Should Know

Now that you have finished reading this chapter, you should know the following:

The purpose of the No Child Left Behind Act
The meaning of *engaged learning*
Some techniques for eliminating boredom from lessons
The characteristics of differentiated learning
How to organize a cooperative learning group
How to implement peer tutoring
The key elements of direct instruction
How direct instruction and differentiated learning differ
How to design a lesson by using theme-based learning and entrepreneurial
    projects
Myths and facts about "brain-compatible" instruction
Ways to organize lessons to minimize disruptive behavior
Some specific ways to modify lessons for students with attention problems
    and other learning difficulties
How to organize a social skills curriculum
The purpose of character education

Applying the Concepts

1. Select a specific social skills curriculum and critique it in terms of the
   following criteria:
   - Does it have a clearly explained research base?
   - How are students' social skills assessed?
   - Does the model presented for teaching social skills incorporate effective
     teaching principles?
   - How does the curriculum fit into a typical school day?
   - Are proactive behavior management strategies described?
   - Would you use the curriculum?

2. Design a cooperative learning activity for students in your college class. Contrast your ideas and select a few for implementation. Critique the results.

3. Survey teachers about how often they use the following instructional methods: direct instruction, differentiated learning, learning strategies, and social skills instruction. Do a pie chart of a typical school day presented by a
   teacher. Divide the day into percentages of time dedicated to these or alternative teaching methods. Discuss your findings.

4. Interview an elementary or a secondary student about boredom. Ask questions such as the following: Are you often bored? What causes you to be

bored? What do you do when you are bored? How much of your school day are you bored? What suggestions do you have for boring teachers?

5. Review the literature on teaching social skills and character education. How are these approaches similar? How do they differ? Interview a teacher about each. Do teachers value teaching social skills or character education? Interview a parent about social skills and character education.

6. At a field site, observe a teacher who uses cooperative learning. How does the teacher's interpretation differ from the description in your text? Ask students how they feel about cooperative learning. Make a list of 10 do's and don'ts for implementing cooperative learning.

7. Select one of the instructional approaches described in this chapter. Compile a 10-article annotated bibliography on your topic.

8. Have a classroom debate on the following topic: Resolved: Direct instruction is superior to differentiated instruction for standardized test performance. Debate the pros and cons of each. At the end of the debate, have a classwide conversation about each position.

9. Interview a classroom teacher about how the No Child Left Behind Act has influenced his or her teaching. Discuss your findings with your classmates.

10. At a field site, observe the effect of different teaching approaches on student behavior. Do students misbehave more at specific times during the day? What is the connection between "good" teaching and students' classroom behavior?

Part III

Positive Behavioral Supports

We ought to regard the breaking of a child's spirit as a sin against humanity.

Erik Erikson

When a man sulks, he becomes passive to his own hurts.

Robert Bly

If we maximize communication, we can minimize coercion.

Edgar Dale

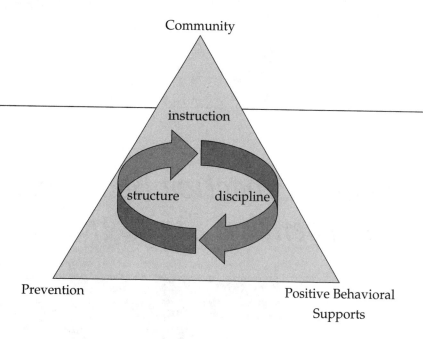

Community

instruction

structure   discipline

Prevention   Positive Behavioral
                                      Supports

Correcting student misbehavior requires a gentle and respectful touch: Be too harsh, and the student will resist. Humiliate, and the student will become resentful. Make a commitment to work together, and the student will respond. Changing student behavior requires time and commitment from both teacher and student.

Various methods are available for making students comply, but the results are superficial. Punishment can stop a misbehavior, but it does not teach new behaviors. Proactive behavioral supports are derived from an analysis of student behaviors and the classroom dynamics that influence these behaviors. When teachers analyze events that trigger problem behaviors, they can adjust classroom variables to promote constructive behavior. Likewise, by reflecting on how they react to student misbehavior, teachers can eliminate responses that escalate misbehavior.

Rather than addressing deficits in student behavior, proactive behavioral supports promote the idea of looking for strengths. Building on individual capacity is the surest path to achieving positive change.

Chapter 8

Using Proactive Behavioral Intervention Strategies

Chapter Outline

 Key Terms

Target behavior

Threats

Time-out

Token economy

Token reinforcers

Tokens

Introduction

Proactive behavioral interventions are methods for positively managing disruptive behavior. No single behavioral intervention will work in every situation. Proactive teachers assess classroom disciplinary issues, and they choose the behavioral intervention that best fits the need. The more behavioral interventions a teacher has to choose from, the more effective he or she will be in dealing with disciplinary problems. Having a sense of humor, accepting and acknowledging feelings, delivering sane messages, and administering logical consequences are examples of verbal interventions that help defuse tension while redirecting students into more-constructive behaviors.

Behavior modification techniques that are used effectively in schools are modeling, positive reinforcement, negative reinforcement, and differential reinforcement. Additional promising practices include life space crisis intervention, bibliotherapy, and cognitive strategies. This chapter also covers the importance of using alternatives to such commonly used behavioral interventions as punishment, threats, time-out, and point and level systems.

Even in the best managed classroom, the teacher sometimes must intervene to correct student misbehavior. The term *behavioral interventions* refers to a cluster of specific techniques for correcting misbehavior in the classroom. When and how the teacher chooses to intervene with a student are key considerations.

Corrections that are direct and respectful are more likely to elicit student cooperation than are corrections that are abrupt and caustic. A correction given in anger can cause a minor misbehavior problem to escalate into a more serious problem. A correction that embarrasses or shames can make a student resentful and damage the student–teacher relationship. A proactive teacher selects interventions that support constructive student behavior and avoids interventions that elicit resentment.

THE PROPER TOOL

Proactive behavioral interventions redirect student behavior with a minimum of disruption to ongoing classroom activities. No single behavioral intervention will fit every situation. Likewise, a behavioral intervention that works one day with a student might have a different effect the next day. Teachers who have a wide range of behavioral interventions at their disposal are more successful than are teachers with a limited repertoire.

Suppose a car is not running properly. Some days it starts up; other days the owner turns the key and nothing happens. The owner has the recalcitrant vehicle towed to a local garage where Bob, the mechanic, opens the hood. From his toolbox, Bob takes out a hammer and bangs on the battery. The shocked car owner looks in the toolbox and sees no screwdrivers, pliers, sockets, or wrenches—only hammers. "Don't worry," Bob tells the owner. "This usually works. If your car does not start, you need a new battery."

A lack of tools limits the mechanic's ability to fix the problem. The battery cannot be removed because he has no wrench. He has no jumper cables to recharge the battery. The mechanic cannot determine the strength of the battery cells because he has no battery-cell tester. The old adage "If all you have is a hammer, you will treat every problem like it is a nail" fits the mechanic's problem and the problems of some teachers as well.

A teacher who handles every behavioral problem with verbal intimidation (i.e., "My way or the highway" attitude) might have limited success, just as a mechanic might get a car started by banging on the battery with a hammer. However, eventually the teacher will encounter a student for whom or a situation in which intimidation does not work. What will happen then?

Unlike the battery, the student will not just sit there waiting to be banged on one more time with a forceful rebuke such as "Sit down and do your work—or else." Such a scenario might unfold in one of myriad ways. The student might talk back to the teacher, or throw a book on the floor, or walk out of the room. In any of these cases, the situation goes from bad to worse because of the teacher's limitations. And, just as the nonresourceful mechanic said the car needed a new battery because banging on it did not work, the nonresourceful teacher will blame the student.

Flexibility

Proactive correction of misbehavior requires flexibility. The more ideas a teacher has for intervening to correct misbehavior, the better suited the teacher will be to manage the problem. Students are more complicated than cars. Sometimes they need a firm hand, other times they need tolerance, and still other times they simply need to know that the teacher cares. Most important, misbehavior must be handled with respect.

Teachers disrespect students by yelling, shaming, or embarrassing them. Such negative tactics might temporarily stop an offending behavior, but with time, the student will become hardened and the teacher will grow more callous. Under such conditions, the student–teacher relationship will deteriorate and all thought of teaching students to be responsible for their behavior will give way to a constant need to enforce compliance.

DISCIPLINE WITH DIGNITY

Curwin and Mendler (1988a) used the term *discipline with dignity* to highlight respectful correction of misbehavior. Constructive student behavior should be nurtured within an ambience of reciprocity. Students learn to respect others when they are treated with respect. The notion of mutual respect is one with which few teachers would disagree. However, dealing with student misbehavior can be stressful, and during times of stress, teachers sometimes have difficulty keeping lofty ideals in mind.

Curwin and Mendler (1988a) offered the following principles as an operational guide to handling student misbehavior with respect:

- **Remember that dealing with students' misbehavior is part of the job.** Inattention, noncompliance, and goofing off are facts of life in school. Recognize that part of teaching is helping students adapt to classroom routines.
- **Treat students with respect.**   Students who grow up in tough neighborhoods know that allowing yourself to be "dissed" (i.e., disrespected) can be dangerous—even fatal. All students have a need to be treated with respect. Lack of respect breeds animosity, which in turn leads to more disciplinary problems.
- **Rather than focusing entirely on retribution for misdeeds, give students the opportunity to consider why they misbehaved and what a suitable consequence might be.**   Learning to understand about behavior is no less preparation for life than learning the causes of the French Revolution or calculating the area of a rectangle.
- **Misbehavior is feedback.**   Sylwester (2000) said that misbehavior in the classroom is like pain in the body—a signal that something is wrong. Perhaps the student has a medical problem, or maybe a serious family problem is influencing a student's behavior. Recognizing the relationship between causes and misbehavior helps the teacher to assess classroom situations that might be contributing agents.
- **Follow the 80–15–5 principle.**   Situations will vary, but in general, 80% of all students rarely engage in misbehavior, 15% of the students occasionally break rules, and 5% are chronic rule breakers. Avoid overbearing disciplinary systems that stifle the ability of the 80% in an attempt to control the 5 percent.

MISBEHAVIOR

The purpose of proactive behavioral interventions is to decrease misbehavior while increasing constructive behavior. Strategies that work best are those that help students learn more about themselves. When responding to a student's misbehavior, the teacher should consider these two questions: How can I redirect

Case Study: John

John does not like his 10th-grade math class. He is failing and believes that there is simply no use in trying anymore. He has started fooling around in class. He talks loudly, teases other students, and generally makes a nuisance of himself. After threatening John a few times, Mr. Langevin sent him to the principal's office. The principal sent John to in-house suspension.

This routine has happened so often that John spends more time out of math class than in math class, which is fine with him. Inadvertently, Mr. Langevin is reinforcing John's misbehavior because math class is more unpleasant to John than in-house suspension is.

If queried, Mr. Langevin would undoubtedly rather have John doing math than sitting in the principal's office. However, Mr. Langevin's response to John is limited—he removes John from class. Teachers with limited behavioral intervention skills usually end up relying mainly on threats and punishment. Such reliance creates an unpleasant classroom experience for everyone—the teacher, the misbehaving student, and the student's classmates. The limits of threats and punishment are explained in more detail subsequently.

this student in a positive fashion? What social skills does this student need to learn?

Problematic behavior in the classroom takes many forms. Sometimes, the student's behavior is passive, such as when he or she sits in a seat quietly and daydreams. Other times, the behavior is acting out—for example, a student who teases another student during a lesson. Acting-out behavior is more public and thus more likely to disrupt the entire class. Because a teacher is attending to 20 or more students at a time, the acting-out behavior gets primary attention. In dealing with misbehavior, whether it is acting out or passive, the teacher must consider how to respond in a way that does not contribute to recurrence of the behavior. Consider the case study of John.

INTERVENTION TIMING

Deciding *when* to intervene is as important a consideration as deciding *how* to intervene. A teacher who immediately acts to solve all misbehavior may be doing the students a disservice. Why? First, doing so limits learning opportunities. For instance, Piaget and Inhelder (1958) pointed out that arguing helps young children learn to look at a situation from another person's viewpoint. Second, some disruptive behavior is developmentally appropriate.

Striking a balance between correcting and tolerating certain behaviors requires experience and a knowledge of how human development influences behavior. A teacher who overreacts each time he or she encounters a boisterous teenager is misplaced in a middle school.

Scenes in the film *The Breakfast Club* humorously depict a teacher wasting time in a futile attempt to impress a group of adolescents with toughness. A group of students are spending Saturday in the school library for detention. The teacher is hell-bent on displaying his tough, no-nonsense approach. "Don't mess with the bull or you will regret it" is his challenge. As you might expect, rather than being cowed by the "bull," the students take on the task of making his Saturday afternoon miserable.

Some behaviors are best ignored. A teacher will rarely have the attention of every student every moment of the school day. Students who are whispering, looking out the window, or engaged in some other type of innocuous behavior do not need to be corrected in each instance.

Still other behaviors may need to be tolerated because a student is grappling with a medical or neurological condition. A student with attention-deficit/hyperactivity disorder (ADHD) will be restless and need to move around. Expecting a student with ADHD to sit still all day is as unreasonable as expecting a student with asthma to not cough.

Long and Newman (1996) offered the following six guidelines for deciding when to intervene to correct misbehavior:

1. **Reality dangers.**   Rough games, fighting, careless behaviors on a field trip, or any other actions that might cause students to hurt themselves or others must be diverted or stopped.
2. **Psychological protection.**   Bullying or teasing others should not be allowed. An inner-city teacher who taught in one of the toughest sections of New York City had only two rules for his fourth graders. Rule one: You can eat food in the classroom if you clean up (many of his students came to school hungry, but he could not stand the smell of stale peanut butter sandwiches). Rule two: No name-calling. When queried about the second rule, he recounted how classmates teased him about being fat in elementary school. He remembered how much their comments had hurt him, and he did not want any of his pupils to endure similar taunts.
3. **Protection against too much excitement.**   Substitute teachers are familiar with how overstimulation can spread within a classroom. Redl and Wineman (1951) coined the term *group psychological intoxication* to describe the phenomenon of contagious excitement (p. 106). An entire class can spin out of control if the ripple effect of group excitement goes unabated.
4. **Protection of property.**   Students cannot be allowed to deface or destroy school property or the property of others.
5. **Protection of an ongoing program.**   One student cannot be allowed to disrupt the learning of others.
6. **Enforcement of school policy or values.**   Typical rules such as "No running in the halls" or "Passes are required for movement outside the classroom" must be equally enforced by all staff.

Once a decision is made to correct a misbehavior, the next consideration is *how* to intervene in a way that will help reduce further disciplinary problems. The purpose of proactive behavioral supports is to teach new, constructive behaviors.

COMMUNICATION ABOUT BEHAVIOR

Classrooms are verbal environments. Therefore, the ability of teachers to communicate clearly and effectively when they are talking with students about their behavior will have a significant effect on the result. An overzealous response could provoke a power struggle as teacher and student verbally spar for control of the situation. An angry response could increase the stress between teacher and student, and the situation might worsen. Corrections must minimize the disruption of an ongoing lesson and demonstrate that the teacher is in control of the situation.

When talking with students about their behavior, teachers should adhere to the following guidelines:

- **Be concrete and specific.**   Describe, do not label, the offending behavior.
- **Avoid judgmental terms such as** *lazy, immature,* **and** *obnoxious.*   Judgmental terms label a youngster and add nothing to the youngster's understanding of his or her behavior.
- **Speak to students directly and emphasize what is happening in the present (i.e., the here and now of the situation).**   Such general statements as "You are always pushing in line" or "You never do what I tell you to do" will put a youngster on the defensive. Instead of getting the message "Stop pushing in line" or following a direction, the student will focus on the demeaning noun *always* or *never.*
- **Speak calmly.**   A calm tone implies control of a situation. Yelling at students is the sign that the teacher is out of control. Teachers who often yell may get students' attention at first, but with time, the students will become conditioned to the harsh volume and will pay less attention.

Following are specific methods for talking with students about their behavior.

Direct Appeal

The best solution to a problem is usually the simplest. This principle of scientific investigation is called *Occam's razor.* For instance, if Althea keeps dropping her pencil during a lesson, the teacher should ask her to stop. If Vincent is upset and he seems ready to bolt from the classroom, the teacher should remind him about school policy on students' wandering the halls. Jason is whispering and distracting Ms. Loop as she addresses her physical education class. Ms. Loop can say, "Jason, please stop whispering" or "Jason, if you keep interrupting me, you are going to sit on the bleacher for the rest of the class." The first option is best because the second option, a threat, may generate resentment and must be acted on for the teacher to maintain credibility. Teachers should assume that students are reasonable individuals who in most cases will comply with respectful requests, or *direct appeals,* to stop an unwanted behavior.

Sane Messages

When a teacher speaks to a student about his or her behavior, how closely the student listens will depend as much on *how* the teacher speaks to the student as on *what* the teacher says. When teachers use sarcasm or belittle students, the misbehavior might subside temporarily because the student is embarrassed. However, the student will resent the teacher, and further misbehavior is likely.

Ginott (1971) called negative statements that humiliate students *insane messages*. He advocated description over criticism. According to Ginott, the teacher should address the situation, not attack the student's character. Statements such as "Stop being lazy" or "I'm tired of your big mouth" might get a student's attention, but at the expense of an insult.

A *sane message* is given without anger. It describes the behavior that is disturbing, it explains why the behavior is disturbing, and it provides the student with an alternative behavior. "Felicia, your talking with Ramón is distracting me; would you please open your book to p. 56 and finish the last two work problems?" is a sane message. "Susan, cut out your jabbering and get back to work" is an insane message.

Sane messages are longer and require patience. However, as with most effective behavioral interventions, the payoff is a decrease in misbehavior with time. Sane messages are also a teaching tool. In addition to explaining what a teacher expects, they provide students with a model of how to express their feelings appropriately.

I Messages

Frustration, disappointment, and fatigue can easily creep into a teacher's response to disruptive events. Such statements as "You are disappointing me" or "You are my main frustration" make the student responsible for the teacher's feelings. These statements are counterproductive because they place blame on students for something outside their control.

At a minimum, such statements embarrass the student; at worst, they infer guilt, which can lead to more-serious student–teacher problems later. Although a student might be the source of a negative feeling such as frustration, the student did not cause the specific feeling.

Consider the paradox of a male student's telling his teacher that she is to blame for his kicking a wastebasket because she made him angry. The teacher would not accept responsibility for the student's feelings or negative actions. In fact, the opposite is true: The teacher would want the student to take responsibility for his feelings and actions.

I messages model the emotionally mature practice of taking responsibility for your own feelings (Ginott, 1971; T. Gordon, 1974). *I* messages demonstrate that teachers are human and experience the same range of emotions as students do. Such messages are nonjudgmental. They describe the how and why of a teacher's feelings. Some examples are as follows: "Luis, I am annoyed by your bickering with Joe" rather than "Luis, you and Joe are ruining my day," and "Shawna, I feel frustrated when you fail to give your best effort" rather than "Shawna, you frustrate me."

An *I* message describes a specific behavior at a particular time and place. This approach keeps the offending behavior in perspective and reduces the need for a student to respond defensively. In contrast, lecturing, preaching, and criticizing student behavior will rarely yield the desired results. When students feel threatened, they put their emotional resources into defending themselves rather than listening to the teacher's message.

Humor

Misbehavior creates tension. *Humor* provides a way to break tension and refocus a student's attention on classroom activities. It helps both teachers and students shift from being in a tense state to relaxing. In fact, Redl and Wineman (1951) used the term *decontamination through humor* to describe the power of humor as a behavioral intervention.

A 1991 survey of high school teachers revealed that they used humor as a way of putting students at ease, as an attention getter, and as a way to show students that their teacher is human (Allen, 2001). Other advantages of using humor as a behavioral intervention tool are as follows (Carlson & Peterson, 1995):

- **Humor permits participants to "save face."**   It provides an exit from a situation that might escalate into a more difficult scenario. Humor offers a way of backing down without the appearance of being defeated.
- **Humor is engaging.**   Humor brings people together. It helps build relationships by providing common experiences of fun and spontaneity.
- **Humor redirects feelings and behavior.**   Humor changes a mood. It can replace tension with an instant feeling of camaraderie. A jovial remark to a student who has just refused a teacher's request eliminates the strain of what will happen next and makes resolving the situation easier for teacher and student.
- **Humor projects confidence.**   A teacher's use of humor demonstrates a strong sense of self. Using humor indicates that the teacher feels secure in his or her position.

Consider the positive use of humor in the case study of Miguel.

Humor is disadvantageous only when it includes sarcasm, "inside jokes" (i.e., jokes that only a few students understand), ethnic jokes, and ridicule. Such humor may be easy to use, but it is inappropriate. It can be devastating to the subject of the jokes, and using it does not set a good example for students.

The best type of humor is self-deprecating. As mentioned previously, when teachers point out their mistakes, they show their humanity and reveal themselves to be secure individuals. When teachers use humor, they should also tailor it to the students' age. Younger students enjoy silly humor, whereas older students like

Case Study: Miguel

A substitute teacher was assigned to a fourth-grade classroom for the day. Because he was a permanent sub for the school, he was aware that most of the youngsters were well behaved. Miguel was another story. Throughout the school, he had a reputation of being difficult to manage. He was easily riled, and his temper tantrums were legendary. The substitute had barely settled into the daily routine when a student asked for the pass to go to the bathroom. The sub rummaged through the teacher's desk, but no pass was to be found.

The missing pass caused quite a stir among the students, who began springing around the room searching for the pass. Feeling that he was losing control of the class, the sub turned his attention to Miguel, who was feverishly leading the search. "Miguel, will you come here for a moment?" the sub asked. When Miguel arrived at the desk, the sub asked him to hold out his hand. When Miguel complied, the sub took a red washable magic marker and wrote "Pass" on Miguel's palm. "You are the official pass for the day," the sub announced.

Miguel grinned, and the rest of the class laughed. For the rest of the day, Miguel escorted students back and forth from class to the bathroom and the drinking fountain. A potential crisis was averted, and Miguel exercised his responsibility with decorum.

spontaneous humor. Some suggestions for blending humor into the regular classroom routine follow (Allen, 2001; Appelstein, 1998):

- Keep a humor file of items related to specific subjects or education in general.
- Remember funny stories and student comments, and relate them at appropriate times.
- Tell students funny anecdotes from your personal life.
- Use buttons, toys, and other props to get students' attention.
- Set up a humor bulletin board and invite students to add jokes and cartoons.
- Do not be afraid to take a few minutes from the regular routine to enjoy a spontaneous laugh with students.
- Look for ways to incorporate humor into the curriculum. For example, assign a humorous topic for a paper or read whimsical poetry. Another suggestion is to research the effects of humor on modern society or how humor played a role in history.

Listening

Communication is a two-way street. What a teacher has to say about behavior is important, but what a student has to say is equally important. When a student misbehaves, the natural tendency is to point out the offending behavior. This response often segues into a "lecture" about what the student did wrong. A more insightful approach is to describe the offending behavior and ask the student to explain why it occurred. Sometimes teachers back off from listening because they believe the student will simply run down a list of excuses. If a student fears punishment, excuses become a student's only defense, but if the student believes the teacher truly cares about his or her point of view, the student will be more likely to present honest information (Morse, 1996a).

Benefits of listening to student include the following:

- **Listening builds trust.** Listening is the cornerstone of many therapy and counseling practices. It demonstrates respect for an individual's point of view and encourages honest dialogue.
- **Teachers who listen to students model an important social skill.** Some disruptive student behaviors are based on the student's inability to listen or care about others' perspectives.
- **Listening is a form of data collection.** Perspective guides behavior (Blumer, 1969). If Cody thinks his peers are teasing him, he will react whether his perception is accurate or not. Listening helps a teacher better understand how a student interprets his or her actions and those of other students.
- **Listening promotes due process.** When students have an opportunity to present their side of a situation, democratic principles are reinforced.

Acceptance and Acknowledgment of Feelings

Imagine the inscription "Expression of Pleasant Feelings Only" posted above a classroom door. This idea is silly because young people experience a range of emotions. However, in school, students sometimes get the message that only pleasant feelings, such as happiness and joy are acceptable, while other feelings, such as anger, resentment, and disappointment, are off-limits.

Students are not told directly to keep unpleasant feelings to themselves, but the adult reaction to the expression of unpleasant feelings makes the point. As a result, some youngsters will act out, rather than verbalize, their feelings. Such acting out creates problems. For example, any of the following reactions can land a student in trouble: Amy refuses to complete a worksheet because she is frustrated; John ignores a teacher directive because he is worried about what other students are thinking about him; Rosita walks out of the classroom because she is angry.

Goleman (1995) called such acting out *emotional hijacking.* The word *emotion* is derived from the French word *emouvoir,* which means "to stir up." Some youngsters are literally at the mercy of their stirred-up feelings. They are emotionally illiterate. They do not understand how their emotions influence their behavior, and they do not see the connections between how they are feeling and how they are acting. Ignorance of the role their feelings play in their behavior handicaps their ability to manage their behavior.

Feeling words describe emotions. When a youngster is unfamiliar with the word *frustration,* he or she has no reference point for understanding how he or she is feeling. The lack of an emotional vocabulary hinders the youngster's ability to deal with the feeling constructively. Knitzer, Steinberg, and Fleisch (1990) referred to students who lack the ability to articulate their feelings as "mad, bad, sad, and can't add" (p. 9). These researchers were referring to the tendency of youngsters with deficient emotional vocabularies to use generalizations to express their feelings inaccurately.

Students need to learn that feelings are neither good nor bad; they simply exist. Young people need to understand that feelings are an internal barometer of what is going on in an individual's life. Acknowledging and *accepting students' feelings* as legitimate helps students understand the role their feelings play in their behavior.

However, accepting that a student is angry does not mean accepting angry behavior. The distinction between feelings and behavior is worth pointing out to students regularly. The comment "I can see that you are angry, but throwing your books on the floor in not acceptable" acknowledges a student's feelings but does not condone the behavior. Helping students learn the distinction between experiencing feelings and behaving constructively is central to teaching responsible behavior (Goleman, 1995; Mendler, 1992; Sylwester, 2000).

Hypodermic Affection

Redl and Wineman (1951) coined the term *hypodermic affection*, which is a method of defusing resistance by giving a shot of caring at the precise time a student is expecting an angry or a punitive response. Maag (1999) said that student resistance is a defensive reaction that protects an individual against his or her anxiety. Resistance can be minor—for example, when a student with reading problems refuses to read an assigned passage—or intense—for instance, when a student refuses to comply with multiple teacher requests to take off a hat and the student is suspended.

One of the most difficult aspects of managing resistance is to avoid responding to the student in a way that replicates the student's behavior (Long & Morse, 1996). For example, one student pushes another student in line and the teacher grabs the offending student by the arm, or a student swears and refuses to follow a teacher directive and the teacher responds with an angry retort. Maag (1999) suggested that rather than attempting to directly change resistance, teachers should focus on redirecting students:

> If you oppose the river by trying to block it, the river will merely go over and around. But if you accept the force of the river and divert it in a new direction, the force of the river will cut a new channel. (p. 9)

Hypodermic affection is not a predictable teacher response to student resistance. Consider how one high school teacher combined humor with hypodermic affection to defuse a tense situation: Alicia, a bright but angry 16-year-old, insulted her geometry teacher with a sarcastic remark in front of the entire class: "You should be in the Who's Who of lousy teachers." Mr. Raker paused and replied, "That is one of the best put-downs I have ever heard, but actually my college professors were more likely to think of me in terms of Who's He?" Expecting an angry retort, Alicia was caught off guard and a potential crisis was defused. "OK, Mr. Raker," she said. "You got me on that one." According to Maag (1999), one of the best ways to manage problem behaviors is through surprise. Surprise eases tension and helps break up rigid thinking. "The unexpected always helps deal with resistant students—never do what is expected" (p. 10).

SANCTIONS

To *sanction* means to approve or disapprove of an action. In schools, sanctions usually follow violation of a rule or a norm. The frequency and severity of sanctions vary depending on student behavior and the viewpoint of the educator who is administering the sanction. Some teachers rely heavily on sanctions or the threat of sanctions to maintain classroom order. Other teachers use sanctions only as a last resort. The following subsections address how sanctions can be best used to promote constructive student behavior. Special attention is given to comparing the relative merits of the three most commonly used school sanctions: consequences, threats, and punishment.

Consequences

Consequences for behavior consist of an event or a series of events that follow a behavior and influence the frequency of the behavior in the future (Alberto & Troutman, 2003). Consequences can be either positive or negative. For instance, a student studies hard for an examination and earns a passing grade; this is a positive consequence. A student stumbles over lines during an audition for a school play and does not get the part; this is a negative consequence. Both positive and negative consequences permeate our lives.

Behaviorists maintain that consequences are the key to behavioral change. Walker and Shea (1999) said, "The consequences and probable consequences of behavior more than any other factor determine the behavior that an individual exhibits" (p. 64). Other educators recognize the effect of consequences, but they also include such factors as heredity, brain function, human development, and temperament as important influences on behavior. Debates about causation of human behavior aside, teachers use consequences frequently in their quest to promote responsible behavior.

In many classrooms, when rules are broken, consequences are used in an attempt to change the student's behavior. Loss of privileges, verbal reprimands, check marks next to a name, and isolation of the student from the classroom are examples of consequences teachers use as sanctions for misbehavior.

In the following four subsections, consequences are first classified as logical or natural. Second, their congruence is discussed. The more congruent consequences are, the more likely students will accept them. Third, the severity of consequences is discussed, and fourth, three key points about administering consequences are given to guide teachers in administering such sanctions.

Logical and Natural Consequences.   Mendler (1992) identified two types of consequences: logical and natural. *Logical consequences* are clearly and rationally connected

Case Study: Julia

Julia was 11 years old and a student in special education in an inclusive sixth-grade classroom. One afternoon, Julia and Frank were tossing paper balls into a nearby wastebasket. Mr. Kramer, their teacher, warned them both to stop or he would send them to the principal's office. Frank went back to his work, but Julia tossed one more. Out of patience, Mr. K escorted Julia to the principal's office. Then, he went back to teaching, confident that Julia's behavior would improve because he had been firm and fair in administering a consequence for her behavior.

However, as Julia was walked down the stairs to the principal's office, she perceived the situation differently. She resented being "picked on," and she was glad to be out of the classroom. Although the consequence removed a troublesome student from the class, any hopes Mr. K had that Julia had "learned her lesson" remained unfulfilled. In fact, just the reverse occurred. What Mr. K thought was a negative consequence that would stop Julia's disruptive behavior was actually a positive consequence that reinforced her acting-out behavior. For a consequence to be effective, it must mean the same thing to the student as to the teacher—the consequence must be *congruent*.

to a behavior. Such consequences are powerful motivators and help individuals make decisions. For instance, a student who is contemplating getting into a fight with another student may decide to walk away because the student understands that regardless of who is "right" or "wrong," he or she will be suspended. The student makes this decision on the basis of a logical consequence. Alternatively, the student might walk away because of the possibility of getting hurt. A bloodied nose is a *natural consequence* of fighting. Natural consequences are so closely tied to a behavior that a minimal amount of adult interpretation is necessary. For example, a natural consequence of dropping a book is to pick it up.

Teachers lean heavily on consequences when they establish behavioral guidelines. They often refer to these guidelines as *limits*. A teacher who states "Students need to know the limits" is referring to the need to have clear behavioral guidelines and consequences. Consequences play a major role in discipline as sanctions for disruptive behavioral. Consequences work best when students understand the connection between the infraction and the sanction as cause and effect. If a student does not perceive the consequence with the same logic as that of the teacher, the consequence will be ineffective and might even achieve the opposite of the intended effect. Consider the case study of Julia.

Congruent Consequences.   *Congruence* means the state of agreeing or coinciding. A *congruent consequence* is interpreted the same way by the teacher as by the students. Natural consequences have more congruence than logical consequences do because the need for interpretation, is minimized. For example, Juan tips back in his chair and falls. This is a natural consequence, and no explanation is needed to connect the action and the reaction. In contrast, logical consequences are more open to interpretation because the teacher is usually enforcing the consequence. The power differential between administering a consequence and receiving a consequence is such that the overall benefit can be lost on a student who sees the effect as punitive. Logical consequences work best when the student has had a say in developing the rules and the consequences (Dreikurs et al., 1982; Gathercoal, 1993; Curwin & Mendler, 1988a, 1988b).

Gathercoal (1993) believed that consequences should be derived from democratic principles and should not be spelled out specifically in a laundry list of rigid behavioral guidelines. For example, Melissa may come to school angry because she found out the previous evening that her parents were getting a divorce. Gathercoal would want the teacher in this situation to be flexible and judge the misbehavior in terms of the bigger picture (Edwards, 2000).

Assertive Consequences.   Canter and Canter (1992) advised against using consequences as a knee-jerk reaction to students' misbehavior. They suggested that consequences must be something that students do not like, but not physically or psychologically harmful. Canter and Canter also said that consequences should be presented to students as a choice they have made. For example, if a student pokes another student, the teacher's response should be, "Okay, Carl, you poked Fred. You have chosen to sit by yourself at the table" (p. 81). Finally, the Canters advised against harsh consequences.

According to the Canters, consequences need not be severe to be effective. For most students, a warning is sufficient. Furthermore, the most effective consequences are the easiest to maintain. For example, having a student work alone for 10 minutes in the classroom is easier than having the student stay in for recess. The Canters developed a hierarchy of consequences that is the foundation of their *assertive discipline* approach to misbehavior. The discipline hierarchy lists four consequences in the order in which they should be used during a day:

1. **First disruption.**   The teacher issues a warning, which gives the student the opportunity to choose a more appropriate behavior.
2. **Second or third disruption.**   The teacher provides a consequence that is easy to implement, such as having a student sit alone for a few minutes.
3. **Fourth disruption.**   The student loses "free time".
4. **Fifth disruption.**   The teacher sends the student to the principal.

The Canters' approach to consequences has been criticized for being too autocratic. For example, Kohn (1993a) argued that assertive discipline is intent on cultivating obedience, and its lockstep procedure does not take into account common causes of misbehavior such as inept teaching.

The Three **Rs**.   Dreikurs et al. (1982) outlined three *R*s that summarize key requirements of using consequences effectively:

1. **The consequence must be** *related* **to the misbehavior.**   A student who throws food in the cafeteria eats lunch in the classroom for 3 days, instead of writing an essay on good manners.
2. **The consequence must be** *reasonable.*   A student who runs in the hallway must back up and walk the distance, not do an extra homework assignment.

3. **The consequence must be *respectfully* applied.**   A student yells out an answer in class, and the teacher responds with a sane message rather than putting the student down with a sarcastic remark.

Keeping the three *R*s of consequences in mind provides a simple framework for administering sanctions.

Threats

Although *threats* are often used in classrooms, classroom management professionals seldom recommend using them. Threats are imperative statements that if a certain behavior is not exhibited, a negative consequence will follow. A child who bickers is threatened with a trip to the principal's office. A student who gets out of a seat is threatened with loss of recess.

In any setting in which adults supervise young people in groups, the use of threats is commonplace. However, if threats are so commonplace, why are experts opposed to their use? Who has not observed a child follow a demand after being threatened with loss of a privilege?

The purpose of a threat is to stop a disturbing behavior. The purpose of discipline is to teach students new, constructive behaviors. A threat carries no learning curve. It imposes authority. It does not teach responsible behavior. After a threat, the student stops the behavior because he or she is intimidated by the imposing *aversive*. The student has no motivation to change. The motivation is to avoid an unpleasant effect. In the best case scenario, a student stops the offensive behavior, but in many cases the disturbing behavior is stopped only temporarily. Suppose Victor is threatened with a loss of free time unless he stops goofing off. We could say the threat had an impact if Victor's goofing off decreased with time, but if Victor stops goofing off only when threatened, what has been accomplished? Victor and the teacher then become enmeshed in a cycle of cat and mouse. Victor's only true motivation is to avoid getting caught.

Threats pose other problems as well. Because threats are so easy to use, they stifle creativity. Some teachers are so accustomed to threatening students that they can think of no other, more effective way of correcting misbehavior. Because they get temporary relief from a problem behavior, these teachers believe they have solved the problem, while in reality they have created a bigger problem—the need to continually enforce the threat.

In addition, once given, a threat must be acted on. Enforcing threats drains time and energy: The *teacher* must find someone to stay with a student during recess. The *teacher* must monitor the student placed in the hallway. The *teacher* must call a parent. The *teacher* must deal with a resentful student who has been deprived of free time. The *teacher* must explain to the principal why he or she keeps sending students to the office.

Threats can also undermine the student–teacher relationship. Using them frequently reveals the teacher to be a person who can lead only through intimidation. Therefore, threats are most useful when used sparingly. A threat should be the last option used when a teacher is confronted with a disturbing behavior, not the first. Frequent threats result in the need to impose frequent punishments. Conversely, a teacher who rarely uses a threat has a potent tool available when it is needed.

Punishment

The use of *punishment* is deeply embedded in school lore. The familiar refrain "School days, school days, dear old golden school days, readin' and writin' and 'rithmetic, done to the tune of a hickory stick . . ." symbolizes the durability of punishment as a standard disciplinary technique.

Nevertheless, Skinner, the architect of modern behavior modification, was opposed to the use of punishment as a behavioral change method. Skinner said,

> What's wrong with punishments is that they work immediately, but give no long-term results. The responses to punishment are either the urge to escape, to counterattack, or a stubborn apathy. These are the bad effects you get in prisons, or schools, or wherever punishments are used. (cited in Goleman, 1987, p. C1)

Punishment can stop a behavior, but, as with threats, it does not teach a suitable replacement behavior. When teachers use punishment, their justification is often based on the principles of behaviorism. However, as Maag (2001b) pointed out, the *effect* of the punishment is often different from the *intention*:

> A teacher may find a student's "obnoxious" behaviors to be aversive. Being sent out of the classroom to sit in the hall or principal's office may be punishing if the student finds exclusion from others aversive. Consequently, the teacher has been reinforced for sending the student out of the room because the act terminated the unpleasantness of the student behavior. Technically, the teacher has been *negatively reinforced*. The principle is in effect whenever any behavior (e.g., sending the student out of the room) results in the removal of an aversion (e.g., a student's obnoxious behavior). . . . In the case of punishment, a vicious cycle is perpetuated: Teachers are negatively reinforced for punishing students, which, in turn, increases the use of punishment, which then reinforces teachers' using it. (p. 176)

The unintended outcomes of punishment can extend further. Suppose LaToya is noncompliant because she wants to avoid doing math. In this case, putting her in the hall is positive reinforcement for her noncompliant behavior, which increases the likelihood that she will engage in more avoidance behaviors to escape unpleasant schoolwork.

Punishment Defined. *Punishment* has two meanings. The first is the everyday usage defined in *Merriam-Webster's Collegiate Dictionary* (2003) as "suffering, pain, or loss that serves as retribution" (p. 1009). The second definition is the more technical behavior modification version. Kazdin (2001) defined *punishment* as "the presentation or removal of events that reduces the probability of the response in the future" (p. 204). From a behaviorist's viewpoint, an aversive response to a student's behavior is not punishment unless it decreases the inappropriate behavior. Maag (2001b) said, "Ironically, if punishment were effective, it would be used less rather than more frequently with a particular student because the desired effect would be to reduce the inappropriate behavior" (p. 179).

When teachers and administrators punish students, the key consideration is whether the punishment will stop the behavior from happening again. When a student is punished and no change in behavior results, the lack of change is a clear sign that punishment is not working and the solution to eliminating the misbehavior lies elsewhere.

Punishment Versus Consequences.   Many misunderstandings about punishment can be traced to misleading terminology (Skiba & Deno, 1991). *Punishment* and *consequences* are frequently used interchangeably. Some teachers use *consequences* as a euphemism for *punishment*—for example, a teacher punishes a student and says, "You have to learn the consequences of your behavior." Consequences for behavior work best when they are generally accepted by students as a reasonable response to misbehavior. A sense of due process accompanies consequences that does not exist with punishment. Punishment is meted out by an authority figure who makes a judgment on the spot concerning the severity and duration of the retribution. When the punishing adult is angry or frustrated, the differences between logical consequences and punishment are more evident. Punishment accentuates the power imbalance between the youth and the adult. Consequences, when developed democratically, level the playing field by giving students a sense of ownership for the governance system.

Overuse of Punishment.   Overuse of punishment in schools is a serious concern, particularly for students with chronic disciplinary problems. Punishing students regularly for misbehavior adds to, rather than detracts from, the problem. Students with chronic disciplinary problems need, more than anything else, to learn new, socially accepted behaviors. They need instruction in the social skills they are lacking. A student who is a bully needs to learn how to relate to peers without intimidation. A student who acts out needs to learn to verbalize feelings. A student who refuses to do work needs to learn how to manage frustration. Punishment does not teach new behaviors; at best, it simply stops a behavior at one point in time.

Controlling students with chronic disciplinary problems through punishment teaches the wrong lessons. The avoidance of punishment becomes the main student concern. Students will use rationalizations, lies, and distortions to defend themselves from punishment. The adult–student relationship deteriorates when the adult is primarily concerned with catching and punishing while the student is mainly concerned with not getting caught. In addition, students who are frequently in trouble become accustomed to aversive reactions, which forces the adults to increase the severity of the punishment. Once a student gets to the point where he or she does not care whether he or she is punished, the adult has lost control of the situation and the student is on the path to even more serious problems.

An additional danger associated with the overuse of punishment is the effect of punishment on children who are emotionally sensitive. Approximately 3 million cases of child abuse and neglect are reported each year (U.S. Department of Health and Human Services, 1999). In states where corporal punishment is legal, the negative impact of paddling an abused child is a serious concern.

Corporal punishment is an accepted legal practice in 23 states. The U.S. Department of Education (2002) reported that nearly 456,000 students were paddled during the 1996–1997 school year. Most of these documented "paddlings" happened in schools in the southeastern and western United States. Jill Eaton, past president of the National Association of Elementary School Principals, said, "Although the research shows that paddling isn't effective discipline, down here in the Bible Belt, the mentality and culture of 'don't spare the rod' still exists to some extent" (cited in Magnuson, 2000, p. 1).

Other less dramatic forms of punishment result in a child's perception that adults cannot be trusted. Cosmos (2001) reported that students with special needs are abused at a higher rate than other students are. Cosmos cited the results of a study in Nebraska in which 33% of children with disabilities were found to have been maltreated, compared with 9% of the children who were nondisabled (p. 2). A sharp comment that humiliates a youngster into being quiet might seem worthwhile at the time, but the small reward of silence is offset by the damage done to a youngster's trust in his or her teacher as caretaker.

Walker and Shea (1999) suggested that when considering punishment, the teacher should use the least aversive intervention first. Braaten, Simpson, Rosell, and Reilly (1988) recommended seven procedures to ensure that teachers carefully consider the use of punishment:

1. Teachers should be provided information about the use and abuse of punishment.
2. Teachers should be trained in the proper use of punishment.
3. School policy makers should approve the punishment procedures.
4. Records of punishment procedures should be maintained.
5. Complaint and appeal due-process procedures should be established.
6. Infractions that warrant punishment should be explained to teachers and students.
7. Procedures for periodic review of punishment should be implemented.

Many alternative behavioral interventions exist that help students behave responsibly without the negative side effects incurred by punishment (Evans & Richardson, 1995). The previous section highlighted ways of talking with students about their behavior. The following section covers a series of proactive correction strategies based on principles of behavior modification.

Behavior Modification

Students behave as they do for many reasons, and many of these reasons are outside the classroom teacher's control. Student temperament, family life, culture, developmental history, and physical health all play a role in how a student behaves. However, the school environment also plays a significant role in influencing behavior. By manipulating elements of the classroom environment, the teacher can increase the frequency of appropriate behavior and decrease the incidence of inappropriate behavior (Cooper, Heron, & Heward, 1990). Such manipulation is the premise behind *behavior modification,* defined by Miltenberger (2001): "Behavior modification is the field of psychology concerned with analyzing and modifying human behavior" (p. 5). The goal of behavior modification is to identify variables within the environment that shape behavior and to systematically control these variables to change behavior.

The U.S. psychologist B. F. Skinner is credited with being the leading contributor to the ascendancy of behavior modification as a tool for behavioral change. Prior to Skinner, classic conditioning researchers emphasized how preceding variables influenced behavior (e.g., a cat that is fed canned food will come bolting out of the blue at the first sound of a can opener's creasing metal). Skinner was more concerned with how behavior was shaped by variables that occurred after an event. He called this *reinforcement* (e.g., a dog is taught to "sit" by a biscuit reward). Most of Skinner's research during the 1930s and through the 1940s consisted of laboratory experiments with rats and pigeons. During World War II, Skinner and his colleagues trained pigeons to guide missiles to enemy vessels (Alberto & Troutman, 2003). His ideas became a springboard for a different way of understanding human behavior. By the mid-1950s, behaviorism had become a major academic discipline.

Three types of behavior modification are covered next. They are positive reinforcement, negative reinforcement, modeling.

Positive Reinforcement

Elements of positive reinforcement are embedded in human interaction both within and outside school. Walker and Shea (1999) defined *positive reinforcement* as the process of reinforcing a target behavior to increase the probability that the behavior will recur (p. 141). For example, when Grandma said "When you finish your spinach, you will get a nice piece of chocolate cake," she was practicing positive reinforcement. Grades, prizes, stickers, and even a teacher's smile following a correct answer are other familiar forms of positive reinforcement.

Types of Positive Reinforcers.   Positive reinforcers are divided into two groups— tangible reinforcers and social reinforcers—which were described in Chapter 6. A *tangible reinforcer* is an object. Food, stickers, and trading cards are examples of tangible reinforcers. Grandma's chocolate cake is also a tangible reinforcer.

If Grandma wanted to use a *social reinforcer* instead of a tangible reinforcer to reinforce her granddaughter for completing the target behavior of eating a vegetable, she might have said, "You are a good girl for finishing your spinach." Praise is a common social reinforcers. A smile, a hug, or any other positive gesture that follows a target behavior is a social reinforcer.

A *target behavior* is an observable behavior that is the objective for behavior modification approaches. Some examples of target behaviors in the classroom are raising a hand to answer a question, working independently for 10 minutes, and completing

Case Study: Alan

Mr. Riley was frustrated with Alan's verbal outbursts in his fourth-grade special education classroom. When Alan knew an answer, he would impulsively shout out an answer without raising his hand. Mr. Riley tried a variety of behavioral interventions, such as sane messages and logical consequences, which resulted in little improvement in Alan's behavior. As a result, Mr. Riley decided to set up a token system for Alan and told Alan that every time he raised his hand to answer a question, he would receive a point. At the end of the morning, if Alan had accumulated 10 points, he could listen to music with a headset for 10 minutes before lunch. Within 2 weeks, Alan's verbal outbursts had diminished, and he was raising his hand an average of 14 times each morning.

homework assignments. Grandma did not have to read a textbook to know that tangible reinforcers like chocolate cake are the strongest type of reinforcer. Tangible reinforcers are more likely to be used with young children or students who require immediate and concrete feedback.

Sometimes teachers use *tokens* in lieu of immediate tangible reinforcers. *Token reinforcers* are specific items that represent tangible reinforcers. Some examples of token reinforcers are check marks, stars, points, and bonus coupons. Token reinforcers are usually accumulated and later traded for tangible reinforcers. For example, a class might earn a pizza party (i.e., a tangible reinforcer) by accumulating 30 bonus coupons (i.e., token reinforcers) for making the transition from recess to afternoon class without misbehaving (i.e., the target behavior). Consider the use of tokens in the case study of Alan.

The advantage of token reinforcers is that they are easier to administer than are tangible reinforcers such as food or beverages. One drawback to using token reinforcers is that they delay gratification. For some students, token reinforcers might not be as strong an inducement as immediate tangible reinforcers because of the waiting period between the target behavior and the reinforcer.

Some teachers take the token system one step further and create a token economy. A *token economy* is a system usually used with an entire group or class. Durable tangible reinforcers such as stickers or poker chips are used to reward behavior. Tokens are paired with backup reinforcers such as toys or trinkets from a "class store." A token is given to a student each time a target behavior is demonstrated. The tokens have no value except that derived from the desirability of the objects for which the tokens are traded.

Anderson and Katsiyannis (1997) designed a token economy for a fifth-grade inclusion classroom. The teachers realized that anything pertaining to automobiles was a strong reinforcer for their students. They chose the theme "Speedway." The token reinforcers were "license plates." Each time the students adhered to seven Speedway rules—for example, drive your own car (do your own work) and use your seatbelt (stay seated)—they were reinforced with paper license plates.

The students exchanged their license plates at the end of the day for both social rewards (privileges) and tangible reinforcers (key chains, car posters, card cars). The teachers then gradually *faded* (i.e., slowly reduced the number of) the tangible reinforcers. Finally, activities and privileges were substituted completely for the tangible reinforcers.

This example of a token economy underscores the importance of selecting reinforcers that are appealing to students. In addition, the theme approach helped maintain the students' interest in the program. At the conclusion of the token economy program, aggressive behaviors had decreased, whereas on-task behaviors had increased.

Positive Reinforcement Considerations.   Teachers who want to use positive reinforcers must first consider the type of reinforcer to use. In most cases, the first option for positive reinforcement should be social reinforcement. Verbal praise, a smile, or a pat on the back is easy to give and does not require any special changes in the classroom routine. For example, when a teacher uses tangible reinforcers, the entire class must be involved or the teacher will need to explain why one student is getting special rewards and the rest are not. Because social positive reinforcement is more natural, it does not draw as much attention to any particular student.

If tangible reinforcers are used, they are best presented along with social reinforcement. As the student begins to demonstrate the target behavior more frequently, the tangible reinforcer can gradually be faded while the social reinforcer continues to support the new behavior.

The second consideration teachers should keep in mind when they use positive reinforcers is to avoid using them inappropriately (Knitzer et al., 1990; Maag, 2001b). Teachers can make three errors in the use of positive reinforcers. One common mistake is rewarding a student for "good behavior" instead of clearly identifying the desired target behavior. A second error is neglecting to identify reinforcers that are attractive to the student or using reinforcers that are desirable but unhealthy, such as candy or soda. Consider the paradox of giving a hyperactive student a soda as positive reinforcement for staying in his or her seat. The combination of caffeine and sugar may add to the problem rather than contribute to the solution. A third mistake is to initiate a behavior modification program without keeping track of how effectively the reinforcers are supporting the development of new behaviors.

Capitalizing on Natural Reinforcers.   The joy of reading an engrossing novel, the feeling of competence from doing a job well, and the fellowship attendant to being part of a team are examples of *natural reinforcers*. When a teacher uses a planned reinforcer to shape a desired behavior, the intention is to eventually maintain the new behavior through natural reinforcement.

Each time Alexis shares materials with another student, Mrs. Ryan praises her. Mrs. Ryan is hoping that soon the enjoyment of socializing will be all the reinforcement Alexis needs. Socializing, student interest, choice, novelty, movement, and fun are powerful natural reinforcers that can be capitalized on in the classroom. Some advantages of natural reinforcers are the following:

- They can be embedded in many collaborative learning activities such as peer tutoring, cooperative learning, and brainstorming.
- They are spontaneous.

- They eliminate the need to keep track of who gets rewarded and who does not.
- They enhance generalization to settings outside the classroom.
- They reduce power inequities between adults and students that sometimes accompany the use of other positive reinforcement.
- They are more enduring in their overall effect than positive reinforcers based on rewards are.

Table 8.1 provides examples of positive reinforcers. They include tangible, social, token, and natural reinforcers.

Group Contingency. *Group contingency* reinforcement is based on the efforts of a group or class rather than on a single individual. Group contingencies can help foster interdependence and build cohesiveness. Ms. Itterly was weary of having to continually remind her third-grade students to come into class quietly after recess. She put a goldfish bowl on her desk and told her students that every time they came into the room and settled down without a reminder, she would put a marble in the bowl. When the bowl was filled, the entire class would have a pizza party. The class greeted this idea enthusiastically and within 2 weeks the bowl was half filled.

Ms. Itterly was careful to tolerate occasional lapses by a few of her students with learning and behavioral disabilities. She recognized that peer pressure can be

TABLE 8.1 *Sample Classroom Positive Reinforcers*

Tangible Reinforcers	Social Reinforcers
Crackers	Praise
Juice	A smile
Fruit	The chance to demonstrate a skill
Pretzels	The chance to sit with a friend
Sugarless gum	A handshake or a pat on the back
Popcorn	A chance to sit with the teacher at lunch
Small toys	A turn at being the line leader
Colored pencils	Free time
Stickers	Extra recess time
Books	Work put on display
Trading cards	A special job
	A special privilege
Token Reinforcers	**Natural Reinforcers**
Check marks	Fun
Points	Socialization
Achievement charts	The opportunity to be a helper
Rubber stamps	Mastery
Play money	Choice
Coupons	Novelty
Poker chips	Movement

a double-edged sword: Getting a reward for working together is one thing. Having the group turn on an individual student for undermining the group effort is entirely different.

One caveat should be mentioned, though. Alberto and Troutman (2003) advised educators to be certain that each group member is capable of attaining the target behavior before starting a group contingency plan.

Negative Reinforcement

Whereas positive reinforcement is a stimulus presented to the student to reinforce a behavior, negative reinforcement is a stimulus removed to reinforce a behavior. Alberto and Troutman (2003) defined *negative reinforcement* as a relationship between events in which the rate of occurrence of a target behavior increases when an aversive condition is removed or reduced in intensity. Note that the aversive condition (i.e., the stimulus) is removed, *not* applied. Negative reinforcement is often confused with punishment, which is the application of an aversive.

Ms. Lewis, a sixth-grade teacher, was having difficulty with several students who were not doing their homework. She understood that most students did not like homework. In behavior modification terms, homework was an *aversive.* On Monday, she instituted a new homework policy. All students who turned in homework from Monday to Thursday would not have to do homework over the weekend. This deal seemed good to the students, and submission of homework assignments during the week improved. Ms. Lewis reinforced homework completion during the week by removing the aversive weekend homework as a reward.

Alberto and Troutman (2003) observed that sometimes teachers inadvertently strengthen an unwanted behavior by using negative reinforcement. Consider the following example: Sheila is a middle school student who does not like to participate in gym. When told to line up for floor exercises, she starts whining about getting sweaty. Mr. Vick, the gym teacher, warns Sheila that unless the whining stops she will have to sit on the bleachers for the remainder of gym class. Sheila continues to whine and Mr. Vick follows through on his threat. By removing the aversive—that is, participating in floor exercises—Mr. Vick has reinforced Sheila's whining. What Mr. Vick interpreted as a logical consequence had the opposite effect. Sheila learned that whining would get her out of gym exercises.

Modeling

Samuel Johnson, the English poet, said, "No man ever yet became great by imitation" (cited in Seldes, 1985, p. 213). A behaviorist rejoinder might be, "No man becomes great without imitation." *Modeling* is teaching by demonstration. The student imitates the model and in the process develops new skills. Walker and Shea (1999) defined modeling as learning by observation and imitation (p. 167).

Instances of the variability of modeling as an influence on behavior can be seen in many naturally occurring behaviors, from the adolescent penchant for dressing the same to the warrior image of a marine used in recruiting. For young children, imitation is a major source of learning. When parents warn their children to avoid certain companions, they are alluding to the power of modeling. Martin and Pear (1996) offered the following examples of modeling:

- For an entire day, speak only in a whisper, and note how often people around you also whisper.
- Yawn conspicuously in the presence of other people, and note the frequency of yawning.
- Stand looking at a window of an empty department store for an hour, and observe how many people stop and also look in the window.

Advertisers take advantage of the power of modeling. We are inundated with messages based on modeling: Drive a sexy car and you will be a sexy person. Use the same basketball shoe as a popular athlete and you will be dunking basketballs. Buy a piece of exercise equipment and in 3 months you will have a body just like the individual on your television screen.

In a classic study of modeling, Jones (1924) taught a young boy, Peter, to overcome his fear of furry objects. Peter was placed in a play situation with three other children and a rabbit. After observing the other children interacting with the rabbit, Peter touched the rabbit, and his anxiety around furry objects diminished. Jones went on to investigate several methods for overcoming anxiety in children (Kazdin, 2001, p. 25).

Within the classroom, teachers who model the behaviors they seek to develop in their students are more effective than teachers who do not. The teacher who states that personal respect is an important value and then humiliates a student for talking out of turn will quickly lose credibility with students.

Providing students with special needs with appropriate models is an effective strategy for helping students develop and maintain social skills. Cooperative learning and peer tutoring, for example, rely on modeling to help teach social skills.

Walker and Shea (1999) recommended the following considerations for teachers making a decision to use peer modeling as a behavioral intervention:

- The child must be developmentally and intellectually capable of imitating the model.
- The child might lack intrinsic motivation and need social or tangible reinforcers to imitate the model.
- Caution should be used in selecting the model. A student who looks like a good model in art class might be an ineffective model in science class.
- The model should be acceptable to the student. Someone whom a student would not normally be attracted to might be an excellent model but be rejected by the target student.

Students will also model inappropriate behavior. One of the difficulties teachers encounter in self-contained special education classes is the tendency of students to imitate disruptive behaviors.

The trend toward establishing alternative high schools for students with chronic disciplinary problems solves one problem and creates another. Students who are disruptive are removed from regular classrooms where they will no longer disrupt their peers' learning. However, the practice of placing 10 or more students with chronic behavioral problems together in one classroom presents a challenge to teachers. The need to maintain control is ever present, and teachers must often rely on unproductive systems of reward and punishment (Knitzer et al., 1990; Kohn, 1993b).

Providing appropriate models for students with special needs is one of the driving forces behind school inclusion programs. In 1997, the Individuals with Disabilities Education Act (IDEA) was amended to promote inclusion. The federal special education law mandates that the first consideration for special education placement is the general education classroom. Within the general education classroom, students with disabilities find more appropriate models than those available within more restrictive special education placements, such as self-contained special classes.

PROMISING PRACTICES

To respond to the challenges presented in educating students with complex problem behaviors, educators have devised a number of specialized interventions for both managing behavior and teaching responsibility. The following section covers three promising practices: life space crisis intervention, bibliotherapy, and cognitive strategies.

Life Space Crisis Intervention

Life space crisis intervention (LSCI) is a guided interview designed to help students gain insight into their behavior (Long, Fecser, & Brendtro, 1998). LSCI is a proactive crisis management tool. A "crisis" is any severe behavioral outburst that signals a student is losing self-control. Long et al. said the following about LSCI:

> In this paradigm, a crisis is perceived as a glass half filled with water rather than half empty. This way of thinking mobilizes the student's resources and potential strengths instead of dwelling on deficits, dysfunctions and disorders. A crisis represents a unique time to help a student come to grips with an important life problem, which the youth has denied. When successfully managed, a crisis can illuminate his or her pattern of self-defeating behavior and provide strength based social skills. (p. 11)

LSCI is designed for specific students who exhibit common patterns of self-defeating behavior. The LSCI approach has six steps (Long, Wood, & Fecser, 2001):

1. **Manage the crisis.**   The student is removed from the classroom to a quiet area. The individual who is conducting the LSCI allows the student to ventilate his or her feelings. The purpose is de-escalation of the student's intense feelings. No judgment is made about the student's verbal outbursts. Such adult statements as "I can see you are angry" or "Tell me how you feel" help establish a climate of mutuality and trust. Once the student has calmed down, the second step is implemented.

2. **Construct the time line.**   The student is asked to describe what happened. As the student presents his or her interpretation, the staff person questions and clarifies details. Many students literally forget what they do to contribute to a crisis situation. Redl and Wineman (1951) called this cognitive omission *evaporation of self-contributing links* (p. 123). During this step, the staff and the student work together to develop a time line of events.

3. **Identify the central issue.**   During this step, the interviewer looks for patterns in the student's behavior. Some questions the interviewer seeks to answer are How often does this particular problem occur? What is the student's typical response to stress? and How effective are the student's coping skills? Also, during this phase, the interviewer assesses the student's perceptions and motivation to change.

4. **Teach insight.**   The interviewer selects one of six therapeutic goals to help a student gain insight into his or her behavioral patterns. See Figure 8.1 for a brief description of each LSCI goal.

5. **Teach new skills (plan for success).**   The goal of this step is to help the student identify specific constructive behaviors for dealing with difficulties. The

---

Red Flag Intervention. The aim of a red flag intervention is to support the student who is acting out because of events that occurred outside school.

Reality Rub Intervention. The reality rub intervention provides insight into how selective attention and errors in perception influence behavior.

Symptom Estrangement Intervention. The symptom estrangement intervention helps aggressive students, who typically justify their actions and portray themselves as victims, to take responsibility for their actions.

Massaging Numb Values Intervention. The massaging numb values intervention is typically used with students who feel guilty about their impulsive actions. The aim is to alleviate feelings of remorse, shame, and inadequacy.

New Tool Intervention. The new tool intervention is geared for students who want to relate more effectively to other people but lack the adequate social skills to do so. Students are counseled about specific constructive behaviors they can use to meet their needs.

Manipulation of Body Boundaries Intervention. The manipulation of body boundaries intervention is designed to help students gain insight into how they are manipulated by their peers.

FIGURE 8.1   Life Space Crisis Intervention (LSCI) Therapeutic Goals
Derived from *Life Space Crisis Intervention: Talking with students in conflict* (2nd ed.), by N. Long, M. M. Wood, and F. A. Fecser, 2001, Austin, TX: PRO-ED.

focus is on what to do. The student and the staff member jointly develop a
written plan.

6. **Discuss the transfer of learning (get ready to resume the activity).**   An
LSCI session can last an hour or longer. At the conclusion, the topic shifts
to how the student will make the transition to ongoing activities. The staff
member and the student discuss what has happened while the student
has been away and what the student will do when he or she returns to
class.

LSCI provides a set of clear and concrete steps for talking with students about
their difficulties. The LSCI emphasis on listening to the student's perspective and
encouraging the student to seek his or her own solutions is a worthwhile crisis intervention (see the LSCI Web site for further information: www.lsci.org).

Bibliotherapy

Bibliotherapy capitalizes on children's and young adult literature to help students
deal with difficult life situations. Divorce, the death of a pet, moving to a new community, and entering a new school are representative plots. Themes include such
issues as grief, loneliness, and learning from mistakes. Sridhar and Vaughn (2000)
advocated bibliotherapy for students with emotional and behavioral problems.
Bibliotherapy enhances self-understanding and promotes reading comprehension.
For optimum results, the reader should be able to identify with the main character,
relate emotionally to situations described in the book, and gain personal insight
from the story.

While reading a story to students or while students are reading, the teacher
asks questions to prompt students to think about events and characters. Henley
(2003) provided the following list of ways to use children's and young adult literature to promote change in student behavior:

- Explore themes in stories. Ask students to identify similar situations in their
  lives.
- Stop reading and ask students what they would do in the main character's
  place, or ask students what they think will happen next.
- Have students rewrite the conclusion to the story.
- Ask students how they felt about the story.
- Ask students about parts of the story they would like to change. Follow-up
  activities such as role-playing and journal writing firm up emerging insights.

Cognitive Strategies

Cognitive strategies is a generic term that encompasses a variety of behavioral
interventions derived from social learning theory (Bandura, 1977) and cognitive
psychology (Barsalou, 1992; Vygotsky, 1978). Cognitive strategies are based on the
assumption that individuals can change their emotions and behavior by changing
the way they think about feelings and behavior (J. Beck, 1995; Webber & Maag,

1997). Two examples of cognitive strategies are rational emotive behavior therapy and self-management skills training.

Rational emotive behavior therapy (REBT) helps students analyze their feelings through the following steps: discriminate between rational and irrational beliefs, distinguish between healthy emotions and unhealthy emotions, and change irrational beliefs that inhibit good choices (Vernon, 1998). REBT can benefit teachers and students in many ways. Zions (1998) said the following about REBT:

> The major purpose of REBT is to teach individuals how to lower the intensity of emotional problems, resulting in less significant and more manageable problems, and their subsequent behavioral consequences. It is an optimistic intervention in that its thesis is that people can learn how to manage their feelings and behaviors. (p. 5)

According to REBT advocates, events themselves do not contribute to behavioral problems; an individual's interpretation of the events does. Behavioral change is predicated on students' acquiring more rational ways of thinking about individuals and events that influence how they feel and behave. Zions (1998) listed some ways irrational thoughts impede constructive behavior:

- Inconsistent evaluation of negative events
- Generalization of "facts" from bits of information
- Belief that feelings are facts
- Consideration of memories as current-day realities
- Perception that remote possibilities are imminent probabilities
- Expectation of immediate or rapid change

The crux of REBT is the belief that more-constructive thinking skills can be learned. Although derived from therapy and counseling techniques, REBT is an educational approach. Deficits in cognition about behavior are treated the same way as cognitive deficits in academics are. The REBT approach is educational, only the emphasis is on the person's thinking process rather than elements of the academic curriculum. Three aspects of the REBT "curriculum" are as follows (Nichols, 1998):

1. **Alternative thinking.**   The ability to think of many possible solutions to a problem
2. **Cause-and-effect thinking.**   Recognition that interpersonal problems have social causes rooted in life experience
3. **Perspective thinking.**   The ability to put yourself in another person's shoes and perceive a problem from the other person's viewpoint

REBT teachers incorporate a variety of teaching methods, including role-playing, modeling, bibliotherapy, social skills, instruction, and rehearsal.

The purpose of *self-management skills training* (Young, West, Li, & Peterson, 1998) is to teach students how to monitor and evaluate their behavior. The teacher and students together identify a specific target behavior, such as "following classroom rules." The teacher provides a rating system on a scale from 1 to 4. A *1* indicates that the student followed rules inconsistently. A *4* indicates that the student followed rules during the entire rating period.

The teacher divides an instructional period into several smaller rating time frames. During a 60-minute academic period, students rate themselves every 15 minutes. The teacher and the students compare ratings. The comparison provides students with feedback about how accurately they perceive their actions.

Commenting on their self-management skills training approach, Young et al. (1998) said,

> If the ratings do not match, students learn that they are not judging their behavior in the same way as the teacher. Usually it is the student who needs to improve accuracy. If a student's behavior needs improvement, he or she is taught to decide on a specific alternative behavior to replace the problem behavior. (p. 92)

Benefits of self-management skills training are twofold: Students gain insight into their behavior, and they acquire tools for self-evaluation.

CONTROVERSIAL PRACTICES

Although time-out and point and level systems are common behavioral intervention strategies, they are controversial. Critics say that time-out is used too often as punishment. Likewise, although point and level systems are used to control students, such systems are criticized for not teaching social skills (Knitzer et al., 1990).

Time-Out

Time-out is the temporary removal of a student from classroom activities because of his or her disruptive behavior. According to Alberto and Troutman (1999), time-out is the denial of a student, for a fixed period, the opportunity to receive positive reinforcement. Alberto and Troutman explained, "Time-out is a shortened form of the term *time-out from positive reinforcement*" (p. 300). During time-out, a student is removed from classroom activities for a specified period. The time-out procedure is based on the assumption that the student finds some elements of the classroom attractive (i.e., the "positive reinforcement" identified by Alberto and Troutman), and he or she wants to stay in the classroom.

Preschool teachers, school psychologists, teachers of students with behavioral disorders, and elementary teachers use time-out (Rose, 1987; Walker & Shea, 1999). Ruhl (1985) reported that 88% of all special educators used time-out. Zabel (1986) surveyed 730 special education teachers, who reported using time-out for the following behaviors: physical aggression, verbal aggression, destruction of property, refusal to work, inappropriate language, failure to follow directions, failure to respond, failure to complete work, and tardiness.

Misuse of time-out is a concern because time-out provides an easy way to avoid dealing with difficult students (Knitzer et al., 1990). Time-out should be reserved for major behavioral infractions such as physical or verbal aggression. Removing a student for minor misbehavior such as failing to complete classroom work is an abuse of time-out.

The Council for Children with Behavioral Disorders (1990) recommended the following implementation procedures for when time-out *is* called for:

- Verbalize the reason for the time-out.
- Provide a warning.
- Locate the time-out area in an appropriate place.
- Limit the duration of the time-out.
- Schedule the time-out appropriately.
- Remove potential sources of positive reinforcement from the time-out area.
- Keep a time-out log.
- Remember that continued exposure to time-outs indicates the procedure is not working.

Point and Level Systems

Point and level systems are often used in special education programs that serve students with emotional or behavioral disabilities. A point and level system provides students with increased benefits as they accumulate points for appropriate behavior. Privileges increase as students earn more points. For example, 20 points might earn a student extra time on the computer, whereas an accumulation of 100 points can earn the right to watch a Friday afternoon video.

In some applications, earned points are deducted and privileges are revoked for misbehavior. However, when a point and level system is the sole behavioral intervention approach, problems can develop. Following are some criticisms of point and level systems (Knitzer et al., 1990; Scheuermann, Webber, Partin, & Knies, 1994):

- If the system works, it can be used to make ineffective, dull, and uninspired teaching appear credible. Students work hard to gain points but lack appreciation for the academic and behavioral tasks they perform to garner points.
- Behavior modification is supposed to provide a temporary bridge to self-sustaining behaviors. In most programs, point and level systems are permanent and institutionalized.
- In some cases, point and level systems might violate federal and state special education laws that require educational programs to be tailored to individual needs.
- Point and level systems do not encourage educators to look for causes of misbehavior.
- Point and level systems overlook an array of contemporary advancements in proactive behavioral management, including social skills training, cognitive instruction, functional assessment of behavior, and positive behavioral supports.

If their deficiencies are kept in mind, point and level systems can serve a useful purpose. They can provide a scaffolding for more proactive behavioral intervention efforts (Henley, 1997). As one teacher in a self-contained class for students with behavioral and emotional problems said, "Point and level helps keep the lid on." Other advantages of point and level systems are their ease of implementation and the fact that behavioral expectations are clear to the students.

Summary

★ No single behavioral intervention fits all situations.

★ Effective teachers are able to use an array of behavioral interventions.

★ Teachers need to develop a variety of verbal intervention skills, including using sane messages, accepting and acknowledging students' feelings, using humor appropriately, and listening to students.

★ Behavior modification offers the possibility of changing student behavior through positive reinforcement, negative reinforcement, modeling, and other approaches.

★ Punishment is often confused with consequences.

★ Punishment and threats have limited ability to change behavior. Consequences provide a rational basis for sanctions.

★ When students can see the connection between behavior and consequences, their behavior will change.

★ Life space crisis intervention, bibliotherapy, and cognitive strategies are promising behavioral intervention strategies.

★ Time-out and point and level systems should be used judiciously and monitored for effectiveness.

What You Should Know

Now that you have finished reading this chapter, you should know the following:

That no single behavior management approach works in all situations

How successful classroom managers incorporate multiple positive behavioral intervention strategies

That behavioral intervention should never embarrass, humiliate, or belittle students

The many positive methods of talking with students about their behavior

The significant differences between punishment and consequences

That punishment stops behavior temporarily but does not help students learn new, constructive ways of behaving

The strategies for modifying students' behavior

What LSCI, cognitive strategies, and bibliotherapy are and how they are used

The precautions that need to be taken when time-out and point and level systems are used so that they are not abused

Applying the Concepts

1. Reflect on your experience as an elementary and a secondary student. Can you recall teachers who frequently used punishment and threats to manage behavior? How did you feel about these teachers? How effective were they? Did students' behavior change? What are some alternative ways these teachers could have dealt with disciplinary problems?

2. Make a checklist of several behavioral interventions described in this chapter. At a field site, do a frequency count of how often teachers use each intervention. Tabulate your results and report them to your class (the teacher's name and the school name should remain confidential). Analyze the ratings. What conclusions can you derive from this mini research project?

3. Interview teachers and principals. Ask them about how students are disciplined. Ask them how they feel about punishment. Ask them if they distinguish between punishment and consequences. Try to determine how many alternative behavioral interventions they use regularly. Ask if they would be willing to come to your class to discuss behavioral interventions.

4. Do a review of several well-known education journals during a 10-year period. Calculate the percentage of articles that deal with discipline or managing disruptive behavior. Survey classroom teachers about their professional preparation for dealing with disruptive students. Summarize your findings and present them to your class.

5. Select a specific type of behavioral problem, such as ADHD, conduct disorder, bullying, violence in schools, oppositional defiant disorder, or acting out. Read 10 articles on the topic and summarize your findings in an annotated bibliography. Present your findings to your class.

6. At a field site, note the type of behavioral problems teachers deal with. Use these samples for a role-playing exercise. In your class, have some of your classmates act out disruptive behavior while others role-play teachers using the positive behavioral interventions described in this chapter. Discuss the results.

7. In your class, list the five behavioral interventions described in this chapter that you would most likely use and the five behavioral interventions you would least likely use. Compare your results and discuss the differences between preferred and nonpreferred interventions.

8. During a brainstorming session, list behaviors that class members find the most disruptive. Match each behavior listed with three behavioral interventions you think would be most effective. Compare your lists with those of your classmates. Discuss your similarities and differences of opinion.

9. Review the film *Dangerous Minds.* Identify the behavioral interventions Ms. Johnson used. Which were effective and which were not effective with her students? Imagine you are Ms. Johnson's supervisor. What recommendations would you give her for working more effectively with her group of "special" students? Discuss the experience of teaching in schools where most students are economically disadvantaged. What different behavioral issues does a teacher need to be able to deal with in an economically disadvantaged school than those a teacher in an affluent school encounters?

Chapter 9

Managing Problem Behaviors

Chapter Outline

Problem Behavior Defined
  Setting
  Duration
  Intensity
Positive Behavioral Supports
  Basic Needs
  Social Skills
  Environmental Support
Functional Behavior Assessment
  Advantages of FBA
  FBA Procedure
  Behavior Management Plan
Emotional Problems
  Undetected Emotional Problems

Types of Emotional Disturbance
  Federal Definition of Emotional
    Disturbance
Five problem Behaviors
  Aggressive Behavior
  Passive-Aggressive Behavior
  Attention-Deficit/Hyperactivity
    Disorder
  Isolating Behaviors
  Nonverbal Learning Disabilities
Discipline and IDEA
Summary
What You Should Know
Applying the Concepts

Key Terms

Asperger's syndrome
Attention-deficit/hyperactivity disorder
  (ADHD)
Behavior management plan (BMP)
Benign confrontation
Contingency contracting
Data collection
Depression
Duration
Emotional disturbance
Externalized behavioral problems

Functional behavior assessment (FBA)
Individuals with Disabilities Education Act
  (IDEA)
Intensity
Internalized behavioral problems
Isolating behaviors
Nonverbal learning disabilities (NLDs)
Positive behavioral supports (PBSs)
Response cost
Setting

Introduction

When a pattern of misbehavior is identified, proactive teachers collect data to determine what events in the classroom might trigger behavioral problems. The intention is to help students learn constructive ways to meet their needs. This approach is called *positive behavioral support*. Positive behavioral support is anchored by the belief that modifications in the classroom environment can promote constructive student behavior. Two useful positive behavioral support tools are a functional assessment of behavior and a behavior management plan. Although some students with emotional problems receive special education services, many remain undetected in general education classrooms. This chapter provides an outline of specific "best practices" to use for students with behavioral and emotional problems. These practices include strategies to positively support students with attention-deficit/hyperactivity disorder, nonverbal learning disabilities, depression, isolating behavior, and aggressive behavior.

A behavior is a "problem" when it interferes with a student's ability to learn. Some problem behaviors are more obvious than others. Externalized behaviors such as aggressiveness and noncompliance are public displays of problems. Meanwhile, internalized problems such as depression and anorexia are subtle and easier to overlook.

Whereas acting-out, externalized behaviors get the most attention from teachers, internalized problems can severely limit a student's ability to participate in classroom routines. This chapter covers the characteristics of internalized and externalized problem behaviors and positive interventions teachers can use to assist such students.

PROBLEM BEHAVIOR DEFINED

At one time or another, almost all youngsters experience difficulty in their lives. Distress can be caused by such events as a divorce, a death, or a move to a new community. After a while, these temporary problems usually dissipate.

In addition to personal difficulties individual student behavior is influenced by the classroom ambience including teacher style. What constitutes a "problem" often depends on the teacher's viewpoint. What one teacher characterizes as an "energetic" student another might describe as "disruptive." Three criteria—setting, duration, and intensity—help determine whether a student's behavior requires positive behavior intervention.

Setting

If the same behavior is replicated in a variety of settings—in school, at home, and in the community—the student has an individual problem, and his or her behavior is not a symptom of a student–classroom environment mismatch. Depression and anorexia are examples of difficult emotional problems that continue to manifest regardless of *setting*. Information about the student's behavior at home and in other classrooms helps the teacher determine whether the problem behavior occurs across settings or is context specific.

Duration

Duration refers to how often a problem behavior occurs: Is the problem behavior temporary or chronic? This key question must be addressed when the teacher is trying to determine the severity of a problem behavior. Developmental phases and circumstantial stressors are two mitigating factors a teacher should consider when he or she is contemplating student behavior.

Parents often use the cliché "the terrible twos" to describe the developmental stage when children explore their world at a breakneck pace. During this time, temper tantrums and tumbles are commonplace. The notion that the child is "going through a phase" helps sustain a concerned parent.

A student who was previously enthusiastic might gradually recede into the background during classroom discussions. A student who is usually task oriented could start arriving at class with incomplete assignments. These signals can alert a teacher to a student's need for more support, but they do not necessarily indicate that the student has developed a serious behavioral problem.

Intensity

Any incident that disrupts an entire class, causes physical or psychological harm, or puts a student in jeopardy is an *intense* behavioral problem. Temper tantrums are an example of an intense behavior. For example, when third-grade student Ramón gets upset, he crawls under tables and desks and physically resists attempts to calm him down. Six-year-old Alicia will bite her arm when frustrated. At least once every month, 17-year-old Lewis skips school and joins some friends in bouts of drinking and marijuana smoking. Each of these episodes, although infrequent, indicates the presence of a serious problem that requires intervention.

Abrams and Segal (1998) said that teachers should be alert to low levels of student frustration that could lead to more-intense behaviors. Sources of frustration for students with emotional and behavioral problems include disorganized teaching, failure, boredom, lack of positive reinforcement, an irrelevant curriculum, overuse of punishment, and feelings of powerlessness.

Proactive teachers deal with intense behavior by remaining emotionally detached. Emotional detachment reduces the possibility that the teacher will say or do something that will increase the *intensity* of an event. A calm response indicates that the teacher is in control of the situation.

POSITIVE BEHAVIORAL SUPPORTS

Positive behavioral supports (PBSs) is a general term for proactive disciplinary methods. Originally, PBSs were developed as alternatives to threats, punishment, and other aversive reactions to disruptive behaviors. PBSs are based on the following principles:

- Nonpunitive approaches to behavioral change are more effective than punitive approaches are.
- Inappropriate behavior is a symptom, not the problem.
- Efforts to change students' behavior should be data based.
- If a behavioral intervention plan does not work, do not blame the student; change the plan.
- Students who exhibit behavioral deficiencies also have behavioral strengths.
- Student behavioral change requires a long-term adult commitment.
- Social skills instruction is fundamental to behavioral change.

The Council for Exceptional Children (Warger, 1999) compared PBSs with traditional disciplinary practices and concluded the following:

> Unlike traditional behavior management, which views the individuals the sole problem and seeks to "fix" him and her by quickly eliminating the challenging behavior, PBS (positive behavior support) views settings and lack of skill as parts of the "problem" and works to change those. As such, PBS is characterized as a long-term approach to reducing inappropriate behavior, teaching a more appropriate behavior, and providing the contextual supports necessary for successful outcomes. (Office of Special Education, 1999, p. 1)

Further support for PBSs has been cited. In an extensive review of research on PBSs, the U.S. Office of Special Education Programs (1999) found that PBS strategies effectively helped change the behaviors of students who had been exhibiting a range of challenging behaviors.

PBSs have evolved into comprehensive systems for analyzing and changing students' behavior. Previous chapters describe an array of behavioral intervention strategies. Developing PBSs involves selecting one or more of these strategies and combining them with an appropriate social skills program. The overall effect is to reduce challenging behaviors (i.e., through positive behavioral interventions) while teaching students replacement social skills (i.e., through the implementation of a social skills curriculum). Effective PBSs respond to individual basic needs, teach appropriate social skills, and provide environmental supports to sustain constructive behavior.

Basic Needs

Rather than taking a one-system-fits-all approach, PBS is based on the premise that individual student needs differ. Some students need more control of their environment, others need improved affiliations with peers, and still others need successful learning experiences. When basic needs are thwarted, students will use any means necessary to meet them. Just as a hungry child will steal to eat, a lonely student will act as class clown to get peer approval.

Different needs require different behavioral interventions. While consistency in classroom routines provides security, flexibility in behavioral interventions is responsive to individual needs.

> *Examples: Incomplete Work.*   Even a minor amount of frustration seems to shut Renée down. She will sit at her desk and stare at a blank paper rather than take the risk of looking foolish because of errors in her work. *PBS approach*: Enlist Renée in a peer-tutoring program. Peer tutoring will encourage Renée to persevere and help relieve the stigma she associates with making mistakes in front of the teacher.
>
> Many of Mr. Churchill's students are turning in incomplete homework. He decides to use negative reinforcement as a group contingency. Students who complete their homework assignments Monday through Thursday are excused from weekend assignments.

Social Skills

For many years, educators believed that teaching social skills was solely the family's responsibility. This view has changed because some students have not learned appropriate social skills.

Sugai and Horner estimated that 15% of all students are deficient in their social skills development U.S. Office of Special Education Programs (1999). For example, some students who are impulsive have difficulty managing frustration. When confronted with a difficult task, they give up or refuse to continue. Other students have not learned how to verbalize their feelings. Instead of describing their anger, they act it out. While the tendency to clamp down on such students to get desired results is understandable, this approach rarely shows long-term benefits. In contrast, Marzano and Marzano (2003) reported a 25% decrease in students' disruptive behavior after social skills instruction.

Social skills instruction aims to produce long-term change that will positively affect a student's behavior outside school as well as in the classroom (U.S. Department of Education, 2001).

> *Example: Following Rules.*   Ms. Lopez was losing instructional time because many of her third-grade students did not follow basic classroom rules such as raising a hand or taking turns. Each time she enforced a rule by taking away a privilege, her students seemed more resentful. After conferring with some colleagues, Ms. Lopez decided to take a social skills approach. She began to weave lessons about rules into her lessons on academic subjects. In language arts, she organized a cooperative learning project with the theme "A Day Without Rules." She gave each group a list of rules, such as speed limit signs are removed, no tickets are necessary to enter a movie theater, and children do not have to wear seatbelts. Each group then devised a list of what they thought the consequences would be. At every opportunity, she encouraged students to

look for rules in their lessons. She read her students the story *No Jumping on the Bed*, by Tedd Arnold (1987). Afterward, the class exchanged ideas about parents, children, and rules. She pointed out rules of nature and rules of government. As time passed, her students no longer personalized their dissatisfaction with rules but began to express an understanding about why rules are necessary. To be sure, problems with classroom rules persisted, but with time, Ms. Lopez saw significant improvement in her students' attitudes toward following rules.

Appendix A is an informal checklist for assessing students' social skills in impulse control, stress management, group participation, social problem solving, and school routines (Henley, 1994b). Teachers can use this checklist to organize a social skills curriculum.

Environmental Support

A comprehensive environmental support system teaches students constructive ways of managing their actions and emotions. Comprehensive supports include the following:

- A schoolwide support system (e.g., administrative support)
- Behavioral support in the classroom (e.g., specific positive behavioral interventions)
- Support for the classroom teacher (e.g., in-service training)
- Individual student support (e.g., counseling)
- Outside-school support systems, including family supports (e.g., access to mental health services) and community supports (e.g., after-school recreational programs)

Culturally appropriate interventions are a key aspect of each support system. Depending on the seriousness of the problem behavior, supports range from minor to major changes in a student's daily program.

Example: Tardiness.   José, a seventh grader, was consistently late for his classes. He often sauntered in 5 minutes after the bell rang, and his late entry disrupted ongoing lessons. At a team meeting, his teachers and the principal hypothesized that the purpose of José's tardiness was to attract peer approval. The educators agreed on a plan. The principal had a private meeting with José and reviewed the school attendance policy. He reminded José that if he accumulated too many tardy slips, he would no longer be eligible to play in the school band. The teachers agreed to use negative reinforcement. They told José that every 10 times he came to class on time, they would delete a previous tardy slip from his attendance record. Also, each teacher agreed to find positive statements to make about his classroom contributions. After 5 weeks, the plan was evaluated and the data indicated a steady decline in José's tardiness.

What distinguished the problem-solving approach of these educators was their data-based solution. The plan provided for keeping a count of improved behavior. If the plan did not work, they would try another. This practical, data-based approach to problem solving is spelled out in more detail in the next section on functional behavior assessment.

FUNCTIONAL BEHAVIOR ASSESSMENT

The purpose of a *functional behavior assessment (FBA)* is to gather information to identify school antecedents and consequences that contribute to a student's behavioral problem. A key premise of functional behavior is that misbehavior serves a practical purpose (i.e., function) for the student. For example, Sam interrupts his eighth-grade teacher with sarcastic remarks because his peers laugh and he gets attention. Joseph acts up during art because he does not like his art teacher, Mr. Melendez. Mr. Melendez then sends Joseph out of the room, which is exactly what he wants. To impress his peers, Nick belittles another third grader about her weight.

Principles of FBA include the following (Ryan, Halsey, & Mathews, 2003):

- The fundamental purpose of functional assessment is to gain insight into why a student misbehaves. This understanding will improve decisions about appropriate PBSs.
- Challenging behavior occurs within the context of a student's interaction with the classroom environment. Changing environmental conditions can change student behavior.
- Descriptive information must be gathered about a student's behavior and classroom variables that influence the behavior.
- Specific data should include a description of the problem behavior, antecedents and consequences to the behavior, and setting events (i.e., meaningful events that occurred earlier).

Fitzsimmons (1998) noted that student misbehavior is motivated by a need to avoid, escape, or get something. Consider the case study of Helene.

Advantages of FBA

Chandler and Dahlquist (2002) outlined the advantages of FBA:

- It is a proactive approach, teaching children what they should do rather than punishing children for engaging in challenging behavior.
- It focuses on prevention as well as remediation by arranging antecedents and consequences that will reinforce positive behavior.
- It provides professionals with a common language (e.g., antecedents, function, and consequence) for discussing challenging behavior.
- It provides professionals with a method for assessing behavior that is useful regardless of the student's age or disability, or the setting.
- It provides professionals with consistent methods for selecting behavioral interventions that address the function of the behavior.

Case Study: Helene

Helene was an overweight high school senior. Physically, she was unable to keep pace with other students, and she was sensitive about her looks. She concocted one excuse after another to avoid physical education. When excuses did not work, she acted up, knowing that the gym teacher would tell her to sit by herself on the bleachers.

Helene's "misbehavior" fulfilled a need: It helped her avoid embarrassment. Nothing was wrong with her wanting to avoid humiliation. The problem was her method. Helene needed physical education, but she also needed to preserve her fragile body image. Helene's homeroom teacher had a heart-to-heart discussion with Helene and uncovered her secret. Her parents were also consulted, and they verified Helene's sensitivity about her weight. Other teachers were consulted, and they revealed that Helene's problem behaviors occurred mainly in the classes that preceded and followed physical education.

Understanding that Helene's actions were an attempt to avoid embarrassment sensitized her teachers to Helene's predicament. Her physical education and homeroom teachers met with the principal to discuss how to support Helene while still ensuring that she met state physical education requirements. They agreed that obesity was a schoolwide problem, so they decided to pilot a physical education class similar to a commercial fitness physical program. The new course emphasized aerobic workouts coupled with nutritional education. Once the program was made available to seniors, Helene and eight other students signed up.

FBA Procedure

As mentioned previously, the goal of FBA is to gather descriptive data that will provide insight into a youngster's behavior. The following two steps describe the FBA *data collection* procedure:

1. **Clearly describe the problem.**   Avoid generalizations and judgmental terms, even if they sound scientific. Rather than saying "Maria is noncompliant" or "Teresa has low self-esteem," say "Maria does not complete assignments" and "During student-centered activities, Teresa avoids contact with other students." The idea is to operationally define the problem behavior in observable terms. Doing so sets the stage for step 2: gathering information about the behavior.

2. **Collect data.**   Stating behavior in observable terms facilitates information gathering. Educators use a variety of methods for collecting data on behavior, including observation checklists, behavior frequency check lists, questionnaires, interviews, and record reviews. The purpose of data collection is to determine the frequency of a problem behavior and to identify environmental events that could be contributing factors. More specifically, data collection addresses the following questions:

   - When and where does the behavior occur?
   - How often does the behavior occur?
   - What is the duration of the behavior?
   - What is the typical adult reaction to the behavior?

- What is the typical peer reaction to the behavior?
- How much does the behavior disrupt normal classroom routines?
- What antecedents trigger the behavior?
- What consequences reinforce the behavior?
- What function does the behavior serve?

See Figure 9.1 for a sample FBA form.

October 28, 2005

Student: Maria Alvarez   *Grade:* 5

Target behavior: Maria refuses to complete assigned work.

	Monday	Tuesday	Wednesday	Thursday	Friday
9:00–10:00	xx	xxx	xxx	xxxxx	xxx
10:00–11:00	xx	xxxx	xxxxx	xx	xxx
11:00–12:00					
12:00–1:00	x		xx	x	x
1:00–2:00		xx		xx	
2:00–3:00	xx				

Data analysis: Maria's noncompliance occurs primarily during morning sessions. Afternoon sessions include more activity-based learning, including arts and crafts activities.

Antecedents: Maria is required to do more passive learning activities during the morning (e.g., textbook/workbook assignments).

Consequences: Primarily negative reprimands and encouragement to try harder

Effect of consequences: Modest increase in effort, which soon dissipates

Function of target behavior: Noncompliance is negatively reinforced because she avoids aversive seat work.

Behavior plan: Include more activity-based learning activities in morning sessions. Alternate textbook/workbook assignments with cooperative learning, role-playing, peer tutoring, and brainstorming sessions.

Evaluate plan: In 2 months, do another behavior frequency count of noncompliant behavior and compare data from the first observation.

FIGURE 9.1   Sample Functional Behavior Assessment Form

Student name: Alfredo Taylor

Age: 11   *Sex:* Male   *Grade:* 5   *Date:* January 25, 2005
Educational setting: James Madison Elementary

Significant student characteristics: Alfredo shows talent in both mathematics and science; however, his effort is often minimal. He spends much of his time trying to avoid schoolwork. He is popular with other students and seems more interested in cultivating peer relationships than excelling in work. His "avoidant" behaviors distract other students.

Target behavior(s): Frequent wisecracks and sarcastic comments
Desired behavior: Constructive classroom comments
Week of: April 15–April 20 *N* = 37 "off-task" comments

During what periods/times of the day is the target behavior most frequently observed? Increase in frequency noted during late morning and early afternoon

What are antecedent events or behaviors that could trigger the target behavior? Subjects during this time involve large-group instruction and independent seat work.

What are the consequences/reactions that could be helping maintain the target behavior? Other students laugh or "egg" Alfredo on; putting Alfredo in time-out has not decreased the behavior but seems to reinforce his perception that the teacher is picking on him.

Hypothesis—What function does the behavior serve or basic need does the behavior attempt to gain? Peer approval. Also, placement in time-out allows him to avoid work.

Modifications to help the student meet the above function or basic need in a constructive way: Incorporate cooperative learning and peer-tutoring lessons to provide socially appropriate ways of interacting with peers. Allow Alfredo to tutor third graders in math three times a week; increase time if successful. Provide more activity-based learning activities that allow Alfredo and other students to move around the room.

Positive behavioral supports: Eliminate time-out and negative reprimands. Use nonverbal interventions—planned ignoring and proximity. Set up a negative reinforcement schedule to encourage completion of work. Use sane messages and logical consequences in place of negative reprimands. Give Alfredo specific classroom responsibilities to help build trust and self-efficacy.

Social skills that would support the generalization of the new constructive behavior into settings outside school: To appropriately verbalize feelings and cooperate in group activities

Date to evaluate behavior management plan: March 15, 2005

FIGURE 9.2   Sample Behavior Management Plan

Behavior Management Plan

After collecting data through observations and interviews, the professionals who know the student best draw up a *behavior management plan (BMP)*. The BMP outlines a specific course of action for helping a student learn constructive behaviors. BMPs are recommended for any student who exhibits chronic classroom management problems. The BMP couples data derived from student observations and interviews with an analysis of classroom variables that could be reinforcing undesirable behavior.

A BMP consists of the following elements (Chandler & Dahlquist, 2002; Ryan et al., 2003; Scott, Liaupsin, Nelson, & Jolivette, 2003):

- A statement of student characteristics, including student strengths and abilities
- A target behavior to change, spelled out in descriptive language
- A desired target behavior to replace the behavior to be changed
- A summary of data collected about the behavior to be changed
- Statements about classroom variables that could be instigating or reinforcing the target behavior (e.g., embedded classroom antecedents and consequences)
- A hypothesis about what function or need the undesired target behavior could be meeting
- A clear statement of classroom modifications, social skills instruction, and PBSs
- A date for re-evaluating the plan after a mutually determined period, usually 2 to 3 months
- A new plan if no change in student behavior is seen

Figure 9.2 shows a sample BMP.

EMOTIONAL PROBLEMS

Undetected Emotional Problems

Emotional problems are a leading cause of school failure. Fifty percent of students with documented emotional disabilities drop out of school (U.S. Department of Education, 2001). While frequent and intense problem behaviors usually attract adult attention, teachers also need to be alert for less obvious signs that a mental health problem exists.

Some students sit silently, staring at their desks, attention fixed inward. Others arrogantly stroll through school corridors alert for any challenge to their fragile self-esteem. Still others are marked more by their absences than by their behavior. These are some of the behaviors that signal a student might be at risk of school failure because of an emotional problem.

One percent of the school population—approximately 600,000 students—receive special education services because of an emotional or a behavioral disability. Yet, according to U.S. Surgeon General David Satcher (2000), most students with emotional problems sit undetected in general education classrooms. The Center for the Advancement of Children's Mental Health (2002) estimated that 80% of children with serious mental health problems go unnoticed and untreated. In fact, a long-term study of 3,700 children with emotional problems revealed that most of the children did not receive special education services (Forness, 2001). Furthermore, those placed in special education were often misidentified as having a learning disability.

Concentration, memory, and perseverance are influenced by a student's emotional state. Within the human brain, the limbic system, the emotional center, and the neocortex, the reasoning center of the brain work in tandem. Strong emotions such as fear, anger, or shame affect rational thought. Even mildly stressful experiences can impede clear thinking. Think of the experience of "going blank" during a test.

When faced with a stressful situation, some students act out, and others withdraw. The situation worsens with fractious interactions with adults or peers. Within school, students who act out are most likely to be identified as having an emotional or a behavioral problem. Meanwhile, more serious mental health problems that do not pose a threat to classroom order, such as depression, are overlooked.

Helping Students.   Research on resilient youths shows that given the support of caring adults, students who are at risk can go on to live productive lives (Benard, 1992; Osher, Kendziora, VanDenBerg, & Karl, 1999; Werner & Smith, 1982). Youths' emotional problems can be treated effectively through the coordinated efforts of mental health and educational agencies. Within school, students who are identified as in need of special education services for emotional disturbance are eligible for counseling and an individual educational program tailored to their specific needs.

Community mental health agencies offer counseling for individuals and families. However, although special education services for emotional disturbance are mandated by federal and state laws, mental health services for children outside school are limited. The availability of such services, family income, and health insurance all play a role in determining whether a young person receives adequate mental health treatment (Epstein, Kutash, & Duchnowski, 1998).

The longer a young person's difficulties go untreated, the less sanguine the prognosis. Satcher (2000) said, "Growing numbers of children are suffering needlessly because their emotional, behavioral and developmental needs are not being met by the very institutions and systems that were created to care for them" (p. 10).

Types of Emotional Disturbance

Emotional disturbance is classified as one of two types: internalized or externalized. *Externalized behavioral problems* are more obvious because a student acts in a way that draws attention to him- or herself. Temper tantrums, physical aggression, and defiance are examples of behaviors that can indicate externalized emotional problems. In contrast, *internalized behavioral problems* are more subtle because the warning signs are less visible, such as sexual abuse that leads to depression and suicidal thoughts.

In a longitudinal study of 812 students aged 9 to 17 with emotional disorders, Greenbaum et al. (1998) found the following distribution of externalized disorders: conduct disorder, 66.9%; attention-deficit disorder, 11.7%; and schizophrenic

TABLE 9.1 *At-Risk Indicators of Emotional Problems*

In School	
Internalized Behaviors	***Externalized Behaviors***
Has no friends	Displays chronic disciplinary problems
Does not complete work	Lacks empathy or compassion
Has mood swings	Has gang attachments
Displays "learned helplessness"	Has angry outbursts
Has an interest in cults	Performs poorly in academics
Has an inordinate attraction to fantasy	Has conflicts with authority figures
Is indolent	Bullies others
Is a bully victim	Is frequently absent
Is frequently absent	Is physically aggressive
Displays inappropriate affect (e.g., crying)	Damages property
Exhibits obsessive-compulsive behaviors	Uses obscene language
Is shy	Ignores teachers' warnings
Outside School	
Was born prematurely	
Mother suffers from depression	
Lives in poverty	
Has been neglected or physically, sexually, or emotionally abused	
Has been placed in foster care	
Displays chronic disciplinary problems	
Has frequent temper tantrums	
Exhibits loss of appetite or overeating	
Engages in long periods of isolation, watching television or on the computer	
Experiences sleep disturbances or nightmares	

Note. Compiled from "'Behavioral Earthquakes': Low Frequency, Salient Behavioral Events That Differentiate Students At-Risk for Behavioral Disorders," by F. M. Gresham, D. L. MacMillan, and K. Bocian, 1996, *Behavioral Disorders, 21*(4), pp. 277–292.

disorder, 4.7%. The internalized disorders that were identified were anxiety disorder, 41%, and depression, 18.5%. Forty-one percent of the youngsters had two or more disorders. Table 9.1 is a guide to early warning signs of emotional disturbance.

Federal Definition of Emotional Disturbance

The *Individuals with Disabilities Act (IDEA)* provides criteria for determining eligibility for special education for an emotional disturbance (Figure 9.3). These criteria provide a functional template for early identification of youths who are at risk and for implementation of proactive classroom supports.

Emotional Disturbance:

A condition exhibiting one or more of the following characteristics over a long period of time and to a marked degree that adversely affects a child's educational performance:

- An inability to learn that cannot be explained by intellectual, sensory, or health factors
- An inability to build or maintain satisfactory interpersonal relationships with peers and teachers
- Inappropriate types of behavior or feelings under normal circumstances
- A general pervasive mood of unhappiness or depression
- A tendency to develop physical symptoms or fears associated with personal or school problems

The term includes schizophrenia. The term does not apply to children who are socially maladjusted, unless it is determined that they have an emotional disturbance.

FIGURE 9.3   Individuals with Disabilities Education Act Definition of *Emotional Disturbance*
From Assistance to States for the Education of Children with Disabilities, 34 C.F.R. § 300.7(c)(4) (1999).

Inability to Learn.   Emotional distress saps motivation. The belief that school has nothing relevant to offer is reinforced by failing grades and teacher reprimands. Noncompliance, disinterest, and avoidance are symptoms exhibited by students whose perseverance is weighted down by their emotional baggage.

> **What Works.**   Students need school success to sustain them. The student who is emotionally distressed is more focused on the concrete here and now than on the abstract future. Establishing links between the curriculum and students' lives injects relevance into lessons. Older students need training that will enhance employment opportunities. Survey students about their interests and how they spend their free time. Use this information as a backdrop for lessons.

Mrs. Samble's fifth–sixth grade inclusion classroom hummed with activity. She summed up her teaching philosophy in one phrase: making connections. A geometry lesson on calculating the perimeter of triangles turned into a class discussion on pyramids, which culminated in a week-long unit on ancient Egypt. One student wore a baseball shirt of his favorite shortstop to school. Mrs. Samble asked how player numbers are selected. This question led to an impromptu discussion on baseball statistics. As follow-up, Mrs. Samble brought in copies of the local newspaper sports page. Her students contrasted statistics of their favorite ball players. Whatever was necessary to keep her students engaged in their learning, Mrs. Samble was ready to try.

Inability to Maintain Satisfactory Relationships.   Peers are second only to family in their influence on a youngster's emotional development. By adolescence, time spent with peers exceeds time spent with family. Relationships with peers provide the main entry into adulthood. Positive peer relationships foster tolerance of others, build effective interpersonal skills, and promote self-confidence. The unwelcome outcomes of negative peer relationships include smoking, alcohol abuse, teenage pregnancy, and delinquent behavior.

What Works.   Teachers enhance peer relationships by structuring routines that foster a sense of classroom community. Cooperative learning, peer tutoring, and classroom meetings promote interdependence. These structured student interactions help dispel the negative effects of cliques while promoting the notion that everyone has something useful to contribute. Many students enter school deficient in the social skills they need for successful participation in classroom routines. Socials skills instruction is a proactive alternative to such reactive disciplinary practices as reprimands and punishment. Integrating social skills instruction with lessons and routines promotes generalization of social skills to other settings outside the classroom (Henley, 2003).

Several teachers at Juniper Park Elementary School were concerned about a rash of teasing among students. The teachers decided to integrate the social skill "understanding how behavior affects others" (Appendix A, Skill #12) into their language arts curriculum. Students were particularly attracted to Shel Silverstein books. Using Silverstein's verses as a model, students wrote and illustrated stories about empathy and human compassion. Teachers decorated a bulletin board in the central school hallway entitled "Acts of Kindness." Each time a student observed an act of consideration, he or she would attach a leaf with the name of the kind student on the "Kindness Tree." The metaphor of branching kindness appealed to students and teachers alike. By the end of the school year, teachers agreed that even though their original concerns were with teasing outside the classroom, behavior within their classrooms had improved as well.

Inappropriate Behavior or Feelings.   Teachers have difficulty understanding why a reasonable request, a minor classroom frustration, or an accidental bump from a peer can prompt sudden rage. Students who have been rejected by or alienated from significant others distrust adults and believe that further rejection is inevitable. In situations that trigger feelings of anxiety, insecurity, or fear, their impulsive response is anger and noncompliance. To justify their behavior, such students develop Teflon-like rationalizations to deflect personal responsibility.

What Works.   Techniques that teach students to reflect on their actions and to use more-constructive ways of managing their emotions promote self-control. Life space crisis intervention (Long, Wood, & Fecser, 2001) is a guided interview that uses spontaneous behavioral outbursts as a platform to teach students personal responsibility. Identifying in-school events that trigger disruptive behavior provides clues about ways of modifying school routines to support constructive actions. Teachers who refrain from personalizing disruptive behavior are most effective at defusing conflict. Recognizing that a reason always exists for misbehavior helps teachers avoid impulsive reactions that can cause a minor episode to explode into a full-blown crisis.

In violation of school rules, Tyrone entered the classroom late and wearing a baseball cap. When Mr. Wade asked to him to remove the hat, Tyrone reacted as if he had been attacked. Mr. Wade calmly asked Tyrone if he recalled the school sanction for wearing hats. Tyrone did not answer but sat down, staring sullenly at his desk. Allowing Tyrone time to save face, Mr. Wade continued his lesson. After 5 minutes, Tyrone stuffed his hat into his desk and opened his text. Later in the afternoon, the principal told Mr. Wade that Tyrone's foster placement had been changed—the 13th time that year.

Pervasive Mood of Unhappiness or Depression.   Two to 4% of young children and 4 to 8% of adolescents experience symptoms of *depression* (CEC, 1999). Persistent sadness or irritability, loss of interest in previously enjoyed activities, disrupted sleep, agitation, loss of energy, feelings of worthlessness or inappropriate guilt, difficulty concentrating, and recurrent thoughts of death or suicide are major symptoms. Depression is identified more often in females than in males. Students with attention-deficit/hyperactivity disorder are prone to depressive disorders. Early identification is the key to successful treatment through a combination of counseling, psychotherapy, and medication.

What Works.   Major depressive disorder is characterized by a pattern of five or more symptoms. If symptoms persist for 6 months, a referral to a school counselor is recommended. A youngster's family may need assistance in engaging the services of a counselor with expertise in depressive disorders. Students cannot "snap out of" depression. Understanding and empathy are more effective than are attempts to change behavior through reprimands, incentives, or heart-to-heart talks. Fatigue is a common classroom complaint. Students' needs include extra time to finish assignments, projects tailored to their interests, and brief breaks. Classroom activities that foster feelings of competence and strengthen social relationships bolster self-efficacy.

Melinda's third-grade teacher was concerned. The bright, energetic student who began school in September was slowly replaced by a child who was whiny and withdrawn. Absences accumulated, and Melinda complained that her schoolwork was too difficult. She would start a task and give up after a few minutes. When reminded that she was falling behind her classmates, she replied, "I don't care." Once an energetic basketball player, Melinda quit the team. Melinda's teacher shared her concerns about Melinda with the school psychologist, and she was surprised to learn that even young children are vulnerable to depression. No local counseling service specialized in childhood depression. The school psychologist, accessed the National Alliance for the Mentally Ill Web site (www.nami.org/helpline/depression-child.html) and gathered the information needed to get Melinda professional help.

Tendency to Develop Physical Symptoms or Fears.   Like steam building in a tightly lidded pot, unvented emotional distress exerts pressure on the body. If the cause is not addressed or effective coping strategies developed, physical symptoms can emerge. Frequent headaches, abdominal pain, asthma, hives, chest pains, and dizziness are common physical complaints. From time to time, students will feign illness to avoid schoolwork. Legitimate psychophysiological ailments persist for 4 months or longer. Only a physician can make an accurate diagnosis. During adolescence, females are 5 times more vulnerable to psychophysiological disorders than males are (Sadock & Kaplan, 2000).

What Works. Using an upset stomach or another physical ailment to escape schoolwork is not unusual. However, when physical complaints are frequent, a student should be referred to a physician to rule out medical origins. Input from family members can help identify unusual stressors. Counseling builds coping strategies. Chronic stress can lead to depression. Local mental health services should be accessed if symptoms persist despite school-based interventions. A combination of coping strategies will alleviate distress, including eliminating the source and providing relaxation training, cognitive restructuring, and medication.

Fourteen-year-old Samantha was a popular and, by all accounts, an average student. Her hectic after-school schedule included soccer, karate, and modeling. Wanting to enhance scholarship opportunities and over Samantha's objections, her parents had her placed in advanced-level courses. Samantha's academic progress did not keep pace with their expectations. She confided to her science teacher that she was afraid of looking stupid. Her class participation, which was always her strong point, went from enthusiastic to apathetic. She began complaining of stomachaches and fatigue.

A prescribed bland diet did not help; neither did a regimen of herbal remedies. When her symptoms continued, the school psychologist met with Samantha's parents and suggested a reduction in her rigorous schedule. The psychologist also recommended a mental health counselor specializing in adolescent stress-related disorders. Samantha went into counseling, dropped an advanced math class, and reduced her after-school schedule. During the next 6 months, Samantha's condition gradually improved.

FIVE PROBLEM BEHAVIORS

The following five subsections provide summaries of practical, research-based strategies for dealing with five of the most common problem behaviors attributed to students with emotional and behavioral disorders. The five problem behaviors addressed are aggressive behavior, passive-aggressive behavior, attention-deficit/ hyperactivity disorder, isolating behaviors, and nonverbal learning disabilities.

Aggressive Behavior

As discussed previously, teachers have difficulty understanding why a reasonable request from an adult, a minor classroom frustration, or an accidental bump by a peer can result in an instantaneous student outburst of anger. The intensity of the

Case Study: Tyrone

Tyrone enters the school wearing a hat, although he knows it is not permitted. A teacher politely asks him to remove it, and Tyrone reacts as if he has been attacked. He shouts, " I'm *!#+* tired of you bossing me around! I'm not taking any more of your @#+**#." His teacher, Mr. Alvarez, is not prepared for this aggressive eruption and begins to argue with Tyrone. The situation quickly escalates into a crisis. Tyrone is removed from the classroom and is suspended. The suspension is fine as far as Tyrone is concerned. He would rather be on the streets than in school.

reaction is out of proportion to the situation. The behavior does not make sense. It is not logical or acceptable, but it often does succeed in creating counteraggressive feelings in staff (Long & Morse, 1996; Maag, 2001a). Unabated, aggressive behavior often leads to a special education referral with a diagnosis of conduct disorder or oppositional defiant disorder (Forness, Walker, & Kavale, 2003). Consider the case study of Tyrone.

The incident in the case study raises a question: How can a teacher defuse aggressive behavior when traditional school-based interventions for students who are aggressive are usually ineffective? (Walker, 1995)

Managing Aggressive Behavior.   The greatest challenge for teachers who deal with students who are aggressive is maintaining their own emotional equilibrium. Emotional objectivity allows time for determining the best method for intervention and alleviates the possibility that the teacher will model the same type of aggressive behavior that he or she is trying to change in the student.

Determining the best intervention varies with individual situations. The following recommendations have proved successful with students in both general and special education:

- Teach students self-management strategies. For example, have students count the number of times they interrupt class. Help students determine a way to reward themselves for appropriate classroom behavior.
- Aggressive behavior usually follows a predictable pattern. Do an FBA to determine classroom events that could be triggering or reinforcing disruptive behaviors.
- Increase positive feedback about appropriate behavior and decrease reprimands about inappropriate behavior.
- Analyze group dynamics to determine how the need for peer affiliation or acceptance might be encouraging maladaptive behavior. Use prosocial instructional methods such as cooperative learning and peer tutoring.
- When sanctions are necessary, use logical consequences rather than threats or punishment. Punishment might temporarily provide relief, but in the long run, it increases student hostility and resentment.
- Systematically teach social skills. Students need to learn replacement behaviors for disruptive behaviors.

- Use exclusion procedures such as time-outs only if the student's behavior is disruptive to the entire class.
- Avoid arguing or being drawn into power struggles.
- Keep rules to a minimum and state each in plain, descriptive language. Instead of "Behave in class," say "Raise your hand before speaking."
- Model the behaviors you want students to exhibit.
- Experiment with behavioral support methods (Chapter 8). Base selection of support strategies on student need rather than teacher style.
- Collaborate with school and community mental health professionals.
- Make data-based decisions about behavioral interventions. If a BMP does not work, do not blame the student. Try another plan.
- Provide consistent routines and schedules and classroom activities to help students manage frustration.

Teachers who are most effective at managing students who act out do not allow themselves to be "hooked" by the students' behavior. These teachers do not allow students to "push their button." "Symptom survival" is a core skill for managing aggressive behavior (Long & Newman, 1996). Emotional objectivity combined with a studied choice of behavioral intervention techniques reduces the possibility that a student's behavior will lure a teacher into counteraggressive behavior.

Passive-Aggressive Behavior

One of the most frustrating problem behaviors teachers deal with is passive-aggressiveness. According to K. Smith (n.d.), "Of all the particular types of behavior problems which exist in students, passive-aggressive behavior is one which most certainly led many teachers to their wit's end" (p. 1). Wentzel (1991) called passive-aggressiveness "sugarcoated hostility." Following are some examples of passive-aggressive behavior:

> **"I can't hear you."**   Karen, a high school sophomore, does not like her geometry teacher. Karen will not initiate conversation with him, and when he talks to her, she pretends she cannot hear him, which constantly makes him repeat his remarks to her.

> **"I can't find it."**   Gary's fourth-grade teacher considers him a frustrating student who always complies with directions but in a slow and bumbling way. Told to get a book from a bookshelf, Gary will look on the wrong shelf and then say, "It's not here!" Told to look on another shelf, he will spend several minutes searching and say, "I can't find it." His teacher has concluded that it is easier to do something himself than to ask Gary.

> **"See what you made me do."**   Second-grader Juanita continually tests her homeroom teacher's patience. Told to line up with the class to go to the library, Juanita will start searching through her desk for her book to return. While everyone is waiting, Juanita says, "I have to clean my desk out." When her teacher tells her "Never mind," she pulls out her library book abruptly, and papers spew on the floor. The class is still waiting and Juanita slowly begins sorting the papers on the floor. She looks up at her teacher and with an accusing tone says, "Now look what you made me do."

"It's not my problem."   Lois is a senior in high school. Her good grades and pleasant demeanor belie her ability to irritate students and teachers alike with her laissez-faire attitude. Her constant response to a request to do something extra such as helping another student is "Why?" Her favorite phrase is "It's not my problem." When challenged by her teachers about her lack of concern for others, she usually responds, "Why are you always picking on me?"

Many adolescents go through a normal and predictable phase of passive-aggressive behavior. Forgetting, failing to complete chores, not hearing, and sulking are examples of typical teenage behaviors that can be expected to change as the teens mature. The development of a passive-aggressive personality is more complex and often begins at an early age when a youngster internalizes anger rather than expressing it through words or behavior.

Students with passive-aggressive behavior are top-notch manipulators. Their intention is to frustrate and irritate, and unless proper proactive interventions are put into place, they usually succeed in doing so. Long and Long (2001) said that passive-aggressive behaviors are learned, conscious behaviors that can be changed.

Managing Passive-Aggressive Behavior.   Following are recommendations for managing passive-aggressive behavior (Long & Long, 2001; Maag, 2001a; K. Smith, 2004):

- Learn the characteristics of passive-aggressive behavior. Knowledge of how students with passive-aggressive behavior manipulate others' feelings helps teachers avoid overreacting.
- Acknowledge your own angry feelings. Use self-talk to remind yourself that anger is a normal reaction. Remind yourself to stay calm in the face of passive-aggressive behavior. Recognize that passive-aggressive behavior often sparks counteraggressive feelings.
- Use *I* messages when talking to students with passive-aggressive behavior— for example, "I am feeling frustrated; perhaps you should think about what you are doing."
- Use benign confrontation as a long-term intervention. *Benign confrontation* is a verbal intervention skill in which the adult gently but openly shares his or her thoughts about the student's behavior and unexpressed anger. Avoid being pulled into a debate or power struggle. Long and Long (2001) described benign confrontation as dropping a pebble of a new idea into a static pool of thought.
- Promote student self-reflection with the question "Guess what I am going to say about your behavior?" This question puts the onus on the student to take responsibility for his or her passive-aggressive behavior.
- Provide logical consequences without anger or hostility. For example, Elaine does not finish her classroom assignment because of a series of avoidance behaviors such as getting out of her seat to sharpen her pencil, organizing her "messy" desk, and feeling "tired." Maintaining emotional objectivity, the teacher tells Elaine that her unfinished work must be completed as home-work and signed by a parent.

- Make a list of annoying behaviors. Target the top three and identify alternative behaviors for social skills instruction. Do an FBA to determine classroom antecedents or consequences that might be reinforcing the passive-aggressive behavior.
- Give students opportunities to express angry feelings through conversations, journals, and literature (i.e., bibliotherapy).

Students must recognize that feelings of anger or resentment are normal and that how they express their feelings is the issue, not the feelings themselves. Teaching students with passive-aggressive behavior acceptable ways of communicating their emotions provides them with a constructive avenue of self-expression.

Attention-Deficit/Hyperactivity Disorder

Attention-deficit/hyperactivity disorder (ADHD) is a presumed neurobiological disorder involving a network of brain structures that control inhibition and focus attention (i.e., frontal lobe, caudate nucleus, and thalamus). While research on the etiology continues, evidence to date suggests that ADHD has a genetic etiology and is likely caused by a chemical imbalance in the brain. ADHD is characterized by inattention, impulsivity, and hyperactivity (Weyandt, 2001). The American Psychiatric Association (1994) estimated that the behavior of 3 to 5% of students matched ADHD criteria.

Some youngsters with ADHD receive special education services; others do not. Students with ADHD who receive special education services are identified as "disabled" under one of the following categories: other health impaired, emotionally disturbed, behavior disordered, or learning disabled. Whether a youngster with ADHD receives special education services depends on several factors, including how vigorous parents are about getting services, how disruptive the student's behavior is, and how the student's behavior affects academic progress.

The *Diagnostic and Statistical Manual of Mental Disorders* (4th ed.; American Psychiatric Association, 1994), specifies the following guidelines for determining whether ADHD is present:

- Some symptoms were present before the child was 7 years old.
- Symptoms are present in two or more settings.
- Symptoms do not occur exclusively during the course of a pervasive developmental disorder, or schizophrenia or other psychotic disorders, and is not better accounted for by another mental disorder.
- Symptoms have been present for the past 6 months.
- Clear evidence of social, academic, or occupational impairment exists.

Public concern about the overuse of medication accelerated after publication of research findings that indicated prescriptions for youngsters aged 2 to 4 years increased two- to threefold in two state Medicaid programs and a health maintenance organization in the Northwest (Goode, 2000). Experts concurred that overdiagnosis of ADHD is a growing problem. "This seems to support the anecdotes that more U.S. children are receiving a diagnosis for attention deficit disorder in the late 1990's than ever before," observed Dr. Julie Zito, associate professor of pharmacy at the University of Maryland (cited in Zernike & Peterson, 2001, p. A1).

Individuals with ADHD have chronic difficulties with planning, staying focused on a task, overriding emotional impulses, and accessing short-term memory. Students with ADHD have special difficulty attending to tasks that are frustrating or uninteresting. Although hyperactivity appears to diminish with age, problems with attention can continue through adulthood.

Managing ADHD.   Following are synopses of educational strategies general and special education teachers use to help students with ADHD.

Cognitive-Behavioral Modification (CBM).   The objective of CBM is to teach students problem-solving strategies and self-control techniques. Students are instructed in a step-by-step procedure to monitor and direct their behavior. For example, students are taught to deal with conflict by (a) calming down before reacting impulsively, (b) identifying feelings and expressing feelings appropriately, (c) setting positive goals for themselves, (d) thinking of alternative solutions to problems, and (e) trying a plan and evaluating its results (Greenberg, 1998). The overall goal is for students to spontaneously think through situations in which they feel the impulse to act quickly.

Social Skills Training.   Students with ADHD develop impulsive habits that interfere with their ability to manage interactions with peers and adults. The purpose of social skills training is to rectify social skills deficits through direct and indirect instruction. This proactive approach seeks to change students' disruptive behavior by focusing on teaching new skills rather than trying to eliminate bothersome behaviors (a reactive approach). For example, a student who acts out impulsively might benefit from learning to verbalize his or her feelings (i.e., proactive), rather than being sent to time-out each time the offending behavior occurs (i.e., reactive). Social skills curricula (see Chapter 7) use a variety of instructional techniques, including modeling, step-by-step scripts, classroom meetings, reinforcement, and emphasis on social skills embedded in the regular curriculum—for example, using science to teach how to anticipate consequences or using children's literature to teach conflict resolution.

Contingency Management.   With contingency management, students are rewarded when they demonstrate socially appropriate behavior. Contingencies include positive reinforcement and consequences. Praise and tangible rewards are frequently used positive reinforcers. Reprimands and ignoring behavior are examples of consequences. Teachers must be vigilant to ensure that consequences are logical. For example, a logical consequence for throwing food in the cafeteria is eating lunch alone in the classroom for 3 days rather than doing additional homework.

Other applications of behavioral theory to ADHD include a token economy (discussed in Chapter 8), response cost, and contingency contracting. *Reponse cost* is the removal of a reinforcer after a problem behavior occurs. Miltenberger (2001) said the following about response cost: "Response cost is a negative punishment procedure when it results in a decrease in the future probability of the problem behavior" (p. 335). Examples of response cost are as follows:

- A fine for parking in a delivery zone
- An Internal Revenue Service fine for underpaying taxes
- A bank deduction for writing a "bounced" check

In each of these examples, the reinforcer that was removed was money earned. In school, teachers use response cost when they revoke a privilege or reward because of undesirable student behavior. Deducting points or tokens that students have earned for positive behavior earlier in the day because of negative behavior later in the day is an illustration of response cost.

Contingency contracting is an agreement, usually written, between a teacher and a student that outlines consequences, either positive or negative, for specific student behavior. For example, a teacher and a student might agree that for every day the student completes assigned classwork, the teacher will allow the student an extra 15 minutes on a computer.

Structured Activity and Movement. Planned classroom activities that allow students to move about, converse with others, and interact with concrete materials help students with ADHD sustain attention and reduce the stress of trying to constantly restrain motor activity. Some frequently used techniques are learning centers, planned student interactions, art, music, kinesthetic activity, games, and authentic learning experiences such as teaching ratios by making orange juice from concentrate.

Self-Management Strategies. Students with ADHD lack organizational skills for sustaining attention and completing projects. Direct instruction in time management helps students learn to divide a task into subunits. By monitoring due dates incrementally, teachers help students set realistic time lines and avoid procrastination. Helping students learn how to organize materials is another key self-management strategy. Filing papers, scheduling, keeping notes in binders, and periodically inventorying materials are frequent self-management organizational objectives. Teaching study skills such as active reading (i.e., writing down questions and comments rather than simply highlighting), webbing chapters, reviewing key topics and subtopics, and developing students' test-taking skills are helpful strategies.

Environmental Accommodations. The physical layout of a classroom is the single most important factor in focusing students' attention. Textbooks with shiny paper are problematic under fluorescent lights. The hum and flickering of fluorescent lights is also a distraction. They should be replaced with incandescent lights. Soft, classical music in the background can be soothing. Sound recordings of nature (e.g., rain) can have a similar effect. Student seating should be adjusted to cut down distractions from high-traffic areas. Sitting at tables may present a problem for some students. Carrels with side panels help eliminate visual distractions. Some teachers report that overhead projectors help cut down on visual distractions by reducing the "clutter" that sometimes fills up chalkboards. Directions should be given slowly, with frequent requests for the student to provide restatements. When worksheets are used, students benefit from fewer problems to complete, lined paper helps with handwriting, and computer software offers myriad possibilities from word processing to games that reinforce academic skills.

Isolating Behaviors

The Columbine High School tragedy triggered an increased awareness among educators about the need to be more attentive to *"outsider" students*—students who exhibit *isolating behavior*. Various terms are used to describe students who spend most of their time alone: *shy, withdrawn, depressed, loner, isolated.* The most serious concern about students who are isolated is that their separation from supportive peer relationships will lead to self-destructive behaviors such as promiscuity, self-abuse, chemical dependency, cult membership, suicide, and violence against others (Chambers & Henrickson, 2002; Larson, 1999).

Kupersmidt, Coie, and Dodge (1990) reported that students who are rejected have double the delinquency and school dropout rates of their peers. Rockwell (1999) said that unabated feelings of negative self-worth and shame among students who are isolated are often the result of physical or sexual abuse. Students who are isolated are often apathetic toward their studies (p. 8). Alchohol abuse and chemical dependency are problems identified with such students (Brophy, 1996).

Managing Isolating Behaviors.   Appropriate classroom interventions combine peer-based activities with structured opportunities for students who are isolated to demonstrate their personal qualities. Brophy (1996) and Rockwell (1999) outlined the following recommendations:

- Talk with students daily.
- Use interest inventories to guide conversations and classroom activities.
- Display student artwork, assignments, and other "islands of competence."
- Assign popular classmates as partners for learning activities.
- Teach students how to be assertive and how to initiate interactions with peers.
- Provide students with a designated role that gives them something to do and increases visibility.
- Encourage families to enroll a student in extracurricular activities.
- Use literature-based assignments and personal journals to help students explore their feelings and learn about how others cope with similar problems.

According to Brophy (1996), the teacher's overall approach is to bolster the student's confidence and encourage the student to learn prosocial behaviors such as listening, nonverbal communication, and assertiveness. Even though their emotional problems are subtle, students who are isolated require interventions that are both thoughtful and consistent.

Nonverbal Learning Disabilities

As a result of presumed impairment in right hemispheric functions in the neocortex, students with *nonverbal learning disabilities (NLDs)* have difficulty interpreting body language and other subtle features of conversation. While their verbal and auditory retention abilities are well developed, students with NLDs exhibit specific dysfunctions in coordination, visuospatial organization, and social relationships. NLDs frequently surface during the late elementary years and cause considerable distress throughout adolescence. *Asperger's syndrome (AS)* is a more severe form of an NLD (Lerner, 2003). It is a neurobiological disorder sometimes described as mild autism. Students with AS have a high IQ but marked deficiencies in social skills. They may have obsessive routines and preoccupations with certain interests such as maps. Impairment of nonverbal behaviors such as eye contact (e.g., avoidant), facial expressions (e.g., disconnection between words and expression), and gestures (e.g., hand flapping) is common (American Psychiatric Association, 2000).

Amanda, a high school sophomore, tries to socialize with her classmates with little success because she appears so self-centered. A conversation with Amanda is a one-way trip through whatever is on Amanda's mind at the time. She interrupts frequently, is unable to interpret facial cues, stands too close to whomever she is talking to and does not seem "to get it" when the other person wants to terminate a conversation. Most of her classmates find simply ostracizing her easier than putting up with her annoying chatter.

According to Foss (2001), students with NLDs concentrate more on details than on the big picture. A student with an NLD will have difficulty comprehending the theme of a story but describe specific scenes or characters in detail. While vocabulary is a strong area, reading comprehension is weak. Part–whole integration problems carry over into mathematics. Mathematical concepts such as fractions, decimals, and percentages are difficult to grasp. Social situations, however, cause students with NLDs the most anguish. Like water pouring through a sieve, their whole-hearted efforts at relating to others just drain away, leaving students with NLDs feeling frustrated and confused.

Managing NLDs.   Students with NLDs are intelligent and strive to do well. They respond to constructive feedback and usually have good memorization skills. Following are some suggestions for helping these students:

- They need the most help with the following social skills: anticipating consequences, learning from past experiences, and conversing with peers.
- Use academic areas such as science and history to buttress the relationship between cause and effect. Carry these academic lessons over to social situations. Help students understand how cause and effect influences peer relationships.
- Teach how to decipher and respond to nonverbal facial and body cues. Also use role-playing to give students practice in analyzing nonverbal communication and taking turns in a conversation.
- Set up cross-age peer tutoring. Use structured interactions with younger students to encourage leadership and personal responsibility.
- Build confidence by using strengths such as memorization, an eye for detail, and facility with language. Use verbal feedback. Ask students to repeat directions, and make sure all steps in a task are understood. Use written outlines to help students learn to prioritize tasks.

- Be alert to classroom situations that will challenge students' social skills. Be ready to intervene, and, if feasible, help interpret social situations and guide students through conversations. Have a prearranged signal that will cue a student about social errors.

Students gauge their self-worth according to their success or failure to maintain satisfactory peer relationships. The diminished abilities of students with NLDs to positively interact with other individuals affects all facets of their lives. By providing these students with structured social skills opportunities, proactive teachers can help students improve their communication skills and promote a positive sense of self.

DISCIPLINE AND IDEA

The 2004 reauthorization of IDEA created a set of mandates that affect disciplinary procedures for students receiving special education services. The revisions were intended to change the perception that a dual system of discipline existed—one for the general education population and another for students in special education. The changes give schools more freedom to remove students who are disruptive when their behavior is not related to their disability. In addition, the revisions to IDEA eliminate the need for excessive administrative hearings and paperwork before a student can be transferred to an alternative setting designed specifically for students with chronic disciplinary problems.

Before the 2004 revisions, school administrators had to build a case to transfer a student to an alternative education setting due to disruptive behavior. The 2004 reauthorization of IDEA allows administrators to remove a student to an alternative placement, and if the parents disagree, they can appeal the decision. Consider the following scenario.

In 2003, a year before the reauthorization of IDEA, Samantha, a 17-year-old high school student, exhibited both academic and behavioral difficulties. Samantha had, among other problems, a record of bullying, being truant, and arguing with her teachers. Because of her academic problems, Samantha's teachers agreed to refer her for a special education evaluation. The evaluation team determined that Samantha met the systemwide criteria for a learning disability because of a severe discrepancy between her IQ and her academic achievement. (*Note:* The severe discrepancy formula for determining a learning disability is not recommended in the 2004 reauthorization of IDEA, but the reauthorization does not change the special education status of students like Samantha who were identified with a learning disability prior to the 2004 reauthorization.)

While special education services appeared to help Samantha with her academic difficulties, her disciplinary problems persisted. The principal suspended her for fighting several times during the 2003–2004 year. After one final episode of disruptive behavior, the principal placed Samantha in a temporary alternative program for students who are disruptive. Her parents hired a lawyer who pointed out that because Samantha was a student with special needs her placement could not be changed without a "manifest determination" hearing. This time-consuming investigation was mandated by IDEA to determine whether a student's misbehavior was related to his or her disability. If the manifest determination found no relationship between her learning disability and her behavior, Samantha would be subject to the same disciplinary codes as the general education population was. However, if her behavior was determined to be a manifestation of her disability, the school was legally required to follow a series of due-process procedures to ensure that Samantha's special education services were not interrupted.

Before the reauthorization, many school administrators complained that mandated legal procedures were too complex. They said that additional hearings, paperwork, individual education plan revisions, and parental consent had become an overwhelming burden. Delays in fulfilling federal requirements also meant delays in keeping schools safe for all students. While still containing protective due-process procedures for students with special needs, the 2004 changes to IDEA were intended to simplify disciplinary procedures. The following items highlight the reauthorization with regard to disciplinary procedures for students in special education:

- On a case-by-case basis, school authorities can consider unique circumstances when determining whether to order a change in placement for a child with a disability who violates a student conduct code.
- School personnel may remove a student to an interim alternative setting, without a hearing, for 45 school days. In addition, school personnel may now remove a student who has caused bodily injury to another student on school premises to an interim placement without a hearing officer ruling.
- Time lines have been added for an expedited hearing in matters related to placement during appeals.

Under the protections for children who are not yet eligible under IDEA, the provisions related to whether school administrator should have known that a student was a child with a disability have been changed as follows:

- Former disciplinary provisions required a parent to put his or her concerns that the child needed special education services in writing to school personnel, with an exception for a parent who was illiterate or had a disability affecting his or her ability to submit concerns in writing. The new bill eliminates this exception.
- Under the new bill, a local education authority shall not be deemed to have knowledge that the student is a child with a disability if the parent of the child has not allowed an evaluation of the child or has refused services, or if the child has been evaluated and was determined not to be a child with a disability.

In response to the IDEA revisions, a nationwide organization of special education professionals, Warger (1999), cautioned its members about interpreting these new requirements. In particular, the Council said more clarification was needed about what is meant by "unique circumstances" for removal of a student and by a school system that does not have to provide "substantial evidence" about the relationship between a student's misbehavior and the presence of a disability (www.cec.sped.org/pp/IDEA_ 120204.pdf).

Summary

★ A "problem behavior" is determined by three factors: the number of settings in which the behavior is exhibited, the frequency of the behavior, and the intensity of the behavior.

★ A functional behavior assessment (FBA) is a data-based method for providing students with positive behavioral support (PBS).

★ PBS is a long-range plan for helping students decrease unconstructive behavior and increase prosocial behavior.

★ If a behavior management plan (BMP) does not work, the teacher should not blame the student but should instead change the plan.

★ Teachers need to be alert for undetected emotional problems in the classroom.

★ Many PBS strategies are available for helping students who exhibit the following behaviors: aggressive behavior, passive-aggressive behavior, depression, isolating behaviors, ADHD, and nonverbal learning disabilities (NLDs).

What You Should Know

Now that you have finished reading this chapter, you should know the following:

Criteria for identifying a problematic behavior
How to develop a behavior frequency checklist
Characteristics of hard-to-detect emotional problems
At-risk signs for emotional disturbance
Specific strategies for managing students with the following problem behaviors: aggressive behavior, passive-aggressive behavior, isolating behaviors, ADHD, and NLDs
The meaning of *positive behavioral support*
How to conduct an FBA
The components of a BMP

Applying the Concepts

1. Interview three classroom teachers. Ask them to explain how they determine when a student's behavior is problematic enough to require special attention. Contrast the teachers' criteria with the criteria described in this chapter. Have a classroom discussion about the types of student behavior that are most likely to be considered serious disciplinary problems.

2. Go to the National Institute of Mental Health Web site (www.nimh.nih.gov/NIMHHome). Review the Web site and select three articles or news releases that provide important information about children's mental health. Share your information with the class.

3. Select one of the following topics for a class presentation: ADHD, childhood depression, passive-aggressive behavior in children, youth suicide, NLDs, isolating behavior, or aggressive behavior. Form cooperative learning groups of four members each. Divide the presentation responsibilities: One person provides audiovisual aids, another researches key factoids, another interviews a mental health professional, and the fourth researches classroom management issues.

4. At your field site, do an FBA of a student. Share your results with the classroom teacher. Write a BMP for the student and share your plan with students in your classroom management class. Solicit feedback and critique the behavior management format used in this text.

5. Do a Web search on "discipline and students with emotional disturbance." Find the answers to the following questions: Are separate disciplinary procedures mandated by IDEA for students receiving special education services for emotional disturbance? What are some precedent-setting court cases that have shaped professional views on discipline and special education students? What are current professional viewpoints about the criteria outlined in IDEA for identifying emotional disturbance?

6. Review the strategies for teaching one of the following: students who are aggressive, students with NLDs, students who are isolated, students with passive-aggressive behavior, students with depression, or students with ADHD. Review the behavior management strategies in another book and add three new strategies to the list. Provide a citation for your research.

7. Interview a mental health or justice professional who works with young people. Ask the individual to identify remediation and prevention strategies in his or her field. How closely does the professional work with school personnel? What does the professional think should be happening in schools to improve mental health services for children and their families?

8. Review films that depict teachers dealing with difficult students. What kind of stereotypes about "good disciplinary practices" can you identify? What films seem to be the most estranged from reality? What movies do a fairly good job of describing school disciplinary issues? Select a movie that the class agrees is a fairly good representation of ideas presented in this text. Contrast the film with the text. Watch the film *Dangerous Minds* and identify interventions that helped positively support student behaviors. Select other features of the film that reflect key ideas presented in this and previous chapters in terms of developing a community, preventing behavioral problems, and positively supporting student behavior.

Chapter 10

Being a Reflective Teacher

Chapter Outline

Emotional Intelligence
  Reflection
  Disposition
  Self-Awareness
Proactive Discipline Beliefs
  Interactional Problem Behaviors
  Reasons for Misbehaviors

Avoidance of Taking Misbehavior
  Personally
Reclamation of the Student–Teacher
  Relationship
Summary
What You Should Know
Applying the Concepts

Key Terms

Conflict cycle
Conflict resolution
Disposition
Emotional intelligence
Mental set
Mini theories

Peer influence
Reclaiming relationships
Reflection
Self-awareness
Teacher style
Temperament

Introduction

Reflection is the process of honestly appraising your beliefs and actions. Reflection enables teachers to examine their disposition toward problem behaviors. Many factors influence disposition, including a teacher's emotional intelligence, values, beliefs, and theories of education. Students' problem behaviors require more than simply trying to make them go away. Reflective teachers look for causes. They understand that students' behavior is influenced by the interaction of teacher style, student temperament, and peer influence. Rather than taking problem behaviors personally, reflective teachers learn to identify their personal pet peeves. Conflicts between teachers and students often begin as minor events that evolve into power struggles. The conflict cycle shows how teachers can learn to de-escalate potential crisis situations.

Classrooms are spontaneous environments, and disciplinary problems are, for the most part, unscripted events. Each school day presents a variety of classroom management decisions: Should a student who is rude be ignored or sent to the principal's office? Should a student who is unruly be challenged or humored? Should a student who is noncompliant be reprimanded or ignored?

Attitude shapes action. What teachers feel, think, and believe about discipline determines how they will respond. A teacher's attitude toward student behavior begins with his or her philosophy. Preceding chapters outlined specific skills for managing student behavior. This final chapter explores the connection between teacher attitude and teacher action.

The reflective teacher is emotionally intelligent, holds proactive discipline beliefs, and works to reclaim relationships with students. Each of these topics is covered next.

EMOTIONAL INTELLIGENCE

If some researchers are correct, a teacher's *emotional intelligence* may be more critical to success than his or her IQ is (Goleman, 1995; Marzano and Marzano, 2003). Emotionally intelligent individuals are self-aware. They identify the feelings they are experiencing and make a conscious decision about how to act on these feelings. Conversely, an emotionally illiterate individual is quick to act on strong feelings such as anger and fear. Goleman (1995) said that when an individual is "emotionally hijacked," his or her behavior is dictated by feelings rather than by thought (p. 59). Reactions are impulsive, often tinged with anger, and then later regretted (Figure 10.1).

Goleman (1995) explained the relationship between emotional intelligence and behavior:

> Those who are at the mercy of impulse—who lack self-control—suffer a moral deficiency: The ability to control impulse is the base of will and character. By the same token, the root of altruism lies in empathy, the ability to read emotions in others;

Just then a little fellow sitting directly before me let drop a slate, which rattled along the floor with that stunning noise which nothing but a slate can make. I lost my self control. I seized my ferule. The poor little fellow shuddered before me; tears trickled down his fair, tender cheek, and his fine lips quivered, as he faintly stammered, "I didn't mean to do it, Sir." "Didn't mean to do it," said I tauntingly, and inflicted on his tender hand several cruel blows. Yet I do not think the boy was badly whipped; for conscience seemed to hold back my arm. The little fellow, however, sobbed and sobbed. . . . How I longed to put my arm about him and tell him I was sorry. But I could not do it; I was a school-master, and my dignity must not be compromised. I returned gloomily to my boarding-place, overwhelmed with a sense of meanness and self-reproach.

FIGURE 10.1   A Teacher's Memoir: 1864
From "A Teacher's Memoir: 1864," 1999, *Massachusetts Teachers Association Today, 30*(1), p. 6. Copyright 1999 by the Massachusetts Teachers Association. Reprinted with permission.

lacking a sense of another's need or despair, there is no caring. And if there are any two moral stances our times call for, they are precisely these, self-restraint and compassion. (p. xii)

During a typical school day, a teacher must deal with numerous emotionally charged events. Split-second decisions about how to respond to student misbehavior can bring out the worst or the best in a teacher. Reflection provides a buffer between strong emotions and impulsive actions.

The emotionally intelligent teacher not only is reflective, but also considers his or her disposition and is self-aware. These three components of emotional intelligence are discussed next.

Reflection

Reflection is the leading edge of emotional intelligence. The reflective teacher recognizes the need to carefully consider how problems with behavior are handled. Handled impulsively or with anger, a minor disciplinary problem can quickly escalate into a major crisis. In contrast, treating students with dignity, even students who are oppositional, strengthens the student–teacher relationship and minimizes student resentment (Brendtro, Brokenleg, & Van Brockern, 1990; Maag, 2001a).

The need for teachers to be reflective in their dealings with students has never been greater. The current-day teacher must be capable of responding not only to students' academic needs, but also to their emotional and behavioral needs (Maholmes, 2002).

Unreflective teachers stagnate. Their classrooms are the same year after year. Mendler (1992) said the following about unreflective teachers: "We have all heard and used the expression 'People are creatures of habit.' This is why people continue to do things even after all of the feedback suggests that what we are doing is ineffective" (p. 35). H. M. Walker (1995) reported that negative reprimands are the most common teacher response to disturbing behavior even though this aversive approach is ineffective in producing positive change.

Socrates said, "The unexamined life is not worth living." When teachers reflect on their belief systems about how and why students behave in a particular way, they enhance their ability to respond to students in a flexible and supportive manner.

A proactive teacher takes time to reflect on the connection between emotions and learning and on how they handle misbehavior in the busy classroom. These two topics are covered next.

Emotions and Learning.   Teachers need to model the emotional and behavioral skills they seek to develop in their students. Within all classrooms are youngsters who require emotional support. These students need more than simply to be told how to behave; they need direct experience with adults who demonstrate how to effectively manage feelings and behavior.

Within every class are students mired in emotional patterns that interfere with their learning (Forness, 2001). Mental illness among young people is on the rise. Depression, bipolar disorder, oppositional defiant disorder, attention-deficit/hyperactivity disorder (ADHD), and nonverbal learning disabilities are being diagnosed among school-aged children at an alarming rate (Hammen & Rudolph, 2003).

Readiness to learn is linked to a student's emotional well-being (Wolfe, 2001). Attention, memory, perseverance, and interest—four key functions of learning—are all linked to an individual's emotional state (Sylwester, 1995). When individuals feel threatened, the emotional center of the brain (i.e., the limbic system) goes on alert and cognition gives way to the more basic emotional requirement: self-protection.

A student who is angered, embarrassed, or humiliated by a teacher's reprimand has difficulty focusing on self-improvement. Emotional stress creates its own agenda. Even the best conceived lesson will wilt in the presence of students who are preoccupied with negative feelings.

Quick Thinking.   When confronted with misbehavior, the teacher's primary objective is to handle the situation and move on to the more important job of teaching. How a teacher deals with a misbehaving student—tone of voice, body posture, and facial expressions—is just as important as what the teacher does. Managing problems with student behavior requires a level of reflection not easily acquired in a busy classroom, where events unfold at breathtaking speed.

Good and Brophy (2000) said,

> The most fundamental factor making it difficult for teachers to assess classroom behavior is that so much happens so rapidly. This problem can be solved in part through training. Awareness of everything that occurs is impossible, but with practice teachers can become more aware of their classroom behavior. (p. 33)

Vignette: Reflection

A new teacher was walking down the hall to her 10th-grade homeroom on the first day of school. A friendly veteran teacher was accompanying her. As they strolled along, the veteran offered some tips for getting through the first day. "One last thing," the veteran whispered as they approached the classroom. "Keep an eye on Lucia Raposa; she will test you."

The new teacher nodded and entered the classroom. She glanced apprehensively around the room at her 28 high school sophomores. "Where is Lucia Raposa?" she asked herself. On a day filled with expectations, one student took center stage. Yet, more was at stake than dealing with Lucia. The young teacher was keenly aware that if a problem with Lucia surfaced, the entire class would take her measure and judge her accordingly.

What thoughts come to mind after reading the vignette on reflection? Was the veteran being fair when she forewarned the novice and perhaps prejudiced her toward Lucia? What should the novice say when she greets Lucia for the first time? If Lucia does present a disciplinary problem, what is the best way to deal with her, and, perhaps most important, what message does the teacher want to send the rest of the class about how she handles behavioral problems?

Simply put, each teacher—in his or her way—must find a method for balancing personal feelings, needs, and values with the students' needs.

Disposition

Effective teachers understand that behavioral expectations are shaped by their value system. *Disposition* refers to the ability to reflect on and, if necessary, adjust your attitude, beliefs, and perspective. The Indian philosopher Bhaktivedanta (1997) said,

> As man believes, so he is. All actions that we take in life, except for instinctive acts, are based on certain conscious and unconscious beliefs and presuppositions. Consequently, it is important that we understand the relationship between our actions and beliefs. (p. 104)

The following questions guide dispositional thinking (Paul & Elder, 2003):

To what extent do my prejudices or biases influence my thinking?
To what extent have I been indoctrinated into beliefs that may be false?
How do beliefs that I have uncritically accepted prevent me from seeing
    things as they are?
To what extent have I analyzed the beliefs I hold?
To what extent am I willing to give up my beliefs when sufficient evidence is
    presented against them?
To what extent do I expect the same of myself as I expect from others?
To what extent am I a conformist?

The key ideas that anchor the discussion in this chapter are reflection and flexibility. Proactive classroom managers think through their actions and make changes to accommodate their students' needs.

Self-Awareness

Self-awareness means getting in touch with your feelings, beliefs, and behaviors. Teachers who are self-aware understand that their personal issues and concerns can undermine their ability to deal effectively with difficult behavior. Self-aware teachers distinguish their needs from their students' needs. For example, when a teacher says to a student "*You* need to do this," what the teacher is really saying is "*I* need you to do this."

The need for security, control, and recognition are examples of teacher needs that, without self-awareness, can be confused with students' needs. Self-awareness enhances a teacher's self-perception, increases his or her problem-solving ability, and promotes flexibility when he or she is dealing with classroom management issues (Carter, 1992; Stoiber, 1991; Winitzky, 1992).

In an extensive review of successful classroom management practices, Marzano and Marzano (2003) identified four key variables: the quality of the student–teacher relationship, knowledge of behavioral interventions, well-organized classroom procedures, and mental set. They said that, of the four, mental set was the most significant. Marzano and Marzano defined *mental set* as a sense of situational awareness and conscious control over your thoughts and behavior relative to discipline (p. 65).

Proactive Discipline Beliefs

Proactive discipline is a positive approach to classroom management. When disciplinary problems erupt, proactive disciplinarians search for causes. Proactive discipline embodies a number of problem-solving techniques to help students learn to manage their emotions and behavior. Maroney (1998) outlined five components of proactive discipline:

1. A supportive classroom environment
2. Achievement-oriented disciplinary plans
3. Positive behavioral change interventions
4. A social skills curriculum
5. A data-based approach to analyzing behavioral difficulties

Proactive discipline emphasizes the same diagnostic-prescriptive approach common to the effective teaching of academics. As educators, we expect to encounter problems in learning. We do not punish students because they cannot multiply, decode words, or discriminate between active and passive voice. When solving academic problems, we are flexible, and we realize that students have different learning styles. If one approach to teaching multiplication of mixed numbers does not work, we try another. Rather than blaming the student for academic difficulties, proactive educators search for solutions (J. E. Walker, Ramsey, & Gresham, 2004). Appendix B contains a comprehensive, proactive classroom management checklist.

Proactive disciplinary practices are bolstered by the following beliefs:

- Behavioral problems are often interactional.
- A reason always exists for misbehavior.
- Teachers need to avoid taking behavioral problems personally.

Interactional Problem Behaviors

Proactive analysis of disciplinary problems requires more than simply trying to identify and rectify individual student deficiencies. When misbehavior occurs, all aspects of the classroom environment are open to analysis.

Individual student contributions to misbehavior include emotional problems, deficiencies in social skills development, and neurological factors (Long & Morse, 1996; Rutter, Giller, & Hagell, 1998; Weyandt, 2001). Teachers contribute to disciplinary problems through low expectations, overreaction to misbehavior, and uninspired lessons (Good & Brophy, 2000). Peer pressure motivates, reinforces, and sustains individual student behavior and misbehavior (Wenz-Gross & Siperstein, 1998).

Proactive analysis of problem behaviors begins with an understanding that both constructive and nonconstructive behaviors are influenced by the interaction of teacher style, individual student temperament, and peer influence (Wang, Haertel, & Walberg, 1993).

Teacher Style.   *Teacher style* is a broad term used to describe how teachers interact with their students. Teacher style lays the foundation for the student–teacher relationship. *Controlling, cooperative, dominant,* and *submissive* are a sample of the adjectives researchers use to describe teacher style (Chiu & Tulley, 1997; Wubbels, Berkelmans, van Tartwijk, & Admiral, 1999; Wubbels & Levy, 1993).

According to Marzano (2003), the optimal teacher style is moderate to high dominance and cooperation. *Dominance* is characterized by assertive guidance and clarity of expectations. *Cooperation* is characterized by a desire to have students function as a team and a concern for all students' needs. The least regarded teacher style is high opposition and low cooperation. This type of teacher is both antagonistic and controlling.

Chiu and Tulley (1997) interviewed 712 elementary students. They queried students about their preferred classroom management style. Students preferred teachers who were assertive and flexible. When sanctions needed to be exercised, preferred teachers showed concern for students' needs and preferences. A consistent finding across research studies on classroom management is that the teacher style that best suits students' needs is a balance between dominance and cooperation (Marzano and Marzano, 2003). These findings highlight the need for teachers to reflect on the quality of their interactions, especially around misbehavior. While teacher style plays a significant role in student behavior, so also does the temperament of individual students.

Student Temperament.   *Temperament* indicates a student's emotional and physical condition. Variability in student temperament includes such factors as motivation, sense of humor, needs, health, and family background. These many overlapping variables require an open mind about which teaching approaches will best suit a student's needs.

Assessment of temperament requires a sincere appreciation for the individual. Observing a student engaged in lessons provides insight into the types of materials and structure a student requires. Moreover, a visit to a student's home or a family conference tightens the bond between student and teacher. A survey of student interests and how the student spends time outside school can lead to novel ideas for lessons. A student's physical well-being, including how much sleep he or she gets, the quality of his or her diet, and his or her general health all affect temperament. Finally, a student's temperament is dictated by his or her emotional stability.

The following questions serve as a guide to gauging a student's emotional stability:

Does the student live in a safe environment?
Is the student moody?
Who are the adults who care about the student?
Is the student often in trouble?
How does the student spend time outside school?

Prizing differences in young people opens the path to mutual respect. Although an individual student's temperament might clash with the institutional norms of school life, the student is still worthy of respect. In fact, the acceptance of individual "deviance" is often the first step toward reconciliation. Sister Mary Rose McGeady, past director of Covenant House International, a crisis and rehabilitation program for homeless youth, said,

> Many of the teenagers we encounter distrust adults and often present a facade which shows little respect and sometimes open hostility. . . . In this program, we see so clearly the relationship between the love and respect that we have poured on each kid and their ability to love and respect themselves. As they gradually grow in their ability to take on the responsibilities of school, work, money management and eventually apartment management, it is like watching a flower bloom. (1997, pp. 9, 13)

Whereas individual temperaments vary, basic needs for affiliation and respect are shared by all. The need for acceptance is just as strong in angry and recalcitrant youths as in youths who exhibit few emotional or behavioral difficulties. In fact, the more difficulties a student experiences (e.g., school failure, dysfunctional family), the more vital is the quality of the student–teacher relationship.

Peer Influence. *Peer influence* increases as youngsters mature. By middle school, peer groups become selective and cliques begin to shape student behavior. Numerous researchers have documented the negative effect of peer relationships on young people's behavior (Asher & Coie, 1990; Asher, Erdley, & Gabriel, 1994; Coie & Dodge, 1997; Rutter et al., 1998). Peer rejection at an early age is a strong predictor of antisocial behavior and delinquency in adolescence (Rutter et al., 1998).

Cairns and Cairns (1994) reported that children aged 10 and 13 kept company with groups that reflected their behavior: aggressive or nonaggressive. Dishion, McCord, and Poulin (1999) suggested that peers reinforced students' beliefs about the benefits of aggressive behavior. These researchers found that aggressive behavior is reinforced through student conversation more than through modeling.

H. M. Walker (1995) said the following about peer-group influence:

> Some teachers attempt to ignore the acting-out child's inappropriate behavior in the hope that if it doesn't receive attention, it won't continue. This would be a sound strategy if the behavior were maintained *only* by teacher attention; however, peers often provide massive support for the acting-out child's misbehavior. (p. 33)

Think of the classroom as a stage and each student as an actor. The audience comprises the other students. Pleasing the audience sometimes means more than pleasing the teacher. To ignore the effect of group dynamics on individual behavior is to overlook a key factor that drives student behavior. This fact is particularly true for students whose need for peer affiliation and recognition outweighs their desire to achieve good grades. Morse (1996) said that group life is a consuming quest for most students of all ages because feedback from the group reaffirms identity (p. 186). Fostering community in the classroom helps mobilize the power of the group to channel individual student energy into constructive behavior.

Reasons for Misbehavior

Proactive teachers do more than simply stop misbehavior; they address causes (Chandler & Dahlquist, 2002; Phi Delta Commission on Discipline, 1984). Causes for misbehavior take many forms. Emotional trauma, metabolic deficiencies, and family dynamics are examples of causes that are usually outside the range of teacher intervention. However, classroom and school events that trigger misbehavior are open to teacher analysis and change. Irrelevant lessons, negative group dynamics, inconsistent routines, and overbearing disciplinary techniques are examples of classroom situations that contribute to problem behaviors.

In searching for causes, professionals also apply their understanding of various theories of human behavior. Theories provide a framework for analysis and provide guidelines for intervention. Although each theory of human behavior is significantly different in focus, all theories share one fundamental principle: Human behavior is not random but causal. In other words, a reason always exists for behavior. Table 10.1 summarizes how a problem behavior might be addressed from the viewpoint of four theories.

Attempting to understand why students behave as they do is a complicated but worthwhile activity. Keeping in mind that a reason exists for misbehavior provides a cautionary buffer against overreacting and an incentive for problem solving.

Mini Theories.   Proactive teachers examine and make adjustments in how they think about students. Albert Camus said, "An intellectual is someone whose mind watches

TABLE 10.1   *Reasons for Misbehavior: Four Theoretical Explanations*

Behavior: Sixth-grader Manuel frequently disrupts class by using attention-seeking behaviors such as making sarcastic remarks and telling inappropriate jokes.

Theoretical Perspective	Hypothetical Explanation
Developmental theory	Manuel is frustrated by his attempts to develop friendships. His attention-seeking behavior is an awkward attempt to gain other students' acceptance. This socioemotional conflict typically surfaces during adolescence in students who are insecure.
Behaviorist theory	Each time Manuel makes a wisecrack, the other students laugh and snicker. Their response provides positive reinforcement for his disruptive behavior.
Biophysical theory	Manuel lives in a rundown area of town. The state freeway bridge runs almost directly over his subsidized public housing unit. During the years, lead has gradually accumulated in Manuel's nervous system. Manuel's impulsivity is caused by lead poisoning.
Psychodynamic theory	Manuel's self-control problems are triggered by situations that remind him of past failures. Most of his inappropriate remarks occur in situations in which he is expected to read. He is insecure about his weak reading skills. This insecurity increases his anxiety, which he acts out through impulsive behavior.

itself." A classroom is a complex environment that requires flexibility in both thought and action. Proactive teachers strive to expand their understanding of how their behavior affects their students and what they can do to be more effective teachers.

When dealing with students, teachers develop personal theories to explain misbehavior. These *mini theories* are collective bits and pieces of information derived from "common sense," study, direct experience, and personal preference. Although mini theories operate in the background of teachers' consciousness, they play a major role in teachers' decisions about how to manage students' behavior.

The teacher who considers an expression of anger in the classroom "inappropriate" will respond to a distraught youngster in a substantially different manner than will a teacher who encourages students to get in touch with their feelings. Proactive teachers continually reassess the alignment of their mini theories with validated theory.

Brian Sheehy (2002), a third-grade teacher in an urban school, said,

I like the idea of choosing an approach that is compatible with your philosophy of education. Of course, this is valid only to the extent that your philosophy is based on an openminded trial and error and honest rumination and reflection. If your philosophy in nothing more than a justification of your own, personal biases and preconceived ideas, then this is an awful place to start. (p. 3)

Theory guides thought and action. A teacher who subscribes to behaviorist theory will respond to misbehavior differently than a teacher who values a developmental viewpoint will. No single theory of human behavior is correct. Various theories highlight different aspects of human behavior. Furthermore, theories of human behavior are never static but always evolving.

Likewise, no theory is totally "objective." Theories are influenced as much by culture as by science. Western theories rely primarily on analysis and rationality. For example, biophysical theory highlights how neurochemicals influence behavior. Psychodyamic theory highlights the role of interpersonal relationships, and behaviorism links behavior to environmental antecedents and consequences.

The dynamics of a classroom are too complex for any single theory to cover. Consequently, experts in the field of classroom management mesh theoretical ideas into practical strategies. This transformation of abstract theory into practical implementation creates useful models for implementation. Sometimes a model for classroom management is associated with a specific title—for example, the psychoeducational approach, which combines psychodynamic principles with various theories on teaching and learning.

Theories, models, and effective classroom management practices are constantly improving. Keeping track of innovations in classroom management theory and models is crucial to success. For example, only since 1995 have social skills instruction, functional behavior assessment, and cognitive psychology enhanced classroom management practices.

Subscribing to educational journals, attending professional conferences, and engaging in professional discourse are some of the ways teachers can continue to review theory and grow as professionals. Teachers not dedicated to their professional development invite stagnation. Teachers who examine their practices allow themselves the opportunity to change. Dedication to self-improvement is the cornerstone of proactive teaching.

Avoidance of Taking Misbehavior Personally

Everyone has pet peeves. Some teachers cannot tolerate teasing; others dislike tattling. Unless restrained, pet peeves, like buttons pushed, can spark an automatic response. Although reacting negatively to unwanted behavior is natural, a subjective, emotional reaction by a teacher restricts creative thinking. Emotional reactions to student misbehavior limit flexibility and reduce options. Teacher anger, resentment, and frustration cannot be eliminated, but they can be controlled or else the teacher will model the same behavior he or she wants the student to change.

Max Fischer (Education World, 2003) taught both elementary and middle school students. Following is what he had to say about teachers' controlling their emotions:

> A teacher risks much when inner rage boils over. Not only might they do permanent damage to the student/teacher relationship, they might also skew the dynamics of the entire classroom for some time to come. (p. 2)

Rezmierski (1987) said,

> I define *discipline* as a response that is, first and foremost, *designed to meet the needs of the child or youth whom we are disciplining*. Such a response carries with it a sense of emotional distance. This does not equate to an absence of emotional feeling. Rather this concept of distance suggests the ability to maintain space between reaction to a behavior and response to that behavior. (p. 8)

Proactive teachers understand the importance of thinking through a response to disruptive behavior. They understand that the wrong adult reaction can cause a minor disruption to escalate into a major confrontation.

The Conflict Cycle.　Many conflicts between teacher and students can be avoided. According to Long (1996), most crisis situations are not instigated by teachers but are accelerated by teachers' overreactions to a minor student disruption.

The *conflict cycle* begins with an event that a student perceives as stressful—an insulting comment, a boring assignment, a school rule. The event incites feelings—anger, apathy, resentment. These feelings lead to a minor transgression—an angry retort, lackluster effort, noncompliance. At this point, the teacher who is observing the student behavior must respond. Teachers who fail to take causes into account or who take misbehavior personally are likely to respond impulsively. An impulsive or angry teacher reaction increases the stress the student experiences, which leads to stronger feelings, more defiant behavior, and a stronger teacher reaction. Unless defused by the teacher, a minor disruption can snowball into a major crisis (Figure 10.2). The conflict cycle reminds teachers that their reaction can either defuse a potential crisis or cause it to escalate. Taking the conflict cycle into account minimizes the potential for misbehavior to disrupt a lesson for the entire class.

Conflict Resolution.　One of the most-difficult-to-achieve, yet critical, forms of positive behavioral supports is *conflict resolution* (Long & Morse, 1996). Stress builds when a teacher confronts a student about misbehavior. Perhaps the student embarrassed the teacher in front of colleagues, or the student hurt another student's feelings. The teacher's perception may be that the offending student is callous or a bully. At the precise moment when the teacher needs to demonstrate maturity and control, his or her emotions may be simmering toward the boiling point. At this point, the teacher needs to use conflict resolution strategies (Figure 10.3).

Controlling your emotional temperature provides stability. Teachers need to be more like a thermostat than a thermometer (Long, 2000). A thermometer reflects

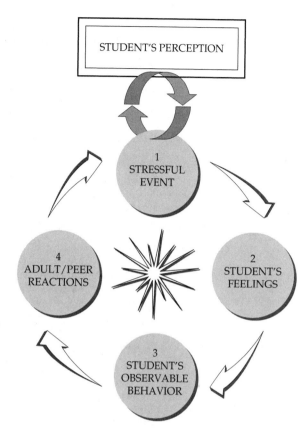

FIGURE 10.2   Conflict Cycle
From *Life Space Crisis Intervention: Talking with Students in Conflict* (2nd ed., p. 25), by N. Long, M. M. Wood, and F. A. Fecser, 2001, Austin, TX: PRO-ED. Copyright 2001 Nicholas Long. Reprinted with permission.

the temperature; a thermostat regulates the temperature. A thermometer is passive; a thermostat is active. Teachers who react to their emotional intensity and that of students around them lose control of the situation and themselves. Teachers who stay calm during turbulent times maintain control and can make better decisions about how to proceed. According to Long (2000),

> When we see ourselves as a thermostat, we will set our emotional temperature at 98.6 degrees. When a student gets hot, we are going to cool him or her down, when a student withdraws, we are going to heat him or her up. (p. 97)

Long (2000) said that student misbehavior does not come by appointment. Classrooms are busy places, and teachers must make on-the-spot decisions. Making the right decision can mean the difference between prolonging or concluding misbehavior. Long (2000) and his colleagues analyzed more than 140 school events in which a student had to be removed from the classroom because of misbehavior. Rather than simply focusing on what seemed wrong with the student, the researchers analyzed the interactions between students and teachers and found that most of the serious behavioral problems occurred during the first 45 minutes of school. Often, the incidents were prompted by transitions from one activity to

Within the school setting, a situation requires a conflict resolution strategy if any of the following three factors is applicable:

1. It is a chronic behavioral problem, with the intensity to disrupt the learning environment.
2. It is a behavior that threatens to spread to other students.
3. The student leaves the room without permission.

Criteria for determining items 1 and 2 are as follows:

- *Reality danger:* Students are engaging in an activity that could result in physical harm.
- *Psychological protection:* Scapegoating, bullying, and instigating behaviors qualify.
- *Protection against too much excitement:* A game or an activity is getting out of hand, for example.
- *Protection of property.*
- *Protection of the ongoing program:* One student is causing a disruption that is distracting the entire group, and he or she shows no sign of relenting.

Proactive behavioral interventions include the following:

- Functional behavioral assessment
- Behavior management plan
- Defusion of the conflict cycle; avoidance of a power struggle
- Sane message—reality appraisal
- Presentation of choices; restructuring of the activity
- Time-out in the classroom as a stress reliever
- Brief removal from the room
- Removal from the room to a quiet area for life space crisis intervention
- Behavior contract
- Peer mediation
- In-house suspension
- Communication with family members to elicit cooperation

FIGURE 10.3   Conflict Resolution Strategies

Adapted from "The Four Choices of Managing Surface Behavior of Students," by N. J. Long and R. G. Newman, 1996, in N. J. Long and W. C. Morse (Eds.), *Conflict in the Classroom: The Education of At-Risk and Troubled Students* (5th ed., pp. 266–273), Austin, TX: PRO-ED.

another, particularly in areas without staff supervision. Long and Morse (1996) reported that a minor issue usually precipitated a more serious problem. In none of the instances did teachers incite the problem, but in 60% of them, a teacher reacted in a manner that made the problem worse. Long and Morse reported, "They refueled it—they reinforced it—they escalated the conflict into a no-win power struggle between the students and themselves" (p. 96). Clearly, the teacher's role in defusing or escalating a problem behavior is significant. Consider the case study of Ms. Adams.

Rather than escalating the initial refusal to work, Ms. Adams could have used any one of the positive behavioral intervention strategies described in Chapter 8. Some possibilities are using planned ignoring, administering logical consequences, and accepting and acknowledging the student's feelings.

Case Study: Ms. Adams

Ms. Adams, a high school algebra teacher, directed her students to calculate some formulas. As she walked around the room, she saw that Abe had a blank sheet of paper in front of him. Rather than keeping in mind that a reason existed for Abe's noncompliance, Ms. Adams took his noncompliance as a personal challenge to her authority.

She said, "You might get away with not working in other classes but not mine—get started now!" A few students took notice and signaled others that an interesting confrontation was brewing. Abe resented what he perceived as an embarrassing reprimand and stood his ground. "This math sheet sucks," he said.

Now the entire class was alerted to a situation that was far more interesting than an algebra worksheet. At the same time, both Ms. Adams and Abe realized they were being scrutinized. Ms. Adams did not want to be viewed as an unassertive teacher, and Abe would not be intimidated. "Leave the room," said Ms. Adams. Abe got up, crumpled his math sheet, and tossed it in the wastebasket. His nifty hook shot drew cheers from his friends in the class. At this point, Ms. Adams was furious. She stalked after Abe and took him to the principal, who gave Abe a week of detention for insubordinate behavior.

RECLAMATION OF THE STUDENT–TEACHER RELATIONSHIP

More than anything else, youths who exhibit problem behaviors need to know their lives can improve. Unfortunately, the symptoms of a student's emotional struggles produce more heat than light. Noncompliance, anger, and aggression do not ordinarily spark acceptance and understanding. Yet, such youths have more right than wrong with them. Teachers who focus on developing student strengths are more successful than those who focus on fixing flaws. By not giving up on youths, proactive teachers help sustain their belief in a brighter future. Ten-year-old Reynaldo said, "A lot of people get shot in my neighborhood, but nothing bad has happened to me yet." By providing a refuge from the "bad" in a student's life, teachers inspire hope that the past is not necessarily a prelude to the future.

Despite overwhelming obstacles, young people who are vulnerable can go on to live successful lives. More than 50% of youths who are vulnerable can overcome the odds and live a normal life (Benard, 1992; Werner & Smith, 1982). Six factors that make a difference in the future of a youth who is at risk are as follows (Crowe, Amsel, & Jensen, 2003):

1. Avoiding peers with negative behavior
2. Being motivated and committed in school
3. Being involved in structured activities
4. Attending religious services
5. Having caring and supportive families
6. Experiencing a caring and supportive school environment

Even though the troubled lives of youths may seem to pose insurmountable barriers to emotional health, time is on the educator's side. Young people spend more organized time with teachers than with any other adult. Educators can help students succeed in school (Benard, 1992; Osher, Kendziora, VanDenBerg, & Karl, 1999; Werner & Smith, 1982). The results of several studies documented the positive effects of teacher support as a protective factor for troubled youths.

For example, Bowen and Bowen (1998) reported that teacher support had a greater effect on student behavior and academic progress than did deleterious home factors. Likewise, a meta-analysis of more than 800 research studies concluded that when teachers use such proactive teaching methods as social skills instruction and positive behavioral interventions, students who are troubled can learn to manage their emotions and achieve success in school (U.S. Department of Education, 2001).

Laursen (2002) used the term *reclaiming relationships* to describe how teachers support youths by forging bonds of trust. Table 10.2 lists seven competencies that help teachers reclaim relationships with a youth who is at risk.

In a 10-year study of school–community change and its impact on student learning, Bryk and Schneider (2003) described how the nature of student–teacher

TABLE 10.2 *Seven Habits of Reclaiming Relationships*

Relationship Component	Teacher Behavior	Teacher Belief
1. Trust	Follow through on what you say you will do.	I'm accountable to young people.
2. Attention	Put the young person in the center of concern.	Children and youths are valuable and worthy.
3. Empathy	See the world through the eyes of young people.	There are many versions of the same story.
4. Availability	Make time for youths a top priority.	Young people are worth an investment of time and energy.
5. Affirmation	Say positive things to youths and mean them.	Even troubled youths have positive qualities and constructive behaviors that can be acknowledged.
6. Respect	Give youths a say in decisions that affect them.	Young people are the best experts on their own feelings.
7. Virtue	Hold youths accountable for their behavior without blame.	Youths must learn self-discipline, and their teachers must be good models.

From "Seven Habits of Reclaiming Relationships," by E. K. Laursen, 2002, *Reclaiming Children and Youth, 11*(1), p. 13. Copyright 2002 by CYC-NET. Reprinted with permission.

relationships bolstered academic progress in failing schools. In highlighting the value of trust, these authors stated,

> Although the arrangement of social exchanges is an important consideration in the overall productivity of any organization, these concerns take on a heightened salience for schools. The social relations of schooling are not just a mechanism of production but are a valued outcome in their own right. We recall, in this regard, John Dewey's long-standing observation that a good elementary school is more akin to a family than a factory. (p. 19)

When queried about how they overcame neglect, abuse, poverty, and other dismal life conditions, many adults who were considered youths at risk during their school years acknowledged that having one or more adults who believed in them was pivotal. Caring adults supported these youths during difficult times and helped sustain the promise of a brighter future. Creating such hope for youths who are disillusioned is one of the most important challenges educators face every day.

Summary

* Beliefs guide actions. Proactive teachers think through their assumptions and values. They examine their own mini theories about human behavior and cultural differences.
* Proactive teachers recognize that emotional objectivity is a critical component of behavior management. They do not take misbehavior personally.
* Proactive teachers understand that various interactional factors influence students' behavior, including teaching style and peer pressure.
* Proactive teachers also understand how crucial defusing crisis situations is by examining their reactions to student behavior.
* The conflict cycle is a visual aid that helps teachers avoid overreacting to a minor transgression in a manner that can cause the situation to escalate into a full-blown crisis.
* Proactive teachers reclaim relationships. By networking with other mental health professionals, proactive teachers extend their advocacy efforts for youths into the community.

What You Should Know

Now that you have finished reading this chapter, you should know the following:

How teachers' mental set influences their behavior management practices
How allegiance to a specific theoretical viewpoint shapes a teacher's response to disciplinary problems
The meaning of the conflict cycle and how teachers inadvertently contribute to crisis situations

Why maintaining emotional objectivity is important when a teacher is managing problem behaviors

How teachers can reclaim relationships through their interactions with students

The value of reflection in maximizing a teacher's potential to work effectively with students

Applying the Concepts

1. Conduct a brainstorming session in your classroom. Each student should reflect on the misbehavior he or she would find most disturbing in a classroom. List these pet peeves and have a class discussion about how you could achieve emotional objectivity when you are dealing with these behaviors. Also discuss how other factors besides student temperament play a role in sustaining the listed disturbing behaviors.

2. Solicit any one of the following mental health professionals for a guest lecture: therapist, counselor, psychologist, social worker, psychiatrist. Ask the person to describe his or her work with youths. Ask questions about school–mental health collaboration. After the guest lecture, brainstorm ways that teachers could work more effectively with mental health professionals.

3. Invite a successful local businessperson to speak about overcoming difficulties on the path to adulthood. Ask the following questions: What are your best memories about school? Your least favorite memories? Can you name one or more teachers who helped you? Did you have support from mental health professionals? How can teachers help youths who are at risk to succeed? Add your own questions to this list. Discuss what the businessperson has to say about the potential for teachers to reclaim relationships.

4. Do a Web search of both governmental and private agencies that support youths and family mental health issues. Locate the answers to the following questions: What is the federal government doing to provide mental health support for families? What is your state and local government doing to advocate for youths? What are the addresses of valuable Web sites? What are some key statistics that reveal youths' mental health needs? Who are some individuals who have taken a leadership role in youth mental health and what are some of their key ideas?

5. Write a brief vignette of a student who exhibits a pattern of behavioral problems. In cooperative groups, analyze the vignette from a variety of theoretical perspectives, including cultural, behavioral, psychodynamic, ecological, biophysical, and developmental. Each person in the group should take responsibility for a single theoretical interpretation. Share your findings with the class. Discuss how different theoretical approaches influence selection of behavior management strategies.

6. The classroom management pyramid served as a visual guide to the organization of this textbook. The conflict cycle diagram illustrated the dynamics of student–teacher interaction. Common to these and other diagrams used in this text is the interactional interpretation of classroom management issues. Select a set of key ideas you have derived from reading this text and draw a diagram to illustrate these ideas. Share it with the class, select the class's best diagrams, and mail them to the author for his feedback.

7. At a field site, find examples of reactive teaching methods; find examples of proactive teaching methods. Compare them with the ideas presented in this text. Analyze each for its relative strengths and weaknesses. Discuss the advantages and disadvantages of each approach.

8. Do a personal analysis of what you consider to be your own classroom management strengths and weaknesses. Develop a plan for building on three strengths and bolstering three weak areas. Share your action plans with the class.

Appendix A

The Self-Control Inventory

Student _____ Age _____

Date _____ Rater _____

Class _____ School _____

The Self-Control Inventory (SCI)

The Self-Control Inventory is a functional guide
for assessing student self-control abilities
and organizing a self-control curriculum.

Directions: *Follow rating procedures listed on bottom of each page. Transfer student
ratings to summary rating below for quick access to student overall self-control skills.*

Self-Control Inventory Summary Rating

Impulse	School Routine	Group Pressure	Stress	Prob. Solve
1. M/S _____	5. A/R _____	9. M/C _____	13. A/N _____	17. F/P _____
2. D/P _____	6. O/M _____	10. A/P _____	14. C/C _____	18. L/E _____
3. V/F _____	7. A/E _____	11. P/G _____	15. T/F _____	19. A/C _____
4. R/O _____	8. C/T _____	12. D/B _____	16. S/A _____	20. R/C _____

The rating system is located on the bottom of each page. A student is rated as
compared to peers. The Self-Control Inventory was standardized on students eight
to sixteen years of age. Uses of the Self-Control Inventory include: clarifying
self-control strengths and weaknesses, targeting self-control skills for instruction,
identifying situations that trigger behavior problems, and comparing teacher judgments about specific students.

From *The Self-Control Inventory,* by M. Henley, 1994, Westfield, MA: Pegasus Center for Enabling
Education. Copyright 1994 by Pegasus Center for Enabling Education. All rights reserved.

GOAL: *TO CONTROL IMPULSES*

Self-Control Skill   *Example*

1. ☐ **MANAGES SITUATIONAL LURE**

   Student resists the impulse to act out (e.g., shout, run, hit people or objects) in such unstructured spaces outside the classroom as hallways, cafeteria, and field trips.

   Student attends a school assembly without becoming overstimulated.

   COMMENTS:

   Sample behavioral objective—*In settings outside the classroom, student maintains composure without teacher intervention.*

2. ☐ **DEMONSTRATES PATIENCE**

   Student adapts to normal classroom procedures that require waiting or taking turns.

   Student raises hand for help and waits for teacher assistance.

   COMMENTS:

   Sample behavioral objective—*When confronted with a delay in an activity, student waits without teacher reminders.*

3. ☐ **VERBALIZES FEELINGS**

   Student verbalizes, rather than acts out, feelings.

   During a private discussion with the teacher, student expresses disappointment and anger.

   COMMENTS:

   Sample behavioral objective—*During a classroom discussion, student verbalizes feelings with teacher support.*

4. ☐ **RESISTS TEMPTING OBJECTS**

   Student resists temptation to misuse objects in situations that could lead to negative consequences.

   Student uses ruler for measuring rather than banging on desk.

   COMMENTS:

   Sample behavioral objective—*When given manipulative learning materials, student uses them for their intended purpose without teacher reminders.*

1 rarely 2 sometimes 3 often 4 mastery N/A not applicable N/O not observable

GOAL: *TO FOLLOW SCHOOL ROUTINES*

Self-Control Skill   *Example*

5. **☐ ACCOMMODATES TO RULES**

    Student accepts clearly stated classroom limits.

    When asked by the teacher to work quietly, student complies.

    COMMENTS:

    Sample behavioral objective—*When asked to follow classroom rules, student obeys without teacher reminders.*

6. **☐ ORGANIZES SCHOOL MATERIALS**

    Student keeps track of items needed for school such as eyeglasses, gym clothes, and pencils.

    Student remembers homework assignments.

    COMMENTS:

    Sample behavioral objective—*During classroom activities, student keeps materials organized.*

7. **☐ ACCEPTS EVALUATIVE COMMENTS**

    Students listens to positive or negative feedback and guides actions accordingly.

    Student uses teacher feedback on math assignment to solve computational problems.

    COMMENTS:

    Sample behavioral objective—*After teacher feedback, student responds appropriately within an acceptable time frame.*

8. **☐ MAKES CLASSROOM TRANSITIONS**

    During the change of lessons or activities within the classroom, student follows classroom procedures.

    Student puts away reading materials and begins working at math activity table.

    COMMENTS:

    Sample behavioral objective—*During transition times, student follows classroom routines with minimal teacher intervention.*

☐1 rarely ☐2 sometimes ☐3 often ☐4 mastery N/A not applicable N/O not observable

GOAL: *TO MANAGE GROUP SITUATIONS*

Self-Control Skill   *Example*

9. ☐ **MAINTAINS COMPOSURE**

    Student maintains control when other
    students are agitated or excited.

    *During a classroom activity, student
    ignores disturbing behaviors of others.*

    COMMENTS:

    Sample behavioral objective—*When other class members are disruptive, stu-
    dent maintains self-control with minimal prompting.*

10. ☐ **APPRAISES PEER PRESSURE**

    When exposed to peer value judgments or
    actions, the student selects an individual
    course of action.

    *Student refuses to join in with class-
    mates who are teasing a new student.*

    COMMENTS:

    Sample behavioral objective—*In a group discussion, the student expresses in-
    dividual opinions without seeking peer approval.*

11. ☐ **PARTICIPATES IN GROUP ACTIVITY**

    Student demonstrates such social group
    skills as contributing ideas, listening to
    others, and offering positive feedback.

    *While working on a group project,
    student assists other members.*

    COMMENTS:

    Sample behavioral objective—*During a cooperative learning activity, student
    helps the group achieve goals with minimal teacher intervention.*

12. ☐ **DESCRIBES EFFECT OF
       BEHAVIOR ON OTHERS**

    Student verbalizes how behavior or
    comments can produce a positive or
    negative reaction in other students.

    *Student acknowledges that an insult
    hurt another student's feelings.*

    COMMENTS:

    Sample behavioral objective—*After tutoring a peer, student discusses positive
    effects of helping role with limited teacher prodding.*

☐1 rarely ☐2 sometimes ☐3 often ☐4 mastery N/A not applicable N/O not observable

GOAL: *TO MANAGE STRESS*

Self-Control Skill	*Example*

13.

☐ **ADAPTS TO NEW SITUATIONS** Student adapts to changes in class personnel, schedule, or routine without withdrawing or acting out problems.	*Student accepts a substitute teacher.* COMMENTS:

Sample behavioral objective—*Confronted with a change in regular classroom routine, student makes adjustments with minimal teacher assistance.*

14.

☐ **COPES WITH COMPETITION** Student participates in competitive activities or games without giving up or boasting.	*Student continues to enjoy a game when on the losing side.* COMMENTS:

Sample behavioral objective—*In a competitive situation, the student participates with minimal teacher support.*

15.

☐ **TOLERATES FRUSTRATION** Student manages moderate amounts of frustration or disappointment within the classroom.	*When a field trip is canceled because of bad weather, student accepts setback and continues with day's activities.* COMMENTS:

Sample behavioral objective—*When confronted with a frustrating situation, the student perseveres with teacher support.*

16.

☐ **SELECTS TENSION-REDUCING ACTIVITY** When confronted with a stressful situation, the student alleviates tension through alternative activities such as games, play, exercise, or other stress-reducing endeavors.	*Student who is having a bad day relaxes by playing a favorite game during free time.* COMMENTS:

Sample behavioral objective—*Given some options, student participates in stress-reducing activity, with minimal teacher prompting.*

☐1 rarely ☐2 sometimes ☐3 often ☐4 mastery N/A not applicable N/O not observable

GOAL: *TO SOLVE SOCIAL PROBLEMS*

Self-Control Skill — *Example*

17. ☐ **FOCUSES ON PRESENT**

Student rebounds from an unsettling prior experience and concentrates on present tasks.

Student regains composure in classroom after an altercation on the school bus.

COMMENTS:

Sample behavioral objective—*After an unpleasant experience, the student regains composure with minimal teacher support.*

18. ☐ **LEARNS FROM PAST EXPERIENCE**

Student uses past mistakes or accomplishments to guide here-and-now decisions.

Student refrains from fighting because a prior incident led to getting in trouble.

COMMENTS:

Sample behavioral objective—*Following a discussion about a pattern of classroom disruptions, the student develops and follows an alternative plan for behavior with teacher guidance.*

19. ☐ **ANTICIPATES CONSEQUENCES**

Student refrains from disruptive behavior because of anticipated loss of privilege.

After a reminder that annoying other students means loss of recess, student resumes individual assignment.

COMMENTS:

Sample behavioral objective—*When reminded of a negative consequence for actions, student changes behavior without further teacher comment.*

20. ☐ **RESOLVES CONFLICTS**

Student appraises misunderstandings or conflicts and seeks alternative solutions.

Rather than fighting, student negotiates a satisfactory settlement to a dispute.

COMMENTS:

Sample behavioral objective—*During a classroom disagreement, student helps work out a compromise with minimal teacher assistance.*

1 rarely 2 sometimes 3 often 4 mastery N/A not applicable N/O not observable

Appendix B

The Proactive Classroom Management Checklist

Proactive classroom management is responsive to the social and emotional needs of young people. The purpose of proactive classroom management is to teach students to work cooperatively, demonstrate self-control, and be accountable for their behavior. Proactive classroom management emphasizes three key elements: classroom as community, preventive discipline, and positive behavioral supports.

CLASSROOM AS COMMUNITY

- The classroom climate is responsive to such basic student needs as trust, belonging, mastery, and control. _____
- Regular classroom meetings give students the opportunity to discuss feelings and opinions. _____
- Space is arranged to encourage student movement. _____
- Activities are designed to promote student interaction. _____
- Cultural diversity is prized and regularly celebrated. _____
- Students with disabilities are included in classroom activities. _____
- Communication with parents is frequent and positive. _____
- Group dynamics are analyzed to limit the negative effects of cliques. _____
- Group dynamics are analyzed to identify and support students with low status. _____
- Classroom space is decorated with student art and academic work. _____
- Students are encouraged to make decisions about classroom events. _____
- Reward systems are structured to recognize the abilities of all students. _____

PREVENTIVE DISCIPLINE

- Students help develop classroom rules. _____
- Direct instruction is balanced with student-centered activities. _____
- Lessons are well organized and presented with enthusiasm. _____
- Cooperative learning is used regularly. _____

- Peer tutoring is used regularly. _____
- Students are given frequent, constructive feedback about their progress. _____
- Students are encouraged to evaluate their own progress. _____
- Lessons are developmentally appropriate. _____
- Classroom activities—both academic and social—are gender neutral. _____
- Students are allowed to make choices about how and what they learn. _____
- Social skills development is embedded within academic lessons. _____
- The teacher moves around the room. _____
- The teacher is aware of events throughout the classroom. _____
- Student motivation methods are regularly reviewed and revised when needed. _____
- Intrinsic rewards are preferred to extrinsic rewards. _____
- Classroom transitions are clear and well organized. _____
- Homework assignments are clear, practical, and brief. _____

POSITIVE BEHAVIORAL SUPPORTS

- The teacher models valued behaviors. _____
- Students are not removed from the classroom for minor disciplinary infractions. _____
- Logical consequences, rather than punishment, are used to maintain limits. _____
- Reprimands are respectful of students' dignity and feelings. _____
- The teacher does not take student misbehavior personally. _____
- The teacher is mindful that the adult reaction to misbehavior can escalate the problem. _____
- Behavioral interventions are aimed at developing constructive behavior rather than punishing students. _____
- The teacher uses a variety of behavioral intervention techniques, such as humor, planned ignoring, redirection, acknowledgment of feelings, reality appraisal, and congruent communication. _____
- Social skills programs are used with students who are at risk. _____
- Students are taught study skills. _____
- Threats are rarely used. _____
- Students are encouraged to reflect on their behavior. _____
- Misbehavior is charted for frequency, duration, and intensity. _____
- The effect of peer pressure on students' behavior is evaluated. _____
- Antecedents and consequences that reinforce or trigger misbehavior are identified. _____
- Behavior management plans are used to develop prosocial behavior. _____
- A variety of behavior modification interventions are used, including positive and negative reinforcement. _____

References

Abrams, B. J., & Segal, A. (1998). How to prevent aggressive behavior. *Teaching Exceptional Children, 30*(4), 10–15.

Adler, A. (1939). *Social interest: A challenge to mankind.* New York: Putnam.

Ainsworth, M. (1989). Attachments beyond infancy. *American Psychologist, 44*(4), 709–716.

Albert, L. (1996). *A teacher's guide to cooperative discipline.* Circle Pines, MN: American Guidance Service.

Alberto, P. A., & Troutman, A. C. (2003). *Applied behavior analysis for teachers* (6th ed.). Upper Saddle River, NJ: Merrill/Prentice Hall.

Alderman, G. L., & Nix, M. (1997). Teachers' intervention preferences related to explanations for behavior problems, severity of the problem and teacher experience. *Behavioral Disorders, 22*(2), 87–95.

Alexander, K. L., & Entwisle, D. R. (1988). Achievement in the first two years of school: Patterns and processes. *Monographs of the Society for Research in Child Development, 53* (2, Serial No. 218).

Allen, R. (2001). Make me laugh: Using humor in the classroom. *ASCD Education Update, 43*(5) 1, 6–9.

American Psychiatric Association. (1994). *Diagnostic and statistical manual of mental disorders* (4th ed.). Washington, DC: Author.

American Psychiatric Association. (2000). *Diagnostic and statistical manual of mental disorders* (Text revision). Washington, DC: Author.

Amrein, A. L., & Berliner, D. C. (2003). The effects of high-stakes testing on student motivation and learning. *Educational Leadership, 60*(5), 32–38.

Anderson, C., & Katsiyannis, A. (1997). By what token economy? A classroom learning tool for inclusive settings. *Teaching Exceptional Children, 29*(4), 65–67.

Appelstein, C. D. (1998). *No such thing as a bad kid.* Weston, MA: Gifford School.

Armas, G. C. (2001, February 12). Schools innovate to teach growing Hispanic population. *Amarillo Globe-News.* Retrieved from http://64.233.161.104/search?q=cache:DzMFw68ezowJ:www.amarillo.com/stories/021201/usn_hispanic.shtml+%22Gaithersburg%22+%22Sharon+Dreyfus%22&hl=en&lr=lang_en&ie=UTF-8

Armstrong, T. (1998). Empower, not control! A holistic approach to AD/HD. *Reaching Today's Youth, 2*(2), 3–5.

Arnold, T. (1987). *No jumping on the bed.* New York: Dial Books.

Aronson, J., Zimmerman, J., & Carlos, L. (1998). *Improving student achievement by extending school: Is it just a matter of time?* San Francisco: WestEd. Retrieved from http://www.wested.org/wested/papers/timeandlearning/

Asher, S. R., & Coie, J. D. (1990). *Peer rejection in childhood.* New York: Cambridge University Press.

Asher, S. R., Erdley, C. A., & Gabriel, S. W. (1994). Peer relations. In M. Rutter & D. Hay (Eds.), *Development through life: A handbook for clinicians* (pp. 456–487). Oxford, England: Blackwell Scientific.

Assistance to States for the Education of Children with Disabilities, 34 C.F.R. § 300.7(a)(4) (1999).

Auden, W. H. (1947). *The age of anxiety: A baroque eclogue.* New York: Random House.

Austin, A. (1984). The relationship among peer acceptance, social impact, and academic achievement in middle childhood. *American Educational Research Journal, 21*(3), 597–604.

Bagwell, C. L., Coie, J. D., Robert, T. A., & Lochman, J. E. (2000). Peer clique participation and social status in preadolescence. *Merrill-Palmer Quarterly, 46*(2), 280–305.

Baker, K. (1985). Research evidence of a school discipline problem. *Phi Delta Kappan, 66*(7), 482–488.

Bandura, A. (1977). Self-efficacy: Toward a unifying theory of behavioral change. *Psychological Review, 84,* 191–215.

Bandura, A. (1986). *Social foundations of thought and action: A social cognitive theory.* Upper Saddle River, NJ: Prentice Hall.

Bandura, A. (2000). Self-efficacy and the construction of an optimistic self. *Reaching Today's Youth, 4*(4), 18–22.

Banks, R. (1997). *Bullying in schools.* Champaign, IL: ERIC Clearinghouse on Elementary and Early Childhood Education. Retrieved from http://www.nldontheweb.org/Banks_1.htm

Banning, J. H. (1992). The connection between learning and the learning environment. In E. Hebert & A. Meek (Eds.), *Children, learning and school design: A first national invitational conference for architects and educators* (pp. 19–30). Winnetka, IL: Winnetka Public Schools.

Banning, J. (2001). Ecology in the lecture hall: How important is the educational environment to the process of learning? *NEA Higher Education Advocate, 18*(5), 5–8.

Barsalou, W. (1992). *Cognitive psychology: An overview for cognitive scientists.* Hillsdale, NJ: Erlbaum.

Bear, G. G. (1998). School discipline in the United States: Prevention, correction, and long-term social development. *School Psychology Review, 2*(1), 14–32.

Beck, J. (1995). *Cognitive therapy: Basics and beyond.* New York: Basic Books.

Beck, M., & Malley, J. (1998). A pedagogy of belonging. *Reclaiming Children and Youth, 7*(3), 133–137.

Benard, B. (1992). Fostering resiliency in kids: Protective factors in the family, school, and community. *Prevention, 12*(3), 1–14.

Benard, B. (1997). Drawing forth resilience in all our youth. *Reclaiming Children and Youth, 6*(1), 29–32.

Bergstrom, J. M., & O'Brien, L. A. (2001). Themes of discovery. *Educational Leadership, 58*(7), 29–33.

Berman, S. (1997). *Children's social consciousness and the development of social responsibility.* Albany: State University of New York Press.

Besag, V. E. (1989). *Bullies and victims in schools: A guide to understanding and management.* London: Taylor & Francis.

Bhaktivedanta, A. C. (1997). *Bhagaved-kita as it is.* Los Angeles: Bhaktivedanta Book Trust.

Billig, S. H. (2000). Research on K–12 school-based service learning: The evidence builds. *Phi Delta Kappan, 81*(9), 658–664.

Blankstein, A. M., & Guetzloe, E. (2000). Developing a sense of the possible. *Reaching Today's Youth, 4*(4), 2–5.

A blueprint for action. (2000, September). *NEA Today.* Retrieved September 11, 2000, from http://www.nea.org/neatoday/0009/cover.html

Blumer, H. (1969). *Symbolic interactionism: Perspective and method.* Upper Saddle River, NJ: Prentice Hall.

Bly, R. (1990). *Iron John: A book about men.* New York: Vintage Books.

Blyton, E. (1989). *Enid Blyton's the night the toys had a party.* New York: Gallery Books.

Boggiano, A. K., Flink, C., Shields, A., Seelbach, A., & Barrett, M. (1993). Use of techniques promoting students' self-determination: Effects on students' analytic problem-solving skills. *Motivation and Emotion, 17,* 319–336.

Bowen, N. K., & Bowen, G. L. (1998). The effects of home microsystem risk factors and school microsystem protective factors on student academic performance and affective investment in schooling. *Social Work in Education, 20,* 219–231.

Bowlby, J. (1973). *Attachment and loss: Vol. 2. Separation, anxiety & anger.* London: Hogarth Press.

Boyd, S. (1997). *Ten ways to break the ice!* Philadelphia: Susan Boyd Associates.

Boyd, W., & Shouse, R. (1997). The problems and promise of urban schools. In H. J. Walberg, O. Reyes, & R. P. Weissberg (Eds.), *Children and youth: Interdisciplinary perspectives*. Newbury Park, CA: Sage.

Braaten, S., Simpson, R., Rosell, J., & Reilly, T. (1988). Using punishment with exceptional children: A dilemma for educators. *Teaching Exceptional Children, 20*(2), 79–81.

Brendtro, L., & Brokenleg, M. (1993). Beyond the curriculum of control. *The Journal of Emotional and Behavioral Problems, 1*(4), 5–11.

Brendtro, L. K., Brokenleg, M., & Van Brockern, S. V. (1990). *Reclaiming youth at risk: Our hope for the future*. Bloomington, IN: National Educational Service.

Brendtro, L., & Long, N. (1997). Punishment rituals: Superstitions in an age of science. *Reclaiming Children and Youth, 6*(3), 130–135.

Brendtro, L., & Ness, A. E. (1995). Fixing flaws or building strengths? *Reclaiming Children and Youth, 4*(2), 2–7.

Brogan, B. R., & Brogan, W. A. (1999, Summer) The formation of character: A necessary goal for success in education. *Educational Forum*, pp. 348–355.

Brokenleg, M. (1999). Native American perspectives on generosity. *Reclaiming Children and Youth, 8*(2), 66–68.

Brophy, J. (1983). Effective classroom management. *The School Administrator, 40*(7), 33–36.

Brophy, J. (1996). *Working with shy or withdrawn students*. Urbana, IL: ERIC Clearinghouse on Elementary and Early Childhood Education. (ERIC Document Reproduction Service No. ED402070)

Brophy, J. (1998). *Motivating students to learn*. New York: McGraw-Hill.

Brown, T. (n.d.). *The broken toy*. Zanesville, OH: A Kids Hope and Summerhill Productions.

Bruer, J. T. (1999). In search of . . . brain-based education. *Phi Delta Kappan, 80*(9), 648–657.

Bryk, A., & Driscoll, M. (1998). *The high school as community: Contextual influences and consequences for students and teachers*. Madison: University of Wisconsin, National Center on Effective Secondary Schools.

Bryk, A. S., & Schneider, B. L. (2003). *Trust in schools: A core resource for improvement*. New York: Sage Foundation.

Bukowski, W. M., Newcomb, A. F., & Hartup, W. W. (1996). Friendship and its significance in childhood and adolescence: Introduction and comment. In W. M. Bukowski, A. F. Newcomb, & W. W. Hartup (Eds.), *The company they keep: Friendship in childhood and adolescence* (pp. 1–15). New York: Cambridge University Press.

Bushweller, K. (1999). Generation of cheaters. *American School Board Journal, 186*(4), 24–32.

Caine, G., Caine, R. N., & McClintic, C. (2002). Guiding the innate constructivist. *Educational Leadership, 60*(1), 70–73.

Caine, R. N. (2000). Building the bridge from research to classroom. *Educational Leadership, 58*(3), 59–65.

Cairns, R. B., & Cairns, B. D. (1994). *Lifelines and risks: Pathways of youth in our times*. New York: Cambridge University Press.

Campbell, P., & Siperstein, G. (1994). *Improving social competence: A resource for elementary school teachers*. Boston: Allyn & Bacon.

Cangelosi, J. S. (2003). *Classroom management strategies: Gaining and maintaining students' cooperation* (5th ed.). Hoboken, NJ: Wiley.

Canter, L., & Canter, M. (1992). *Assertive discipline: Positive behavior management for today's classroom* (3rd ed.). Santa Monica, CA: Canter & Associates.

Carlson, P. M., & Peterson, R. L. (1995). Using humor with troubled youth. *Reclaiming Children and Youth, 4*(3), 22–25.

Carnegie Corporation of New York. (2001). Creating powerful interdisciplinary curricula. In *Great transitions: Preparing adolescents for a new century* (Chapter 4, Educating young adolescents for a changing world). New York: Author. Retrieved from http://www.carnegie .org/sub/pubs/reports/great_transitions/ gr_chpt4.html

Carter, K. (1992). Toward a cognitive conception of classroom management: A case of teacher comprehension. In J. Shulman (Ed.), *Case methods in teacher education* (pp. 111–130). New York: Teachers College Press.

Center for the Advancement of Children's Mental Health. (2002). *Developing mental health indicators for U.S. children and adolescents.* New York: Author. Retrieved from http://www.kidsmentalhealth .org/documents/warningsignsphaseI.pdf

Centers for Disease Control and Prevention (2004). *Suicide: Fact sheet.* Washington, DC: Author. Retrieved from http://www.cdc.gov/ncipc/ factsheets/suifacts.htm

Chambers, J. C., & Henrickson, T. (2002). "Drugships": How kids make relationships with addictive behaviors. *Reclaiming Children and Youth, 11*(3), 130–133.

Chandler, L. K., & Dahlquist, C. M. (2006). *Functional assessment: Strategies to prevent and remediate challenging behavior in school settings* (2nd ed.). Upper Saddle River, NJ: Merrill/ Prentice Hall.

Chang, H. (1992). *Adolescent life and ethos: An ethnography of a U.S. high school.* London: Falmer Press.

Charles, C. M. (1996). *Building classroom discipline* (5th ed.). White Plains, NY: Longman.

Charles, C. M. (1999). *Building classroom discipline* (6th ed.). New York: Longman.

Charles, C. M. (2000). *The synergistic classroom: Joyful teaching and gentle discipline.* New York: Longman.

Charles, C. M. (2002). *Building classroom discipline* (7th ed.). Boston: Allyn & Bacon.

Charney, R. S. (2002). *Teaching children to care: Management in the responsive classroom* (Rev. ed.). Greenfield, MA: Northeast Foundation for Children.

Cheers for Kensington. (1999, December 27). *Springfield Morning Union,* p. A10.

Children's Defense Fund. (2004, August). *Key facts about American children.* Washington, DC: Author. Retrieved from http://www.childrensdefense .org/data/keyfacts.asp

Children's Defense Fund. (2005). *2005 Gun report.* Washington, DC: Author. Retrieved from http://www.childrensdefense.org/education/ gunviolence/gunreport2005/default.aspx

ChildStats.gov. (1999). *America's children 1999.* Retrieved from http://www.childstats.gov/ ac1999/highlight.asp

Chiu, L. H., & Tulley, M. (1997). Student preferences of teacher discipline styles. *Journal of Instructional Psychology, 24*(3), 168–175.

Coalition for Community Schools. (2004). Community school and social capital [Special issue]. *Coalition for Community Schools Newsletter, 3*(7). Retrieved from http://www .communityschools.org/newsletterv.3.7.html

Coie, J. D., & Dodge, K. A. (1997). Aggression and antisocial behavior. In W. Damon & N. Eisenberg (Eds.), *Handbook of child psychology: Vol. 3. Social, emotional, and personality development* (5th ed., pp. 779–862). New York: Wiley.

Coleman, J. (1990). *Foundations of social theory.* Cambridge, MA: Harvard University Press.

Coloroso, B. (1994). *Kids are worth it! Giving your child the gift of inner discipline.* New York: Avon Books.

Comer, J. P. (1986). Parent participation in the schools. *Phi Delta Kappan, 67*(6), 442–446.

Comer, J. P., Zigler, E. F., & Stern, B. M. (1997). Supporting today's families in the elementary school: The CoZi initiative. *Reaching Today's Youth, 1*(3), 37–43.

Committee for Children. (1992). *Second Step: A violence prevention curriculum.* Seattle, WA: Author.

Cooper, J. O., Heron, T. E., & Heward, W. L. (1990). *Applied behavior analysis.* Upper Saddle River, NJ: Merrill/Prentice Hall.

Copeland, E. P., & Hess, R. S. (1995). Differences in young adolescents' coping strategies based on gender and ethnicity. *Journal of Early Adolescence, 15*(2), 203–219.

Corbett, D., & Wilson, D. (2002). What urban students say about good teaching. *Educational Leadership, 60*(1), 18–22.

Cosden, M., Gannon, C., & Haring, T. G. (1995). Teacher-control versus student-control over choice of task and reinforcement for students with severe behavior problems. *Journal of Behavioral Education, 5,* 11–27.

Cosmos, C. (2001). Abuse of children with disabilities. *Today, 8*(2), 1–15.

Costa, A. L., & Kalick, B. (2000). Getting into the habit of reflection. *Educational Leadership, 57*(7), 60–65.

Cotton, K. (2000). *The schooling practices that matter most.* Alexandria, VA: Association for Supervision and Curriculum Development.

Cotton, K. (2001). *Expectations and student outcomes* (School improvement research series). Northeast Regional Educational Laboratory. Retrieved from http://www.nwrel.org/scpd/sirs/4/cu7.html

Council for Children with Behavioral Disorders. (1990). Position paper on use of behavior reduction strategies with children with behavioral disorders. *Behavioral Disorders, 15*(4), 243–260.

Council for Exceptional Children. (1986). In search of excellence: Instruction that works in special education classrooms [Special issue]. *Exceptional Children, 52*(6).

Council for Exceptional Children. (1999). The hidden problem among students with exceptionalities—Depression. *Today, 5*(5), 1, 5, 15.

Cox, R. D., & Gunn, W. B. (1980). Interpersonal skills in the schools: Assessment and curriculum development. In D. P. Rathjen & J. P. Foreyt (Eds.), *Social competence: Interventions for children and adults* (pp. 1–23). New York: Pergamon Press.

Craig, S., Hull, K., Haggart, A. G., & Perez-Selles, M. (2000). Promoting cultural competence through teacher assistance teams. *Teaching Exceptional Children, 32*(3), 10.

Craigen, J., & Ward, C. (1996). *What's this got to do with anything? A collection of group/class builders and energizers.* Ajax, Ontario, Canada: VISUtronX.

Crowe, M., Amsel, L., & Jensen, P. S. (2003). Language matters: Communicating with parents and teachers about mental health care for youth. *Emotional & Behavioral Disorders in Youth, 3*(4), 87–91.

Csikszentmihalyi, M. (1990). *Flow: The psychology of optimal experience.* New York: Harper & Row.

Curwin, R. L., & Mendler, A. N. (1988a). *Discipline with dignity.* Alexandria, VA: Association for Supervision and Curriculum Development.

Curwin, R. L. & Mendler, A. M. (1988b). Packaged discipline programs: Let the buyer beware. *Educational Leadership, 46*(2), 68–71.

Curwin, R. L., & Mendler, A. N. (1997). Beyond obedience: A discipline model for the long term. *Reaching Today's Youth, 1*(4), 21–23.

Darch, C. (1998). Instructional classroom management: A proactive model. *Beyond Behavior, 9*(3), 18–27.

Deci, E. L., Koestner, R., & Ryan, R. M. (1999). A meta-analytic review of experiments examining the effects of extrinsic rewards on intrinsic motivation. *Psychological Bulletin, 125,* 627–688.

Derman-Sparks, L. (1989). *Anti-bias curriculum: Tools for empowering young children.* Washington, DC: National Association for the Education of Young Children.

Diamond, M., & Hopson, J. (1998). *The magic trees of the mind: How to nurture your child's intelligence, creativity, and healthy emotions from birth through adolescence.* New York: Dutton.

Dishion, T. J., McCord, J., & Poulin, F. (1999). When interventions harm: Peer groups and problem behavior. *American Psychologist, 54,* 755–764.

Donald, B. (2002, December 10). Students still afraid despite fewer school weapons, crime. *Detroit News.* Retrieved from http://www.detnews.com/2002/schools/0212/10/schools-32460.htm

Dreikurs, R., & Cassel, P. (1972). *Discipline without tears: What to do with children who misbehave.* New York: Hawthorn Books.

Dreikurs, R., & Cassel, P. (1995). *Discipline without tears* (Reissued ed.). New York: Penguin–NAL.

Dreikurs, R., Grunwald, B. B., & Pepper, F. C. (1982). *Maintaining sanity in the classroom: Classroom management techniques* (2nd ed.). New York: Harper & Row.

Drew, N. (1987). *Learning the skills of peacemaking: An activity guide for elementary-age children on communicating, cooperating, resolving conflict.* Rolling Hills, CA: Jalmar Press.

Duffet, A., Johnson, J., & Farkas, S. (1999). *Kids these days '99: What Americans really think about the next generation.* New York: Public Agenda.

Dweck, C. S. (1999). *Self-theories: Their role in motivation, personality, and development.* Philadelphia: Psychology Press.

Edmonds, R. (1979). Some schools work and more can. *Social Policy, 9,* 28–32.

Edmonds, R. (1982). Programs of school improvement: An overview. *Educational Leadership, 40*(3), 4–11.

Edwards, C. H. (2000). *Classroom discipline and management* (3rd ed.). New York: Wiley.

Eggert, L. L. (1994). *Anger management for youth: Stemming aggression and violence.* Champaign, IL: Research Press.

Eggert, L., & Nicholas, L. (n.d.). *Reconnecting Youth: A peer group approach to building life skills* (2nd ed.). Bloomington, IN: National Educational Service.

Elam, S., Rose, L., & Gallup, A. (1996). The 28th annual Phi Delta Kappa/Gallup poll of the public's attitudes toward the public schools. *Phi Delta Kappan, 78*(1), 41–58.

Eliot, S. N. (1993). *Caring to learn: A report on the positive impact of a caring curriculum.* Greenfield, MA: Northeast Foundation for Children.

Emmer, E. T., Evertson, C. M., & Anderson, L. M. (1980). Effective classroom management at the beginning of the school year. *The Elementary School Journal, 80*(5), 219–231.

Epstein, H., Kutash, K., & Duchnowksi, A. (1998). *Outcomes for children and youth with behavioral and emotional disorders and their families: Programs and evaluation best practices.* Austin, TX: PRO–ED.

Ericson, N. (2001, June). *Addressing the problem of juvenile bullying.* Retrieved from http://www.ncjrs.org/txtfiles1/ojjdp/fs200127.txt

Erikson, E. (1950). *Childhood and society.* New York: Norton.

Erwin, J. C. (2003). Giving students what they need. *Educational Leadership, 61*(1), 19–23.

Evans, E. D., & Richardson, R. C. (1995). Corporal punishment: What teachers should know. *Teaching Exceptional Children, 27*(2), 33–36.

Evertson, C. M., & Harris, A. H. (1995). *Classroom Organization and Management Program: Revalidation Submission to the Program Effectiveness Panel (PEP), U.S. Department of Education* (Tech. Rep.). Nashville, TN: Peabody College, Vanderbilt University. (ERIC Document Reproduction Service No. ED403247)

Evertson, C. M., & Emmer, E. T. (1982a). Effective management at the beginning of the school year in junior high school classes. *Journal of Educational Psychology, 74*(4), 485–498.

Evertson, C., & Emmer, E. (1982b). Preventive classroom management. In D. Duke (Ed.), *Helping teachers manage classrooms* (pp. 2–31). Alexandria, VA: Association for Supervision and Curriculum Development.

Fahlberg, V. (1991). *A child's journey through placement.* Indianapolis, IN: Perspective Press.

Fischer, K. W., & Rose, T. L. (2001). Webs of skill: How students learn. *Educational Leadership, 59*(3), 6–12.

Fischer, M. (2003). Taming the three T's. *Education World,* pp. 1–4. Retrieved from http://www.educationworld.com./a_curr/voice/voice098.shtml

Fitzsimmons, M. K. (1998). *Functional assessment and behavior intervention plans.* Urbana, IL: ERIC Clearinghouse on Elementary and Early Childhood Education. (ERIC Document Reproduction Service No. ED429420)

Fleming, D. (1996). Preamble to a more perfect classroom. *Educational Leadership, 54*(1), 73–76.

Forness, S. (2001). Schools and the identification of mental health needs. In *Report of the Surgeon General's Conference on Children's Mental Health: A National Action Agenda.* Retrieved December 19, 2003, from http://www.hhs.gov/surgeongeneral/topics/cmh/childreport.htm

Forness, S. R., Walker, H. M., & Kavale, K. A. (2003). Psychiatric disorders and treatment. *Teaching Exceptional Children, 36*(2), 42–49.

Foss, J. M. (2001). *Nonverbal learning disability: How to recognize it and minimize its effects.* Arlington, VA: ERIC Clearinghouse on Disabilities and Gifted Education. (ERIC Document Reproduction Service No. ED461238)

Foster, E. S. (1989). *Energizers and icebreakers.* Minneapolis, MN: Educational Media Corporation.

Freiberg, H. J. (1996). From tourists to citizens in the classroom. *Educational Leadership, 54*(1), 32–37.

Freiberg, H. J. (1998). Measuring school climate: Let me count the ways. *Educational Leadership, 56*(1), 22–26.

Frymier, J. (1983). *Bad times–Good schools.* Bloomington, IN: Phi Delta Kappa.

Gallup, A. (1984). The Gallup poll of teachers' attitudes toward the public schools. *Phi Delta Kappan, 66*(2), 97–107.

Garbarino, J. (2000). *Lost boys: Why our sons turn violent and how we can save them.* New York: Anchor Books.

Gardner, H. (1993). *The unschooled mind: How children think and how schools should teach.* Boulder, CO: Perseus Books Group.

Garrity, C., Jens, K., Porter, W., Sager, N., & Short-Camilli, C. (1995). *Bully proofing your school: A comprehensive approach for elementary schools.* Longmont, CO: Sopris West.

Garrity, C., Jens, K., Porter, W., Sager, N., & Short-Camilli, C. (1996). Bully-proofing your school: A comprehensive approach. *Reclaiming Children and Youth, 5*(1), 36.

Gates, R. (2001). *Questions every teacher should answer.* Guilford, CT: McGraw-Hill/Dushkin.

Gathercoal, F. (1993). *Judicious discipline* (3rd ed.). San Francisco: Caddo Gap Press.

Gaustad, J. (1992). *School discipline.* Eugene, OR: ERIC Clearinghouse on Educational Management. (ERIC Document Reproduction Service No. ED350727)

Gehring, J. (2003). Report examines motivation among students. *Education Week, 23*(15), 5.

Gewertz, C. (2002, November 20). No racial gap seen in students' school outlook. *Education Week,* p. 5.

Gibbon, P. H. (2002). A hero of education. *Education Week, 21*(38), 33, 36.

Gibbs, J. (1995). *Tribes: A new way of learning and being together.* Sausalito, CA: CenterSource.

Gibbs, J., Potter, G., & Goldstein, A. P. (1995). *The EQUIP Program: Teaching youth to think and act responsibly through a peer-helping approach.* Champaign, IL: Research Press.

Gilbert, S. (1999, August 10). Bully or victim? Studies show they're much alike. *The New York Times,* p. F7.

Ginott, H. (1971). *Teacher and child.* New York: Macmillan.

Glasser, W. (1986). *Control theory in the classroom.* New York: Harper & Row.

Glasser, W. (1990). *The quality school: Managing students without coercion.* New York: Harper & Row.

Glasser, W., & Wubbolding, R. (1997). Beyond blame: A lead management approach. *Reaching Today's Youth, 1*(4), 40–42.

Glenn, J. (2001, January/February). The benefits of service-learning. *Harvard Education Letter.* Retrieved from http://www.edletter.org/past/issues/2001-jf/glenn.shtml

Goleman, D. (1987, August 25). Embattled giant of psychology speaks his mind. *The New York Times,* p. C1.

Goleman, D. (1995). *Emotional intelligence: Why it can matter more than IQ.* New York: Bantam Books.

Good, T. L., & Brophy, J. E. (2000). *Looking in classrooms* (8th ed.). New York: Longman.

Goode, E. (2000, February 23). Rising use of psychiatric drugs in toddler cases called alarming. *The New York Times,* p. A13.

Goodlad, J. (1984). *A place called school: Prospects for the future.* New York: McGraw-Hill.

Goodlad, J. I. (2000). Education and democracy: Advancing the agenda. *Phi Delta Kappan, 82*(1), 86–89.

Goodnough, A. (2003, January 19). Fearing a class system in the classroom: A strict curriculum, but only for failing schools, mostly in poor areas of New York. *The New York Times,* pp. A25, A27.

Gordon, D. T. (1999, September/October). Turning frustration to fulfillment: New teachers need more help with discipline. *Harvard Education Letter, 15*(5), 2–3.

Gordon, T. (1974). *Teacher effectiveness training.* New York: Wyden.

Gottfredson, G. D., & Gottfredson, D. C. (1985). *Victimization in the schools.* New York: Plenum Press.

Goulet, L. (1997). Maintaining respect under fire. *Reaching Today's Youth, 1*(4), 17–20.

Graber, J. (1996). Growing up female: Navigating body image, eating and depression. *Reclaiming Children and Youth, 5*(2), 76–80.

Greenbaum, P. E., Dedrick, R. F., Friedman, R. M., Kutash, K., Brown, E. D., Lardieri, S. P., et al. (1998). National Adolescent and Child Treatment Study (NACTS): Outcomes for children with serious emotional and behavioral disturbance. In M. H. Epstein, K. Kutash, & A. J. Duchnowski (Eds.), *Outcomes for children and youth with behavioral and emotional disorders and their families: Programs and evaluation best practices* (pp. 21–54). Austin, TX: PRO-ED.

Greenberg, G. (1998). Answers to six most frequently asked questions about AD/HD. *Reaching Today's Youth, 2*(2), 16–18.

Gresham, F. M., MacMillan, D. L., & Bocian, K. (1996). "Behavioral earthquakes": Low frequency salient behavioral events that differentiate students at-risk of behavior disorders. *Behavioral Disorders, 21*(4), 277–292.

Gunter, P. L., & Denny, K. R. (1996). Research issues and needs regarding teacher use of classroom management strategies. *Behavioral Disorders, 22*(1), 15–20.

Gunter, P. L., & Denny, K. R. (1998). Trends and issues in research regarding academic instruction of students with emotional and behavioral disorders. *Behavioral Disorders, 24*(1), 44–50.

Hall, C. S., Lindzey, G., & Campbell, J. B. (1998). *Theories of personality* (4th ed.). New York: Wiley.

Hammeken, P. A. (2000). *Inclusion: 450 strategies for success: A practical guide for all educators who teach students with disabilities.* Minnetonka, MN: Peytral.

Hammen, C., & Rudolph, K. D. (2003). Childhood mood disorders. In E. J. Mash & R. A. Barkley (Eds.), *Child psychopathology* (2nd ed., pp. 233–278). New York: Guilford Press.

Hansen, J. M., & Childs, J. (1998). Creating a school where people like to be. *Educational Leadership, 56*(1), 14–21.

Harmon, J. M., & Katims, D. S. (1999). Helping middle school students learn with social studies texts. *Teaching Exceptional Children 32*(1), 70–75.

Harter, S. (2000). Is self-esteem only skin-deep? The inextricable link between physical appearance and self-esteem. *Reclaiming Children and Youth, 9*(3), 133–138.

Hartup, W. (1992). *Having friends, making friends, and keeping friends: Relationships as educational contexts.* Urbana, IL: ERIC Clearinghouse on Elementary and Early Childhood Education. (ERIC Document Reproduction Service No. ED345854)

Harvard Graduate School of Education. (2001). *Dropouts concentrated in 35 cities, while federal data on dropouts underestimates problem.* Retrieved July 14, 2003, from http://www.gse.harvard.edu/news/features/conf01132001.html

Haskell, D. H. (2000, March). Building bridges between science and special education: Inclusion in the science classroom. *Electronic Journal of Science Education, 4*(3).

Hauck, W. E., & Thomas, J. W. (1972). The relationship of humor to intelligence, creativity, and intentional and incidental learning. *Journal of Experimental Education, 40*(4), 52–55.

Hawkins, J. D., Catalano, R. F., Kosterman, R., Abbot, R., & Hill, K. G. (1999). Preventing adolescent health-risk behaviors by strengthening protection during childhood. *Archives of Pediatric and Adolescent Medicine, 153*, 226–234.

Hayden, C. (1997). *Teaching about values: A new approach.* London: Cassell.

Heard, P. F., Divall, S. A., & Johnson, S. D. (2000). Can "ears-on" help hands-on science learning for girls and boys? *International Journal of Science Education, 22*(11), 1136–1146.

Hebert, E. A. (1998). Design matters: How school environment affects children. *Educational Leadership, 56*(1), 69–70.

Henderson, N. (1997). Resiliency in schools: Making it happen. *Principal, 77*(2), 10–17.

Henley, M. (1994a). A self-control curriculum for troubled youngsters. *The Journal of Emotional and Behavioral Problems, 3*(1), 40–46.

Henley, M. (1994b). *The self-control inventory.* Westfield, MA: Pegasus Center for Enabling Education.

Henley, M. (1997). Points, level systems, and teaching responsibility. *Reaching Today's Youth, 1*(4), 24–29.

Henley, M. (2000, September 13). Unpublished survey.

Henley, M. (2003). *Teaching self-control: A curriculum for responsible behavior* (2nd ed). Bloomington, IN: National Educational Service.

Henley, M. (2004). *Creating successful inclusion programs.* Bloomington, IN: National Educational Service.

Henley, M., & Long, N. (1999). Teaching emotional intelligence to impulsive-aggressive youth. *Reclaiming Children and Youth, 7*(4), 224–229.

Henley, M., Ramsey, R., & Algozzine, R. (2003). *Characteristics of and strategies for teaching students with mild disabilities* (4th ed.). Boston: Allyn & Bacon.

Henton, M. (1996). *Adventure in the classroom.* Dubuque, IA: Kendall/Hunt.

Hersch, P. (1998). *A tribe apart: A journey into the heart of American adolescence.* New York: Ballantine Books.

Hewett, F. (1968). *The emotionally disturbed child in the classroom.* Boston: Allyn & Bacon.

Hewitt, M. B. (1998). Helping students feel like they belong. *Reclaiming Children and Youth, 7*(3), 155–159.

Hochschild, J., & Scovronick, N. (2003). Our looming "racial generation gap." *Education Week, 22*(42), 40–41, 56.

Hodges, E., & Perry, D. (1996). Victims of peer abuse: An overview. *Reclaiming Children and Youth, 5*(1), 23–28.

Hodgkinson, H. (2001). Educational demographics: What teachers should know. *Educational Leadership, 58*(4), 6–11.

Hoffman, L. M. (2002). What students need in the restructured high school: Hints from the yearbook. *Education Week, 22*(7), 34, 38.

Holloway, J. H. (2002). Research link/Extracurricular activities and student motivation. *Educational Leadership, 60*(1), 80–81.

Holt, J. C. (1964). *How children fail.* New York: Dell.

Hoover, J. H., & Oliver, R. (1996). *The bullying prevention handbook: A guide for principals, teachers, and counselors.* Bloomington, IN: National Educational Service.

Hyland, N. E. (2000). *Threatening discourse: Cultural and contextual challenges to constructing antiracist narrative and practice among one elementary school staff.* Unpublished doctoral dissertation, University of Illinois at Urbana–Champaign.

Hyman, I., & D'Alessandro, J. (1984). Good, old-fashioned discipline: The politics of punitiveness. *Phi Delta Kappan, 66*(1), 39–45.

Irujo, S. (1989). Do you know why they all talk at once? Thoughts on cultural difference between Hispanics and Anglos. *Equity and Choice, 5*(3), 14–18.

Jensen, E. (1998). How Julie's brain learns. *The Best of Educational Leadership 1998–1999,* pp. 11–14.

Jensen, E. (2000a). Brain based learning: A reality check. *Educational Leadership, 57*(7), 76–79.

Jensen, E. (2000b). Moving with the brain in mind. *Educational Leadership, 58*(3), 34–37.

Jobe, D. A. (2003). Helping girls succeed. *Educational Leadership, 60*(4), 64–66.

Joint Economic Committee. (1991, August). *Doing drugs and dropping out: A report prepared for the use of the Subcommittee on Economic Growth, Trade, and Taxes of the Joint Economic Committee* (102nd Congress, 1st session). Washington, DC: U.S. Government Printing Office. (ERIC Document Reproduction Service No. ED344153)

Jolivette, K., Wehby, J. H., Canale, J., & Massey, N. G. (2001). Effects of choice-making opportunities on the behavior of students with emotional and behavioral disorders. *Behavioral Disorders, 26*(2), 132–145.

Jones, B., Valdez, G., Nowakowski, J., & Rasmussen, C. (1994). *Designing learning and technology for education reform.* Oak Brook, IL: North Central Regional Educational Laboratory.

Jones, F. (1979). The gentle art of classroom discipline. *National Elementary Principal, 58,* 26–32.

Jones, F. (1987). *Positive classroom discipline.* New York: McGraw-Hill.

Jones, M. C. (1924). The laboratory study of fear: The case of Peter. *Pedagogical Seminary, 31,* 308–315.

Jones, V., & Jones, L. (2004). *Comprehensive classroom management: Creating communities of support and solving problems* (7th ed.). Boston: Allyn & Bacon.

Josephson Institute of Ethics. (2004). *2004 Report card on the ethics of American youth.* Los Angeles: Author.

Judson, S. (1984). *A manual on nonviolence and children.* Philadelphia: New Society.

Kagan, J. (1998). Biology and the child. In W. Damon & N. Eisenberg (Eds.), *Handbook of child psychology* (5th ed., Vol. 3, pp. 177–235). New York: Wiley.

Kagan, S. (1994). *Cooperative learning.* San Clemente, CA: Kagan Publishing & Professional Development.

Katims, D. S., & Harmon, J. M. (2000). Strategic instruction in middle school social studies: Enhancing academic and literacy outcomes for at-risk students. *Intervention in School and Clinic, 35*(5), 280–289.

Katz, S. R. (1999). Teaching in tensions: Latino immigrant youth, their teachers, and the structure of schooling. *Teachers College Record, 100*(4), 809–840.

Kazdin, A. (2001). *Behavior modification in applied settings* (6th ed.). Belmont, CA: Wadsworth.

Kea, C. (1998). Focus on ethnic and minority concerns. *Council for Children with Behavior Disorders Newsletter, 11*(6), 4–5.

Kelly, G. (1955). *The psychology of personal constructs.* New York: Norton.

Kielsmeier, J. C. (2000). A time to serve, a time to learn: Service learning and the promise of democracy. *Phi Delta Kappan, 81*(9), 652–657.

Knitzer, J. (1982). *Unclaimed children: The failure of public responsibility to children and adolescents in need of mental health services.* Washington, DC: Children's Defense Fund.

Knitzer, J., Steinberg, Z., & Fleisch, B. (1990). *At the schoolhouse door: An examination of programs and policies for children with behavioral and emotional problems.* New York: Bank Street College of Education.

Knoblock, P. (1973). Open education for emotionally disturbed children. *Exceptional Children, 39,* 338–355.

Koestner, R., Ryan, R. M., Bernieri, F., & Holt, K. (1984). Setting limits on children's behavior: The differential effects of controlling versus informational styles on intrinsic motivation and creativity. *Journal of Personality, 52,* 233–248.

Kohn, A. (1993). *Punished by rewards: The trouble with gold stars, incentive plans, A's, praise, and other bribes.* Boston: Houghton Mifflin.

Kohn, A. (1996). *Beyond discipline: From compliance to community.* Alexandria, VA: Association for Supervision and Curriculum Development.

Kohn, A. (2002). Education's rotten apples. *Education Week, 22*(3), 36–48.

Kordalewski, J. (1999). *Incorporating student voice into teaching practice.* Washington, DC: ERIC Clearinghouse on Teaching and Teacher Education. (ERIC Document Reproduction Service No. ED440049)

Korinek, L., Walther-Thomas, C., McLaughlin, V. L., & Williams, B. T. (1999). Creating classroom communities and networks for student support. *Intervention in School and Clinic, 35*(1), 3–8.

Kounin, J. S. (1970). *Discipline and group management in classrooms.* New York: Holt, Rinehart & Winston.

Kozol, J. (1991). *Savage inequalities.* New York: Crown.

Kupersmidt, J., Coie, J., & Dodge, K. (1990). The role of poor peer relationships in the development of disorder. In S. Asher & J. Coie (Eds.), *Peer rejection in childhood* (pp. 274–308). New York: Cambridge University Press.

Kyle, P., Scott, S., & Kagan, S. (2001). *Win–win discipline course workbook.* San Clemente, CA: Kagan.

Ladd, G. W. (1984). Expanding our view of the child's social world: New territories, new maps, same directions? *Merrill-Palmer Quarterly, 30,* 317–320.

Landers, A. (2000, December 20). Ann Landers. *Springfield Union-News*, p. B10.

Landfried, S. E. (1989). Enabling undermines responsibility in students. *Educational Leadership, 47*(3), 79–83.

Langdon, C. A. (1996). The third annual Phi Delta Kappa poll of teachers' attitudes toward the public schools. *Phi Delta Kappan, 78*(3), 244–250.

Langdon, C. A. (1997). The fourth Phi Delta Kappa poll of teachers' attitudes toward the public schools. *Phi Delta Kappan, 79*(3), 212–220.

Langdon, C. A., & Vesper, N. (2000). The sixth Phi Delta Kappa poll of teachers' attitudes toward the public schools. *Phi Delta Kappan, 81*(8), 607–611.

Lantieri, L., & Patti, J. (1996). *Waging peace in our schools*. Boston: Beacon Press.

Larrivee, B. (2005). *Authentic classroom management: Creating a learning community and building reflective practice* (2nd ed.). Boston: Allyn & Bacon.

Larson, S. J. (1999). When inward pain turns outward. *Reaching Today's Youth, 4*(1), 31–35.

Laursen, E. K. (2002). Seven habits of reclaiming relationships. *Reclaiming Children and Youth, 11*(1), 10–14.

Leakey, R., & Lewin, R. (1977). *Origins: What new discoveries reveal about the emergence of our species and its possible future*. New York: Dutton.

Leitch, L. M., & Tangri, S. S. (1988). Barriers to home–school collaboration. *Educational Horizons, 66*(2), 70–74.

Leming, J. S. (1993). Synthesis of research: In search of effective character education. *Educational Leadership, 51*(3), 63–71.

Lepper, M. R. (1988). Motivational considerations in the study of instruction. *Cognition and Instruction, 5*(4), 289–309.

Lepper, M. R., & Greene, D. (1975). Turning play into work: Effects of adult surveillance and extrinsic rewards on children's intrinsic motivation. *Journal of Personality and Social Psychology, 33*, 479–486.

Lerner, J. W. (2003). *Learning disabilities: Theories, diagnosis, and teaching strategies* (9th ed.) Boston: Houghton Mifflin.

Lewin, K. (1936). *Principles of topological psychology*. New York: McGraw-Hill.

Lewis, B. L. (1992). Do conduct disordered gang members think differently? *Reclaiming Children and Youth, 1*(1), 17–20.

Lewis, C. C., Schaps, E., & Watson, M. S. (1996). The caring classroom's academic edge. *Educational Leadership, 54*(1), 16–21.

Lickona, T. (1991). *Education for character: How our schools can teach respect and responsibility*. New York: Bantam Books.

Lindsley, O. R. (1990). Precision teaching: By teachers for children. *Teaching Exceptional Children, 22*(3), 10–15.

Litsky, D., & Gardner, A. (1991). Restructuring quality. In J. Lloyd, N. Singh, & A. Repp (Eds.), *The regular education initiative: Alternative perspectives on concepts, issues, and models* (pp. 43–56). Sycamore, IL: Sycamore Press.

Lloyd, J. W., Crowley, E. P., Kohler, F. W., & Strain, P. S. (1998). Redefining the applied research agenda: Cooperative learning, prereferral, teacher consultation, and peer-mediated interventions. *Journal of Learning Disabilities, 21*(1), 43–52.

Long, N. (1986). The nine psychoeducational stages of helping emotionally disturbed students through the reeducation process. *The Pointer, 30*(3), 5–20.

Long, N. J. (1996). The conflict cycle paradigm on how troubled students get teachers out of control. In N. J. Long & W. C. Morse (Eds.), *Conflict in the classroom: The education of at-risk and troubled students* (5th ed., pp. 244–266). Austin, TX: PRO-ED.

Long, N. (2000). Personal struggles in reclaiming troubled students. *Reclaiming Children and Youth, 9*(2), 95–98.

Long, N. J., Fecser, F. A., & Brendtro, L. K. (1998). Life space crisis intervention: New skills for reclaiming students showing patterns of self-defeating behavior. *Healing Magazine, 3*(2), 2–27.

Long, N., & Long, J. (2001). *The angry smile: Managing passive-aggressive behavior of children and youth at school and home*. Austin, TX: PRO-ED.

Long, N. J., & Morse, W. C. (1996). *Conflict in the classroom: The education of at-risk and troubled children* (5th ed.). Austin, TX: PRO-ED.

Long, N. J., & Newman, R. G. (1996). The four choices of managing surface behavior of students. In N. J. Long & W. C. Morse (Eds.), *Conflict in the classroom: The education of at-risk and troubled students* (5th ed., pp. 266–273). Austin, TX: PRO-ED.

Long, N., Wood, M. M., & Fecser, F. A. (2001). *Life space crisis intervention: Talking with students in conflict* (2nd ed.). Austin, TX: PRO-ED.

Longwill, A. W., & Kleinert, H. L. (1998). The unexpected benefits of high school peer tutoring. *Teaching Exceptional Children, 30*(4), 60–65.

Lovitt, T. C., & Curtis, K. A. (1969). Academic response rate as a function of teacher and self-imposed contingencies. *Journal of Applied Behavior Analysis, 2,* 49–53.

Lumsden, L. S. (1994). *Student motivation to learn.* Eugene, OR: ERIC Clearinghouse on Educational Management. (ERIC Document Reproduction Service No. ED370200)

Lunde, J. P. (n.d.). *101 Things you can do in the first three weeks of class.* Retrieved from http://www.unl.edu/gradstudies/gsapd/instructional/101things.shtml

Maag, J. W. (1999). Why they say no: Foundational premises and techniques for managing resistance. *Focus on Exceptional Children, 32*(10), 1–16.

Maag, J. W. (2001a). *Powerful struggles: Managing resistance, building rapport.* Longmont, CO: Sopris West.

Maag, J. W. (2001b). Rewarded by punishment: Reflections on the disuse of positive reinforcement in education. *Exceptional Children, 67*(2), 173–186.

Maag, J. W. (2004). *Behavior management: From theoretical implications to practical applications* (2nd ed.). Belmont, CA: Wadsworth/Thomson Learning.

Magnuson, P. (2000, April). Spare the rod, but don't spoil the child. *Communicator,* pp. 1, 3. Retrieved from http://www.naesp.org/ContentLoad.do?contentId=154

Maholmes, V. (2002). What school is all about: Restoring the heart and soul of education. *Education Week, 22*(8), 30.

Maroney, S. (1998). *Pro-active discipline.* Retrieved September 9, 2003, from http://www.wiu.edu/users/mfsam1/ProactiveDiscipline.html

Marriott, D. M. (2002). His name is Michael. *Education Week, 22*(6), 35.

Marrow, A. J. (1969). *The practical theorist: The life and work of Kurt Lewin.* New York: Teachers College Press.

Martin, G., & Pear, J. (1996). *Behavior modification: What it is and how to do it* (5th ed.). Upper Saddle River, NJ: Prentice Hall.

Marzano, R. J. (2003). *What works in schools—Translating research into action.* Alexandria, VA: Association for Supervision and Curriculum Development.

Marzano, R. J., & Marzano, J. S. (2003). The key to classroom management. *Educational Leadership, 61*(1), 6–13.

Marzano, R. J., Marzano, J. S., & Pickering, D. J. (2003). *Classroom management that works: Research-based strategies for every teacher.* Alexandria, VA: Association for Supervision and Curriculum Development.

Maslow, A. H. (1970). *Motivation and personality* (2nd ed.). New York: Harper & Row.

Maslow, A. (1971). *The farther reaches of human nature.* New York: Viking Press.

Mastropieri, M., & Scruggs, T. (1998). Constructing more meaningful relationships in the classroom: Mnemonic research into practice. *Learning Disabilities Research and Practice, 13*(3), 138–145.

May, M. (2000, October 24). School's success story—It's pride restored, Stege Elementary in Richmond shows stunning advancement three years after arrival of principal. *San Francisco Chronicle,* p. A-21. Retrieved from http://sfgate.com/cgi-bin/article.cgi?file=/chronicle/archive/2000/10/24/MN109186.DTL

McCall, N. (1994). *Makes me wanna holler: A young Black man in America.* New York: Random House.

McGeady, M. R. (1997). Delivering respect, developing responsibility. *Reaching Today's Youth, 1*(4), 6–13.

McGinnis, E., & Goldstein, A. P. (1997). *Skillstreaming the elementary school child: New strategies and perspectives for teaching prosocial skills* (Rev. ed.). Champaign, IL: Research Press.

McIntyre, R., & Tong, V. (1998). Where the boys are: Do cross-gender misunderstandings of language use and behavior patterns contribute to the over-representation of males in programs for students with emotional and behavioral disorders? *Education and Treatment of Children, 21*(3), 321–333.

McLaughlin, M. W. (2001). Community counts. *Educational Leadership, 58*(7), 14–18.

Mendler, A. (1992). *What do I do when? How to achieve discipline with dignity in the classroom.* Bloomington, IN: National Educational Service.

Mendler, A. N. (2000). *Motivating students who don't care: Successful techniques for educators.* Bloomington, IN: National Educational Service.

Merriam-Webster's collegiate dictionary (11th ed.). (2003). Springfield, MA: Merriam-Webster.

Meyers, D. E., Milne, A. M., Baker, K., & Ginsburg, A. (1987). Student discipline and high school performance. *Sociology of Education, 60,* 18–33.

Miller, R., Brickman, P., & Bolen, D. (1975). Attribution versus persuasion as a means of modifying behavior. *Journal of Personality and Social Psychology, 31,* 430–441.

Miltenberger, R. (2001). *Behavior modification: Principles and procedures* (2nd ed.). Belmont, CA: Wadsworth.

Moles, O. C. (Ed.). (1989). *Strategies to reduce student misbehavior.* Washington, DC: U.S. Department of Education, Office of Educational Research and Improvement. (ERIC Document Reproduction Service No. ED311608)

Morse, W. C. (1987). Introduction. *Teaching Exceptional Children, 19*(4), 4–6.

Morse, W. C. (1996b). The power of group forces in the classroom: Strategies and skills of promoting positive group behavior. In N. J. Long, W. C. Morse, & R. G. Newman (Eds.), *Conflict in the classroom: The education of at-risk and troubled students* (5th ed., pp. 186–191). Austin, TX: PRO-ED.

Morse, W. (2001). A half century of children who hate: Insights for today from Fritz Redl. *Reclaiming Children and Youth, 10*(2), 75–88.

Moustakas, C. (1971). *The authentic teacher: Sensitivity and awareness in the classroom.* Cambridge, MA: Doyle.

Mueller, C. M., & Dweck, C. S. (1998). Intelligence praise can undermine motivation and performance. *Journal of Personality and Social Psychology, 75*(1), 33–52.

National Center for Education Statistics. (2002a). *The condition of education 2002.* Washington, DC: Author. Retrieved from http://nces.ed.gov/pubsearch/pubsinfo.asp?pubid=2002025

National Center for Education Statistics. (2002b). *A profile of the American high school sophomore in 2002: Initial results from the base year of the longitudinals study of 2002.* Washington, DC: Author. Retrieved from http://nces.ed.gov/pubsearch/pubsinfo.asp?pubid=2005338

National Center for Education Statistics. (2002c). *Public high school dropouts and completers from the common core of data: School years 1998–99 and 1999–2000.* Washington, DC: Author. Retrieved from http://nces.ed.gov/pubsearch/pubsinfo.asp?pubid=2002382

National Education Association. (2000, September). Getting help from home. *NEA Today.* Retrieved September 11, 2000, from http://www.nea.org/neatoday/0009/cover.html

National Institute of Education. (1978). *Violent schools–Safe schools: The Safe School Study report to Congress.* Washington, DC: U.S. Government Printing Office.

National Longitudinal Study of Adolescent Health. (1994). Retrieved from http://www.cpc.unc.edu/addhealth

National Research Council & Institute of Medicine. (2004). *Engaging schools: Fostering high school students' motivation to learn.* Washington, DC: National Academies Press.

National School Safety Center. (n.d.). *Set straight on bullies.* Malibu, CA: Author.

Nelson, J. L., Lott, L., & Glenn, H. (2000). *Positive discipline in the classroom* (3rd ed.). Rocklin, CA: Prima.

Nichols, P. (1992). The curriculum of control: Twelve reasons for it, some arguments against it. *Beyond Behavior, 3*(2), 5–11.

Nichols, P. (1998). Teaching thinking skills—A class act. *Beyond Behavior, 9*(1), 13–19.

Noddings, N. (1984). *Caring: A feminine approach to ethics and moral education.* Berkeley: University of California Press.

Norton, R. (1995). *The quality classroom manager.* Amityville, NY: Baywood.

Oliver, R., Hoover, J., & Hazler, R. (1994). The perceived roles of bullying in small town Midwestern schools. *Journal of Counseling and Development, 72*(2), 416–420.

Olson, L. (2002, May 29). Detachment starts in middle school, study finds. *Education Week,* p. 9.

Olweus, D. (1993). *Bullying at school: What we know and what we can do.* Cambridge, MA: Blackwell. (ERIC Document Reproduction Service No. ED384437)

Osher, D., Kendziora, K. T., VanDenBerg, J., & Karl, D. (1999). Growing resilience: Creating opportunities for resilience to thrive. *Reaching Today's Youth, 3*(4), 38–45.

Pajares, F. (n.d.). *But they did not give up.* Retrieved from http://www.emory.edu/EDUCATION/mfp/index_html

Pajares, F. (2000, January 27). *Schooling in America: Myths, mixed messages, and good intentions.* Lecture delivered at Emory University, Atlanta, GA. Retrieved from http://www.emory.edu/EDUCATION/mfp/pajaresgtl.html

Panico, A. (1997). The classroom community model. *Reaching Today's Youth, 2*(1), 37–40.

Patrick, B. C., Skinner, E. A., & Connell, J. P. (1993). What motivates children's behavior and emotion? Joint effects of perceived control and autonomy in academic domain. *Journal of Personality and Social Psychology, 65,* 781–791.

Patrick, H. (1997). Social self-regulation: Exploring the relations between children's social relationships, academic self-regulation, and school performance. *Educational Psychologist, 32*(4), 209–220.

Patrick, H., & Townsend, M. A. R. (1995, April). *The influence of perceived social competence on a school beginner's emergent academic intrinsic motivation.* Poster session presented at the annual meeting of the American Educational Research Association, San Francisco, CA.

Paul, R., & Elder, L. (2003). *The thinker's guide for students on how to study & learn a discipline: Using critical thinking concepts & tools.* Dillon Beach, CA: Foundation for Critical Thinking.

Peters, T. G. (1984). *In search of excellence.* New York: Warner Books.

Phillips, B. N. (1993). *Educational and psychological perspectives on stress in students, teachers, and parents.* Brandon, VT: Clinical Psychology.

Piaget, J. (1954). *The construction of reality and the child.* New York: Basic Books.

Piaget, J., & Inhelder, B. (1958). *The growth of logical thinking from childhood to adolescence.* New York: Basic Books.

Pierce, S. (1999). *Steve's primer of practical persuasion and influence.* Retrieved from http://www.as.wvu.edu/~sbb/comm221/primer.htm

Pikas, A. (1989). The common concern method for the treatment of mobbing. In E. Roland & E. Munthe (Eds.), *Bullying: An international perspective* (pp. 132–144). London: Fulton.

Pikes, T., & Daniels, V. I. (2000). Listen to us! Voice of despair. *Reaching Today's Youth, 4*(4), 6–8.

Prater, M. A. (1999). Impact of peer teaching on the acquisition of social skills by adolescents with learning disabilities. *Education and Treatment of Children, 22*(1), 19–35.

Purkey, W. W., & Novak, J. M. (1996). *Inviting school success: A self-concept approach to teaching learning and democratic practice* (3rd ed.). Belmont, CA: Wadsworth.

Qualities that count with employers. (1995, February 20). *The New York Times,* p. A13.

Redl, F., & Wineman, D. (1951). *Children who hate: The disorganization and breakdown of behavior controls.* New York: Free Press.

Reeve, J., Bolt, E., & Cai, Y. (1999). Autonomy-supportive teachers: How they teach and motivate students. *Journal of Educational Psychology, 91*(3), 537–548.

Reid, K. S. (2004). Report focuses on graduation-rate gaps. *Education Week, 23*(25), 5.

Resnick, M. D., Bearman, P. S., Blum, R. W., Bauman, K. E., Harris, K. J., Jones, J., et al. (1997). Protecting adolescents from harm: Findings from the National Longitudinal Study on Adolescent Health. *Journal of the American Medical Association, 278,* 823–832.

Rezmierski, V. E. (1987). Discipline: Neither the steel nor the velvet, but the maturity inside the glove, that makes the difference. *The Pointer, 31*(4), 5–13.

Rhodes, W., & Tracy, M. (1975). *A study of child variance.* Ann Arbor: University of Michigan.

Rockwell, S. (1995). *Back off, cool down, try again: Teaching students how to control aggressive behavior.* Arlington, VA: Council for Exceptional Children.

Rockwell, S. (1997). Building responsibility through entrepreneurship and service. *Reaching Today's Youth, 1*(4), 44–48.

Rockwell, S. (1999). Ghost children: Uncovering distress and depression in a typical middle school. *Reaching Today's Youth, 4*(1), 8–13.

Rogers, S., & Renard, L. (1999). Relationship-driven teaching. *Educational Leadership, 57*(1), 34–35.

Rose, T. L. (1987). *Current disciplinary practices in American public schools.* Washington, DC: Educational Resources Information Center. (ERIC Document Reproduction Service No. ED309560)

Rosenthal, R., & Jacobson, L. (1968). *Pygmalion in the classroom: Teacher expectations and pupils' intellectual development.* New York: Holt, Rinehart & Winston.

Rothstein, R. (2001). *Of schools and crimes, and gross exaggeration.* Washington, DC: Economic Policy Institute. Retrieved from http://www.epinet.org/content.cfm/webfeat_lessons20010207

Ruhl, K. (1985). Handling aggression: Fourteen methods teachers use. *The Pointer, 29,* 30–33.

Rutherford, R. B., Mathur, S. R., & Quinn, M. M. (1998). Promoting social communication skills through cooperative learning and direct instruction. *Education and Treatment of Children, 21*(3), 354–369.

Rutter, M. (1981). *Maternal deprivation reassessed.* London: Penguin Books.

Rutter, M., Giller, H., & Hagell, A. (1998). *Antisocial behavior by young people.* New York: Cambridge University Press.

Ryan, A. L., Halsey, H. N., & Matthews, W. J. (2003). Using functional assessment to promote desirable student behavior in schools. *Teaching Exceptional Children, 35*(5), 8–15.

Sadock, B., & Kaplan, V. (2000). *Kaplan and Sadock's comprehensive textbook of psychiatry* (7th ed., Vols. 1 & 2). Philadelphia: Lippincott Williams & Wilkins.

Saltman, J. M. (1995). The humor connection. *Reclaiming Children and Youth, 4*(3), 4–5.

Satcher, D. (2000). *Remarks at the news conference held at the Surgeon General's Conference on Children's Mental Health.* Washington, DC: U.S. Department of Health and Human Services. Retrieved September 19, 2000, from http://www.surgeongeneral.gov/library/history/satcherarchive/speeches/ChildMentalHealth.htm

Sauter, C. (1995, January). *Standing up to violence: Kappan special report.* Bloomington, IN: Phi Delta Kappa.

Sautner, B. (2001). The safe and caring schools initiative. *Reclaiming Children and Youth, 9*(4), 197–201.

Schab, F. (1980). Cheating among college and non-college bound pupils, 1969–1979. *The Clearing House, 53*(8), 379–380.

Schaps, E. (2000). Building community from within. *Principal, 80*(1), 14, 16.

Scherer, M. (2000a). The discipline of hope: A conversation with Herb Kohl. *The Best of Educational Leadership 1998–1999,* pp. 2–6.

Scherer, M. (2000b). Standardized instruction—Effects may vary. *Educational Leadership, 58*(1), 5.

Scherer, M. (2001). The brain and learning. *Educational Leadership, 59*(3), 5.

Scherer, M. (2002). Who cares? And who wants to know? *Educational Leadership, 60*(1), 5.

Scheuermann, B. (1998). Curricular and instructional recommendations for students with emotional/behavioral disorders. *Beyond Behavior, 9*(3), 3–4.

Scheuermann, B., Webber, J., Partin, M., & Knies, W. (1994). Level systems and the law: Are they compatible? *Behavior Disorders, 19*(3), 205–220.

Schneider, B., & Stevenson, D. (1999/2000). The ambitious generation. *Educational Leadership, 57*(4), 22–25.

Schumaker, J. B., Pederson, C. S., Hazel, J. S., & Meyen, E. L. (1983). Social skills curricula for mildly handicapped adolescents: A review. *Journal of Learning Disabilities, 17*(7), 422–431.

Scott, T. M., Liaupsin, C. J., Nelson, M. C., & Jolivette, K. (2003). Ensuring student success through team-based functional behavioral assessment. *Teaching Exceptional Children, 35*(5), 16–21.

Seldes, G. (1985). *The great thoughts.* New York: Ballantine Books.

Seligman, M., Gillham, J., & Reivich, K. (2000). Learning the ABCs of accurate optimism. *Reaching Today's Youth, 4*(4), 9–13.

Sheehy, B. (2002). *Reflection and teaching.* Unpublished term paper, Westfield State College, Education Department, Westfield, MA.

Sheets, R. H., & Gay, G. (1996). Student perceptions of disciplinary conflict in ethnically diverse classrooms. *NASSP Bulletin, 80*(580), 84–94.

Shellard, E., & Protheroe, N. (2000). *Effective teaching: How do we know it when we see it?* (Informed educator series). Arlington, VA: Education Research Service.

Shepard, C. (1964). *Small groups: Some sociological perspectives.* Scranton, PA: Chandler.

Shores, R. E., Gunter, P., & Jack, S. L. (1993). Classroom management strategies: Are they setting events for coercion? *Behavioral Disorders, 18,* 92–102.

Sileo, T. W., & Prater, M. A. (1998). Creating classroom environments that address the linguistic and cultural backgrounds of students with disabilities: An Asian Pacific American perspective. *Remedial and Special Education, 19*(6), 323–327.

Silverstein, S. (1974). *Where the sidewalk ends.* New York: HarperCollins.

Simon, K. G. (2002). The blue blood is bad, right? *Educational Leadership, 60*(10), 24–28.

Skiba, R. J., & Deno, S. L. (1991). Terminology and behavior reduction: The case against punishment. *Exceptional Children, 57*(4), 298–313.

Skiba, R. J., & Peterson, R. (1999). The dark side of zero tolerance: Can punishment lead to safe schools? *Phi Delta Kappan, 80*(5), 372–382. Retrieved from http://www.pdkintl.org/kappan/kski9901.htm

Skinner, B. F. (1978). *Reflections on behaviorism and society.* Upper Saddle River, NJ: Prentice Hall.

Sloane, P., & MacHale, D. (1994). *Great lateral thinking puzzles.* New York: Sterling.

Smith, K. (n.d.). *Tip sheets: Positive ways of intervening with challenging behavior: Passive aggressive behavior. . . Preventing and dealing with challenging behavior.* Minneapolis: University of Minnesota, College of Education, Institute on Community Integration. Retrieved January 11, 2004, from http://ici2.umn.edu/preschoolbehavior/tip_sheets/passagg.htm

Smith, P. K., & Sharp, S. (1994). *School bullying: Insights and perspectives.* London: Rutledge.

Snow, C. E., Burns, M. S., & Griffin, P. (Eds.). (1998). *Preventing reading difficulties in young children.* Washington, DC: National Academy Press. Available from http://books.nap.edu/catalog/6023.html

Sridhar, D., & Vaughn, S. (2000). Bibliotherapy for all: Enhancing reading comprehension, self concept, and behavior. *Teaching Exceptional Children, 33*(2), 74–82.

Stallings, J. A. (1980). *Classroom research: Implications for mathematics and science instruction.* Paper presented to the Biological Science Curriculum Study Conference, Boulder, CO, November 7. (ERIC Document Reproduction Service No. ED211355)

Stanford, G. C. (2000, October 30). A discussion on school reform—An introduction: Substantive change versus superficial change: A look at two urban middle schools. *Teachers College Record.* Available from http://www.tcrecord.org/Content.asp?ContentID=10618

Stein, N. (2000). Listening and learning from— Girls. *Educational Leadership, 57*(4), 19–20.

Sternberg, R. (2002). Teaching for wisdom in our schools. *Education Week, 23*(11), 42, 56.

Stevenson, H., & Stigler, J. (1992). *The learning gap: Why our schools are failing and what we can learn from Japanese and Chinese education.* New York: Summit Books.

Stoiber, K. (1991). The effect of technical and reflective preservice instruction on pedagogical reasoning and problem solving. *Journal of Teacher Education, 42*(2), 131–139.

Strauss, V. (2001, April 27). Synergy yields dividends for all. *The Washington Post*, p. A09.

Stringfield, S., & Teddlie, C. (1988). A time to summarize: The Louisiana School Effectiveness Study. *Educational Leadership, 46*(2), 43–49.

Strong, R., Silver, H., Perini, M., & Tuculescu, G. (2003). Boredom and its opposite. *Educational Leadership, 61*(1), 24–29.

Stronge, J. H. (2002). *Qualities of effective teachers.* Alexandria, VA: Association for Supervision and Curriculum Development.

Sugai, G., Horner, R. H., Dunlap, G., Hieneman, M., Lewis, T. J., Nelson, C. M., et al. (1999). *Applying positive behavioral support and functional assessment in schools.* Washington, DC: Office of Special Education Programs, Center on Positive Behavioral Interventions and Supports.

Swanson, C. B. (2004). *Who graduates? Who doesn't? A statistical portrait of public high school graduation, class of 2001* (Executive summary). Washington, DC: Urban Institute. Retrieved February 27, 2004, from http://www.urban.org/url.cfm?ID=410934

Sylwester, R. (1995). *A celebration of neurons: An educator's guide to the human brain.* Alexandria, VA: Association for Supervision and Curriculum Development.

Sylwester, R. (2000). *A biological brain in a cultural classroom: Applying biological research to classroom management.* Thousand Oaks, CA: Corwin Press.

Taylor, G. R. (1997). *Curriculum strategies: Social skills intervention for young African-American males.* Westport, CT: Praeger.

Taylor, J. M., Gilligan, C., & Sullivan, A. (1996). *Between voices and silence: Women and girls, race and relationships.* Cambridge, MA: Harvard University Press.

Taylor, Q. L. (1990). *Cross-cultural communication: An essential dimension of effective education* (Rev. ed.). Chevy Chase, MD: The Mid-Atlantic Equity Center. (ERIC Document Reproduction Service No. ED325593)

Taylor, P. B., Gunter, P. L., & Slate, J. R. (2001). Teachers' perceptions of inappropriate student behavior as a function of teachers' and students' gender and ethnic background. *Behavioral Disorders, 26*(2), 146–151.

Taylor-Greene, S., Brown, D., Nelson, L., & Longton, J. (1997). School-wide behavioral support: Starting the year off right. *Journal of Behavioral Education, 7*(1), 99–112.

A teacher's memoir: 1864. (1999). *Massachusetts Teachers Association Today, 30*(1), 6.

Teachers.net. (2005). *Latest buzz on the Classroom Humor Chatboard.* Retrieved from http://teachers.net/mentors/humor/

Teddlie, C., & Stringfield, S. (1993). *Schools make a difference: Lessons learned from a 10 year study of school effects.* New York: Teachers College Press.

The ten worst ways to make a school parent-friendly. (2000, September). *NEA Today.* Retrieved September 11, 2000, from http://www.nea.org/neatoday/0009/cover.html

Thorson, S. (2003). *Listening to students: Reflections on secondary classroom management.* Boston: Allyn & Bacon.

Tomlinson, C. A. (2000). Reconcilable differences? Standards-based teaching and differentiation. *Educational Leadership, 58*(1), 6–11.

Tuckman, B. (1965). Developmental sequence in small groups. *Psychological Bulletin, 63*, 384–389.

Tully, F. G., & Brendtro, L. K. (1998). Reaching angry and unattached kids. *Reclaiming Children and Youth, 7*(3), 147–154.

Turner, J. C., Midgley, C., Meyer, D. K., Gheen, M., Anderman, E. M., Kang, Y., et al. (2002). The classroom environment and students' reports of avoidance strategies in mathematics: A multi-method study. *Journal of Educational Psychology, 94,* 88–106.

U.S. Department of Education. (2000). *Twenty-second annual report to Congress on the implementation of the Individuals with Disabilities Education Act.* Washington, DC: Author.

U.S. Department of Education. (2001). *Twenty-third annual report to Congress on the implementation of the Individuals with Disabilities Education Act.* Washington, DC: Author.

U.S. Department of Education. (2002). *Twenty-fourth annual report to Congress on the implementation of the Individuals with Disabilities Education Act.* Washington, DC: Author.

U.S. Department of Health and Human Services. (1999). *Report of the Surgeon General's Conference on Children's Mental Health: A National Action Agenda.* Washington, DC: Author. Retrieved from http://www.surgeongeneral.gov/topics/cmh/childreport.htm

U.S. Office of Special Education Programs. (1999, Winter). Positive behavioral support: Helping students with challenging behaviors succeed. *Research Connections in Special Education, (4),* 1–5. Retrieved from http://ericec.org/osep/recon4/rc4cov.html

Valenzuela, A. (1999). *Subtractive schooling: U.S. Mexican youth and the politics of caring.* Albany: State University of New York Press.

Van Allsburg, C. (1990). *Just a dream.* New York: Houghton Mifflin.

Vernon, A. (1998). Promoting prevention: Applications of rational emotive therapy. *Beyond Behavior, 9*(2), 14–21.

Viadero, D. (2003). Studies illuminate self-defeating behavior by students. *Education Week, 22*(28), 8.

Vyogtsky, L. (1978). *Mind and society: The development of higher psychological processes.* Cambridge, MA: Harvard University Press.

Wagmeister, J., & Shifrin, B. (2000). Thinking differently, learning differently. *Educational Leadership, 58*(3), 45–48.

Walberg, H., & Greenburg, K. (1997). Using the learning environment inventory. *Educational Leadership, 54*(8), 45–47.

Walker, H. M. (1995). The acting-out child: Coping with classroom disruption (2nd ed.). Longmont, CO: Sopris West.

Walker, H. M., Todis, B., Holmes, D., & Horton, G. (1988). *The Walker social skills curriculum: The ACCESS program.* Austin, TX: PRO-ED.

Walker, J. E., & Shea, T. M. (1999). *Behavior management: A practical approach for educators.* Upper Saddle River, NJ: Merrill/Prentice Hall.

Wallace, M. (2000). Nurturing nonconformists. *Educational Leadership, 54*(4), 44–46.

Walters, L. S. (2000). Putting cooperative learning to the test. *Harvard Education Letter, 16*(3), 1–6.

Wang, M. C., Haertel, G. D., & Walberg, H. J. (1993). Towards a knowledge base for school learning. *Review of Educational Research, 63*(3), 249–294.

Warger, C. (1999, September). *Positive behavior support and functional assessment.* Arlington, VA: ERIC Clearinghouse on Disabilities and Gifted Education. Retrieved from http://ericec.org/digests/e580.html

Wayson, W., DeVoss, G., Kaeser, S., Lasley, T., Pinell, G., & Phi Delta Commission on Discipline. (1982). *Handbook for developing schools with good discipline.* Bloomington, IN: Phi Delta Kappa.

Webber, J., & Maag, J. W. (1997). Thinking our way to improved performance and psychological health. *Reclaiming Children and Youth, 6*(2), 66–67.

Webster-Doyle, T. (1991). *Why is everybody always picking on me? Guide to handling bullies.* Middlebury, VT: Atrium Society.

Wehlage, C. G., Rutter, R., Smith, G., Lesko, N., & Fernandez, R. (1989). *Reducing the risk: Schools as communities of support.* Philadelphia: Falmer Press.

Wehmeyer, M., & Schwartz, M. (1997). Self-determination and positive adult outcomes: A follow-up study of youth with mental retardation or learning disabilities. *Exceptional Children, 63*(2), 245–255.

Weinstein, C. S., Tomlinson-Clarke, S., & Curran, M. (2004). Toward a conception of culturally responsive classroom management. *Journal of Teacher Education, 55*(1), 25–28.

Wentzel, K. R. (1991). Relations between social competence and academic achievement in early adolescence. *Child Development, 62*(5), 1066–1078.

Wenz-Gross, M., & Siperstein, G. N. (1998). Students with learning problems at risk in middle school: Stress, social support, and adjustment. *Exceptional Children, 65*(1), 9–100.

Werner, E. E., & Smith, R. S. (1982). *Vulnerable but invincible: A longitudinal study of resilient children and youth.* New York: Adams, Bannister, & Cox.

Weyandt, L. (2001). *An ADHD primer.* Boston: Allyn & Bacon.

Whitehead, J., & Hoover, J. (2000). The link between body issues and behavioral problems. *Reclaiming Children and Youth, 9*(3), 130–132.

Wilson, S., & Mishra, R. (1999, April 28). In high school, groups provide identity. *The Washington Post,* p. A1.

Winitzky, N. (1992). Structure and process in thinking about classroom management: An exploratory study of prospective teachers. *Teaching and Teacher Education, 8*(1), 1–14.

Wolfe, P. (2001). *Brain matters: Translating research into classroom practice.* Alexandria, VA: Association for Supervision and Curriculum Development.

Wood, M. M. (1996). *Developmental therapy— developmental teaching: Fostering social-emotional competence in troubled children and youth* (3rd ed.). Austin, TX: PRO-ED.

Woolfolk, A. (1990). Teachers' sense of efficacy and their beliefs about managing students. *Teaching and Teacher Education, 6*(2), 137–148.

Wubbels, T., Berkelmans, M., van Tartwijk, J., & Admiral, W. (1999). Interpersonal relationships between teachers and students in the classroom. In H. C. Waxman & H. J. Walberg (Eds.), *New directions for teaching practice and research* (pp. 151–170). Berkeley, CA: McCutchan.

Wubbels, T., & Levy, J. (1993). *Do you know what you look like? Interpersonal relationships in education.* London: Falmer Press.

Wyne, M., & O'Connor, P. (1979). *Exceptional children: A developmental view.* Lexington, MA: Heath.

Young, R., West, R., Li, L., & Peterson, L. (1998). Teaching self-management skills to students with learning and behavior problems. *Reclaiming Children and Youth, 6*(20), 90–96.

Zabel, M. K. (1986). Timeout use with behaviorally disordered youth. *Behavioral Disorders, 12*(1), 15–21.

Zernike, K., & Peterson, M. (2001, August 19). Schools' backing of behavior drugs comes under fire. *The New York Times,* p. A1.

Ziegler, A., & Heller, K. A. (2000). Effects of an attribution retraining with female students gifted in physics. *Journal for the Education of the Gifted, 23*(2), 217–243.

Zionts, P. (1998). A classroom mental health curriculum. *Beyond Behavior, 9*(1), 5–11.

Zionts, P., & Fox, R. W. (1998). Facilitating group classroom meetings: Practical guidelines. *Beyond Behavior, 9*(2), 8–13.

Zittleman, K., & Sadker, D. (2002). Teacher education texts: The unfinished gender revolution. *Educational Leadership, 60*(4), 59–63.

Name Index

Subject Index